FUNDAMENTAL VALUES

Fundamental Values

Edited by
KIM ECONOMIDES, LAMMY BETTEN,
JOHN BRIDGE, ANDREW TETTENBORN
AND VIVIEN SHRUBSALL

HART PUBLISHING
OXFORD AND PORTLAND, OREGON
2000

Hart Publishing
Oxford and Portland, Oregon

Published in North America (US and Canada) by
Hart Publishing
c/o International Specialized Book Services
5804 NE Hassalo Street
Portland, Oregon
97213-3644
USA

Distributed in Netherlands, Belgium and Luxembourg by
Intersentia, Churchillaan 108
B2900 Schoten
Antwerpen
Belgium

Hart Publishing is a specialist legal publisher based in Oxford, England. To order further copies of this book or to request a list of other publications please write to:

Hart Publishing, Salters Boatyard, Folly Bridge, Abingdon Rd, Oxford, OX1 4LB
Telephone: +44 (0) 1865 245533 Fax: +44 (0) 1865 794882
email: mail@hartpub.co.uk
WEBSITE: http//:www.hartpub.co.uk

British Library Cataloguing in Publication Data
Data Available
ISBN 1 84113-118-0 (Hardback)

Typeset in Sabon
by Best-set Typesetter Ltd., Hong Kong
Printed and bound in Great Britain by
Biddles Ltd, www.biddles.co.uk

Preface

Fundamental Values completes a trilogy of volumes associated with Exeter investigating the foundational character of law, its predecessors being *Fundamental Rights* (London, Sweet & Maxwell, 1973) edited by J W Bridge, D Lasok, R O Plender and D L Perrott, and *Fundamental Duties* (Oxford, Pergamon, 1980) edited by D Lasok, A J E Jaffey, D L Perrott and Christina Sachs. This latest collection brings together essays by current (or recent) members of the School together with those of a distinguished group of former Exeter alumni. It celebrates three significant milestones in the history of the Exeter Law School: its establishment in 1923, the creation of the Bracton Chair in 1948 and its seventy-fifth anniversary in 1998 when, once again, it adopted the title School of Law.

As editors we have organised the essays into four sections but have left individual contributors the freedom to decide how best to connect with the overarching theme of fundamental values. The volume does not aim to provide a comprehensive analysis of values associated with law but does seek to explore the ethical basis of law within certain peripheral, mainstream and emerging areas of modern legal scholarship. Having been a driving force for the introduction of European law at both undergraduate and postgraduate levels since the 1970s, and one of the select few "old" universities actively teaching and researching legal practice in the 1990s, these essays hopefully will provoke discussion and continue our tradition of contributing to innovation in legal education and scholarship.

Kim Economides
Lammy Betten
John Bridge
Andrew Tettenborn
Vivien Shrubsall

Contents

List of Contributors

John Alder is Professor of Law at the University of Newcastle Upon Tyne, and was (Senior) Lecturer at Exeter from 1973–91.

Mervyn Bennun was Lecturer in Law at the University of Exeter and is currently Honorary Research Associate at the University of Cape Town, South Africa.

Lammy Betten is Jean Monnet Professor of European Law and Director of the Centre for European Legal Studies, University of Exeter.

John Bridge has been Professor of Public Law since 1974 and is a former Dean, Head of the School of Law and Deputy Vice Chancellor of the University of Exeter.

Indira Carr is Reader in International Commercial Law at the University of Kent, Canterbury. She was a (Senior) Lecturer at the University of Exeter where she also received her PhD.

Bob Drury is Senior Lecturer in Law and Director of Postgraduate Studies, University of Exeter.

Kim Economides is Professor of Legal Ethics and Head of the School of Law at the University of Exeter.

Christopher Harding is Professor of Law at the University of Wales, Aberystwyth. He was part of one of the earliest cohorts of the European Legal Studies LLM Programme in Exeter in the early 1970s.

Jackie Heath was a Lecturer in the Centre for Legal Practice, University of Exeter, from 1994–9 and is currently living in Bermuda.

Simon Honeyball is Senior Lecturer in Law and Director of Undergraduate Studies, University of Exeter, and Barrister of the Middle Temple.

Paul Lasok QC specialises in European Community law. He studied at Exeter for an LLM in European Legal Studies in 1975–6 and obtained a PhD in 1986. From 1980–4 he was a legal secretary at the Court of Justice of the European Communities.

Robert Mitchell was Lecturer in the Centre for Legal Practice, University of Exeter, and now practises law in Exeter.

Anthony Musson is Lecturer in English Law, University of Exeter, and Barrister of the Middle Temple.

Istvan Pogany is Professor of Law at the University of Warwick, and taught at Exeter from 1979–90 where he also received his PhD.

Harry Post is Professor of International Law, University of Exeter and Adjunct Professor, Department of Political Science, University of Victoria, Canada.

Vivien Shrubsall is Professor of Law and Director of the Centre for Legal Practice, University of Exeter.

Erika Szyszczak is Jean Monnet Professor of European Law, University of Nottingham. She followed the LLM in European Studies in the late 1970s.

Andrew Tettenborn is Bracton Professor of Law, University of Exeter, and Barrister of Lincoln's Inn.

Carola Thielecke was Lecturer in German Law at the University of Exeter and is eurrently following a legal practice course in Berlin.

Hans van der Wouw is an Honorary Research Fellow in the School of Law, University of Exeter.

Foreword
Fundamental Values

Exeter School of Law has long been at the forefront of innovation in legal scholarship. Let me give two illustrations. It became an early driving force for the introduction of the study of European Law when the United Kingdom joined the European Community in 1973. More recently it has developed a programme to teach and research legal practice. Now it is exploring the ethical basis of law as it applies to a wide range of topics of increasingly great importance.

The law is not just a series of technical disciplines although these are obviously important. A legal system is an essential framework for the successful functioning and development of society and at its heart lie moral, ethical, economic and social judgments. Ethics, values, rights and duties are all integral to the teaching and practice of lawyers. The work of both academics and practitioners is critical to achieving sound footings for our legal system and it is important that they should illuminate each other.

Our legal system is going through a time of immense challenge and changes almost everywhere you look. The overdue but most welcome introduction of the European Convention on Human Rights into our domestic law. The reshaping of the way in which people may be granted (or denied) access to justice. The growth of mediation and arbitration. The Woolf reforms to the way litigation is conducted are a brave attempt to reduce delay and costs. The internationalisation of law firms and the opportunities for mixed interdisciplinary practices. These and many other changes span both the substantive law and the way in which it is practised.

The essays in this book attack the question and dilemmas inherent in shaping and maintaining core values across much of the field of contemporary legal study. They do so both at the level of domestic and international law. Key but tough topics are confronted: they include the basic elements of ethics and professionalism, the principles of non-discrimination and quality, the right to trade, employment and tax, company law, together with important public law (including the environment) and private law issues. All are topics at the leading edge of contemporary legal thought.

This book commemorates the seventy-fifth anniversary of the establishment of the School of Law. When it reached its half century, Lord Denning, who played an unrivalled part in exploring the moral values of the law and adapting it to reflect our post Second World War society wrote of *Fundamental*

Rights, a predecessor to this work: "the essays show a range of knowledge, and a depth of research, which is worthy of the highest praise. They prove beyond doubt that Exeter is in the van of legal scholarship in the country". I believe the same is true of this ground-breaking and stimulating volume which I warmly commend.

Lord Alexander of Weedon QC,
Chancellor of the University of Exeter.

Part 1

Fundamental Legal Values

1

What are Fundamental Legal Values?

KIM ECONOMIDES*

1. INTRODUCTION

This essay explores the relationship between law, lawyers and their values; and the particular question of whether there is anything distinctively "legal" or "fundamental" in the underlying values which lawyers, when pressed, may claim to defend or uphold. While the remaining essays in this volume concentrate on surveying values within particular legal contexts, I wish to draw attention to the role of ethical values in shaping contemporary legal consciousness and professional legal ideology. These intellectual spaces define the boundaries of legal thought and may be expected to influence the pace and direction of changes taking place elsewhere in the legal system. We might begin by asking why it is that ethics and values have for so long been excluded from formal legal education, analysis and decision-making all of which give primacy not to values but to the creation, interpretation and application of legal rules.[1]

Almost everywhere rules tend to eclipse the underlying values they express by becoming the natural and immediate focal point of lawyers' attentions and it is perhaps unsurprising therefore that within legal discourse legal rules should appear in a permanent state of flux while values commonly associated with law (e.g. order, justice and personal freedom)[2] remain fairly constant resurfacing regularly across different cultures and generations. Rules commonly offer lawyers, their clients and the public at large a measure of predictability and security through articulating formal standards governing human relationships while values, on the other hand, create instability if not havoc in these

* This essay is dedicated to the memory of my colleagues Professors Clifford Parker and Dominik Lasok, both former Deans, Peter English, a former Head of School, and Tina Sachs all of whom in different ways were deeply committed to educational and legal values at Exeter. I should like to thank Professor Andreas Kapardis and his class at the University of Cyprus, and members of the 4th Colloquium on "Legal Theory and Legal Education" for reacting to ideas explored in this essay.

[1] See K Economides, "Learning the Law of Lawyering" in M D A Freeman (ed.), *Current Legal Problems 1999* vol. 52 (Oxford, OUP, 1999), p. 392.

[2] P Stein and J Shand, *Legal Values in Western Society* (Edinburgh, Edinburgh University Press, 1974). See also G P Fletcher, *Basic Concepts of Legal Thought* (Oxford, OUP, 1996) chs.5–8 discussing four "ultimate values": justice, desert, consent and equality.

relationships by enabling individuals or groups to re-open legal decisions which, while technically correct, may from a more subjective standpoint be considered morally flawed. In modern societies legal rules tend to be ubiquitous while legal values, though by no means invisible, hide in the shadows.[3] Lawyers typically seem much more at home ascertaining the precise meaning of rules in the latest statute or judgment, yet feel awkward when discussing ultimate values such as truth, justice or freedom. Such big ideas appear almost too large for the majority of lawyers to grasp, most of whom prefer analysing established authorities (precedent) or making hair-splitting distinctions (interpretation), and those lawyers who might be inclined to philosophical reflection probably lack the time to indulge their habit. This no doubt reflects disciplinary preferences and pressures deeply embedded within lawyers' education as well as their professional culture, both of which militate against "navel-gazing" theorising in favour of pragmatism and solving the immediate case arising out of the so-called "real world".[4] Paradoxically, positivism could lay claim to being among the most fundamental of legal values.

Immediately we confront some quite complex epistemological and methodological problems: how can we know what are the fundamental values underpinning law, do they really exist, and in what sense are they either "fundamental" or "legal"? I shall not be so rash as to answer my question "What are Fundamental Legal Values?" with reference to my own definitive, yet incomplete, list of values (though I believe the essays in this volume do provide at the very least a satisfactory if partial start to such an answer). Rather than conjure up an arbitrary list of *what* are, or could become, fundamental legal values I prefer to approach this key question indirectly by considering two *a priori* issues: first, *why* are values becoming less neglected within legal science and professional practice and, secondly, *how* might future lawyers establish closer contact with fundamental legal values, whatever these may turn out to be? My aim is to expose and understand better the intellectual or psychological blocks obstructing lawyers from debating, and thereby developing, those values which are significant if for no other reason than that they hold the potential to inform both the study and practice of law.

2. WHY FUNDAMENTAL VALUES?

If values have been neglected within legal education and practice for much of the past two centuries there are some welcome signs that this is now changing.

[3] M Galanter, "Laws Abounding: Legislation Around the North Atlantic" (1992) 55 *Modern Law Review* 1.

[4] P S Atiyah, *Pragmatism and Theory in English Law* (London, Sweet & Maxwell, 1987). See also, P S Atiyah and R S Summers, *Form and Substance in Anglo-American Law* (Oxford, Clarendon Press, 1987) and F Schauer, *Playing by the Rules* (Oxford, Clarendon Press, 1991) for insights on how lawyers apply rules in practice.

In the United Kingdom at the close of the last century there was a new wave of interest in human rights and access to justice stimulated by the new Human Rights Act 1998 and the Access to Justice Act 1999. The principal driving force behind this legislation may have been government or economic policy but the implications for professional legal values are, I suggest, very considerable. This new legislation is without doubt having a profound impact on the market for legal services but is also influencing indirectly the curriculum of future law schools and the scholarship produced by them. At a deeper level lawyers will be confronting difficult questions about their priorities and will no longer be able to rely on precise rules remaining divorced from moral, social or political principles. This new legislation opens up a whole new world for English lawyers forcing them to become familiar with general principles and open-ended values such as those enshrined in the European Convention on Human Rights (ECHR). Looking at what lies immediately ahead of us, Michael Freeman has said, "It is not difficult to predict, or even in this case foolhardy to do so, that human rights and ethics will dominate legal thinking in the new decade".[5]

While lawyers may well become the new "oracles of human rights", rescuing rights through substituting well-established legal techniques and practical reason for the philosophical emptiness or incoherence which has in the past prevailed, we should not ignore or underestimate the impact of human rights, ethics and values on traditional legal relationships and methods of reasoning.[6] Values may be used not only by clients, but also by judges, to upset established legal relationships, as Feldman explains, "The value [of dignity] offers judges an instrument with which they could subvert the proper relationship between themselves and the legislature in a democracy, or undermine respect for individual autonomy".[7] Lawyers are already under enormous pressure to think, and behave, differently as a result of recent reforms restructuring their intellectual and institutional legal frameworks. It will be interesting to observe just how quickly and deeply both litigation practices and legal method evolve as they absorb the jurisprudence of the ECHR. If the impact of European Union law is anything to go by, the changes we are about to witness in the field of human rights will be radical and inexorable.[8]

The positivism which has served lawyers for so long has come under fire from external challenges arising out of the needs of new markets, as well as

[5] Preface to *Current Legal Problems 1999* (Oxford, OUP, 1999), p. vi.

[6] David Feldman has explored this in relation to the impact of dignity as a legal value in public law: D Feldman "Human Dignity as a Legal Value – Part 1" (1999) *Public Law* 682. See also D Oliver, "The Underlying Values of Public and Private Law" in M Taggart (ed.), *The Province of Administrative Law* (Oxford, Hart Publishing, 1997), p. 217; *Common Values and the Public-Private Divide* (London, Butterworths, 1999), pp. 56–70 discussing five "key" values: autonomy, dignity, respect, status and security.

[7] D Feldman "Human Dignity as a Legal Value – Part 2" (2000) *Public Law* 61, at 76.

[8] See also changes arising out of the EU Charter on Fundamental Rights: Dominik Lasok Lecture delivered by EU Commissioner Antonio Vitoríno at Exeter School of Law, 19 May 2000.

internally by various developments taking place within legal education.[9] Apart from the international, and emerging domestic, human rights movements forcing lawyers to engage with new thinking on core human and professional values,[10] the globalisation of professional ethics could further inspire the incubation of new values, though this may turn out to be far less significant than the impact of human rights or international commercial arbitration on the future market for legal services.[11] Lawyers regularly promote and defend, often with considerable creativity and imagination, commercial values while simultaneously serving the needs of corporate and domestic clients, as well as satisfying, apart from financial reward, their thirst for personal status and respect. While élite groups of international lawyers resolve international business disputes through private arbitration, and their precise position in the global marketplace is determined by intense competition among arbitrators over who has the highest reputation for virtue,[12] at the other end of the spectrum legal aid and other lawyers in the provinces operating conditional fee arrangements must also be seen as virtuous and trustworthy if these systems are to function properly.[13] Ethics and values have, quite suddenly, become fashionable within law schools and the wider legal profession.

The link between lawyers and ethics is however complex and elusive. It does not follow that just because lawyers may be reading or talking about ethics and human rights their ethical commitments run very deep. It may even be true that familiarity breeds contempt. Some sceptics dismiss lawyers' ethics as a cynical ploy designed to enhance professional status and market share rather than promoting genuine altruism.[14] It is easy to pour scorn on lawyers' ethics as little more than an oxymoron and indeed much humour about lawyers derives from the fact that in the eyes of the public this professional group is largely ignorant

[9] K Economides, "Introduction: Legal Ethics – Three Challenges for the Next Millennium" in Economides (ed.), *Ethical Challenges to Legal Education and Conduct* (Oxford, Hart Publishing, 1998), p. xvii; R Brownsword, "Ethics in Legal Education: High Roads and Low Roads, Mazes and Motorways" (1999) 33:3 *The Law Teacher* 269.

[10] M Hunt, "The Human Rights Act and Legal Culture: The Judiciary and the Legal Profession" (1999) 26 *Journal of Law and Society* 86. See also V Olgiati, "Risk, Professions, and the Claim for Human Rights" in Oligiati et al (eds.), *Professions, Identity, and Order in Comparative Perspective* (Oñati, The International Institute for the Sociology of Law, 1998).

[11] See J Flood and A Boon, "Globalization of Professional Ethics? The Significance of Lawyers' International Codes of Conduct" (1999) 2:1 *Legal Ethics* 29; H W Arthurs, "A Global Ethics for the Transnational Legal Field" (1999) 2:1 *Legal Ethics* 59.

[12] Y Dezalay and B Garth, *Dealing in Virtue: International Commercial Arbitration and the Construction of a Transnational Legal Order* (Chicago, Chicago University Press, 1996).

[13] R J Maiman, C A McEwen and L Mather, "The Future of Legal Professionalism in Practice" (1999) 2:1 *Legal Ethics* 71; R O'Dair, "Legal Ethics and Legal Aid: The Great Divorce?" in *Current Legal Problems 1999*, vol.52, p. 419. See further K Economides and J Flood (Special Issue), "The Political and Ethical Economy of the New Lawyering" (1999) 2:2 *Legal Ethics* 105.

[14] R L Abel, "Why does the ABA promulgate ethical rules?" (1981) 59 *Texas Law Rev.* 639; "The Politics of Professionalism: The Transformation of English Lawyers at the End of the Twentieth Century" (1999) 2:2 *Legal Ethics* 131.

of, or hostile towards, the idea of values.[15] Other commentators point to significant differences within legal professions, both in terms of attitudes and social composition, highlighting the impact of social origins, gender or politics on lawyers' ethical commitments, all of which undermine traditional stereotypes.[16] The fact that the legal profession is becoming increasingly diverse makes the quest for unifying values more difficult and yet all the more important: what does it mean to be a lawyer in the twenty-first century and what difference does law make?[17] If the nature, content and scope of legal work varies as much as those carrying it out, and both product and producer are undergoing fundamental change, it is tempting to deny that there is any common reference point or valid concept of professional "core" left to explain the essence of modern lawyering.[18] But if legal values, common and fundamental to lawyers regardless of status or workplace, persist and can be identified then these could be of considerable practical importance in strengthening both professional identity and cohesion, even though academic debates over the relationship between law and morality may have become tired or irrelevant.[19]

3. IN SEARCH OF FUNDAMENTAL LEGAL VALUES

If lawyers, like many others, are gradually acclimatising to the idea of ethics and values, where are these to be found? Furthermore, if a source for legal values is discovered, what tools are available to enable lawyers to see and handle them?

I suggest that there are four principal arenas which merit further investigation before we attempt to draw up and categorise any comprehensive list of fundamental legal values, and that legal scholarship could help clear some pathways for those seeking access to fundamental legal values. First, we need to examine *legal texts* more closely in order to expose the latent values and inter-

[15] T Overton, "Lawyers, light bulbs, and dead snakes: the lawyer joke as societal text" (1995) 42 *UCLA Law Rev.* 1069; C Puma, "The Missing Link: Does Lawyer-Bashing Warrant Additional Protection for Lawyers?" (1995) 19 *J. Legal Prof.* 207; M Galanter, "Predators and Parasites: Lawyer-Bashing and Civil Justice" (1994) 28 *Georgia L. Rev.* 633; "The faces of mistrust: the image of lawyers in public opinion, jokes, and political discourse" 66 *Univ. Cincinnati Law Rev.* 805 (1998).

[16] R Jack and D C Jack, *Moral Vision and Professional Decisions: The Changing Values of Women and Men Lawyers* (Cambridge, Cambridge University Press, 1989); C Menkel-Meadow, "The Causes of Cause Lawyering. Toward an Understanding of the Motivation and Commitment of Social Justice Lawyers" in A Sarat and S Scheingold (eds.), *Cause Lawyering. Political Commitments and Professional Responsibilities* (Oxford, Oxford University Press, 1998), p. 31.

[17] B Garth and A Sarat (eds.), *How Does Law Matter?* (Chicago, Northwestern University Press, 1998).

[18] A T Kronman, *The Lost Lawyer. Failing Ideals of the Legal Profession* (Cambridge, Harvard University Press, 1993); A Alfieri, "Denaturalizing the Lawyer-Statesman" (1995) 93 *Mich. L. Rev.* 34.

[19] But see T D Campbell, *The Ethics of Legal Positivism* (Aldershot, Dartmouth, 1996).

ests they may contain. Critical legal scholarship and various forms of linguistic analysis have been performing precisely this task since the 1970s and indeed many of the essays in this volume also examine legal values inside specific legal contexts which cross the borders separating international, European and domestic law. Legal texts are undoubtedly a rich source and are receptacles of legal values whether or not they express them overtly.[20] Second, the *professional behaviour* of those who work within, and alongside, the legal professions should inform us of a range of values currently upheld across a variety of practice settings in formal and informal legal institutions.[21] What values lie at the core of professional practice and how, if at all, do these tie in with values associated with academic legal scholarship? Is respect for truth a core value in both evidential proof presented in court as well as in legal argument carried out in scholarly journals? Here socio-legal studies, whether focused on the traditional legal profession or newer forms of legal practice, could reveal the extent to which values such as independence, trust and integrity are common and fundamental to liberal professions associated with law. If legal texts and practice need further investigation neither should we neglect two other arenas, both of which are also likely to shape legal values in the future. The professions' *codes of conduct* present us with a third source of values, which for some could be seen as a kind of constitutional showcase for legal professionalism and, finally, *law schools* and the education which they promote act not only as a fountain of knowledge but as a resource potentially capable of guiding, informing and even transforming our future understanding of professional responsibility.[22]

Each of these four legal fields offers different routes towards finding and understanding legal values both at present and in the future. Although we can approach legal values from either the standpoint of doctrine ("the law in books") or from what judges, lawyers and legal workers actually do, or should do, in practice ("the law in action") we should not neglect one of the basic intellectual values, so dear to virtually all lawyers linking their education and conduct, namely that of "thinking like a lawyer". In the United Kingdom, at least since Ormrod reported in the early 1970s, this phrase "thinking like a lawyer" expresses one of the most basic legal values and is something to which

[20] See D L Perrott, " Has law a deep structure? – The Origin of Fundamental Duties" in D Lasok, A J E Jaffey, D L Perrott and C Sachs, *Fundamental Duties* (Oxford, Pergamon, 1980), ch.1; B S Jackson, *Semiotics and Legal Theory* (London, Routledge, 1985); P Goodrich, *Languages of Law. From Logics of Memory to Nomadic Masks* (London, Weidenfeld and Nicolson, 1990). See also S Pinker, *The Language Instinct* (London, Penguin, 1995); L Solan, *The Language of Judges* (Chicago, University of Chicago Press, 1993).

[21] On the masculine values embedded in law schools and legal practice see R Collier, "'Nutty Professors', 'Men in Suits' and 'New Entrepreneurs': Corporeality, Subjectivity and Change in Law School and Legal Practice" (1998) 7:1 *Social and Legal Studies* 27.

[22] See R Granfield and T Koenig, "The Fate of Elite Idealism: Accommodation and Ideological Work at Harvard Law School" (1992) 39 *Social Problems* 4; J Cooper and L Trubek (eds.), *Educating for Justice: Social Values and Legal Education* (Aldershot, Dartmouth, 1997).

every law student aspires and every good practitioner seeks to refine throughout the course of a legal career. "Thinking like a lawyer" is much more than method or habit and has been elevated to the status of a unique value differentiating lawyers from other liberal disciplines or professions. It suggests that there is something very special, particular – even peculiar – about the way in which lawyers approach and interpret the world they inhabit.[23]

If "thinking like a lawyer" is something truly *sui generis* this raises two rather important considerations. The first is this: in what sense are fundamental legal values specifically *legal*? If there are certain basic values which are distinctively legal could this be simply because of the way in which lawyers habitually conceptualise law? Or could it be that what is specifically *legal* about core legal values has more to do with legal practice and the particular social environments within which law, law students and lawyers function? Whatever values we may choose to classify as *legal* might in fact be linked to law only by association. Could it be that the values we as lawyers believe lie at the root of our discipline are in fact shared with several other liberal disciplines and professions, and that the only thing that makes a value *legal* is that lawyers assert it as such?

A related point which deserves further consideration can also be put in the form of a question: in what sense can we say that certain legal values are *fundamental*? Again, do the values we associate with law become *fundamental* simply because of the vigour or regularity with which lawyers voice them? If, for example, lawyers habitually talk about "justice", whether from the standpoint of its practical administration or from Aristotelian or equitable principles, is it mere usage which confers fundamental status on the value? Are other values such as "fairness", "reasonableness" or "equality" fundamental to law just because of their ubiquity as a tool of legal decision-making or legal reasoning? Could other values crucial to the authority of the legal process such as "certainty", "consistency", "independence" or "integrity", be considered fundamental to legal practice because wherever law is practised in the world these process values are, or should be, present? The fundamentality of a so-called *legal* value could be linked more to the fact that it is regularly associated with legal thought or action rather than having any intrinsic claim to status within legal hierarchies. In order to be able to state objectively that any particular legal value is *fundamental* implies that there is an established normative hierarchy within which such a value can be placed. Although lawyers may construct such hierarchies for positive laws by grading them in a pyramidal structure under a Kelsenian *grundnorm* it is much more difficult, though not impossible, to achieve this for values.[24]

[23] See R Rosen in Economides, *supra* n.9. See also G Teubner, "How the Law thinks: Toward a Constructivist Epistemology of Law" (1989) 23 *Law & Society Rev*. 727; M King, "The 'Truth' About Autopoiesis" 20:2 *Journal of Law and Society* 218 (1993); A L James," An Open or Shut Case? Law as an Autopoietic System" 19:2 *Journal of Law and Society* 271.

[24] Perrott, "The Logic of Fundamental Rights" in J W Bridge, D Lasok, D L Perrott and R Plender (eds), *Fundamental Rights* (London, Sweet & Maxwell, 1973), ch.1.

Professional values, for example, could be and often are "*positivised*" by being expressed in a professional code of conduct which elevates them to an exalted position commanding respect from all those who wish to claim allegiance to shared professional ideals expressed by the code. But here legal values in effect become legal rules and fundamentality is a consequence of their codification. Interestingly codifications of professional conduct are beginning to emerge not simply at the domestic level but also at the transnational level with the goal of applying to lawyers everywhere.[25] The values expressed in these transnational codes could lay claim to fundamental status on account of their global reach or inherent moral validity while simultaneously remaining peripheral to lawyers' work at the local level. But if fundamental status rests purely upon abstract aspirational goals detached from actual practice or subjective experience inevitably this must call into question the basis of the claim to fundamentality, at least from a practitioners' standpoint.

Why any particular value should be labelled as either *legal* or *fundamental* is a question which raises complex issues taking us to the core of law as both an academic and professional discipline. If one accepts that such a core exists (or could be found) then clearly it should be possible to assert the existence of fundamental legal values by reference to that core. On the other hand, should it turn out that this core is mere chimera, and that there is nothing particularly unique about values linked with the discipline of law, we might then begin to see "fundamental legal values" more as a mirage whose primary function is to differentiate law from other academic or professional disciplines in order to stake out and defend territorial claims to intellectual space or market share.[26]

At a time when traditional reference points of professional identity have come under critical scrutiny – from reformers seeking to abolish wigs, arcane language, formal procedures etc. – fundamental legal values may retain a certain appeal for conservative forces as a first line of defence against modernisation programmes geared to changes designed to keep up with the demands of technology, demography or consumerism. Similarly, for those wishing to resist interdisciplinary, critical or nihilist tendencies in legal thought – or the application of socio-legal or social science methodologies within legal scholarship – fundamental legal values upholding traditional legal method and formal elegance might be welcome buffers protecting the so-called "core" of the discipline.[27] On the other hand, the idea of fundamental legal values may be used by reformers to assert new, higher standards of professional behaviour aimed at opening a visible gap between ideals and reality. Furthermore, as many

[25] See Flood and Boon, Arthurs, *supra* n.11.

[26] W Twining, "Pericles Regained?" (1999) 1:2 *Legal Ethics* 131 and *Blackstone's Tower: The English Law School* (London, Sweet & Maxwell, 1994), ch.7.

[27] See the account of proceedings of the Oslo Law Faculty by Thomas Mathiesen, in *Law, Society and Political Action* (London, Academic Press, 1980), ch.3.

of the essayists in this volume illustrate, interdisciplinary perspectives drawn from other disciplines and legal cultures have much to contribute if we wish to explain the nature and scope of legal values. What we have to understand more clearly are the processes through which underlying values associated with law evolve. How, and why, do fundamental legal values change within particular contexts and are there any universal values common to lawyers everywhere which remain fairly constant?

4. LEGAL VALUES: FUNDAMENTAL OR EPHEMERAL CHANGE?

The essays which follow are all concerned with exploring change and how legal values which have arisen in one context could have applicability or relevance to another. One way of appreciating the fundamentality of a legal value is to consider its endurance and relevance across time and space. The essays which follow come at different legal values from contrasting perspectives and inevitably raise as many questions as they answer. One of the more interesting points to emerge is that values are not only necessary but essential if we are to have the opportunity of influencing, guiding and managing change effectively. If an unpredictable future is all we can be sure of, legal values offer lawyers a rudder with which to navigate the uncharted, possibly turbulent, waters which lie ahead.

Musson and *van de Wouw* open by considering lawyers' commitment, and access, to justice from medieval times onwards and both stress the need to communicate something of this heritage to modern lawyers who, they warn, ignore values at their peril. *Heath* also considers professional values such as competence, independence and integrity but from a practitioner's standpoint.[28] Justice emerges as a virtue of recurring significance for lawyers but one which until very recently has been neglected within formal legal education.[29] *Honeyball* and *Betten* analyse principles of non-discrimination and equality as legal values, while *Lasok*, *Carr* and *Szyszczak* focus on changing values associated with the rule of law, free trade, prosperity and the environment within the European Union and other supranational organisations. At the transnational level *Harding* and *Post* focus on how traditional values of international law, particularly those defining the relationship between individuals and the State, are undergoing change in the context of inter-dependent nation states and globalisation. Citizenship, legitimacy and sovereignty are presented as fluid concepts which interact with dynamic legal orders opening up new possibilities for participation if not emancipation.

[28] See also J Webb and D Nicolson, "Institutionalising Trust: Ethics and Responsive Regulation of the Legal Profession" (1999) 2:2 *Legal Ethics* 148.

[29] J Webb, "Developing Ethical Lawyers: Can Legal Education Enhance Access to Justice?" (1999) 33:3 *The Law Teacher* 284, Economides, *supra* n.1.

At the domestic level, legal values seem either to be born out of traumatic political, economic and cultural unrest – as positive reactions to the evils of corruption, pollution, racism and xenophobia – or, more commonly, are the product of evolutionary change calmly taking place within legal doctrine and relatively stable institutional frameworks. Values seem to surface whenever rights are tested or asserted. *Bridge* examines values recently associated with public service (selflessness, integrity, objectivity, accountability, openness, honesty and leadership) emerging from the Nolan Committee which are rapidly being absorbed into our political and legal culture. *Alder* discusses environmental values and the extent to which ethical concerns and concepts such as sustainability are recognised in public law. The impact of the Truth and Reconciliation Commission on pluralism and change in the new South Africa is considered by *Bennun* while *Pogany* also looks at the transition process but in post-Communist societies as experienced by Gypsy communities. Multiculturalism provides a common link between these essays while the theme of culture is taken further by *Thielecke* in her discussion of the *Kulturstaat* debate in German constitutional law. On the borders of the public-private divide, *Tettenborn* creates a novel distinction within the law of negligence concerning the duty of care while *Mitchell* surveys fairness as a legal value in relation to tax law. Finally, *Shrubsall* reviews values and tensions attaching to workers' and managers' rights within the sphere of employment, while *Drury* also touches upon these and other rights when searching for values in English, French and German company law.

5. FUNDAMENTAL LEGAL VALUES: A CONCLUDING PARADOX

Fundamental legal values, although excluded as a discrete topic in the traditional law school curriculum, nonetheless pervade legal, political and economic developments in many societies and at many different levels. For lawyers, the values which are inherent in principles such as justice, fairness, reasonableness and equality, for example, operate at both the macro- and micro- levels. These values have become central reference points embedded in professional and legal ideologies but are also familiar tools of legal decision-making in constant use by lawyers. Words expressing these legal values are no doubt repeated several times in every hour in virtually every law school and court in every country. But are these words really understood and valued by the law students, law teachers and practitioners who utter them and, if not, are we entitled to describe them as *fundamental*? Would lawyers be prepared to defend and uphold these values as *legal* values and to what extent do lawyers really identify with them? Is it true that lawyers prefer rules to values and is there a danger that we confuse familiarity with commitment when discussing fundamental legal values?[30]

[30] See R Granfield, *Making Elite Lawyers* (New York, Routledge, 1992).

Whether one is a first year law student or a seasoned practitioner, I suspect most of the time lawyers are preoccupied with the façade of justice rather than its underlying meaning. That is not to say lawyers are oblivious to values but that many values, especially in their practical application, take on new meanings which may close down others. Reasonableness and fairness, for example, are common legal values which remain deeply ambiguous: they express intrinsic professional values but at the same time have evolved as practical decision-making tools used as terms of art by lawyers and judges whenever they review discretion, resolve conflict or determine liability. This phenomenon, which I shall call "*value devaluation*", seems quite natural and could well be common to several other professions – medicine, the church or the military – whereby practitioners develop a kind of intellectual detachment, or even immunity, from core values they are employed to uphold in order to be able to concentrate on performing key skills competently. I do not wish to suggest that doctors fail to think about health, nor that priests fail to put into practice Christian or other religious values, but it may well be the case that fundamental values are not uppermost in their minds in the performance of everyday professional duties. With a value such as "Justice", which is seen, read and heard constantly in almost every legal environment, could it be that lawyers have become shut off from its essential meaning and are therefore unable to appreciate its true significance? Or has this value become so embedded in professional ideology that it functions almost at an unconscious level?

If lawyers have become detached from their fundamental values it should do no harm to find ways of reminding them of their existence and importance. At the point of admission to a profession there is often a *rite de passage* whereby neophytes swear allegiance to the fundamental values of their new profession. In the case of medicine, new doctors take the Hippocratic oath, a kind of manifesto expressing (though by no means exhausting) the fundamental values associated with their profession since the time of its inception. Professional codes of conduct may contain aspirational norms expressing fundamental legal values but more often than not these seek to guide conduct and regulate etiquette through detailed rules and are designed to promote or protect collective rather than individual responsibility. A judicial oath may require a judge to repeat words upholding both the law and justice but the significance of these words may easily be lost in the ceremony surrounding the occasion with the risk that what is said is reduced to little more than empty rhetoric. Lawyers need to be vigilant about processes and practices which may devalue values and try to find new ways of refreshing their professional commitments. Legal education and scholarship, as the following essays illustrate, have a vital role to play in both detecting and protecting our fundamental legal values.

2

Legal Ethics in the Age of Bracton

ANTHONY MUSSON

The closing decades of the twentieth century witnessed the enunciation of concerns from many quarters about the accessibility and operation of justice in Britain. The judiciary and the legal profession were also in the firing line, with criticisms voiced about judicial prejudice, professional conduct, the professions' supposed money-making interests, and the provision of legal education. Those calling for reform highlighted the essential importance of ethical modes of thinking and stressed the need for inexpensive and easy access to the courts and legal services.[1]

Looking back into the thirteenth and fourteenth centuries, at a crucial phase in the evolution of the judicial system and the birth of the English legal profession, it is significant that serious concerns were similarly voiced by contemporaries, both inside and outside the legal profession. While the historian must be fully aware of the dangers of reading back into the past the concerns of the present, it is clear that during this formative period emphasis was placed on certain fundamental values, which underpinned the moral attitude and practical behaviour of the developing legal profession. In the "preface" to his revised version of the influential treatise *On the Laws and Customs of England* which bears his name, Henry Bracton criticises the judiciary of his day – those greater men who are "foolish and insufficiently instructed, who climb the seat of judgment before learning the laws" – for perverting the laws and customs by deciding cases more by their own will than by the authority of the laws.[2] It is not clear whether Bracton had particular individuals within his sights or whether he simply intended a general condemnation, perhaps as justification for the book's existence and its format. Nevertheless, the statement implicitly reveals a concern for the importance of legal education and the application of judicial

[1] The Government's reforms and proposals on access to justice, now enacted (Access to Justice Act 1999) are intended to alleviate the stress on the courts, make the legal system more approachable and justice more readily obtainable.

[2] *Bracton De Legibus et Consuetudinibus Angliae*, ed. & trans. S E Thorne (4 vols., Cambridge, MA, 1968–77), vol. 2, p. 19; P Brand, "The Age of Bracton", in J Hudson (ed.), *The History of English Law*, Centenary Essays on "Pollock and Maitland", *Proceedings of the British Academy*, 89 (1996), p. 77.

power; and provides an exhortation to the nascent legal profession to think about its duties and raise its standards.

This essay accordingly investigates the quality and expression of these values, while exploring the implications and veracity of Bracton's indictment and its applicability to the legal profession as a whole for the century or so following his death in 1268. It looks, first, at the provision of legal education and the growth of the concept of precedent as a curb on inconsistency. Secondly, it assesses the profession's ethical awareness, focusing on the standards of behaviour within the profession and the level of impartiality expected of judges. Third and finally, the essay considers the extent to which the attitudes displayed towards moral responsibility facilitated or hindered access to justice.

It is really only from the mid-1270s that we have direct evidence for the existence of oral instruction in the common law, though the proximity of the courts and the royal justices together with the availability of possible "course texts" provide circumstantial evidence of law teaching in London in the early thirteenth century.[3] An informal, practical education was necessarily a feature of training in the common law and is probably exemplified most readily in the way judge's clerks learned through their immersion in the plea rolls and attendance at sessions held by their masters.[4] The survival of manuscript lectures and "do-it-yourself" manuals, however, is symptomatic of a growing awareness in the later thirteenth century of the need for oral and written instruction in law. In addition to the two main existing works on law and procedure, *Glanvill* (written 1187–9 and revised in about 1229) and *Bracton* (compiled in the late 1220s/30s by William Raleigh and revised by Henry Bracton),[5] a number of treatises were drawn up especially to meet the rapid expansion in the ranks of men desiring legal training. Some texts, such as the *Mirror of Justices*, *Britton* and *Fleta*, are in effect further revisions or updated versions of *Bracton*.[6] The provision of texts and lectures on how to conduct litigation (surviving texts such as *Brevia placitata* and *Casus placitorum*), on writs (*Natura brevium*) and how to compose them (*Modus componendi brevia*) and the procedural rules applicable to actions in the king's courts (*Fet asaver*) fulfilled some of the demand for legal education, at least at a fairly elementary level.[7]

More advanced courses and materials were available for those who aspired to the elite world of pleading. In fact from at least the late 1280s it is apparent

[3] *Close Rolls, 1234–37*, p. 26; P Brand, "Legal Education in England before the Inns of Court", in J A Bush and A Wijffels (eds.), *Learning the Law* (London, Hambledon Press, 1999), pp. 52, 56–8.

[4] R V Turner, *The English Judiciary in the Age of Glanvill and Bracton, c. 1179–1239* (Cambridge, Cambridge University Press, 1985), p. 213.

[5] Brand, "Bracton", pp. 66–79.

[6] *The Mirror of Justices*, eds. W J Whittaker and F W Maitland, *Selden Society [SS]* 7 (London, 1895); *Britton*, ed. F M Nichols (London, 1865); *Fleta*, eds. H G Richardson and G O Sayles, *SS*, 72, 89, 99 (London, 1955–84).

[7] Details of manuscript and published versions of these treatises can be found in Brand, "Legal education", pp. 76–80.

that there was a body of students known as "apprentices of the bench" (learning from the court rather than being tied to an individual serjeant as would be the case with a traditional apprenticeship) who in 1291 were provided with a special vantage point in the courtroom ("en le cribbe") from which they could listen to and study the proceedings.[8] The number of students taking part had expanded so much that permission for the construction of a second crib was requested from Edward II in 1310.[9] The apprentices were clearly afforded a special status in the court and it may have been that they were also provided with other privileges and facilities.[10] The judges themselves took part in the instruction of apprentices, providing comments on points of law to the assembly often while the serjeants were consulting with their clients.[11] Chief Justice Bereford, for instance, is reported as ironically telling a serjeant that he was obliged for his challenge "not for the sake of us who sit on the bench, but for the sake of the young men (*les joevens*) who are here".[12]

This body of advanced students was able to take advantage of other educational aids and opportunities. The compiling of law reports (examples of interesting cases occurring in the eyre and the central courts which form what are known as the Year Books), which began from at least the late 1260s, provided another way of teaching and assimilating law. In lectures based on these law reports, the factual situation was set out first so that the student could be oriented as to the nature of the case. Then the ingredients of the pleadings, the directions in argument taken by the serjeants and the opinions of the judges were expounded, before the items to be noted were summarised.[13] The dictation of reports and the addition of comments both by teachers and their pupils indicates not only that these manuscripts were regularly used as a form of teaching aid, but also that, in making notes, both the teacher and the learner were reflecting on the points being made. By the 1340s commentaries on the statutes and learning exercises of the kind used in the Inns of Court (and which were forerunners of the "readings" provided in the Inns), were also offered, which enabled students to focus on single (or closely related) points of law and gain skills in presenting oral argument.[14]

[8] *YB 2 & 3 Edward II*, pp. xv–xvi; Brand, "Legal education", pp. 62–4.

[9] Public Record Office, Special Collections, Ancient Petitions, SC 8/189/9409 printed in *YB 3 & 4 Edward II*, p. xlii.

[10] P Brand, "Observing and recording the medieval bar and bench at work", *SS*, 1998 Selden Society Lecture (London, 1999), p. 17.

[11] For example, *YB 5 Edward II*, p. 90: "And I say something for the young men that are around us . . ." (*et jeo die une chose par les jeones qe sont environ*) followed by a mini lecture on avowry for services.

[12] *YB 3 Edward II*, p. 36.

[13] P Brand, "The beginnings of English law reporting" in C Stebbings (ed.), *Law Reporting in England* (London, Hambledon Press, 1995), p. 7. For examples see *The Earliest English Law Reports [EELR]*, ed. P Brand, *SS*, 111 & 112 (2 vols.; 1996), vol. 1, p. 151 and vol. 2, pp. 205–6.

[14] J H Baker, *The Legal Profession and the Common Law* (London, Hambledon Press, 1986), pp. 11–16; Brand, "Legal education", pp. 66–9.

Private reading and reference was aided and encouraged through the provision of legal literature in the form of statute books. These books, which achieved wide dissemination through a pool of commercial copyists, were handy, pocket-sized volumes that were tailored to suit the needs of the practitioner. They generally comprised a textual core of statutes from Magna Carta up to and including Edward I's great enactments, instructional treatises (such as *Hengham Magna* and *Parva* and *Placita corone*), a section devoted to apocryphal texts from the same period, and some blank leaves so the books could be updated.[15]

The breadth of the lawyers' experience, knowledge and reading is sometimes revealed in the arguments used, comparisons with other areas of law, and in the citation of cases, especially where points of interest are recalled from cases before the eyre justices or at provincial assize sessions.[16] The misquotation, wrongly attributed statutory provision or half remembered citation is,[17] however, as illuminating as the lawyer giving the correct one in that it reveals the emphasis placed on memory and the pressure under which many lawyers worked. The apparent ignorance or lack of erudition betrayed on occasion by some men of law was nevertheless compensated for by a growing concern for the provision and subsequent consultation of accurate and authoritative texts. In court judges asked to see a copy of the relevant portion of a statute,[18] while judicial officers such as Andrew Horn, the chamberlain of London's Guildhall, carried out research in order to correct legal records and obtain reliable statements of the law.[19] Many judges carried their plea rolls around with them. This provided a ready archive of past cases, which were available either as an official record or for private reference. Geoffrey Scrope (CJKB, 1324–38), for instance, kept some rolls in York and some in London.[20] When William Shareshull (CJKB 1350–61) retired from his post, he handed over to Henry Green, his successor, "rolls, records, processes and indictments and all other memoranda touching the king's bench" stretching back to 1339. There were also seventy-five bags and 189 boxes full of indictments, bills and items that had been sent into or related to the court.[21]

[15] D C Skemer, "Reading the law: statute books and the private transmission of legal knowledge in late medieval England" in Bushand Wijffels (eds.), *Learning the Law*, pp. 113–32.

[16] For example, *YB 15 Edward III*, p. 386 (*Thorpe*: "witness the case of Gervase Bray in the third year of the present king"); *YB 16 Edward III*, pt. 1 p. 74 (*Pole*: "and this you might have seen at York between the Lord of Mowbray and John de Haveryintone" – *YB 9 Edward*, Mich. no. 43); *YB 14 & 15 Edward III*, pp. 82, 96 (W Thorpe refers to an oyer and terminer case and an assize at Beverley), 114 (*Thorpe*: "and so it was adjudged in the Northampton eyre").

[17] For various examples see T F T Plucknett, *Statutes and their Interpretation in the First Half of the Fourteenth Century* (Cambridge, Cambridge University Press, 1922), pp. 37, 103–6.

[18] *YB 2 & 3 Edward II*, p. 33; *YB 3 Edward II*, pp. 75–6.

[19] J Catto, "Andrew Horn: law and history in fourteenth-century England", in R H C Davis and J M Wallace-Hadrill (eds.), *The Writing of History in the Middle Ages* (Oxford, Clarendon Press, 1981), pp. 367–87.

[20] *Calendar of Close Rolls 1323–7*, p. 2.

[21] *Select Cases from the Court of King's Bench [SCCKB]*, ed. G O Sayles, *SS*, 55, 57, 58, 74, 76, 82, 88 (London, 1936–71), vol. 6, pp. 128–9.

The reporting of cases provided a fund of information and example that proved useful not only for the student, but also appealed to experienced practitioners, who were able to use them for their own record or to refresh their memory concerning a case.[22] There seems to have been a growing awareness among the judges and serjeants of the royal courts that they might refer to points of law argued in previous cases, and that the information could indeed be relevant, if not crucial, for the outcome of a case in progress. This trend should be coupled with a growing reliance on the written word for evidence and, moreover, litigants' desire for consistency. The circulation of details concerning how things had gone in X's case could cast doubt on the integrity, not to say the infallibility, of royal judges if the decision was the reverse in Y's case.

The concept of binding precedent is something with which every modern common lawyer is thoroughly conversant. Indeed, it is a doctrine upon which the common law system is based, complete with its own rules and method of application.[23] At this date there was no formal structured theory (*stare decisis*) imposed on the courts. For many judges (at least in the twelfth and early thirteenth centuries when the details of court sessions were not recorded either formally by clerks or informally by other lawyers) each case was to be approached individually and dealt with on its own merits.[24] Even with the advent of court record keeping, the rolls themselves rarely reveal general statements of legal principles, and even where they do it is difficult to pin down the authority to any single judge owing to the impersonal language of the court record. It is unlikely that early thirteenth century judges consciously saw the judgments of their forebears as influencing the way they approached the cases before them.[25] It is noticeable, however, that specific reference was made to the concept of precedent in court proceedings as early as 1287. "On what basis should we give judgment: under the ancient laws customary in the time of those who preceded us, or under the laws alleged by you and others?", a justice in the court of common pleas asked.[26] Indeed, there were signs that the benefits of precedent, in providing for certainty, uniformity and consistency, were appreciated. In another case reported in the same year, William Bereford, then a serjeant-at-law, made clear to the judge his belief: "I have seen it adjudged before you yourself; and there ought to be one law for all people in this kingdom".[27]

[22] Occasionally it is the reporter who has got things wrong: Plucknett, *Statutes*, pp. 106, 112.

[23] J A Holland and J S Webb, *Learning Legal Rules*, 2nd ed. (London, Blackstone, 1993), pp. 103–24; R Cross, *Precedent in English Law*, 4th ed. (Oxford, Clarendon Press, 1991).

[24] M T Clanchy, *From Memory to Written Record: England 1066–1307*, 2nd ed. (Oxford, Blackwell, 1993), p. 97.

[25] R V Turner, *Judges, Administrators and the Common Law in Angevin England* (London, Hambledon Press, 1994), pp. 205–7.

[26] *EELR*, vol. 2, p. 349.

[27] *Ibid.*, p. 293.

The longevity of tenure enjoyed by the justices of king's bench and common pleas and their previous service to the court as serjeants facilitated a strong sense of collective memory and an awareness of past decisions. The medieval Year Books provide evidence that cases were cited and discussed in court by counsel and judges alike.[28] Some concept of precedent clearly obtained and its value was felt in bolstering arguments and justifying decisions.[29] Authority and respect could be accorded a decision by naming the particular judge responsible.[30] Individual judges were also known to have excellent memories. William Herle (CJCP, 1327–9, 1331–5) was highly regarded in this respect. A copious memory was not only a useful faculty, but one prized by contemporaries and considered as providing a natural foundation for ethical judgment.[31] The dangers of allowing precedent to dominate all decision-making, however, was felt by Shareshull (JCP, 1334–40, 1342–50; CJKB, 1350–61), who, while demurring from too much judicial innovation, believed that "right" (or reason) remained a powerful influence. "No precedent is of such force as that which is right".[32] (The notions of equity inherent in judicial decisions will be discussed below).

The ethical behaviour and general conduct of members of the legal profession was also the subject of deliberation and official scrutiny in the profession's early years. This was partly a symptom of the Crown's desire for accountability among its servants, but also the exhibition of a genuine concern for impartiality in judicial circles and the prevention of practices which would serve to undermine the operation of the law. In order try to prevent judicial wrongdoing and ensure that practitioners were not behaving unethically a number of safeguards were initiated in the thirteenth and fourteenth centuries.

The main brake on misbehaviour was the psychological, spiritual and chivalric device of an oath: an appeal to honour and a pledge of good faith, backed up by the foundation of religious belief. In the Middle Ages the swearing of an oath had an aura of sanctity, indeed such a pledge was usually described as *sacrum juratum* (sacred oath). Oaths were generally taken on gospel books, which were sacred objects in themselves.[33]

Royal justices took some form of oath on appointment from at least the late twelfth century onwards. According to the earliest surviving example (in *Bracton*) probably in use during the third decade of the thirteenth century, judicial obligations were of a fairly vague nature: the first two clauses concerned

[28] *YB 15 Edward III*, pp. 160, 260, 350.

[29] *YB 14 Edward III*, pp. 246, 252; *YB 1 Edward II*, p. 109.

[30] For example, *YB 11 & 12 Edward III*, pp. 412, 498, 612.

[31] M Carruthers, *The Book of Memory: A Study of Memory in Medieval Culture* (Cambridge, Cambridge University Press, 1992), pp. 99, 109, 112–13, 154, 205–6: it was expected of canon lawyers that they had committed to memory the entire set of Decretals.

[32] *YB 19 Edward III*, p. 376; B.H. Putnam, *The Place in Legal History of Sir William Shareshull* (Cambridge, Cambridge University Press, 1950), pp. 105–6.

[33] Clanchy, *Memory*, p. 256.

the straightforward diligent exercise of their duties as the king's justices. The third one, however, enunciates a particular ethical standard in the performance of these duties: the royal judge is to uphold "right justice" (*rectam justiciam*) and swears to do so (in what is a far-sighted recognition of human fallibility) "to the best of his ability" (*pro posse suo*). An additional element was introduced around 1257 when it was required that royal justices (and barons of the exchequer) swear that they would not accept (either directly or indirectly) any gift or service (excluding customary hospitality of food and drink) from anyone whom they knew was a litigant in the king's court in connection with their litigation.[34]

In the later years of Henry III's reign or possibly at the beginning of Edward I's a remodelling of the judicial oath occurred. In contrast to the previous versions there was a more comprehensive promise with an explicit concentration on standards of judicial conduct. The justice swore:[35]

> to do justice to the best of his ability to all as well poor as rich . . . not to disturb or respite justice against right or against the law of the land either for the great or the rich, nor for hatred nor for favour nor for the estate of anyone nor for a benefit, gift or promise given or to be given to him nor in any other way; but loyally to do right to all according to law and custom.

By the 1290s, it is clear that the same judicial oath was taken by *all* royal justices on their admission to office and that the complaints of judicial misconduct arising at the end of the previous decade (see below) had correspondingly influenced its content. Though similar to the one recorded in 1278, there were significant differences. It contained a promise not to receive anything (except food and drink) *without the king's permission* and, more significantly, a clause designed to prevent complicity in misconduct by putting the onus on an individual to dissuade his colleagues from embarking on or continuing with any perceived wrongdoing, if he failed in this respect he was bound to report it to the king's council or, in the absence of an appropriate response, to the king himself.[36]

Half a century later, the Ordinance of Justices (1346) focused on the actions and behaviour of those exercising power in a judicial capacity,[37] enshrining in statute law standards of conduct applicable to the pursuance of their duties. The oath prescribed under the Ordinance was itself remarkably similar to its thirteenth century predecessors in its emphasis on equal justice to rich and poor alike and its prohibition of reward (either in cash or by way of a gift or

[34] P Brand, *The Making of the Common Law* (London, Hambledon Press, 1992), p. 149.

[35] *Ibid.*, p. 150: Dr Brand notes that although the oath first appears in letters close of 1278 directed to the eyre justices, it is possible that it had already been used by other royal justices and its recording was merely coincident with the reorganisation of the eyre which occurred in 1278.

[36] Brand, *Making*, pp. 150–1.

[37] The requirements of the oaths extended equally to the barons of the exchequer, the justices of oyer and terminer and to the justices of assize and gaol delivery.

anything from which profit might be gained). Hospitality in the form of meat and drink was again exempted provided that it was of negligent value. There was equally a duty placed on those in a position of judicial responsibility to inform the king of any "damage or disherison". A significant divergence from earlier oaths was the onus placed on justices when holding office to accept neither payment nor robes from anyone but the Crown. To make up for this restriction on earnings the king agreed to increase the judges' salaries and there is evidence from the wardrobe accounts that they were provided with new robes (in the royal livery) for both summer and winter.[38]

The seriousness with which the Crown viewed any transgression of these solemn undertakings can be gauged initially from the nature of the punishment envisaged. In 1257 the sanction against a judge's violation of his oath was dismissal from his position and forfeiture of a year's wages.[39] Ninety years later, the stakes had been raised considerably. It was not merely his judicial position and wages which could be lost: upon conviction the offender's lands, goods and even his life were placed at the king's will.

This overt stand upon standards of judicial conduct could only be effective if there was widespread recognition of the level of behaviour that was expected and the remedies for breaches or injustices that could be claimed accordingly. An important element in the desired success of the Ordinance, therefore, lay in the requirement that it be published openly and exhibited in such places in his bailiwick as the sheriff thought appropriate. Relief was also offered: anyone who thought that they had a grievance under the Ordinance concerning the misdemeanours of judges and local officials could complain to the assize justices or pursue the matter in chancery before the chancellor and treasurer. The king was thus encouraging his subjects to scrutinise and report upon the ethical behaviour of royal servants performing judicial functions with an eye to benefiting both the complainant and the Crown: to ensure that justice really meant fairness and that miscreants were not allowed to continue in office unless the king willed otherwise. The Ordinance of 1346 was reaffirmed by Richard II in 1384, demonstrating the royal regime's commitment to justice following the hostility to lawyers demonstrated during the Peasants' Revolt three years earlier.[40]

In addition to oath-taking, basic principles of practical behaviour were enunciated a generation or so after the death of Bracton. It is apparent that the Crown and judiciary were in agreement as to the potentially disruptive effect of the behaviour of certain members of the nascent legal profession and aware of the negative impact it could have on public confidence in the judicial system.

[38] 20 Edward III (*Statutes of the Realm [SR], 1101–1713*, ed. A Luders et al., 11 vols (London, 1810–28), vol. 1, pp. 303–6).

[39] Brand, *Making*, pp. 149–50.

[40] 8 Richard II c. 3 (*SR* vol. 2, p. 37).

Regulation was initially confined to a somewhat unspecific, though fundamental, professional obligation formulated in the First Statute of Westminster (1275).[41] The 1275 legislation created a duty on legal practitioners not to mislead the court or litigants and established harsh penalties for demonstrable malpractice: imprisonment for a year and a day, together with complete disbarment or permanent suspension from practising. In practice the statute's enforcement was left to the judges, who through their presidency of the courts elaborated on its terms to provide norms of professional behaviour equating to an ethical standard. It appears that serjeants and professional attorneys alike were expected to conform to this code, and to observe it whether they acted in the customary or royal courts. The existence of this private regulatory code and, indeed, its practical application is confirmed by instances of professional misbehaviour coming to the attention of the justices either during a trial itself or as a result of complaints brought against court personnel by disgruntled litigants.[42]

Analysing such evidence it is possible to see certain key precepts at work in the courts. First, a serjeant-at-law owed a primary duty of loyalty to his client.[43] He was not allowed to leave the client's service before the conclusion of litigation unless informed that his services were no longer required or the client failed to pay his fee. There was also a continuing obligation to the client once the particular case had finished: the serjeant could not be employed by his client's opponent without the former's permission, nor could he appear against his client in subsequent litigation. Secondly (in line with the 1275 statute), he was under a duty not to deceive the court and was liable to be punished if he made an untrue statement in court or advised his client to sue more than once on the same matter. Thirdly, a serjeant's general conduct was subject to scrutiny, whether he was pleading for a client or undertaking his own business. Wasting the court's time or persisting with an unconvincing argument were particularly frowned upon and received discouragement.[44]

A professional attorney was similarly bound in terms of his relations with clients. It was expected, for instance, that he would exercise due diligence in his preparation and handling of the case: obtaining the necessary writs and ensuring that there was a minimum of delay in pursuing the various stages of litigation. Like the serjeant, he was under a continuing obligation to his client and could be punished for deliberate fraud, negligence or incompetence. There were also obligations in respect of a client's opponent (such as taking account of legitimate grounds for absence and not suing in default), a duty to third parties, and to the court itself (such as following the correct procedures).

[41] 3 Edward I c. 29 (*SR* vol. 1, p. 34).

[42] For this and the following three paragraphs see P Brand, *The Origins of the Legal Profession* (London, Blackwell, 1992), pp. 120–37.

[43] For the oaths of serjeants-at-law and king's serjeants see *SCCKB*, vol. 7, xxxii.

[44] Judges did not always need to control pleading by using words: a wink or a nod could suffice (*YB 4 Edward II*, pt. 1, p. 132).

The fact that this code of professional ethics emerged out of, and may be effectively reconstructed from, the breaches of good conduct exposed in court does, of course, provide direct evidence that abuse and malpractice continued to occur. Was it rife though? While the relative infrequency of such cases cannot in itself be taken to indicate that levels of integrity and misconduct altered, they do demonstrate that blatant deviation from the acceptable standards of good conduct was acknowledged and punished by the courts. Indeed, if anything, it suggests that the judiciary regarded conformity to a code of ethics as a necessary corollary to professional status and to the "special relationship" which lawyers enjoyed with the courts. Allegations were usually tried by juries of fellow professionals and the punishments reflected the seriousness with which each particular breach was viewed. If the conduct point arose during the trial itself, a warning or some form of judicial guidance might be given. In other instances men were fined (the money being split between the client – as a form of compensation – and the royal coffers) or spent brief periods in gaol (which would undoubtedly affect their reputation and curtail earning capacity). Others were punished by temporary suspension, by receiving the statutory period of imprisonment, or (in really serious cases, where perhaps a forged writ had been used or an entry in the plea roll had been falsified) by permanent suspension from practising in court.

The evidence compiled by Dr Brand relates mainly to the thirteenth century. It is clear, though, that the courts remained concerned for practitioners' ethical behaviour and that during the fourteenth century, the provisions of the First Statute of Westminster were still being enforced.[45] Judges combined a mixture of winks, warnings, and exasperation to ensure the etiquette of pleading was observed.[46] Practitioners, too, recognised their professional duties: "We must serve our clients according to the law of the land".[47] By the mid fourteenth century, dissatisfied litigants began to use other remedies against their legal representatives, couching their complaints in terms analogous to assumpsit: negligence in carrying on the profession of attorney or pleader.[48]

It can therefore be said with some assurance that there was definite concern both from within (and outside) the legal profession during the thirteenth and fourteenth centuries that the law should be upheld and its practices revered. In addition to competence, a reputation for probity was paramount for employment (and of course for re-employment) in the sphere of court activity. Trustworthiness was also a necessary prerequisite for appointment in a number of other legal contexts, such as acting in arbitrations and as feoffees in feoffment to uses. The frequency with which lawyers were called upon to act as a feoffee

[45] For example two cases in 1347: *SCCKB*, vol. 6, pp. 54–5, 62.

[46] *YB 4 Edward II*, p. 132; *YB 12 & 13 Edward III*, p. 350; *YB 8 Edward III*, pl. 9, f.21.

[47] *YB 3 Edward II*, p. 80.

[48] *Calendar of Plea and Memoranda Rolls [CPMR], 1323–64*, ed. A H Thomas (Cambridge, Cambridge University Press, 1926), p. 218 (attorney – 1345); *CPMR 1381–1412*, ed. A H Thomas (Cambridge, Cambridge University Press, 1932), pp. 16–17 (pleader – 1382).

in the late fourteenth century, for example, suggests that a high standard of honesty existed and that landowners relied upon a practitioner to perform his duties in good faith.[49]

Rules for practitioners are one thing, but who blew the whistle on misbehaviour by the judiciary? How secure were royal judges' positions? According to contemporary political theory, the judges were the king's servants to appoint or dismiss at will (*judices non habentur nisi per regem*). There was thus an element of arbitrariness, which could be expected at times of political stress. When there were complaints about royal judges, the Crown was not slow to act. The dismissal in 1289–90 of eleven members of the higher judiciary following allegations of misconduct could be seen as a defining moment in the early history of the judicial profession.[50] Their convictions in what have been referred to as "state trials" and the subsequent imposition of substantial fines totalling at least twenty thousand pounds (equitable with almost a whole year's normal income for the Crown) appeared to signal corruption on a grand scale. With regard to professional standards, the purge of 1289 undoubtedly provided a valuable precedent for Edward III sixty years later: in what amounted to another aggressive strike at the judiciary he sacked a total of seven of his judges in 1340–1.[51]

In the years immediately following both instances the threat of further measures may have hovered menacingly over holders of judicial offices. The only other significant judicial dismissals in the period were isolated occurrences.[52] A particular *cause célèbres*, however, was the case of William Thorpe (CJKB, 1346–50), who admitted to accepting money from a litigant and whose very life was put at the king's mercy in 1350.[53] Although there was ultimately a change of heart in terms of his punishment, Edward III's treatment of Thorpe indicates a definite concern to stamp out any allegations of corruption and that, in order to uphold his "anti-sleaze" campaign, he was prepared to make an example of someone as exalted as his chief justice. While some judges found guilty of wrongdoing were re-accepted into royal service, those who were generally did not retain their existing status and were normally moved to another department.

When examining official responses to allegations of judicial corruption that surfaced during the thirteenth and fourteenth centuries it is necessary to bear several points in mind. We should resist the temptation to judge medieval justice purely from a modern ethical standpoint and consider the extent to which judges in fact aimed to provide impartiality. Rather than taking these en masse

[49] N Ramsey, "What was the legal profession?" in M Hicks (ed.), *Profit, Piety and the Professions in Later Medieval England* (Gloucester, Alan Sutton, 1990), p. 65.

[50] For detailed discussion of the events see Brand, *Making*, pp. 101–12.

[51] N M Fryde, "Edward III's removal of his ministers and judges, 1340–1", *Bulletin of the Institute of Historical Research* 48 (1975), pp. 159–61.

[52] These occurred in 1251, 1317, 1350 and 1365.

[53] *SCCKB* vol. 6, pp. xxv–xxvi.

dismissals at face value as necessarily indicating a manifest lack of ethics among the higher judiciary, we must seek to understand their context and the complicated political and social framework within which royal justices operated. Moreover, any criticisms made ought to distinguish individual wrongdoing from that attributable to the entire judiciary. Finally, attention should be paid to the outcome of the particular judicial "crises" and the capacity of the judicial system to alter its practices as well as rehabilitate its personnel.

Public antipathy towards the legal profession (manifested in the assassination of Chief Justice John Cavendish and the targeting of other lawyers during the Peasants' Revolt of 1381)[54] stemmed partly from the perceived proximity of relations between lawyers and landowners (both individual and corporate) and partly from the perennial view that lawyers were making large sums of money out of the fees paid by litigants. The retaining of lawyers for advice and assistance, which over course of the thirteenth and fourteenth centuries was increasingly regarded as a necessity both for individuals and corporations, may have brought about closer relations resulting in friendships subsisting outside their official connection. Judging from their letters to each other, John Stonor and the Bishop of Exeter, for example, enjoyed a close association.[55] Links established prior to a man of law's rise to serjeant and before a serjeant's elevation to the ranks of the central court judiciary frequently remained intact and could even be strengthened as a consequence of the new position.[56] Both judges and lawyers, however, had a plurality of associations, rarely did they give anyone their sole, overriding allegiance.

The earning power of judges and lawyers made them targets for those who regarded them simply as "fat cats", without necessarily discerning the reality. While some judges, such as Hengham or Scrope G did manage to earn vast amounts, it was usually as a result of very hard work or shrewd investments.[57] In fact the Crown was frequently in arrears with judges' salaries, which themselves have been described as "absurdly low".[58] Attorneys' fees varied with the length of the case and the amount of work involved, but an ordinance of 1356 for the City of London considered 3s 4d a "reasonable fee". Payment did not have to be wholly in cash: some attorneys accepted payment in kind (for example in cheese and butter).[59] In comparison with attorneys, the fee-scale for

[54] A Harding, "The revolt against the justices", in R H Hilton and T H Aston (eds.), *The English Rising of 1381* (Cambridge, Cambridge University Press, 1981), pp. 165–93.

[55] *Register of John de Grandisson, Bishop of Exeter, 1327–69*, ed. F C Hineston-Randolph, 2 vols. (London and Exeter, 1894–8), vol. 1, pp. 210, 235–6.

[56] J R Maddicott, "Law and lordship: royal justices as retainers in thirteenth and fourteenth century England" *Past & Present* supplement, 4 (Oxford, 1978), pp. 19, 21, 24; N Ramsay, "Retained Legal Counsel, c.1275–c.1475" *Transactions of the Royal Historical Society*, 5th series, 35 (1985), p. 102.

[57] *SCCKB*, vol. 1, p. lxxviii; B Vale, "The profits of the law and the 'rise' of the Scropes: Henry Scrope (d.1336) and Geoffrey Scrope (d.1340)" in Hicks (ed.), *Profit, Piety and the Professions*, pp. 98–100.

[58] *SCCKB*, vol. 4, p. xxi.

[59] *Select Bills in Eyre, 1292–1333*, ed. W C Bolland, *SS*, 30 (London, 1914), p. 119.

serjeants was generally higher, but they were not all the grasping fee-earners the poet Langland would have us believe in a satirical passage in the Prologue to *Piers Plowman*:[60]

> Serjeants it seemed that serveth at the Bar
> Pleaden for pennies and pounds the law
> And not for love of Our Lord (for charity) unlose their lips once.
> Thou mightest better mete (measure) mist on Malvern Hills
> Than get a mum (murmur) of their mouth but money be shewed.

The grumblers were probably those who had lost their case and resented someone profiting at their financial expense or who had an axe to grind against the justices. In fact only modest remuneration was levied from some litigants and it was not unknown for serjeants to undertake work *pro bono*.[61] Indeed, there was an ad hoc system of "legal aid" provision in place long before the *in forma pauperis* legislation of Henry VII.[62]

It is easy to make gibes at lawyers' expense when everyone knows they need to finance their livelihood. Chaucer's Serjeant-at-Law is not quite the same easily condemned, stock literary character, nor are we required to make moral judgments. The satirical comments on his ethical stance are subtly mixed with admiration for his professional skills. We are told that "of fees and robes hadde he many oon" (emphasising his connection with landowners) and he regards everything as "fee simple" (in monetary terms). But he obviously has a busy practice and the words "fee simple" themselves (referring to a technical term in land law) taken on another level point towards "his science" and "high renoun" and remind us not only that legal knowledge was essential, but also that reputation was important.[63]

Laicisation of the profession, which was occurring during the thirteenth century, may have brought the issue of the payment of lawyers to a head. The trappings of wealth were more observable when lands were bought and sold and estates accumulated in the provinces. Lawyers very often wanted to appear to be part of landed society and so themselves contributed to a blurring of distinctions between the two and fostered perceptions of a collaboration between justices and landowners. Closer relations thus were a natural corollary of the increased technicality of the law and legal procedure, but were frequently portrayed as having sinister implications, even though the receipt of money, or

[60] William Langland, *Piers Plowman*, ed. A V J Schmidt (London and New York, 1995), p. 19, C text, lines 160–4. (I have modernised the spelling and translated some words).

[61] Boland, *Select Bills in Eyre*, p. 21; Brand, *Origins*, pp. 104–5.

[62] J A Brundage, "Legal aid for the poor and the professionalization of law in the Middle Ages" *Journal of Legal History* 9 (1988), 173; A Musson, "Social exclusivity or justice for all? Access to justice in late medieval England" in R Horrox and S Rees Jones (eds.), *Ideals, Utopias and Institutions, 1200–1630* (Cambridge, Cambridge University Press, forthcoming); J M Maguire, "Poverty and civil litigation" *Harvard Law Review* 36 (1923), 361–404.

[63] *SCCKB*, vol. 7, p. xxxvii; S H Rigby, *Chaucer in Context* (Manchester, Manchester University Press, 1996), pp. 43–5.

another form of gift from an individual, was not necessarily an indication of corruption. In the vast majority of cases it was unlikely to significantly advance a cause or prejudice a reasoned judgment in court. In a society where gift giving was customary and a mark of politeness, the proportionality mattered, not the mere fact of reward or apparent sweetner.[64] High profile examples of serious misdeeds arising from a close proximity of relations, however, may have underlined people's fears and undermined their belief in the impartiality of royal justice.[65]

The chronology of perceptions is interesting. Henry III tolerated close relations between his nobles and leading members of the judiciary. The granting of fees and robes was a natural expression of their relationship.[66] Although the money and possessions acquired by lawyers over the course of their lives were commented upon in the thirteenth century,[67] it was not until later in the century that the connection between justice and wealth was made explicitly in *A Song on the Venality of the King's Judges*. The complaints concerning lawyers "on the take" seem to have coincided with the period when many members of the profession were "on the make". It is not surprising that by the fourteenth century the abundance of lawyers should be accounted for in some way either by those jealous of their new found wealth and acquired social status or those who were in fact critical of them precisely because they were "self-made" men. The *Scrope* v. *Grovesnor* case in 1385, a dispute about bearing arms heard in the Court of Chivalry, highlighted the contemporary feeling among some in the upper stratum that lawyers were socially inferior: Richard Scrope was told that he could not be a "gentilhomme" because his father had been a lawyer.[68]

The expression of "popular" attitudes in late fourteenth century literature clashes with the dedicated picture of professionalism and intellectual rigour that is preserved in the legal records and marked the great bulk of their work. They may have been the views of individuals, but frequently struck a chord with a wider audience. The fact that feelings against lawyers run as strong today as they did in the Middle Ages must surely confirm that the love/hate attitude needs to be addressed in chronological terms as well as with regard to influencing factors. Personality may have played a large part. Two of the justices named in *An Outlaw's Song of Trailbaston* (a poem complaining about a set of judicial commissions in 1305) appear to have been respected. They are described in

[64] *SCCKB*, vol. 1, lxxvii; R C Palmer, *The Whilton Dispute, 1264–1380* (Princeton, NJ, Princeton University Press 1984), pp. 10–11.

[65] N. Fryde, "A medieval robber baron: Sir John Molyns of Stoke Poges, Buckinghamshire", in R F Hunnisett and J B Post (eds.), *Medieval Legal Records Edited in Memory of C A F Meekings* (London, HMSO, 1978), pp. 197–222.

[66] *SCCKB*, vol. 7, p. xxxiii; D Carpenter, *The Reign of Henry III* (London, Hambledon Press, 1996), pp. 83–4.

[67] Matthew Paris, *Chronica Majora*, ed. H Luard, *RS*, 7 vols (London, 1872–84), vol. 4, p. 49; vol. 5, p. 138.

[68] Vale, "Profits of Justice", pp. 100–1.

terms of their piety and concern for the poor and are clearly contrasted with two of their colleagues, whose discretion, it is implied, was unlikely to be exercised in the litigant's favour.[69]

The accessibility of the judicial system was marked not only by whether the less well off litigants were able to afford representation and the costs of going to court, but whether they could achieve balanced treatment within it. The moral responsibility of the legal profession was uppermost in this respect, especially in their acceptance of the need to provide legal services through individual favour and charity. The justices' oath placed on them an onus to intervene and use their discretion where it mattered. A practical manifestation of this might be to assign counsel to poor litigants and thus counteract any advantage which a litigant of higher status might wield.[70] This might be particularly pertinent in the case of a poor litigant unable to provide the customary gifts for judges and jurors. It is significant that in a late fourteenth century case it was argued that the cost of a long trial would be prohibitive for the plaintiffs and that to deny them justice merely because they were poor and unable to afford the cost was "against law and conscience".[71]

The capacity to look at an individual's situation and go behind the strict letter of the law to the underlying morality characterised the term in office of several judges of the period and was a vital factor in the beginnings of "equity" and the chancellor's "court of conscience". Towards the end of Edward I's reign, for example, royal judges Staunton, Hengham and Howard were quite prepared to override a statute where hardship might result.[72] Staunton also refused to let a woman lose her dower through a tenant's deviousness and by distinguishing between the heir's inheritance and his purchase achieved "justice" for her.[73] Even Chief Justice Weyland (who went into exile after his dismissal in 1289) sought to make equitable decisions (*Je regarde en ce cas un equite*).[74] Bereford CJ in particular must have gained a reputation for his humanity. He was not averse to urging counsel to admit a fact that had not been proved if it rescued the situation ("You must not allow conscience to prevent your doing law"). Where he felt unable to intervene, he made it clear that, in his opinion, good faith was on the losing side. ("It is a dishonest thing for an honourable man to demand what his predecessor has released").[75] Bereford's sense of fairness and proportion included the suggestion that lack of formal written proof was not

[69] R B Dobson and J Taylor, *The Rymes of Robin Hood: An Introduction to the English Outlaw*, rev. edn. (Stroud, Alan Sutton, 1997), p. 253.

[70] Brundage, "Legal aid", 173.

[71] *SCCKB*, vol. 7, pp. lxv–lxvi. The plaintiffs were clearly asking for an equitable remedy, but it was felt that since they could afford serjeants to act for them their alleged poverty was a fiction.

[72] *YB 33 & 35 Edward I*, p. 380.

[73] *YB 4 Edward II*, pp. 25–6.

[74] *EELR*, vol. 2, p. 254.

[75] *YB 1 & 2 Edward II*, p. xix.

necessarily detrimental to a claim ("Would you have his estate and the estate of his wife perish because he has no charter? It may be that he had a deed which is lost, but thereby he has not lost his right").[76] Although the judges just mentioned were predominantly men of the late thirteenth and early fourteenth centuries, there were others in the mid-to late fourteenth century who carried this spirit forward. Mowbray, for instance, believed the law (judicial decisions) needed to be in accord with reason and to remedy "mischief" (injustice).[77]

This essay has offered an historical appreciation of values fundamental to the administration of justice and provided a reflection on areas of current concern not only to the Government and legal profession, but to the wider population of this country. If we look back to the age of Bracton and examine the legal profession and its growth over the following century or so, it is possible to appreciate the concern that certain moral and ethical qualities be placed at the forefront of professional activities. The problems faced by the profession today are obviously very different ones, but the need for simplifying the ethical code or going back to first principles, the fundamental values recognised in the thirteenth century, is now regarded by some leading commentators as a prerequisite, especially in the field of advocacy:[78]

> What is required is a cultural change . . . That will only come about if some fundamental ethical questions are answered . . . In order to lay those foundations, fresh debate is needed on the ambit of the advocate's duty not to mislead the court . . . [which itself] derives from the commitment to justice.

This commitment to justice is enshrined in one of the chapters of Magna Carta still on the statute book today, one that provides the touchstone of ethical behaviour and symbolises access to justice: "To no one will we sell, to no one will we deny or delay right or justice". (c. 40, 1215, c. 29, 1225). This provision was almost contemporary with early drafts of *Bracton* and was very much in the minds of early thirteenth century lawyers and politicians. We live in a different era with different requirements and public demands, but we must retain a similar concern for justice and a profession that upholds the law to the best of its ability, free from error, negligence, prejudice and bias. Revisiting the earliest days of the legal profession offers the opportunity to reflect on and rekindle those fundamental values.

[76] *YB 2 & 3 Edward II*, p. 171.

[77] *YB 15 Edward III*, p. 126. Technically Mowbray was not a judge at the time he made this remark, but it illustrates his thinking. He became a justice of common pleas in 1359.

[78] M Blake and A Ashworth, "Some ethical issues in prosecuting and defending criminal cases", [1998] *Crim LR*, pp. 16–34 (quotation at p. 32).

3

Justice as Virtue: A Subject in the Law Curriculum?

HANS VAN DE WOUW

1. The purpose of this essay is to make a very modest contribution to the discussion on the role of ethics in legal education.[1] It is a rather personal contribution: allow me to make clear why I chose this subject, and in which context my remarks should be situated. Although I have a degree in law, I am not a lawyer. Neither am I a legal philosopher. Although I have taught legal history, I am not a legal historian. My interest lies with medieval law texts, in Latin and translated from Latin into French, and in the manuscripts and books that transmit them. To put it succinctly, I am not interested in the Digest because it tells me something on Roman law, I think it is necessary to know something of Roman law to be able to read the Digest.

My father was an antiquarian bookseller. My birth place, 's-Hertogenbosch in the Netherlands, has a magnificent cathedral, the St-John the Evangelist, the most beautiful gothic building of the country.[2] That church was to me, as well as to many of my fellow citizens, a kind of second home. The liturgy used to be very elaborate, with beautiful Gregorian and polyphonic music.[3]

The local "City Gymnasium" was an old-fashioned grammar school with seventy-five pupils when I arrived in 1950 and one hundred when I left in 1956. In the first form: seven hours of Latin per week, the minimum to let the Latin etymology sink into the then still receptive heads of eleven- and twelve-year-olds. In the last two forms eight hours of Greek and eight hours of Latin a week,

[1] See now K Economides (ed.), *Ethical Challenges to Legal Education & Conduct* (Oxford, Hart Publishing, 1998).

[2] It has two Michelin-stars (worth a detour). Strangely, Antwerp Cathedral has three stars (worth the journey): just for the tower and the Rubens paintings? For the rest, it is rather dull compared with the St John.

[3] A high point was the *triduum sacrum*, Maundy Thursday, Good Friday and Easter Eve. The "dark mattins" sung Thursday evening in a sombre church, the altar denudated, with the lamentations of Jeremiah, the Passion according to St John on Friday, sung in plainchant by three priests (Christ, Evangelist, others), alternating with the texts of "the people" in the setting of Tomás Luís de Vitoria, the Easter Vigil with the Exultet, a piece for which, allegedly, Mozart would have given his own compositions, all that made a thorough impression.

taking time also for authors who would not be subject of the final examination but who were considered essential for one's classical education. In my last year, a rabbi came just for me early every Friday to give me lessons of Hebrew. That is why I never accepted that the rules of higher education economy ask for a minimum number of students for a course. After my studies at Utrecht University I started to teach Roman law: then all law students in The Netherlands knew Latin,[4] and we could read Digest texts in the original.

Then, during the 1960s, all this came to an end. As I was just married, fathering children and writing a dissertation I was not strong enough in the defence of the old values, and I repent of that. Still, I feel sad for the destruction of culture that can only be compared with the Great Migrations in the fifth century, a destruction that has lead us into a period that has to be compared with the Dark Ages between the fall of the Western Roman Empire and the Renaissance of the twelfth century.[5] And where some of the changes in the universities were at least partially comprehensible (although I wonder why people wanted more law students: the less lawyers the better for society), the betrayal by the Roman Catholic Church of its liturgical and musical tradition, against the teaching of the Second Vatican Council,[6] is one of the most disturbing developments of the twentieth century.

Furthermore, I owe a debt to the medieval learned law, the *ius commune*, and the way the law texts are used in that law. One should forget concepts as "valid" or "in force": for the medieval romano-canonist, the texts are an eclectic collection of argument based on various sources, not all of which are legal, including the texts of the Church Fathers in the *Decretum* of Gratian. All of these texts could be used indiscriminately in every context; there were no strict boundaries between public and private law, land law and the law of contracts, and, especially in the twelfth century, between law and moral theology.[7]

When I, rather late in my life, started to visit England I was astonished by the glory, the beauty and the continuity[8] of the Anglican liturgy: it made me

[4] They all had in their grammar school also been taught in Greek, French, English and German.

[5] C H Haskins, *The Renaissance of the Twelfth Century* (Cambridge, Harvard University Press, 1927).

[6] See the Liturgy Constitution *Sacrosanctum Concilium* n. 36 § 1.

[7] An example of how the medieval reader would look at a text: in D. 50.13.1.5 Ulpian states that the governor of the province does not give judgment in cases concerning the salaries of law professors. The medieval reader would forget about the context, and just look at the sequence: "est quidem res sanctissima civilis sapientia, sed quae pretio nummario non sit aestimanda nec dehonestanda, dum in iudicio honor petitur, qui in ingressu sacramenti offerri debuit": knowledge of civil law is indeed a most hallowed thing, but something which is not to be valued in terms of money or dishonoured by seeking in court a fee which should have been offered voluntarily when someone began to follow such a calling (translation by M Crawford in *The Digest* (see n. 12) vol. V). Strangely the translation omits the last sentence: "quaedam enim tametsi honeste accipiantur, inhoneste tamen petuntur": "although one can accept some things honourably, not so ask for them". Imagine the possible influence of this sentence on the problem of legal costs!

[8] How grateful I am for the Church of England (Worship and Doctrine) Measure 1974 (1974 No. 3), s. 1 (1). Is there a better argument for Establishment?

feel at home in a church for the first time in twenty years. Now that I am contributing to a volume on "Fundamental Values" I would like to use this opportunity to plead for a little attention to a part of our tradition. I think that there are some indications that this tradition could play a useful, albeit small part in the legal education.

In § 2 I will point to some factors that make the relation between law and justice easier to be seen for some continental jurists than for the English. In § 3 and 4 I will dwell shortly on virtue in legal and in ethical literature. In § 5 I will present three thirteenth-century texts which might be unknown to most readers, and in § 6 I will say why I think that a little bit more attention for justice as virtue might be useful in legal education.

2. One of the best British films of all time, a film that pleases me more every time I see it again, is Powell and Pressburger's *A Matter of Life and Death*, from 1946. As the appeal of a British pilot against the Office of Records of the hereafter is heard, the counsel for the pilot remarks: "This is a court of justice, not of law". And an English jurist whose reputation is as great on the Continent as in England, Alfred (later Lord) Denning begins his book *The Road to Justice*[9] with a story about William Temple, Archbishop of Canterbury, saying "I cannot say that I know much about the law, having been far more interested in justice". Law and justice are obviously different, almost contrary concepts for the English. It might be useful to give some indications why continental jurists, and especially those who know Latin, either from their education or from their religion, find themselves in a different situation.

Let us start with the beginning of the most sacred of all law texts, Justinian's Digest. The first title of the first book is inscribed "*De iustitia et iure*", "Of justice and law".[10] The first fragment is by Ulpian, a jurist who died in 228 AD, from the first book of his Institutes:

> *Iuri operam daturum prius nosse oportet, unde nomen iuris descendat. est autem a iustitia appellatum: nam, ut eleganter Celsus definit, ius est ars boni et aequi.*
>
> A law student at the outset of his studies ought first to know the derivation of the word *jus*. Its derivation is from *justitia*. For, in terms of Celsus' elegant definition, the law is the art of goodness and fairness.[11]

Imagine that Ulpian had written in English: he would not have said: "a law student . . . the derivation of the word *jus*", but "of the word law". There we see immediately that for English-speaking lawyers the relationship between law and justice is not as obvious as for Latin-speakers, or better, Latin-thinkers. In

[9] London, Stevens and Sons, 1955.

[10] Note that justice is mentioned first, before law, while we speak of "law and justice".

[11] Translation by D N MacCormick, in *The Digest of Justinian*, Latin text edited by Theodor Mommsen with the aid of Paul Krueger. English translation edited by Alan Watson. Vol. I (Philadelphia, University of Pennsylvania Press, 1985).

fragment ten of the same title Ulpian (in his first book of *regulae*, rules) gives a definition of justice:

> *Iustitia est constans et perpetua voluntas ius suum cuique tribuendi. Iuris praecepta sunt haec: honeste vivere, alterum non laedere, suum cuique tribuere.*
>
> Justice is a steady and enduring will to render unto everyone his right. The basic principles of right are: to live honorably, not to harm any other person, to render to each his own.

Two things are here to be noted. The first is that justice is seen by Ulpian as a quality of a person ("steady and enduring will"). The second is that the translator had a problem with the *iuris praecepta*. They are indeed the precepts of law, not the principles of right. The word *jus* is here translated differently from fragment one. Is it because especially the "to live honorably" is difficult to accept as a precept of law, for the English speaking, whereas it was no problem for Ulpian, who derived "law" from the personal quality "justice"? And could the word "right", especially in combination with the "principles", be connected with the word "righteousness"?

The words "righteousness" and "righteous" bring us to another point which I would like to mention here shortly. Nobody doubts the influence the Bible has had on the thinking of the Europeans during the last two thousand years. Especially when the Bible texts were used in the liturgy they could become very familiar and indeed also to those people who were not regular Bible readers. St Jerome translated the very frequent word "*tsaddiq*" with "*iustus*", and in the New Testament, "*dikaios*" likewise. This was the cause that in the perception of the people the importance of justice as a kind of general virtue was very much enhanced. But where the King James version often had "just", the Revised Standard version mostly has "righteous". A few examples:[12]

Gen. 6.9 Noe vir iustus atque perfectus fuit in generationibus suis, cum Deo ambulavit. Noah was a just man and perfect in his generations, and Noah walked with God. Noah was a righteous man, blameless in his generation; Noah walked with God.

Prov. 4.18 Iustorum autem semita quasi lux splendens procedit et crescit usque ad perfectam diem. But the path of the just is as the shining light, that shineth more and more unto the perfect day. But the path of the righteous is like the light of dawn, which shines brighter and brighter until full day.

Prov. 10.7 Memoria iusti cum laudibus et nomen impiorum putrescet. The memory of the just is blessed: but the name of the wicked shall rot. The memory of the righteous is a blessing, but the name of the wicked will rot.

[12] First the Vulgate, then the King James Version, then the Revised Standard Version.

Prov. 21.15 Gaudium iusto est facere iudicium et pavor operantibus iniquitatem. It is joy to the just to do judgment: but destruction shall be to the workers of iniquity. When justice is done, it is a joy to the righteous, but dismay to evildoers.
Eccl. 7.21 (20) Non est enim homo iustus in terra qui faciat bonum et non peccet. For there is not a just man upon earth, that doeth good, and sinneth not. Surely there is not a righteous man on earth who does good and never sins.
Mat. 13.49 Sic erit in consummatione saeculi: exibunt angeli et separabunt malos de medio iustorum. So shall it be at the end of the world: the angels shall come forth, and sever the wicked from among the just. So it will be at the close of the age. The angels will come out and separate the evil from the righteous.
Act. 3.14 Vos autem sanctum et iustum negastis, et petistis virum homicidam donari vobis. But ye denied the Holy One and the Just, and desired a murderer to be granted unto you. But you denied the Holy and Righteous One, and asked for a murderer to be granted to you.
Rom. 1.17 Iustus autem ex fide vivit. The just shall live by faith. He who through faith is righteous shall live.

Some examples from liturgical texts:

Os justi meditabitur sapientiam, The mouth of the righteous speaketh wisdom.[13]
Laetabitur justus in Domino, The righteous shall be glad in the Lord.[14]
Justus ut palma florebit, The righteous shall flourish like the palm tree.[15]
Justorum animae in manu Dei sunt, The souls of the virtuous are in the hands of God.[16]

These examples may suffice to show that in the Latin tradition the *iustus* was seen as say that I know much about the law, having been far more interested in "justice". Law and justice are obviously different, almost contrary concepts for the English.

[13] Introit from the first Mass for a Confessor non-bishop; Gradual from the Mass for the Doctors of the Church; Ps. 36 (37) 30.

[14] Introit from the second Mass for a Martyr non-bishop; Communion-verse from the Mass for a Martyr during Easter; Ps. 63.11 (64.10).

[15] Introit from the second Mass for a Confessor non-bishop; Gradual from the first Mass for the same; Alleluia-verse from the Mass for the Abbots; Communion-verse from the Mass for the Doctors of the Church; Ps. 91.13 (92.12).

[16] Offertory from the third Mass for more Martyrs; Gradual and Communion-verso in the octave of a virtuous man and *iustitia* could be readily understood as a virtue. St Peter and St Paul; Wisd. 3.1. Translation according to *The Jerusalem Bible* (London, 1966); the *New Jerusalem Bible* (London, 1985) has for "virtuous" "upright".

3. In modern literature on legal philosophy the virtue of justice has a rather restricted place. Although there is much attention for the relationship between law and morals[17] and for legal ethics,[18] the concept of justice that is now prevailing is that of "social justice".

A classical formulation is that of John Rawls:[19]

> Many different kinds of things are said to be just and unjust: not only laws, institutions, and social systems, but also particular actions of many kinds, including decisions, judgments, and imputations. We also call the attitudes and dispositions of persons, and persons themselves, just and unjust. Our topic, however, is that of social justice. For us the primary subject of justice is the basic structure of society, or more exactly, the way in which the major social institutions distribute fundamental rights and duties and determine the division of advantages from social cooperation.

This is a kind of justice that is not covered by Ulpian's definition.[20] But looking for justice as virtue, we can turn to other authors. Roscoe Pound[21] starts, with the Greek philosophers, with justice as an individual virtue. He cites Ulpian's definition (from Justinian's Institutes), mentions the cardinal virtues, and continues:

> From this we got analogical uses such as the rightfulness or uprightness of something. . . . By further development we get the idea of the maintenance or administration of that which is just, and hence the regime of rendering to everyone his due or his rights . . . From this we get the idea of a regime of establishing or determining rights in accordance with law.

C K Allen[22] also starts with "Justice as Pure Virtue". In discussing Ulpian's definition he, rightly, stresses the importance of the words *constans et perpetua voluntas* (firm and perennial disposition). That disposition "is the moral attitude . . . without which justice cannot manifest itself, and, as we shall see, it is not merely a matter of facile intuition, but of intuition ripened by experience

[17] It is remarkable that in Lon Fuller, *The Morality of Law* (Revised edition, New Haven and London, Yale University Press, 1969), "justice" is not even an entry in the Index.

[18] As recently as 1998, illustrated by the appearance of a new international and interdisciplinary journal, "*Legal Ethics*".

[19] J Rawls, *A Theory of Justice* (Oxford, Clarendon Press, 1972), p. 7.

[20] A Ross, *On Law and Justice* (London, Stevens & Sons, 1958), p. 276 is extremely critical of this definition and the following principles (note that Ross does not write "precepts"). "It has often been repeated as the quintessence of wisdom. But it is pure delusion which achieves an appearance of obviousness because it says nothing at all". Ross seems to think that a text of the Digest can be read as a mathematical formula. In a different province of learning one could say "littera in textu occidit, spiritus in glossa vivificat" (the letter in the text kills, the spirit in the gloss gives life). For a different understanding of Ulpian's text see Ch. Perelman, "Les trois aspects de la justice", in Ch. Perelman, *Justice et raison*, 2nd ed. (Bruxelles, Editions de l'Université, 1972), p. 155 at p. 174 (English translation by J Petrie, "The three aspects of justice 2, in Ch. Perelman, *The Idea of Justice and the Problem of Argument*, with an introduction by H L A Hart (London, Routledge & Kegan, 1963), p. 61 at p. 77).

[21] *Justice according to law* (New Haven, Yale University Press, 1951), p. 3.

[22] *Aspects of Justice* (London, Stevens & Sons, 1958), p. 5 sq.

and by anxious cultivation". Is that last sentence not an argument for a somewhat more explicit attention for justice as virtue in legal education?

4. It is time to make here one remark, which, if superfluous, may do no harm, if not, be of some use to understand why a virtue is important. During the centuries that the Christian religion[23] was dominant in our civilization, people believed that they were on earth for a certain time, to prepare for the eternal life after death. Every individual would be judged individually, and the judgment meant for the immortal soul (and for the body after the resurrection) eternal beatitude or eternal damnation. The way one lived influenced the judgment.[24] If we forget this it becomes very difficult to understand what all the thinking and writing on virtues and vices was about. Even if we do not accept the beliefs that were fundamental in former times, we should know that they existed; alas, one sometimes gets nowadays the impression that all this is so far from us, that we have lost our capacity for empathy.[25] The concept of virtue that is adopted here is the classical Christian one (which had its roots mainly in Greek philosophy).[26] The definition of St Thomas Aquinas[27] is "*bona qualitas mentis qua recte vivitur, qua nullus male utitur*", "a good habit of the mind productive of good living and incapable of abuse".[28] Therefore, I shall look at the virtue of justice as one of the four so-called cardinal virtues, and not dwell on the treatment of the subject by some of the great writers on ethics of the past,[29] nor on some of the modern works on this subject,[30] who are for the most part going their own way.

The four cardinal virtues, prudence, justice, temperance and fortitude were first discerned by Plato, and became through Aristotle, Cicero and the Church Fathers a common element of the European tradition. They were known to the

[23] One religion, most of the time manifesting itself in different churches.

[24] Allow me to ignore some details of predestination theology.

[25] There are, nevertheless, still people who believe the old Creed.

[26] Much historical material (not only on justice) can be found in G del Vecchio, *Justice. An Historical and Philosophical Essay*. Edited with Additional Notes by A H Campbell (Edinburgh, University Press, 1952), especially pp. 18–41. For the early development in Hellas see E A Havelock, *The Greek Concept of Justice. From Its Shadow in Homer to Its Substance in Plato* (Cambridge, Mass. and London, Harvard University Press, 1978).

[27] *Summa Theologica*, I II qu.55 art.4. (University Press, 1978).

[28] R C Mortimer, *The Elements of Moral Theology* (London, Adam and Charles Black, 1947), p. 102. Cf. T C O'Brien, *New Catholic Encyclopedia* 14 (1967) 704: "a habitual, well-established, readiness or disposition of man's powers directing them to some specific goodness of act".

[29] Like Hume: see J Harrison, *Hume's Theory of Justice* (Oxford, Clarendon Press, 1981); D Wiggins, "Natural and Artificial Virtues, A Vindication of Hume's Scheme", in R Crisp (ed.), *How Should One Live? Essays on the Virtues* (Ibiden, 1996); Kant: see A D Rosen, *Kant's Theory of Justice* (Ithaca and London, Cornell University Press, 1993); O O'Neill, "Kant's Virtues", in *How should one live*; H Sidgwick, *The Methods of Ethics*, 5th ed. (London, Macmillan, 1893).

[30] Like M Slote, *Goods and* Virtues (Oxford, Clarendon Press, 1983); N J H Dent, *The moral psychology of the virtues* (Cambridge University Press, 1984); J W Chapman and W A Galson (eds), *Virtue* (Nomos, Yearbook of The American Society for Political and Legal Philosophy 34, New York and London, New York University Press, 1992); O O'Neill, *Towards Justice and Virtue. A constructive account of practical reasoning* (Cambridge University Press, 1996).

Judaic wisdom literature too:[31] Wisd. 8.7 "or if it be virtue you love, why, virtues are the fruits of her labours, since it is she who teaches temperance and prudence, justice and fortitude".[32] Terminologically it is interesting that the first "virtue" is "*dikaiosunè*" in Greek and "*iustitia*" in Latin; the second "virtues" "aretai" and "virtutes", "fortitude" "andreian" and "virtutem". Here we see a good example of justice as the universal virtue.[33]

There is another traditional number of virtues: seven. Then we have next to the cardinal virtues the theological virtues of faith, hope and charity. These virtues are "infused", that is, "implanted in us by God".[34] Christian authors tend to stress the links between the theological and the cardinal virtues.[35] But "in this secular age"[36] we can restrict our view to the cardinal virtues. P T Geach inscribes the first chapter of his *The Virtues*[37] "Why men need the virtues" and writes:

> The definite article in my title is significant. I am concerned with why men need the seven virtues to which tradition gives pre-eminence: the theological virtues of faith, hope and charity, and the cardinal virtues of prudence, temperance, justice and courage. I commit myself to the thesis that all of these *are* virtues: and I shall argue that this thesis cannot rationally be doubted so far as the four cardinal virtues are concerned.[38]

We will take a short look at two totally different works, that speak of justice, adopting the system of the cardinal virtues, one strongly fixed in the broad tradition of Anglicanism, the other highly personal.

The first work is Mortimer's *The Elements of Moral Theology.*[39] After general chapters (The End of Man, Law, Human Action, The Morality of Actions, Conscience, The Virtues) he discusses the different theological and cardinal virtues, whereby justice takes more room than fortitude, temperance and prudence together. After citing the traditional definition of justice Mortimer discusses the three prerequisites for every act of justice: a person whose right is being respected; a right, something strictly owed and due; the fact that the right must be rendered fully, completely and exactly (185–6). What is a right and what is

[31] But we should not jump to the much misused term "judaeo-christian". If we want to assign the elements from which our so-called cultural heritage is directly derived we should speak about Hellenistic, Roman and Christian elements, the Jewish culture essentially passed on by the Christian.

[32] Translation according to the *Jerusalem Bible.*

[33] Del Vecchio, *Justice* 18.

[34] Mortimer, p. 105.

[35] For example, H R Williamson, *The Seven Christian Virtues* (London, SCM Press, 1949), p. 50.

[36] Tom Lehrer, *This Was The Week That Was*, Reprise RS 6179.

[37] The Stanton Lectures 1973–4 (Cambridge University Press, 1979, repr. with corrections 1979), p. 1.

[38] At the end of his book he states: "All virtues, however, are in the end vain for a man without the theological virtues of faith, hope and charity" (p. 168). I am not that pessimistic, and would not have written this article if I were.

[39] See note on R C Mortimer, who was Bishop of Exeter from 1949 to 1973, see B G Skinner, *Robert Exon* (Bognor Regis, New Horizon, 1979).

its base? The basis of rights is the sanctity of the individual, the ultimate basis of rights is God (186–8). Starting from the distinction between a right *in* a thing and a right *to* a thing there follows a digression on property (188–94). Then rights in general are distinguished into three classes: internal or personal rights, . . . such as life, health and the exercise of one's faculties; external rights, i.e. property and so forth; quasi-external rights, such as reputation and honour; something is said about the obtaining of external rights (194–7).

The three kinds of justice are distinguished: general, distributive and commutative (the latter two species of particular justice) (197–8). "Of these three kinds of justice, distributive covers the smallest field, and may conveniently be dealt with first" (198). Remarkable his opinion: "He who offends against distributive justice only is not obliged to make any restitution, for he has not offended against anyone's strict right" (200). The question if a judge has to deliver judgment in accordance with the evidence or in accordance with the truth is touched upon (203–4). The part on general justice (204–8) summarises the moral duty of man in this point as follows:

> It is the duty, then, of every individual, in the interest of the common good, to lead a moral life, to respect the rights of others, to defend the State against aggression, and to make his contribution to its common wealth. In this way he plays his part in achieving the true aim of a State . . . (206–7).

The discussion on commutative justice is mainly devoted to restitution, as "the distinctive feature of commutative justice" (209). In the last paragraph, justice is put in its proper place, albeit somewhat contradictory:

> Upon the practice of justice is based all virtuous living, and the duties of love cannot be either known or performed except the humbler and less exalted concept of justice be understood . . . Justice . . . is rightly called a cardinal virtue, and the queen of the virtues (223).

The second work we will consider is Geach's *The Virtues.*[40] Geach sees justice as "an immensely problematic concept", and starts, somewhat surprisingly, with "veracity and fidelity: telling the truth and keeping promises" (110). The problem of lying is treated first (111–17), then he reaches promises (117–22). then "covenants, promises exchanged . . . Without covenants' being made and generally observed, the amenities of civilized life would be largely made impossible" (122–3). He turns to Hobbes to make clear what justice in civil society consists in (125–8). At the end, he makes clear that his book is not aimed at the atheist: "I have said little in this chapter of the now much agitated topic of justice as fair distribution. I find the topic too difficult to discuss in this work if it regards justice as between men" (129).

5. Let us now take a look at three works from the Middle Ages, to get an idea of the insights and stimuli one could get from reading those texts. "One could

[40] See n. 38 *supra*.

get": I can understand that some people might find these things totally out of date, fundamentally erroneous and utterly irrelevant. That is why I made some personal remarks in § 1. Two works are of English origin; the third is continental, but presented here in an English seventeenth century translation, out of veneration for antiquarian books and Exeter University Library.

The first work is the *Summa de commendatione virtutum et extirpatione vitiorum* of Thomas de Chobham, who studied in Paris under Petrus Cantor, was back in England 1190–2, became Subdean of Salisbury ca. 1208, was in Paris again somewhere between 1222 and 1228, died between 1233 and 1236.[41] This work is dated by its editor as 1220 or somewhat later.

Thomas' *Summa* belongs to a type of literature that was very popular in the Middle Ages, both in Latin and in the vernacular.[42] The main function of this literature was educational and devotional.[43] It is divided into a prologue and five books: the commendation of the virtues is in book four. Thomas[44] systematises this book according to the principal virtues: the theological virtues charity, faith and hope, and the cardinal virtues prudence, justice, temperance and fortitude. The treatise on justice is the most elaborate of those on the cardinal virtues: it takes more space than the other three together.[45]

Thomas starts his treatise on justice[46] with a very familiar-sounding definition: justice is a virtue which gives everyone his own (*unicuique reddens quod suum est, 1290*).[47] Human society could not exist, if everyone took the possessions of others. Worse still, if someone wanted to usurp the things pertaining to God, he would seem to chase God from his realm (1290–3). But does justice not presuppose injustice, because if there were no injustice, there would be no place for justice? No, Wisd. 1.15: Justice is eternal and immortal (1294–1300).

Justice has many meanings: firstly, when a man subjects himself to a superior, as Christ the man to God the Father; secondly when a man subjects himself to his peer, as Christ the God to God the Father; thirdly, when a man subjects himself to an inferior, as Christ to John the Baptist. But these two last kinds of justice are more properly humility, as to give almonds to the poor, which is

[41] Edition of the *Summa de commendatione virtutum* by F Morenzoni, Corpus Christianorum, Continuatio Mediaevalis 82B (Turnhout, Brepols, 1997). Two other works by Thomas had been edited by the same in the same series: *Summa de arte praedicandi*, CCCM 82, 1988 (there biographical details) p. xxxi; *Sermones*. CCCM 82A, 1993. His work with the greatest circulation, the *Summa confessorum*, has been edited by F Broomfield, Analecta Mediaevalia Namurcensia 25 (Louvain-Paria, 1968).

[42] R Newhauser, *The Treatise on Vices and Virtues in Latin and in the Vernacular*, Typologie des sources du Moyen Age occidental, Fasc. 68 (Turnhout, Brepols, 1993), with bibliography.

[43] Newhauser, 65, 135, 155.

[44] And the editor. The rubrication of medieval manuscripts is seldom constant or complete, therefore an editor almost always has the task to fill in systematical elements.

[45] Like in Mortimer.

[46] Of course, I give only some of the barest outlines of his exposé.

[47] The numbers are those of the lines of the Latin text of book four.

improperly called justice, properly mercy (1326–38). Another distinction is that between weighing justice (*iusticia appendens*) and due-giving justice (*justicia reddens*). Weighing justice is that with which we weigh on the same scale our own sins and the sins of the others (1341–4). Due-giving justice is fourfold: to give to God and our neighbour what is his; to give hate to sin; to give contempt to the world; and to give resistance to the devil (1356–60).

For the conservation of human society through justice, we must consider a threefold status: firstly, that of the superiors (*maiorum*); secondly, that of the inferiors (*minorum*); thirdly, that of all. For every status, justice is threefold: for the superiors, in judging, in punishing, in showing mercy; for the inferiors, in obedience, in patience, in holding-on; for all, in paying wages and debts, in giving back what is entrusted, in telling the truth (1482–91). In consequence of this distinction Thomas lets follow three chapters on the justice of the superiors, the justice of the inferiors, the justice of all. Concerning the justice of the superiors, the first and obviously most important duty in giving judgment is to avoid *acceptio personarum*, all kinds of giving in to the favours of dignity of the people who are accepting judgment. A judge has to give judgment according to the truth and according to divine wisdom, not according to his own power (1495–1509).

An interesting opinion is that found in ll. 1514–25, on 1 Cor. 6.4: what St Paul meant was that in secular proceedings, where the hail of the soul is not involved, people who should lead a monastic life or preach should not act as judges, but they should leave those causes to less worthy people who cannot read and write and know the customs and laws of the realms or the regions ("*indigniores qui sunt illiterati et nouerunt consuetudines et constitutiones regnorum uel uillarum*"). In punishing, the judges must imitate God, who always punishes less and rewards more than deserved (1566–8). Certainly he who judges without mercy should know that he is like the devil (1599–1600). In showing mercy: injustice in showing mercy is no less sin than injustice in punishing (1685–6). All these theses are elucidated by a wealth of references to Holy Scripture, Church Fathers and philosophers. A very beautiful sentence is *aliis sepe indulgeas, tibi numquam*, "forgive others often, never yourself" (1669), where the note of the editor shows the popularity of this saying.

The justice of the inferiors consists firstly in obedience. Obedience is a very important part of this virtue, because the first man sinned through disobedience, and all his progeny fell with him (1758–62). It is noteworthy that some prelates commit heavy sins against their subjects, in making too many laws and precepts, so that the subjects are breaking the law often. Who would obey so many precepts? This was one of the reasons why the Old Testament was changed for the New (1834–7).

Secondly their justice consists in patience. Patience takes place in the suffering of injustice, because, although self-defence is permitted, nobody should take vengeance in his own hands. In the secular world (*secundum uitam humanam*)[48] it is therefore stated that nobody can be judge in his own cause and that lost possessions should be sought through a judge, not taken back by violence (1894–1902).

Finally, there is sustainment (*sustinentia*). The difference between patience and sustainment is that patience has to do with actual bad things, sustainment with the expectation of good things (2035–8). Thomas then gives illustrations which are mostly formulated for the relation between God and man: the waiting for wages, for vengeance, for the positive answer to a prayer, for the healing from an illness.

In the chapter about the justice of all Thomas writes first about restitution, that is to give back that which one has taken from someone else. This obligation is suspended as long as the debtor has insufficient means, so that it is impossible for him to pay his debts; one has to wait until he is in better circumstances (2201–4). The concept of restitution, to give back, *reddere*, is very large: it encompasses rented, borrowed, stolen goods, wages for work, the price for goods bought, found goods, taxes imposed, goods received in custody (2220–3). The question of self-help is discussed (2240–58). Then follows a long treatise about special cases of restitution, about the obligation of the heir, what to do if the person to whom things should be given back cannot be found, if the obligation of the debtor can be stretched so far, that he after restitution has nothing, and if a thing obtained by robbery in some cases can be retained after penance.[49]

The last part,[50] about truth, is very short, and shows that probably the wish of the author to divide concepts into three has been the fundament of taking up the telling of the truth as the third aspect of the justice of all. He states, rather bluntly, that truth is a special kind of justice, but that he has little to say in this place about the commendation of truth, because he is speaking here only about virtues, and he will reserve the treatment of lies for the book on vices (2547–50).

The second work is an anonymous one, written in England shortly after 1241, the *Summa virtutum de remediis anime*,[51] called *Postquam* by the editor (after its incipit). This work belongs to the same category as Thomas' *Summa*, but has a different starting point. Attention is centred on the vices, and the virtues are treated as the remedies that correspond to the vices. So the greater part of *Postquam*, chapters ii–ix, deal with the so-called "remedial" virtues; only the first chapter is devoted to the theological and cardinal virtues.[52] *Postquam* starts with some remarks on virtues in general:[53]

[48] Here we can clearly see that the readers Thomas was addressing were clerics.

[49] This text would suffice for a one-term legal history course.

[50] This part has been made into a separate one by the editor, there is no manuscript evidence; but it must be admitted that in commenting on the threefold "justice-of-all" Thomas has taken the first two aspects together, so that the third aspect stands out more.

[51] Edited by S Wenzel (The Chaucer Library, Athens, University of Georgia Press, 1984). With an English translation, but, alas, no *apparatus fontium*.

[52] Wenzel, pp. 7–8.

[53] The numbers are those of the lines of the Latin text of chapter I.

"Before we define virtue, we must present a division of the virtues, for division is the way toward definition. Virtues are divided into natural virtues, political virtues, and virtues of grace. Natural virtues are the powers of the soul and the body . . . (5–8). A political virtue is a virtue acquired through the exercise of deeds that are good by their nature . . . (22–3). Now we turn to the virtue of grace, which can be considered in two ways: either as *gratis data*, 'gratuitously given', or as *gratum faciens*, 'rendering acceptable'. The first comprises not only the virtues of grace proper but also the political and natural virtues, as well as spiritual and temporal gifts . . . The second kind of virtue of grace, which 'renders acceptable', comprises the theological virtues and the cardinal virtues inasmuch as they are formed with grace, because before the coming of grace they are numbered among the political virtues" (156–63).

The treatment of the cardinal virtues is rather short, but there is some etymology: "The political virtues also include the cardinal virtues as long as these are unformed, because once they have been formed with grace, they belong to the virtues of grace. There are four cardinal virtues: prudence, justice, fortitude, and moderation (*temperancia*). They are called 'cardinal' as if of the heart, because according to Isidore '*cardias*' in Greek means heart . . . Or else they are named after *cardo*, 'hinge', because just as a hinge supports the door, so these virtues support the mind in its workings . . ." (31–42). (The last etymology is right).

The short treatise on justice shows a distinction we have seen in Thomas de Chobham: "Justice is the virtue 'by which each is given his own', according to Augustine . . . Or according to Tullius [Cicero], justice is 'the virtue which gives everyone his right'. Its acts are to subordinate the lower to the higher, to serve only God spiritually, to worship and to fear him . . . Moreover, this virtue teaches us to give reverence and obedience to men of higher rank . . . It also teaches to give counsel and aid to one's equals, to unite oneself with one's equals, not to desire to be like others, and to do unto others as we would have them do to us . . . It also teaches us to show compassion and sympathy to our inferiors, so that we may judge of the disposition of our neighbours by ourselves . . . And it teaches us to help the suffering and to punish evil habits . . . We should know that justice is twofold: one is general and embraces all virtues and has its subject what is owed and what is worthy; the other is a special virtue, on the same level with the other three cardinal virtues, and has as its subject what pertains to each individual" (106–24).

That is all *Postquam* has to say; in the end we can notice a certain systematic weakness.

The third text is an English translation of a work (wrongly) ascribed to Albertus the Great (ca. 1200–1280), the *Paradisus animi*.[54]

[54] See on this work M W Bloomfield, *Incipits of Latin Works on the Virtues and Vices, 1100–1500 A.D.* (Publications of the Mediaeval Academy of America 88), Cambridge, Mass., 1979, nr. 0677 (p. 72); P Glorieux, *Répertoire des Maîtres en théologie de Paris au XIIIe siècle* (Études de Philosophie Médiévale, 17–18), Paris 1933–4, vol. I. notice 6, cq (p. 72).

> The Paradise of the Soul: or, A little Treatise of Virtues. Made by Albert the Great, Bishop of Ratisbon, who died in the year 1280. Translated out of Latin into English. By N.N.[55] Printed for William Brooks, 1682.[56]

It is a very simple work, which gives the impression of being more devotional than educational. The four cardinal virtues are treated in chapters 8 to 11, in the order: prudence, fortitude, justice, temperance. The most important elements of the author's scheme are: True and perfect [Prudence etc.] is . . . He has true [Prudence etc.] . . . The Office of [Prudence etc.] is . . . *The Paradise of the Soul* distinguishes between Justice to God ("True and perfect Justice to God, is, a rendering of due praise to the Divine Nature in all things . . . He has true Justice to God, who is faithful to him, always, and every where, in keeping all Precepts and Vows" (63–4)) and Justice to our Neighbour. That Justice to our Neighbour is clearly formulated in moral terms, echoing the Golden Rule:

> True Justice to our Neighbour lies in two things. Tob. 4. Never to do to our Neighbour what we would not justly have to be done to our selves; that is, never to hurt or offend him, by Word, or Deed, or Sign, or Counsel, in his Goods, in his Body, or in his Honour; never to suspect ill of him; never to detract from him; never to misinterpret or diminish his Good; never to hinder his Good; for these things no Body, according to Justice, would have to be done to himself. Also, to do good to his Neighbour, as he justly would have to be done to himself; that is, to honour his Neighbour, to think well of him, to interpret well all his Actions, even his bad ones; always to rejoice with him in his Good, and to condole with him for his Misfortunes; always to excuse his Innocence and to defend him being absent: for every one, according to Justice, would have these things done to himself (64–5)

For those who noticed that there was added a small interpolation in the Golden Rule, the explanation follows:

> And it is said according to Justice, because a Judge would not be hanged by a Thief, and yet he ought to hang a Thief; because not to Will that, is according to Justice. And a Robber would willingly be robbed so he might be permitted to rob, which notwithstanding, he ought not to do, because to will that, is not according to Justice (65–6).

After these thoughts, which are totally clear also to the non-believer, God is put into the centre again:

> The Office of true Justice is, to rectify our Thoughts and Affections, that they be always set upon God; our Will, that it be conformed to the Divine Will; our

[55] The Exeter copy has in manuscript: Constantin.

[56] D Wing, *Short-Title Catalogue of Books Printed in England . . . 1641–1700*, 2nd ed., Vol. I (New York, The Modern Language Association of America, 1994) no. 875 H. I used the copy (not in Wing, the only copies in England he gives are in the British Library and in Downside Abbey) of Exeter University Library, signature 1682/ALB, from Syon Abbey, Chudleigh (there signature K.31).

> Intentions, that they always eye God, and that we refer all things to his Praise. In like manner, to direct all our Words and Deeds, that they be always done for some special and right end. And these things are an Argument of true Justice (67–8).

The three texts we have looked at show a mixture of education and devotion. I think that "education" and "devotion" could be seen as complementary, in a way, and that this view could have some relevance for legal (and other) education.

6. Why do I think that some more attention for justice as virtue might be useful in legal education? One reason, I must be honest, is that I love tradition, that I deeply deplore the loss of sense for it, and that I would like to see every opportunity taken to reintroduce it. Another reason is that I believe that a university has to take a responsibility to make good, complete and well-disposed human beings out of its students, especially the young ones. I might in this respect think too much, maybe, of the college system of the old English universities: but I have the impression that over here, somewhat more than on the Continent, it is indeed "life at university", and not as much "life in a university city or town". And, of course, as a continental I see the university as the primary place to get your education (factually, that is: I think that most legal, especially the professional, education should take place elsewhere).

A third, and maybe the most important reason is this: I think that more attention to virtue might contribute to a better ethical development of the individual, because of "the importance of enabling individual moral growth as a basis for fostering ethical understanding and behaviour".[57] And the concept of virtue promotes the acceptance of ethical standards as above all personal standards, and with that a higher degree of realism.

I would like to conclude with a citation of John Cottingham:[58]

> The result of this depersonalizing tendency in what are still the two leading branches of modern ethical theory [utilitarianism or consequentialism and deontological ethics] is that much of the work done by philosophers of ethics has little relation to the way nearly all of us live . . . The point . . . is that many ethical writers, whether working at an abstract level or on concrete problems, are officially subscribing to accounts of rightness and goodness which simply do not impinge on, or make contact with, the partialistic commitments and preferential ties that deeply and pervasively inform their own lives . . . There is a serious instability in any moral theory which urges on us attitudes that we could not in honesty conceive of incorporating into our ordinary blueprint for daily living. . . . (T)he ethical excellences unfolded in the

[57] J Webb, "Conduct, Ethics and Experience in Vocational Legal Education" in *Ethical Challenges*, *supra* n. 1, 271 at 283.

[58] J Cottingham, "Partiality and the Virtues", in *How Should One Live?*, *supra* n. 29, 57 at 58.

classical Aristotelian conception of the virtuous life presuppose, for the most part, a preexisting network of preferences and partialities . . . (T)he presupposition of such networks is the basis of that rootedness in the real world which gives virtue theory a decisive edge over its competitors; the "autocentric" perspective . . . can be seen as one of the hallmarks that confer worth and authenticity on virtue theory as against its impersonally oriented rivals.

4

The Principle of Non-Discrimination as a Fundamental Value

SIMON HONEYBALL*

Is the principle of non-discrimination a fundamental value? By "the principle of non-discrimination" I mean that idea which finds legal form in the race, sex and disability discrimination legislation of Great Britain rather than any other broader conception.[1] In that the categories of discrimination law are now set to widen, following the Treaty of Amsterdam, to include age, sexual orientation and religion and beliefs, we are perhaps moving towards a general conception of the ground of discrimination. The time is therefore ripe to consider how fundamental the principle of non-discrimination as a value is.

It is not at all clear that the principle of non-discrimination, framed in that way, is one instantly recognisable as a fundamental value. There is no great body of literature in the history of moral thought that argues that it is. At least, there would appear not to be. However, if one were to view the principle of non-discrimination as synonymous with, or at least entailed by, the concept of equality then, if one could make the further claim hold that the concept of equality itself is a fundamental value, then it necessarily follows, of course, by definition that the principle of nondiscrimination is a fundamental value. If we cannot do any of this, then the claim must be made on independent grounds that the principle is fundamental.

1. THE DEFINITIONAL RELATIONSHIP BETWEEN NON-DISCRIMINATION AND EQUALITY

Let us begin with an examination of the relationship between the principle of non-discrimination (POND) and equality, as that would appear to be much the

* I would like to thank Mr David Perrott and Professor Jenny McEwan for reading a draft of this article, and for their comments. I am, of course, solely responsible for this final version.

[1] The most important relevant legislation is the Race Relations Act 1976 (the RRA), the Sex Discrimination Act 1975 (the SDA), the Equal Pay Act 1970 (the EqPA) and the Disability Discrimination Act 1995 (the DDA).

easiest route to establish POND as a fundamental value. We must start by seeing if the definitions of POND and equality are the same. This is an attractive idea, for does POND amount to anything more than the notion that like cases should be treated alike, and that unlike cases should be treated unalike? This is the principle of formal (as opposed to substantive) equality recognised since Plato and Aristotle.[2] Certainly, that POND does mean this would seem to be indicated by the definitions in the anti-discrimination legislation. Section 1(1)(a) of the Sex Discrimination Act 1975, for example, defines discrimination as occurring where a person treats another, on the grounds of her sex, less favourably than he treats, or would treat, a man, or alternatively, under section 1(1)(b), where he applies a requirement or condition which a smaller proportion of one sex can comply with than the other.[3] Here we have all the elements of the principle of formal equality. We have the element of comparison, with the categories identified as to what makes one person like another (sex) and the manner in which inequality can come about (treatment or the application of a requirement or condition with disproportionate impact). If this is correct, then POND is part of the classical concept of justice as, Aristotle wrote, equality and justice are synonymous. "To be just is to be equal, to be unjust is to be unequal".[4]

The issue, however, is far from settled. Catherine Barnard, for example, sees a distinction between POND and equality in that POND fills the vacuum in the principle of equality as the latter provides no internal guidance as to the relevant characteristics to be compared. She calls this the "hidden value". POND provides a framework within which equality can be given substance.[5] But there surely is nothing in the general nature of POND itself that does this: it is merely that in its legal manifestation the necessary detail is provided.

There is an obvious close relationship between POND and equality in that all who come within the ambit of POND must be treated equally. But it is not clear if this is only because POND is entirely an equality-based notion, or whether it is because it is a principle, encapsulated in law at least, through the technique of rules. In other words, there is a requirement that anyone whose case falls under a rule is entitled to be treated equally with anyone whose case also falls under it, and may be entitled to be treated differently from anyone whose case does not fall under the rule. But this is something that is entailed in

[2] Aristotle, *Ethica Nicomachea* V.3.1131a–1131b (W Ross, ed. 1925). See Westen, "The Empty Idea of Equality" (1982) 95 *Harvard Law Review* 537 at 543.

[3] There are similar definitions in the other legislation – see RRA s.5 and DDA s.5. There is a small difference between them in that the SDA and the DDA require the ground of discrimination to be the applicant's own sex or disability as appropriate, but the RRA merely states that the discrimination must be "on racial grounds" which, of course, need not refer to the applicant's own race. This distinction is immaterial for present purposes.

[4] Aristotle, *Ethica Eudemia* VII.9.1241b. See Westen, *supra* n.2.

[5] Barnard, "The Principle of Equality in the Community Context: *P Grant*, *Kalanke* and *Marshall:* Four Uneasy Bedfellows?" [1998] *CLJ* 352 at 363.

the moral and logical foundations of deciding cases under rules. It is not something that arises from the content of those rules. And, of course, the concept of non-discrimination is something that takes effect through the content of the rules that manifest it. To put it another way, it may be because POND is enforced through rules that the importance of equality is clear or, at least, POND is no different from any other concept that takes effect through rules in that precepts of equality necessarily pertain.

It might be thought that there is a fundamental distinction between POND and the principle of equality in that POND may operate so as to protect inequalities. This can happen in two ways. First, the principle itself may be used to give certain advantages or protections to a group which otherwise does not have it. So, for example, the sex discrimination legislation, although ostensibly designed to ensure equal protection of the sexes, is actually also used to give women preferential treatment in certain circumstances, namely when they are pregnant or have given birth. In considering whether there has been discrimination against a male applicant, no account may be taken of special treatment afforded to women in connection with pregnancy or childbirth.[6]

In some circumstances women are given benefits and protections not afforded to men, not through the discrimination legislation, but by virtue of positive rights. So, to take but one example, women are given rights to maternity leave which are not enjoyed by men. This, of course, is not best viewed as an application of the principle of *non*-discrimination, but a legislative recognition (normally considered anathema) of justified direct discrimination. Although positive rights would seem to be the route by which this should be done, some commentators are wary of this because of perceived difficulties. Sandra Fredman identifies four of these.[7] First, although the rights exist without making reference to a male comparator, she sees a male norm continuing to lurk beneath the surface. Secondly, these rights take a lower place to the perceived dictates of the market, employers' needs and government economic policies. Thirdly, the rights are inaccessible because they must be enforced by individuals in the absence of class actions and lastly, by giving rights to women, this reinforces the differences between men and women, particularly the assumption that women are primarily responsible for child-care. Therefore the anti-discrimination legislation is instead often prayed in aid to protect women who are treated in particular detrimental ways, even though no comparable man can be found. Indeed, the European Court of Justice has said on several occasions, and this has been mirrored also in the English courts, that no comparison *should* be attempted.[8] Without a comparison with a man, it would seem that POND cannot be said to be rooted in the principle of equality at all. There

[6] SDA s.2. See too the Pregnancy Workers Directive 92/85/EEC.

[7] Fredman, *Women and the Law* (Oxford, Clarendon Press, 1997), p. 192 et seq.

[8] See *Dekker* v. *Stichting Vormingscentrum voor Jong Volwassenen (VJV-Centrum) Plus* Case C-177/88 [1990] ECR I-3941 and (applying this principle into English law) the decision of the House of Lords in *James* v. *Eastleigh Borough Council* [1990] ICR 554, [1990] IRLR 288.

must, after all, be at least two people involved in the picture for equality to be relevant – there has to be something to be equal to.

However, it seems that this view may be mistaken. That it is not necessary to have a comparative element in equality would seem to be unarguable. But it would also seem to be untenable in so far as discrimination is concerned too. After all, to be discriminated against would seem to involve the idea that one is being treated not just badly, but *worse*, and this involves a comparison. But what it need not involve is a comparison with someone else, even a hypothetical person as the discrimination legislation allows.[9] Indeed, perhaps it should not, because it is important in deciding equality issues, and in identifying discrimination, that all irrelevant factors are stripped away leaving as much identical as possible in order to be secure that the cause of the disadvantageous treatment lies where it is claimed to lie, and nowhere else. Thus, is not the right approach in deciding if someone has been discriminated against on the grounds of their sex to ask, not if someone else of the opposite sex would have been treated differently (because there may be another reason for that), but if *that* person themself would have been treated differently but for their sex?[10]

It is interesting, however, that while this sits well with the vocabulary of discrimination, it is less comfortable to take this approach with the language of equality. We do not tend to refer to equality in this way because the principle of equality is concerned with the relative positioning of individuals. This is not the case with POND, as we have seen, where it is the relationship between the individual and the reason for their treatment that is the focus of concern. This is not just a difference in the language that is used but can be seen to pinpoint a fundamental distinction between POND and the principle of equality.

The second way that POND may secure unequal treatment is in the case where it is used to protect proportionate value. This occurs where the relevant parties are not equal nor do they claim to be. However, their inequality should be such as to reflect a scale which can be considered fair and logical, and where this does not occur, what might be termed the principle of proportionate value (as a limb of POND) can be invoked. So, for example, a man and a woman doing the same job should, all other things being irrelevant, be paid the same rate according to the principle of equality. However, if a woman is, let us say, three grades higher than the men in the same employment, but she nevertheless gets paid just a few pounds more a year than they, the principle of proportionate value is clearly breached. This, it might be thought, indicates how POND is not a species of, nor identical with, the principle of equality. However, this would be to make a mistake. The classical doctrine of formal equality, it should

[9] But this is not the case under the Equal Pay Act 1970 s.1 which protects against discriminatory treatment in contracts of employment. Under this legislation only comparison with real cases is permitted.

[10] See further on this point Honeyball, "Pregnancy and Sex Discrimination" 29(2000) *ILJ* 43.

be remembered, not only requires that like cases be treated alike, but also that like cases be treated unalike to the extent that they are relevantly different.[11] The irony is, however, that the principle of equal pay as it appears in the British legislation, being the one statute that does rely on the principle of equality rather than POND, does not reflect the principle of proportionate value, but extends only to identical equality outcomes. Under this legislation the applicant has to show that she is doing the same work as her comparator, or a job that has been rated as equivalent under a job evaluation scheme, or one that becomes so rated by virtue of her case where she claims that her job is of equal value (though different) to that of her comparator. The term "equal" in each case means "the same".[12]

It should not be thought that it is an easy ride for POND in its quest to be treated as a fundamental value for it to be seen to be entailed by equality. It is not self-evident that equality is a fundamental value, and some have gone so far as to imply that it is not a value, in the sense that it is something independently to be valued, at all.[13] Peter Westen, for example, constructs a convincing argument.[14] The principle of equality, he says, entails the Aristotelian idea that like cases be treated alike – the principle of formal equality. What is involved in treating like cases alike? It cannot involve the argument that the fact that people are alike entails that they ought to be treated alike, for that breaches Hume's Law against deriving an ought-statement from an is-statement.[15] The answer is that there is no is-statement involved in this process. To determine that two examples are alike cannot involve a view that they are alike in *all* respects (which can only be said of immaterial symbols and forms) nor that they are alike in

[11] There should, of course, be no actual requirement that unalike cases be treated differently, but they cannot be treated the same for all the *same* reasons – there must be some other relevant reason that makes the like treatment appropriate. An example here would be where equality of outcome is seen to be secured by balancing out differences. If male employees get time off to watch the World Cup and this is matched, say, by the female employees' extra time off to do the school run, under the principle of equality identical treatment would be permissible. But note that both concessions would appear to be discriminatory (let alone sexist). It is interesting that this balancing approach is not one taken in the EqPA where a term-by-term comparison must be undertaken, but this is possibly due more to accidents of drafting and construction rather than a stand on philosophical principle – see the decision of the House of Lords in *Hayward* v. *Camell Laird Shipbuilders Ltd. (No.2)* [1988] ICR 464.

[12] EqPA s.1. See the Court of Appeal's decisions in *Pointon* v. *University of Sussex* [1979] IRLR 199; *Benveniste* v. *University of Southampton* [1989] IRLR 122.

[13] Gladstone said: "there is no political idea which has entered less into the formation of the political system of this country than the love of equality". See Thomson, *Equality* (Cambridge, Cambridge University Press, 1949), p. 1. Some have argued that inequality is the "source of everything that is good" – see Dahrendorf, "On the Origin of Social Inequality" in Laslett and Runciman (eds.), *Philosophy, Politics and Society* (Oxford, Basil Blackwell, 1964), ch.5. Dahrendorf is here echoing Kant's remark about Rousseau.

[14] *Supra* n.1 at p. 542 et seq.

[15] *Cf.* Margolis, "That All Men Are Created Equal" (1955) 52 *Journal of Philosophy* 337 at 338: "It is clear . . . from the very nature of an alleged right as something which permits a common human nature to be explored in an ethically important way by different individuals that *the concept of normative equality depends on the conviction of some fundamental and actual equality of all men*" (original emphasis).

only *some* respects, for that is true of everything. There must therefore, if the idea is to have any usefulness at all, be a normative judgment involved in the identification stage – identifying who are alike. In that categories of morally alike objects do not exist in nature, but are man-made, the principle that like cases should be treated alike thus collapses into a vacuous tautology. But, is this so? It is not enough to show that there is a normative element in the identification stage. It must also be shown that this is the same value judgment. That all cases which should be identified as alike should be treated alike may be false, but it is not tautological. It requires the further claim that the morality of like treatment is involved in what it is to identify people as morally alike. However, that is a claim that would not seem to be hard to substantiate. The concept of equality is thus circular. As Westen himself puts it:

> It tells us to treat like people alike; but when we ask who "like people" are, we are told they are "people who should be treated alike". Equality is an empty vessel with no substantive moral content of its own. Without moral standards, equality remains meaningless, a formula that can have nothing to say about how we should act. With such standards, equality becomes superfluous, a formula that can do nothing but repeat what we already know.[16]

There is one final difference between POND and the principle of equality that we should notice. This is that equality is not a concept that can be graduated, but discrimination is. In other words, one thing is either equal with another or it is not. It cannot be said to be very equal, or only just equal, partially equal or half-equal. Where there is not equality there is inequality complete. We cannot say the same of discrimination. The language of degree is quite apposite to it. We can recognise levels and the extent of discrimination, recognise that something is more discriminatory than another, or less. The mistake should not be made that this can also be said of the principle of formal equality because it recognises that cases should be treated unequally according to the degree that they are not alike. Rather, we are here referring to the notion that there can be varying degrees to which something may not accord with actual parity *or* with the principle of proportionate value. While the language of equality does not run here, the language of discrimination does, and this suggests that POND is not entailed by equality. Indeed, in this way, it suggests that POND is a wider concept than equality.

2. CONSEQUENTIAL DIFFICULTIES ON A LOGICAL RELATIONSHIP BETWEEN POND AND EQUALITY

Let us turn from the differences between POND and the principle of equality to the difficulties that arise were POND to be considered to be entailed by the

[16] At p. 547.

principle of equality. First, it is a difficult notion in that it is clear that not all people are equal, differing to a large extent in their physical and intellectual achievements and potentialities, as well, perhaps more importantly, differing markedly in their moral and ethical integrity. What an entirely egalitarian approach does is not to deny this, but to take the view that these differences are not matters which *should* be taken into account in assessing what each person is due, and what is due from each person, being a form of fundamental entitlement. In other words, egalitarianism views these types of difference as irrelevant, and actual inequality does not matter in this assessment. Alternatively, the view may be taken that these are relevant distinctions and actual inequality does matter in the assessment, and to such a degree that each person is to be treated *as if* they were equal with everyone else.[17] This is an easier line to take with regard to the application of POND in procedural matters, but harder to justify in considering substantive issues. This is because we recognise the importance of inequality in outcome which equality, which we seek to secure, in treatment will not remove, but rather maintain in its proper degree. Indeed, it may be the only way to secure a proportionate outcome. We do consider that differential treatment is justified if this reflects differing worth of individuals, so long as the differences are reflective of a proportionate scale of differential. Perhaps it is for this reason that the application of POND in British legislation has been restricted to matters which are entirely outside the control of those subject to it, thus removing considerations of moral worth. One's race and sex are determined at birth, and a disability is not a life-choice. One's religion, however, is not, and there has been a widespread feeling, only latterly gradually being dispelled, that sexual orientation is also a matter of volition. These are not grounds that presently found an action in law, although the position may soon change.[18]

Further difficulties in founding POND on equality of outcome (including proportionate equality) is that it is subject to two major variables. The first is that one's worth or dessert (moral or objective/non-moral) will change from

[17] This is fundamental to some moral theories such as utilitarianism which treats each person as one unit and one unit only in the felicific calculus. This is paradoxically so even if the sum of human happiness may be seen to be increased by securing inequalities of outcome. See further on this principle Berlin, *Concepts and Categories* (London, Hogarth Press, 1978), ch.5.

[18] Religion was expressly excluded from the race discrimination legislation having originally been included in earlier stages of the Bill's progress. It was not, therefore, as is sometimes thought, an oversight. It should be noted, however, that religious discrimination is a protected ground in Northern Ireland, and that religion and beliefs as well as age and sexual orientation may be the subject of legislation following the Treaty of Amsterdam. Interestingly, age discrimination is not illegal as the law stands, although again this may alter following the Treaty of Amsterdam, despite having a non-volitional basis. The matter is not clear cut, therefore, and it may be that the prohibited grounds are as they are for the most obvious reason, namely that these were the grounds which were giving most cause for public concern at the time of the legislation. But these concerns were not necessarily moral-based. As France had had sex discrimination legislation since before the foundation of the European Communities, she wished for economic reasons to secure a level playing field with other Member States. It is therefore not surprising that this was the object of British governmental thinking at the time of its own membership bids.

time to time depending on financial success, increasing age and a host of other very obvious factors. The second is that there will be aberrations of outcome, even if worth or dessert remain static. A system of non-discrimination designed to preserve equality of outcome may be drawn into a constant battle of redistribution. Moral theories of justice as equality have had to grapple with this difficulty for many years,[19] but its translation into POND is even more problematic, for it might require not just constant reassessments of the justification of discriminatory treatment under otherwise static criteria, but may involve a constant reassessment of those criteria themselves. This would mean a realisation that the *grounds* on which it is right to discriminate would perpetually shift in order to achieve substantive equality. In that the grounds are instrumental in producing substantive equality, this would necessarily follow. A further fundamental difficulty with outcome equality, however, is that it is economically inefficient in that it leads towards lack of incentive as advantage is forever being clawed back and neutralised. But the most fundamental objection to this from the point of view of POND is that we do not view as morally acceptable that the grounds of discrimination should be subject to constant revision, even for the ultimate goal of equality (including proportionate equality) of outcome.

What POND seems to demand concentration on more is equality of treatment leaving outcomes to take care of themselves or, alternatively, to be subject to the application of other principles. So, the discrimination legislation looks to see if, on the grounds of sex, race or disability a person is *treated* less favourably than people of another sex, race or the able-bodied. This is curious to some degree, for POND would seem to be concerned to right unfavourable outcomes, but instead uses a method which concentrates as much on the act rather than the ultimate substantive outcome. But this should only *seem* curious, for concentration on the act does not mean that one concentrates on the motives or desires of the discriminator. Even the justification defences (when available) do not rest on the moral worth of the discriminator's act but instead on the objective nature of the reason for it.[20] And the term "discrimination"

[19] Compare the differing positions of the two leading modern writers on justice, John Rawls and Robert Nozick here. The parties in the Rawlsian original position choose a system of the distribution of societal benefits and burdens based on inequality which, either by definition or heuristically, is the most just solution. So, although Rawls' theory of justice is one of patterned distribution, it is not based on equality. (See Rawls, *A Theory of Justice*, Oxford, Clarendon Press, 1972 esp. p. 504 et seq. and Gutmann, *Liberal Equality* (Cambridge, Cambridge University Press, 1980), pp. 129–35.) Nozick, on the other hand, bases his theory of justice, the theory of entitlements, on the notion that no patterned-distribution theory is tenable, because no pattern could be sustained in a society which values freedom in the use of benefits and burdens allocated to its citizens, thereby resulting rapidly in the pattern disintegrating. This, of course, includes patterns based on equality. (See Nozick, *Anarchy, State and Utopia,* Oxford, Basil Blackwell Ltd, 1974) esp. p. 232 et seq.) This is not just a practical point in that rights and competition are not morally incompatible – see e.g. Wollheim, "Equality and Equal Rights" in Olafson (ed.), *Justice and Social Policy* (New Jersey, Prentice-Hall, 1961), p. 119.

[20] See for example SDA s.7 which provides a "genuine occupational qualification" defence to an employment sex discrimination claim, and the case law on the justification defence to an indirect discrimination claim under SDA s.1(1)(b)(ii).

itself would appear, in the way that the term "equality" does not at all, to primarily refer to an *act* (including a volitional omission) that is differential.

3. IS THE PRINCIPLE OF NON-DISCRIMINATION A VALUE?

Is POND a value? The answer to this may seem self-evident, even if POND were not to be considered to be entailed in the principle of equality. If by "value" we mean in essence something that is valued in society, then it is clear that it is, as it is equally clear that it is something which should be valued. So the crux of the issue is whether it is a value which is fundamental. Leaving aside the meaning for the moment of what "fundamental" means, we can make several observations on POND as a value.

The first observation is that, although we clearly value POND, there are limitations on the extent that we do so value it. It is not just that there are several other competing values which are of wider application and yet can at times be in conflict with POND, such as liberty,[21] justice and wealth.[22] We may value wealth more and tolerate discrimination if we are wealthy as a worthwhile price to pay. We may value freedom more, and dislike the legislative methods by which non-discrimination could be achieved. We may, as with Rawls, feel the most just distribution of benefits and burdens entail inequality of outcome in order that the least-advantaged in society can have their lot improved. We may value more the free speech that would be lost if racist or sexist remarks were to be considered discriminatory. The list could be very lengthy. The limitations on POND even extend to the fact that we at times value discrimination. We recognise that, in its place, discriminatory treatment is morally justified and at times even morally required. I do not refer merely to discrimination which is based on moral or other worth. There is a distinction between differential treatment and discrimination. Of course it is right to have different pay scales for employees with varying qualifications, abilities or experience, for example. This we have already seen can be considered to be part of the principle of formal equality in what I have called the principle of proportionate value. Rather, I refer here to those occasions when it is right for us to discriminate in favour of people who are of no greater worth than any others looked at objectively. Ronald Dworkin has addressed a form of this idea when he referred in *Law's Empire* to what he termed "associative" or "communal" obligations.[23] This is the idea that we have special responsibilities which social practice attaches to membership of social or biological groups, such as families and friends. There is nothing in the nature of dessert or worth in these relationships, some of which are based on volition but others not. The obligations arise not because of any particular value in the

[21] See Fletcher, *Basic Concepts of Legal Thought* (Oxford, Oxford University Press, 1996), pp. 126–30.

[22] *Cf.* Dworkin, *A Matter of Principle* (Cambridge Mass., Harvard University Press, 1985), ch.12.

[23] Dworkin, *Law's Empire* (London, Fontana Press, 1986), pp. 195–206.

other members of the group but rather because of the value we place on these groups in society justifying preferential treatment. Of course, there are limits to this, and we condemn nepotism. But we also applaud, and even require, that family members look after each other before looking to the needs of others. A non-discriminatory approach between these groups and others in society is considered misplaced. These groups can be very wide. We see no need, for example, for any special justification for discriminatory treatment in favour of human beings as against other species. It is hard to defend logically, but is a given in our moral make-up. Biological and other factors perhaps require this form of attitude if the species is to survive.

A further observation we can make about the limitations of POND as a value is that it does not necessarily promote a moral good of itself. To treat people equally is not necessarily to treat them well. It may mean that we treat them equally badly.[24] What POND and the principle of equality both involve is that, although there can be no perfectly moral treatment or distribution unless done so without irrelevant differentials, achieving this does not guarantee of itself any particular moral quality. However, this view is controversial. Lon Fuller argued that principles of procedural practice if satisfied, regardless of the content of the rules to which they were applied, guaranteed an outcome that is thereby value-laden. But it is hard to see a tyrant who terrorises his entire population equally as being a better moral person, or performing lesser immoralities in so doing, than terrorising a small segment of his community.[25]

4. CONCLUSION

Does it follow from the above observations that POND, if it is a value, is not fundamental? It depends, of course, on what is meant by "fundamental" in this context. I shall adopt here David Perrott's analysis of fundamentality.[26] If we are thinking of the fundamental values of a legal system, as we are here, then one sense in which something can be fundamental is if it is basic or pre-eminent in that system. This need not be enshrined but must be necessary for the working of the constitution. Alternatively, something can be fundamental if it is part of the basic law of the system in the sense that the validity of all law is dependent on it. This is the sense in which we might talk of the fundamentality of the Kelsenian Grundnorm or Hart's rule of recognition.[27] We can obvi-

[24] See Fredman, *supra* n.7 at p. 350.

[25] See Fuller, *The Law in Quest of Itself* (Boston, Beacon Press, 1940), pp. 11–16. However, see Summers, *Lon L Fuller* (London, Edward Arnold, 1984), pp. 33–4 where the author argues that Fuller's use of the term "value" here does not translate into moral rightness or goodness.

[26] See Perrott, "The Logic of Fundamental Rights" in Bridge, Lasok, Perrott and Plender (eds.), *Fundamental Rights* (London, Sweet and Maxwell, 1973), ch.1.

[27] Although Perrott is surely right to include the rule of recognition in his description of rules giving rise to fundamental rights (*ibid.*, p. 8), it seems doubtful that this can be said of all other secondary rules. Some of these may be quite minor in relative terms.

ously discount for present purposes both these meanings. Even if the principle of equality were to be considered fundamental in the former sense, it can hardly be said of POND. The workings of the constitution do not depend upon it. It would also, of course, be ludicrous to argue that the validity of any law is dependent upon POND.

It is when we turn to morality that better claims can be made. Perrott refers to a legal right which is fundamental *because* it embodies a moral right or value.[28] We can turn that on its head and say that the value is fundamental because it is a moral value embodied in the law.[29] But this then means that we are not referring to the *legal* fundamentality of POND, but its moral fundamentality. We should be clear, too, that the claim to fundamentality in this sense should not be equated with importance, for moral ideas can be embodied in laws that are relatively unimportant while much more morally important ideas may be ignored. This claim, then, would not be a significant one.

We can perhaps see a value as having legal fundamentality if it is one which the legal system is not free, according to its own moral[30] lights, to ignore but must include at points. This would not seem to entail any notion of overridingness[31] in that there need be no rights, rules or values that it must be seen to trump. All that is required is that it is a necessary value ingredient recognised by the system. It may, however, be itself trumped from time to time by other values, such as justice, free speech and wealth. In that discrimination legislation is a product of only the last thirty years, and the fact that it appears to have been largely driven by economic and political factors rather than moral rectitude, it is hard to see it as a value the legal system has felt to be important, let alone overriding. And yet it is not one that anyone could now envisage being removed. Indeed, in that the European Court of Justice has recognised discrimination rights as fundamental to the legal system of the European Union, it may be legally unthinkable so to do.[32] But this leaves open the question – is it a value the legal system is *morally* required to include within its law? Even if it does not override many other values, or if it does not do so as often as it is overridden itself, or it is dependent upon other values such as the principle of equality, and even if its scope is still woefully limited to just a few areas of human activity and concerns, we can surely credibly make the claim that it can no longer be ignored. At least in these two senses, then, the principle of non-discrimination makes a credible claim as a fundamental value of our own legal system.

[28] At p. 9.

[29] Perrott also does this, and he interestingly uses the example of a sex discrimination right (at p. 9).

[30] Let us assume that we need to consider only moral values here.

[31] Cf. Perrott at p. 10.

[32] See Docksey, "The Principle of Equality as a Fundamental Right under Community Law" (1991) 20 *ILJ* 258, and Barnard n.5 *supra*.

5

Competence, Independence and Integrity: the Essence of Professionalism?

JACKIE HEATH

1. INTRODUCTION

The law has traditionally been recognised as a noble calling, a mantle which denotes high ethical standards. A recent discussion paper published by the Law Society[1] addressing broad issues about the future shape of regulation of the solicitors' profession, reiterated the importance of the solicitors' ethical code. It stated that an implicit acceptance of the code was at the heart of the solicitor/client relationship and essential to attracting client business. Any such statement begs the question "What ethical code"? A seemingly simple enquiry but not, in fact, one it is easy to answer satisfactorily.

As the guardian of the professions' collective integrity, one would expect the Law Society to be able to provide appropriate guidance and there is a partial answer in the discussion document on regulation, which refers to the core of the lawyers' ethical code as: "the client interest, the wider public interest and the correct relationship between them . . .".[2] But the problem of pinning down the airy notion of "public interest" is notorious, and the phrase "client interest" can be equally ephemeral. The "correct relationship" between the client interest and the public interest is necessarily a moveable feast. It is arguable, however, that recognition and expression of the profession's values has never been more important. This is a time of increasing diversity, competition and instability for the profession, a time when its continued existence is being called into question. There are those who claim that the era of professionalism is dead, while others believe that the legal profession will break up into a number of smaller and more specialised groupings. Finally, there are those

[1] Cooper and Willis, *A Strategic Discussion Paper*, February 1999.
[2] *Ibid.*, at p. 4.

who argue that since they are no longer able to protect their traditional markets, solicitors should discard the trappings of "professionalism" and compete in the marketplace unhampered by the need to comply with the extra tier of regulation that comes with the professional package.[3]

This essay will look first at some definitions of "professionalism" in order to assess the qualities that have traditionally characterised the professions, before looking more closely at the core values of the modern solicitors' profession.

2. DEFINING A PROFESSION

There are three principal theoretical approaches to studying the professions, namely the Weberian approach, the Marxist approach and the approach of the structural functionalists.[4] Weberian analysis focuses on distribution, looking at the way players compete in the marketplace. In Marxist theory, production is key and the role of the professional group is marginalised, becoming a question of whether "professionals" are properly considered part of labour or capital. The third approach is the most helpful for the purposes of this essay, in that the structural functionalist breaks down the professional body into its different component parts. The characteristic features of a professional have been enumerated as intellectual skill acquired through learning and training, institutionally recognised and validated, and applied in a socially responsible manner. Traditionally it has been these attributes which have enabled a final distinguishing feature to exist, namely, that of autonomy.

The approach of the structural functionalists highlights the importance of educational attainment, status, independence and an awareness of wider obligations to society. It is a method which has been favoured by many legal commentators[5] and it has formed the basis of studies commissioned into the legal profession by successive governments. It has, however, been challenged by David Maister, a leading management consultant, who takes the position that: "professionalism is predominantly an attitude, not a set of competencies".[6] His

[3] A useful review of the papers in this area can be found in A Paterson, "Professionalism and the legal services market" (1996) 3 *International Journal of the Legal Profession* 137 at 157. See also R Abel, "Ten Years On: Changes in the Regulatory Framework" in *Proceedings from the Annual Research Conference, Governing the Profession* (London, The Law Society, 1998).

[4] R Abel, *The Legal Profession in England & Wales* (Blackwell, 1988), ch. 1.

[5] An impressive list of its supporters can be found in P A Thomas, "Introduction" in P A Thomas (ed.), *Law in the Balance: Legal Services in the Eighties* (Oxford, Martin Robertson, 1982).

[6] D H Maister, *True Professionalism* (The Free Press, 1997), p. 16. Its validity has also been questioned by some legal academics on the basis that trait ideology is discredited by contemporary sociology of law: see, for example, P A Thomas, *ibid.* R Abel prefers the Weberian approach because professional practice is essentially an economic activity: R Abel, *The Legal Profession in England & Wales* (Oxford, Blackwell, 1988).

view is that the respect and trust of clients must be earned, it is no longer the automatic adjunct of a particular status. A true professional is dedicated to the interests of his client.

It would be possible to dismiss Maister's practical definition (which enshrines the notion that anyone can be a professional), and his exhortations to do whatever it takes to get the job done, as irrelevant to the legal profession on the basis that they fail to encompass the niceties of the professions' special obligation to uphold the rule of law. To do so, however, would be to miss a valuable lesson. The right attitude is fundamental to good practice, solicitors can only improve their service by adopting the commitment to excellence and willingness to assume responsibility extolled by Maister, nor is his approach so different from traditional legal analysis.

It has always been recognised that the first and particular responsibility of a professional person is his client.[7] A solicitor may have a responsibility to society and the rule of law which means that there are occasions when, rather than being able to give clients what they "want", the lawyer's role is to resist their pressures and get them to realise the hard facts of their situation,[8] but this obligation has never precluded doing an excellent job. Enabling the client to achieve the optimum result permissible is getting the job done and getting it done well. Moreover, in the era of mandatory continuing education, few would argue that basic qualification should command respect throughout a professional life. While the successful completion of a demanding professional examination is an achievement that deserves acknowledgement, maintaining and developing clients' respect must necessarily depend on expertise displayed during the retainer.

Recognition of the need to earn respect as a professional is reflected in the theory of neo-contractualism.[9] Neo-contractualism proceeds from the basis that professionalism is "a socially constructed, contingent and dynamic concept".[10] It emphasises the negotiated essence of the professional bargain, the need to balance the lawyer's desire for status, reasonable reward, limited competition and autonomy, with the client's need for access to competent technicians with a service ethic who recognise their responsibility to the public interest. Neo-contractualists do not believe that the era of legal professionals is ending, but rather that the nature of professionalism is changing. The traditional "bargain" was too slanted in favour of the profession. An appropriate balance must be determined by the public interest and must reflect the

[7] This is noted as one of the five main features of a profession in the *Royal Commission on Legal Services* 1979, vol.1: 28, 30.

[8] A position advocated by Talcott Parsons and quoted by R Abel, see *supra* n.4 p. 26.

[9] A Paterson, "Professionalism and the legal services market" (1996) 3 *International Journal of the Legal Profession* 137. That any privileges the profession sustains must be based on "negotiation" with its customer base is also recognised by M Burrage, "From a Gentlemen's to a Public Profession: Status and Politics in the History of English Solicitors" (1996) 3 *International Journal of the Legal Profession* 45.

[10] A Paterson, *Ibid.* at p. 137.

demands of the state and the consumer movement as much as those of lawyers themselves. The current restructuring of the profession is a re-balancing of the equation.

3. THE VALUES

It has been recognised that the solicitor's ethical code is vital to the solicitor/client relationship and essential to attracting client business.[11] The neo-contractualist position involves a re-basing of the solicitor/client relationship but retains, and indeed calls for a strengthening of, the protection of the public interest. While fully accepting the need for other interested groups to feed into the equation if any new "professional bargain" is to be sustainable, this essay seeks to clarify the lawyers' input at this stage. What are the values, common to the profession, that should be more loudly espoused as part of the justification for professional status?

The obvious place to start a search for common values is the profession's own professional conduct guide. Although a professional code of conduct is not the same thing as a statement of a profession's ethical values,[12] it is equally clear that key aspects of the solicitors' code enshrine core values of the profession. It has been said that "[professional codes of practice] identify the main lines of the profession's thinking on professional responsibility"[13] and this is recognised within the Law Society where individuals working on regulation have stated that "underlying the maze [of regulations], there are fundamental principles of legal professional ethics . . .".[14] That this is also the view of those responsible for compiling the Guide to the Professional Conduct of Solicitors is clear in their statement that Solicitors' Practice Rule 1, which "sums up the basic principles of conduct governing the professional practice of solicitors", stems from "the *ethical* duties imposed on solicitors by the common law"[15] (emphasis added).

The ethical duties imposed by the common law evolved with the law of obligations, in particular the rules of agency and fiduciary duties. In addition, the courts relied on their inherent jurisdiction to control lawyers to develop behavioural standards to protect the reputation of the profession and defend the public from incompetent practitioners.

[11] *Supra*, opening text and accompanying notes.

[12] See further, Sheinman, "Looking for Legal Ethics" (1997) 4 *International Journal of the Legal Profession* 139.

[13] R Cranston, "Ethics and Professional Responsibility" in R Cranston (ed.), *Legal Ethics and Professional Responsibility* (Oxford, Clarendon Press, 1995), p. 4.

[14] A Crawley and C Bramall, "Professional Rules, Codes, and Principles Affecting Solicitors (or What Has Professional Regulation to do with Ethics?)" in R Cranston (ed.), *Legal Ethics and Professional Responsibility* (Oxford, Clarendon Press, 1995), p. 99.

[15] The Law Society, *The Guide to the Professional Conduct of Solicitors* (7th edition 1996) at para.1.02.

The current version of Practice Rule 1, which was formulated in the mid-1980s, is as follows:

> "Practice Rule 1 (basic principles)
>
> A solicitor shall not do anything in the course of practising as a solicitor, or permit another person to do anything on his or her behalf, which compromises or impairs or is likely to compromise or impair any of the following:
>
> (a) the solicitor's independence or integrity;
> (b) a person's freedom to instruct a solicitor of his or her choice;
> (c) the solicitor's duty to act in the best interests of the client;
> (d) the good repute of the solicitor or of the solicitor's profession;
> (e) the solicitor's proper standard of work;
> (f) the solicitor's duty to the court".

Guidance notes on the rule provide that "where two or more of the principles in Practice Rule 1 come into conflict, the determining factor in deciding which principle should take precedence must be the public interest, and especially the public interest in the administration of justice".[16]

Competence, independence and integrity are frequently quoted as a shorthand for the values contained in Solicitors' Practice Rule 1, but are they the values that should be aspired to in modern professional practice?

4. COMPETENCE

No one would take issue with the need for a lawyer to have the ability and skill required to do the job in hand. Indeed, there is a strong argument that bad work is unethical.[17]

It has been said that: "the fundamental mark of professional information or advice is the expectation engendered that it is reliable: that it reaches a standard of skill".[18] That there are occasions when this expectation is not satisfied is all too apparent from the rising volume of complaints made to the Office for the Supervision of Solicitors and from the recent annual reports of the Legal Services Ombudsman. It seems that too often competence assumes its meaning of "moderate, no more than adequate", rather than "having adequate skill, properly qualified, *effective*"[19] (emphasis added).

Technical competence is indispensable to professional practice. Aspiring to competence is not enough. Modern professionals must aspire to excellence,

[16] *Ibid.*
[17] A Abraham, "Ethical issues and Solicitor's Practice" in (1998) 1 *Legal Ethics* 23.
[18] D Partlett, *Professional Negligence* (The Law Book Company Limited, 1985), p. 4.
[19] Definitions from the *New Shorter Oxford English Dictionary* (Oxford, 1993).

reach out for responsibility and do what it takes to get the job done.[20] The pursuit of quality is a necessity not a luxury.[21]

5. INDEPENDENCE

The autonomy of the profession has traditionally been seen as a counterweight to state authority. The right to independence, justified on the basis of the objectivity of the practitioner who serves the interests of justice and the rule of law as well as those of his client, has been strongly defended by the profession.[22] But it is hard to see how autonomy and independence can remain defensible standards for the future.

The professions' jealously guarded right to self-regulation was first compromised when the Courts and Legal Services Act 1990 required the Law Society to seek the advice of the Lord Chancellor's Advisory Committee on Legal Education and Conduct before introducing certain new rules or amendments to existing rules. Self-regulation is now again in the spotlight. The proposed transfer of supervisory authority for the activities of solicitors engaged in investment business away from the Law Society to the Financial Services Authority under the Financial Services and Markets Bill, is initiating a wider debate on the longevity of self-regulation generally.

State authority over the profession has expanded with the development of Legal Aid, most recently the setting of standards in the Legal Aid franchise introducing an aspect of control more direct than the influence of the paymaster.

The independence of lawyers has frequently been challenged by academics positing the concept of lawyer as "hired gun", and a recent study concluded that "competition and commercialism has increased the service orientation of some lawyers with corporate clients in the shape of a greater willingness to be a 'hired gun'".[23] The impact of the introduction of conditional fees on the objectivity of the lawyer is obvious.

The growing trend for in-house lawyers means that increasing numbers of solicitors are employees rather than in independent practice. Moreover, as law firms get bigger many solicitors in private practice are employees rather than principals of their firm. It is arguably only full equity partners who can claim to be "independent" and even then few are so ensconced in their position that

[20] See further, D H Maister supra n.6.

[21] The Law Society, *Quality: a Briefing for Solicitors* (London, Law Society, 1991); J Jenkins *The Quality of Solicitors Practice Management* (London, Law Society, 1993).

[22] There has, in fact, been little research to substantiate the assertion that solicitors act altruistically and in the interests, not only of their clients, but also of the wider public interest in the administration of justice. Instead, solicitors have been given the benefit of the doubt and research and lobbying has tended to focus more on challenges to the autonomy of the profession: R Abel, supra n.4.

[23] A Paterson, "Professionalism and the legal services market" (1996) 3 *IJLP* 137 at 152.

they can afford to act without regard for the general health and benefit of their firms and co-partners. It has been said that the "ideals of professionalism may be harder to preserve when a majority of lawyers are employees"[24] and the ideal of independence must be most at risk.

6. INTEGRITY

As with the need for technical competence, the value of integrity, or soundness of moral principle, is universally recognised and supported.

Confidentiality, diligence and loyalty have historically been accepted as the basic responsibilities that a solicitor owes to his clients.[25] They represent the essence of the fiduciary obligation owed by those in positions of authority and influence.[26] Unless clients can be assured of the integrity of their advisor, it is impossible for an effective client/solicitor relationship to exist.

True competence and integrity are keystones of any profession and a modern way to achieve them is to adopt Maister's practical definition of the professional. Nevertheless, a solicitor will additionally be required to satisfy his duty to uphold the rule of law.

7. JUSTICE

The overriding obligation imposed pursuant to Solicitors' Practice Rule 1 is the duty to apply the principles in the manner that will promote the administration of justice, but what is meant by "justice"?

It is relatively easy to achieve a level of agreement as to the value of procedural justice and the need to treat like cases alike, but it is an entirely different matter when it comes to trying to achieve a common understanding of the essence of substantive justice. Rawls developed the concept of the "original position" working on the basis of justice as fairness, encompassing liberty, opportunity and equality.[27] Nozick offers an "entitlement" theory of justice.[28] Marx and Engels expounded communal egalitarianism and distribution according to need. Legal feminists have asserted that an ethic of justice simply does not reflect feminine values. The feminist ethic of care is necessarily contextualised and as such renders concepts such as equality and equal rights irrelevant.[29]

[24] R Abel, *The Legal Profession in England & Wales* (Blackwell, 1988), p. 306.

[25] R Cranston, supra n.13, traces these duties back to an address to the new serjeants at law in 1648.

[26] The solicitor/client relationship is one where the presumption of undue influence arises: *Wright v. Carter* [1903] 1 Ch. 27.

[27] J Rawls, *A Theory of Justice* (Oxford, Oxford University Press, 1971).

[28] R Nozick, *Anarchy, State and Utopia* (Oxford, Basil Blackwell, 1974).

[29] S Gibson, "The Structure of the Veil" in (1989) 52 *MLR* 420 at 436.

At this point it would be possible to develop an argument for one of two diametrically opposed positions. One could either search for the common thread and espouse a belief in justice as the fundamental value of the legal professional, unifying the profession and benefiting society or, more cynically, conclude that the only distinctive value in modern legal practice could mean "all things to all men" so as not to be a common value at all.

There is strength in both positions, but the rule of law is too important to allow the cynical view to prevail. As changes in the law and to the structure of the profession accelerate, it becomes ever more important to articulate and develop the fundamental ethics of the profession, its integrity and belief in justice.[30] An onus rests on policy-makers, educators, academics and practitioners to keep the ideal of justice at the forefront of legal professional activity.

8. CONCLUSION

The increasing diversity of the profession is undeniable, but there are fundamental values common to good practice: belief in justice and integrity in application. When combined with the pursuit of excellence in day-to-day practice these values are the essence of legal professionalism and sound commercial practice. These are the values we should be seeking to develop in our legal education and defend through our professional associations. They are values worthy of respect.

[30] A position argued strongly in ACLEC, *First report on legal education and training* (London, 1996).

Part 2

Fundamental Values in International Law

6

New Equality Provisions in European Law: Some Thoughts on the Fundamental Value of Equality as a Legal Principle

LAMMY BETTEN

1. INTRODUCTION

In the aftermath of the atrocities committed during the Second World War it was established as a principle of international law that all persons are born equal and that they should not be discriminated against simply because of their race, gender, creed, nationality or any other status. A large number of post Second World War universal and regional declarations and treaties stipulate that discrimination should be abandoned from all areas of life.[1]

At European regional level, it took until the turn of the millennium before the principles of equality and non-discrimination were incorporated as autonomous and self-executing general principles in the text of the European treaties. It was not the Council of Europe, founded after the War to protect democratic principles and fundamental rights, but the European Union, established to enhance economic co-operation,[2] which was the first to include a general non-discrimination principle.

The existing non-discriminatory provision of the 1950[3] European Convention for the Protection of Human Rights and Fundamental Freedoms (ECHR,

[1] Apart from the *Universal Declaration of Human Rights* and the two *International Covenants on Civil and Political Rights (ICCPR)* and *Economic, Social and Cultural Rights (ICECSR)* which form together the International Bill of Rights, there are a number of specific Conventions, e.g. the *International Convention on the Elimination of All Forms of Racial Discrimination*, the *Convention on the Elimination of All Forms of Discrimination against Women* and a number of ILO Conventions which deal with the prohibition of discrimination in employment and education.

[2] In the original version of the EC Treaties fundamental rights were deliberately excluded.

[3] As amended by Protocol No. 11 in 1998.

European Convention, the Convention), Article 14, can be called upon only in combination with the substantive provisions of the Convention. The European Convention, one could say, lags thus somewhat behind the 1966 International Covenant on Civil and Political Rights (ICCPR) which, in Article 26, recognises equality and non-discrimination as autonomous, legally enforceable principles.

The original equality provisions of the European Community Treaty (TEC) are limited in personal as well as material scope; moreover, they were included in the Treaty as market principles, not as human rights. Article 119 TEC (now Art 141)[4] on equal pay of men and women was included to avoid distortion of competition. Article 48(2)TEC (now Art 39 (2)) prohibiting discrimination on the basis of nationality was meant to avoid obstacles to the free movement of persons, one of the pillars of the Common Market.[5] Later legislation[6] as well as the case law of the EC Court of Justice (ECJ)[7] have broadened and deepened the above principles, but they still fall short of a general principle of equality.

Recently, in both the Council of Europe and the European Union, steps have been taken to remedy these lacunae in the European treaties. The 1997 Amsterdam Treaty contains the addition of a general non-discrimination principle in the European Community Treaty (TEC). Article 13 TEC reads that the Council, within the limits of the Community's power and on proposal of the Commission, "may take appropriate action to combat discrimination based on sex, racial or ethnic origin, religion or belief, disability, age or sexual orientation".[8]

In July 1999, the Council of Europe adopted a proposal to add a non-discrimination Protocol to the Convention. This (Draft) Protocol (No. 12) contains a general, autonomous provision prohibiting discrimination similar to Article 26 ICCPR.[9]

[4] After the adoption of the 1997 Amsterdam Treaty, all articles of the EU Treaties were renumbered.

[5] The same applies to the free movement of goods, services and the freedom of establishment. On the confusion around the significance of the different concepts of discrimination in these areas, see. e.g., Nicolas Bernard "Discrimination and Free Movement in EC Law" (1996) *International and Comparative Law Quarterly*, 82; Chris Hilson, "Discimination in Community free movement law" 24 *European Law Review 1999*, 445.

[6] Notably the Equal Pay and Equal Treatment Directives 75/117/EEC, 76/207/EEC, 79/7/EEC, 86/378 and 86/613/EEC.

[7] On the development of sex equality law in the European Union, see e.g., Evelyn Ellis, *EC Sex Equality Law*, (Oxford, Clarendon Press, 1998, 2nd ed.); Tamara Hervey and David O'Keeffe, *Sex Equality Law in the European Union* (Chicester, Wiley, 1996); G More, "Equal Treatment of the Sexes in European Community Law: What Does Equal Mean?" (1993) 1 *Feminist Legal Studies* 45; C Docksey, "The principle of equality between men and women as a fundamental right under Community law" (1991) 20 *Industrial Law Journal* 258; S Peers, "Social Advantages and Discrimination in Employment: Case Law Confirmed and Clarified" (1997) 22 *European Law Review*, 157; David O'Keeffe, "The Free Movement of Persons and the Single Market" (1992) 17 *European Law Review* 3.

[8] The omission of nationality as a prohibited ground for discrimination is deliberate. It is included in Article 12 TEC (new) which prohibits discrimination on the basis of nationality within the scope of application of the Treaty.

[9] Article 1 of the Protocol reads *(1) The enjoyment of any right set forth by law shall be secured without discrimination on any ground such as sex, race, colour, language, religion, political or other*

The question is whether these new developments in European law[10] will improve the equality record in the region. In this essay I want to focus on one aspect of the question of how far legal provisions on equality or non-discrimination contribute positively to achieving equality in society. More cynically phrased, my question would be whether this whole exercise will make the slightest difference for those who suffer the effects of unequal treatment.

There are many avenues along which to examine this question. The literature on equality, one of the most fundamental value(s) in society, can easily fill a library of respectable size. It is a subject which fascinates political scientists as well as lawyers and economists. In this essay I will focus on one issue only: the validity of the concept of equality as a separate legal rule. It questions the necessity of an autonomous principle of equality[11] in view of the hypothesis that the concept of equality is inherent in the principles of social justice and the rule of law. I will examine this question in the context of the case law of the European Court of Human Rights (the ECHR or "Strasbourg Court") and the EC Court of Justice (ECJ or "Luxembourg Court"). The first part focuses on the significance of Article 14 ECHR; the second part questions the confusing application of the concept of equality as a general principle of Community law. The exercise will obviously focus on existing case law, but this leads inevitably to conclusions as to the question of the significance of the new equality provisions.

1.1. The significance of the legal concept of equality

There is, apart from, possibly, "social justice", no other term which has caused more confusion than the word "equality".[12] The law has been instrumental in adding to this by declaring, for instance, that "All men are (born or created) equal". If taken at face value, these words form, as Nietzsche would have it, the biggest lie ever told.[13] The first time it was laid down, in the 1789 American

opinion, national or social origin, association with a national minority, property, birth or other status. (2) No one shall be discriminated against by any public authority on any ground such as mentioned in paragraph 1.

[10] The term refers to European international public law as developed within the European Union and the Council of Europe.

[11] It also questions, of course, the necessity of an accessory principle of equality as that, too, requires, as we shall see later, a separate examination of the equality issue.

[12] I do not pay attention to the differences between the principle of equality and that of non-discrimination. I consider them to be two sides of the coin, or one (a prohibition to discriminate on irrelevant grounds) the consequence of the other (to treat like cases alike and unalike cases unalike). See also Paragraph 15 of the Explanatory Memorandum to the Draft Protocol No. 12 to the ECHR which recognises that the two principles are "closely intertwined". I am not implying that there is no disagreement on this issue. Ellis points out that discrimination is a narrower concept than (the promotion of) sex equality: "whereas discrimination is an individualised and essentially comparative concept", "notions of sex equality and equality of opportunity for all are much more generalised": Evelyn Ellis, *EC Sex Equality Law*, 2nd ed. (Oxford, Clarendon Press, 1998), p. 321.

[13] Friedrich Nietzsche, Gesammelte Schriften. XV, 488, XVI 200, quoted by Warwick McKean, *Equality and Discrimination under International Law* (Oxford, Clarendon Press, 1983), p. 3.

Declaration of Independence, the term "men" certainly did not mean all men and women: blacks and women were not included, witness also a famous discussion between the American Senator Stephen Douglas and candidate for the Senate Abraham Lincoln in which the first strongly denied that the declaration that all men were created equal included anyone but white men: "(. . .) it has no reference either to the negro, the savage Indian, the Fejee, the Malay, or any other inferior and degraded race (..)".[14]

When laid down in the United Nations Charter and the 1948 Universal Declaration on Human Rights (UDHR) it did include all men and women but, taken at face value, it was still a great piece of nonsense. Some have stated that it should be read in the sense that people should be shown equal respect,[15] whatever their station at birth. Others point at the normative aspect of the declaration: it does not state the fact that, in effect, men are treated equal, but that they ought to be treated equal. That may be so, it does not make the formula as such less nonsensical. For a vast majority of the people inhabiting this world, the statements that everyone is born or created born equal,[16] should be treated equally and, in particular, should be given equal opportunities must, indeed, be very cynical ones.

It must be clear to everyone that, in reality, all men are not born equal, nor do they have equal opportunities or are they being treated equally. Fifty years after its adoption in international law as a binding principle upon civilised nations, it may be concluded that as a political principle it has largely failed the majority of people. As a legal principle, it suffers from inexactitude and vagueness which makes it of limited use to those who rely on it and a fertile ground for interpretation for those in the power to do so. Indeed, as critical lawyers have suggested, it has, so far, served only to reaffirm the inequality in society.[17]

This essay does not focus on the criticism of law as an instrument to fight, for instance, inequality although I will come back to it in my conclusion. Hereafter I will focus on the practical implications of the theoretical assumption that equality is an "empty vessel".

2. IS EQUALITY AN EMPTY VESSEL?

The core of this question is whether separate equality provisions add a new dimension to the just application of legal rules. If they do not, the addition of

[14] Quoted by Peter Westen "The Meaning of Equality in Law, Science, Math and Morals: A Reply" (1983) 81-1 *Michigan law Review*, 604, at 606. Lincoln conceded that may be the colour of the blacks was not equal to the white colour, so that men might not be equal in some respects, they were equal in "their right to life liberty and the pursuit of happiness". *(Ibid).*

[15] See, for example, John Rawls, *A Theory of Justice* (Oxford, Clarendon Press), p. 511.

[16] Since the introduction of methods of artificial insemination, even in the strictest biological sense it is no longer true that men are created equal. It is, however, the circumstances in which men and women are born which make the suggestion of equality of opportunity such nonsense.

[17] See *infra*, para. 2.

autonomous general principles of equality would have very limited, if any, significance for those who are still on the receiving end of unequal treatment. The suggestion is that the rule itself must be applied equally and that all differential treatment must be justified. In other words, the principle of equality is implicit in each rule.

The question whether "equality" is an empty term formed the subject of a highly interesting discussion in the United States in the early 1980s. It followed a provocative article by Peter Westen the core of whose argument was that the term "equality" is both empty and confusing; empty in that it derives its entire meaning from normative standards that precede it, and confusing in that it obscures the context of the normative standards that logically precede it. For the principle of equality to have meaning, it must incorporate external values that determine which persons and treatments are alike. Once those external values are found, the principle of equality becomes redundant. Equality, according to Westen, should be abolished from moral and legal discourse as an explanatory term. Transforming simple statements of rights into statements of equality "not only involves unnecessary work but also engenders profound conceptual confusion".[18] It is true that rules should be applied equally, consistently and impartially, but it is "wrong to think that equality has something additional to say about the scope of the rule – something that is not already inherent in the substantive terms of the rule itself".[19] Westen follows to say that equality, like the idea of justice, is entirely formal.[20] "It requires that a person be given their due but does not in itself define what is their 'due'".[21] Referring to Locke, he submits that equality is entirely circular. ("Who are like people? People who should be treated alike"). According to Locke, the principle of equality "seems to collapse into shattering triviality that cases are alike (. . .) unless they are different".[22] The equality analysis logically collapses into a rights analysis and, therefore, "analysing legal problems in terms of equality is essentially redundant".[23] Accordingly, fundamental rights cases must be decided by direct reference to the substantive right.[24] In a response to the criticism on his theory, Westen emphasised that the submission that equality is an empty term, does

[18] Peter Westen, "The Empty Idea of Equality" (1982–3) 95-1 *Harvard Law Review*, 537, at 542.

[19] *Ibid*., at 551.

[20] Not to be confused with the concept of "formal equality" as part of the Aristotelian concept of equality. Westen's definition of a formal statement is a statement "containing one or more variable terms (. . .) that remain unspecified until filled with specific 'substantive', features". Peter Westen, "To Lure The Tarantula From Its Hole: A Response" [1983] *Columbia Law Review*, Vol. 83, 1186, at 1187 (footnote 4).

[21] *Loc cit*. n. 18, at 556/7.

[22] J Locke, "The Trivializability of Universalizability" (1968) 77 *Philosophical Review* 25, at 25, quoted by Westen, *ibidem*, at 547, footnote 30).

[23] *Ibid*., at 560.

[24] Westen gives, *inter alia*, the following example in the steps involved in solving an "equality problem": (1) persons who are alike should be treated alike (2) the State shall not deny persons the right to free speech (3) persons who are treated differently from others solely by virtue of regulations that violate their right of free speech are necessarily "like" others and hence must be treated alike. Steps (1) and (3) are superfluous. Westen, *loc cit*. n. 18, 568.

not mean that it is meaningless, but that it is a derivative formula possessing no independent normative context apart from the anterior rights and rules they incorporate by reference.[25] For instance "equal protection" does not explain "the right to be free from stigmatic classification, and in the context of stigmatic classification, it does not exist as an independent norm. We can preserve the right to be free from racial stigma and yet banish equality as an explanatory norm. We not only can. We should".[26]

In this context one should also look at Rawls, who does not argue as such that equality is an empty concept but who does make the point that like decisions be given in like cases is a precept of the rule of law guaranteeing equal liberty. It forces judges *et al* to justify distinctions that they make between persons "by reference to the relevant rules and principles".[27] This seems to suggest that a separate principle of equality is not necessary as it is implicit in the rule of law. It does not prevent arbitrary decision in a particular case, but when cases multiply it becomes more difficult to construct a "plausible justification" of biased judgment.[28]

Rawls reminds us that discrimination is not necessarily the result of corruption or bribery but it can also consist of "subtle distortions of prejudice and bias as these effectively discriminate against certain groups in the judicial process".[29]

This subtle reminder of class prejudice finds a much stronger voice in the writings of representatives of Critical Legal Studies (CLS). In the context of their criticism on the formalism and objectivism of the existing system, Critical Legal Studies theorists also criticise the liberal concept of equality as a method of maintaining the social order as it stands. By the term "formalism" is understood a method of legal justification of the system as opposed to open ended disputes about the basic terms of social life. The term "objectivism" refers to the belief that authoritative legal materials "embody and sustain a defensible scheme of human association. They display . . . an intelligible moral

[25] Peter Westen, *Loc cit.* n. 14, 604–663, 604. His reply was an answer to two articles, in the same volume of the *Michigan Law Review*, one by Erwin Chemerinsky, "In Defense of Equality: A Reply to Professor Westen", 575–99 and one by Anthony d'Amato, "Is Equality a Totally Empty Idea?", 600–03. Both these articles were a reaction to Westen's original article "The Empty Idea of Equality" *loc cit.* n. 16. Another contribution to the discussion was made by A Greenawalt, "How Empty is the Idea of Equality?" (1983) *Columbia Law Journal*, Vol. 83, 1167, to which Westen replied in the same volume, *loc cit.* n. 19, 1186.

[26] *Ibid.*, at 663.

[27] John Rawls, *op cit.* n. 15, at 237.

[28] *Ibid.*

[29] *Ibid.*, at 235. See also John F Dovido and Samuel L Gaertner (eds.), *Prejudice, Discrimination and Racism* (Orlando, Academic Press, 1986) in their chapter on The Aversive Form of Racism, p. 61 in which they argue that there is evidence that blatant forms of racial bigotry are declining but subtle and insidious types are still pervasive. See also chapter 9 of this book on Racism in the Courtroom, 255 by Stephanie Nickerson, Clara Mayo and Althea Smith, who examined the prejudicial attitudes in *voir dire* procedures which are intended to select a fair and impartial jury.

order. Alternatively they show the results of practical constraints upon social life . . . that have a normative force".[30] The laws are not seen as "an outcome of contingent power struggles or of practical pressures lacking in rightful authority".[31] Critical Legal Studies theorists emphasise the importance of power relations in employing and developing the law.[32] According to them the law is used as an instrument to maintain current relations, not to question them. The dominating and dominated class belief that the existing order is the most desirable one. The law fulfils a constituent role in this process.[33]

Although one could say that the CLS argument deals with the moral emptiness of the concept of equality, it is basically different from the one we are concerned with here. The logical conclusion of the CLS would be that the law blocks rather than promotes achievement of equality. Westen's argument is that separate consideration of equality obscures rather than promotes just application of (other) substantive rights. Yet, as we shall see in the following, both arguments are relevant for the method of application of the equality principle by the European judiciary.

3. THE CONCEPT OF EQUALITY IN EUROPEAN LAW

In this section, I want to examine the case law of the European Court of Human Rights (Strasbourg) and the EC Court of Justice (Luxembourg) in the context of the empty vessel theory. In doing so, I will focus on four cases which illustrate the problematic character of applying the concept of equality as a separate "test".

3.1. The European Court of Human Rights

According to Westen's view, it would not make much difference whether the principles of equality or non-discrimination are autonomous or accessory. In his view it is the separate consideration of the principle of equality in the

[30] Roberto Mangabeira Unger, *The Critical Legal Studies Movement* (Cambridge, Mass., and London, Harvard University Press, 1986), p. 2. See also 1983 *Harvard Law Review*, Vol. 96, 561.

[31] *Ibid.*

[32] Mark Tushet, "Critical Legal Studies, An Introduction to Its Origins and Underpinnings," 36 *Journal of Legal Education* (1986), 505.

[33] This version of Gramsci's concept of hegenomy – referring to "a system of attitudes and beliefs, permeating both popular consciousness and the ideology of elites, reinforcing existing social arrangements and convincing the dominated classes that the existing or is inevitable" – has been criticised by Crenshaw, one of the most important representatives of the Critical Race Studies. The idea that the dominated classes have consented to their place in the social order, is, as far as racism is concerned an unrealistic picture as "black people are coerced into living in worlds created and maintained by others". Kimberlé Crenshaw, "Race, Reform and Retrenchment: Transformation and Legitimation in Antidiscrimination Law" 101 (1988) *Harvard Law Review*, 1331, at 1357. I would submit that this observation applies to all dominated classes.

context of the application of substantive rules which is superfluous. It is this very assertion with which the European Court of Human Rights has struggled over the years.

In spite of its accessory character, Article 14 ECHR is a separate rule prohibiting discriminatory application of the substantive provisions of the Convention. The Strasbourg Court's standing case law is that, if a violation of the substantive provision is found, it does not have to examine separately whether there is a violation of Article 14, unless a clear inequality of treatment is a fundamental aspect of the case. If, however, the substantive provision is found not to be violated, a separate examination of Article 14 does take place. In other words, although Article 14 can be invoked only in combination with a substantive provision, the latter does not have to be violated for Article 14 to be applied.[34] Article 14 is particularly important in relation to those cases which give states a discretionary power to ensure the rights and freedoms set forth in the Convention. In this view, measures taken by states do not necessarily have to constitute a breach of the Convention's substantive provision, but an individual might, as a result of an infringement of Article 14, "not enjoy the right or freedom in question on the conditions or to the degree laid down in the Convention viewed as a whole".[35]

The Strasbourg Court speaks sometimes of the complementary nature of Article 14, which is autonomous only in the sense that it "does not necessarily presuppose a breach" but not independent in that it has effect only in relation to (or "within the ambit of") one of the substantive provisions.[36] So, it is an autonomous but not independent principle of non-discrimination . . .

Similar confusion is created when the Court speaks sometimes of the complementary nature,[37] when in other judgments it expresses the opinion that Article 14 forms "an integral part" of each of the Convention's substantive provisions.[38] Sometimes it does both within the same (paragraph of a) judgment.[39]

In the context of the empty vessel theory, the confusion in terminology suggests that the Court has, for itself, not entirely solved the question of whether unequal application of a provision in itself is a violation of the rule of law, or that it must be considered separately under a principle of equality or non-discrimination.

[34] For example, *Airy Case*, Judgment of 9 October 1979, Series A No. 32, para. 30; *X and Y* v. *The Netherlands* Judgment of 26 March 1985, Series A No. 91, para. 32; *Dudgeon Case* Judgment of 22 October 1981, Series A No. 45, para. 67.

[35] *Belgian Linguistic Case*, Report of the Commission of 24 June 1965, B.3 (1967), 306.

[36] For example, *Van der Mussele*, Judgment of 23 November 1983, Series A No. 70, para. 43; *Rasmussen*, Judgment of 28 November 1984, Series A No. 87, para. 29; *Inze*, Judgment of 28 October 1987, Series A No. 126, para. 36; *Karlheinz Schidt*, Judgment of 18 June 1994, Series A No. 291-B, para. 22; *Abdulaziz, Cabales and Balkandali*, Judgment of 28 May 1985, Series A, 35.

[37] *Ibid.*

[38] *Belgian Linguistics Case*, Judgment of 23 July 1968, Series A No. 6 para. 10.

[39] *National Union of Belgian Police*, Judgment of 27 October 1975, Series A No. 19, para. 44.

Equally important is the inconsistency of the method used by the Court when applying the equality test. Van Dijk's and Van Hoof note that the Court "not infrequently" skips the comparability test and "merges" it with the justifiability test. The authors point at the difficulty of the first (which may be the reason why the Court "skips" it) which requires that "the criteria used have to be adequately related to the object of the provision which prescribes equal treatment" and "the comparison which is inherent in the equality test puts in focus the goals underlying the provisions concerned". If the comparability test is ignored, "the danger arises that the interests protected and/or the goals envisaged in the provisions embodying equality become underexposed".[40]

Let me illustrate this with the help of two British cases, the *Dudgeon* case and the *Abdulaziz* case. These demonstrate Westen's point of how the equality test can obscure the objective of the underlying rule. Although Van Dijk's and Van Hoof's starting point is different – they assume the useful function of an equality test, but warn against its incomplete application – their point is basically the same.

In the *Dudgeon* case, the issue was the inequality in the age of consent for, on the one hand, heterosexual and lesbian encounters and, on the other, male homosexual encounters. For heterosexual encounters, the age of consent was sixteen, while it was twenty-one for male homosexual encounters.[41] The plaintiff argued that this was a violation of Article 14 in relation with Article 8 ECHR. In its judgment, the Court ignored the element of the age-difference completely and went immediately to the justification argument holding that there was a legitimate necessity in a democratic society for some degree of control over homosexual conduct, "notably to provide safeguards against the exploitation and corruption of those who are specially vulnerable by reason, for example, of their youth".[42] By emphasising the protection of youth, an objective which was not disputed, it entirely overlooked examining what possible purpose could be served by upholding different age limits to achieve that objective; in effect, the Court upheld discrimination between heterosexual and male homosexual encounters.

In the *Abdulaziz* case, one of the issues was a differentiation in British immigration rules between female residents who themselves or whose parents were born in the United Kingdom and those who did not fulfil these conditions. Non-British spouses of the first group only could settle in the UK, while the gates remained closed for the foreign spouses of the second group. Britain's justification that the distinction was meant to avoid hardship for women who had close ties with Britain if, when married, they had to move abroad to join their

[40] P van Dijk and G J H van Hoof, *Theory and Practice of the European Convention on Human Rights* (The Hague, Kluwer Law International, 1998), pp. 720–9, at 720.

[41] Entirely in the style of Queen Victoria, who did not believe in the possibility of lesbian relationships, there is no age of consent for lesbian relationships. They are still ignored by the law.

[42] *Dudgeon Case*, Judgment of 22 October 1981, Series A 45, 25.

husband. The Court accepted this justification,[43] and, in doing so, again failed to address the completely unnecessary hardship caused by the unequal treatment of the two groups: a woman, born outside Britain, who subsequently lived all her life within the country had to move away on marriage if she wanted to join her husband (which is supposedly the idea of marriage) while the woman whose parents were born in the UK but who herself has lived all her life somewhere else could – if she so wished – enter Britain with her new spouse. The distinction could, in other words, hardly be justified with a hardship argument as it simply did not meet that objective.[44]

These are only two examples in which the objective of safeguarding the enjoyment of a right or freedom for everybody was missed by focusing on the equality test. If, in the example of the *Dudgeon* case, the protection of youth is better served by a lower age limit for sexual content than twenty-one, why should this apply to male homosexual relationships only? Are heterosexual (and lesbian) youth better protected against sexual abuse than male homosexual youth? Are they less vulnerable, weaker in body or mind or more inexperienced? The difference in age for consent strongly suggests prejudices against homosexuals which, with this judgment, the Court did nothing to dispel.

Equally, in the *Abdulaziz* case there was no justifiable ground for differential treatment of the two groups of women. The difference created hardship instead of avoiding it.[45]

The two cases illustrate Westen's point that a separate equality analysis might confuse the just application of the anterior substantive rule. As argued above, the equality argument and, in particular, the justification of the differential treatment obscured the real objective of the rule.

According to the empty vessel theory, also without Article 14, the European Convention's normative standards must be applied equally to everybody unless differentiation can be justified. Differentiations must be made if that is necessary to avoid harmful effects of the rule of equal application. These principles are inherent in the concepts of the rule of law and social justice and separate reference to Article 14 is not necessary.

[43] Even though the judges did recognise that the second category of women (in case Mrs Balkandali) could also "form close ties" with Britain, the Court held that there were nevertheless, "general persuasive reasons for giving special treatment to those whose link with the country stems from birth within it". (Para. 88 of the judgment).

[44] Although this aspect of the Immigration rules had been amended before the judgment was published, it did not influence the Court's judgment.

[45] The Court did conclude to a violation of Article 14 on the grounds that it was more difficult for the wives than for the husbands to obtain a permit to stay with their spouses in Britain for which the (protection of the) labour market argument used by the UK Government did not strike the Court as a sufficient justification. The point here was that this was discrimination based on sex, for which, because of the advancement of equality of sexes is a major goal in the Member States of the Council of Europe, "very weighty reasons would have to be advanced" before the Court would regard this as compatible with the Convention. (Para. 78 of the judgment). This was seen, not as a violation of Article 8 as such, but as a violation of Article 14, in combination with Article 8.

Where does this leave the newly proposed autonomous non-discrimination Protocol? I assume that Westen would argue that such a provision is an anomaly. However, in the context of the European Convention, an autonomous non-discrimination provision would expand considerably the area it covers, as that provision would apply to situations which are presently not covered by the Convention. For instance, if and when the Protocol becomes effective, cases of sex discrimination in employment and social security which fall presently outside the Convention would then fall within the Strasbourg Court's jurisdiction.[46]

This does not mean that it is not an anomaly as cases brought before the Court come from the domestic context from which it should be clear that – to keep within the example – men and women workers should be treated equally unless there is a reason not to treat them equally. That is inherent in the rule itself and no separate equality test is needed.

If this argument is accepted, then the main function of an autonomous equality provision might be that it increases the awareness of the fundamental importance of abandoning discrimination. This psychological function may be very valuable. A good example of this are the sex equality provisions in Community law, which, although their success is limited, have undeniably contributed to the awareness that there are no acceptable reasons for sex discrimination.

3.2. The EC Court of Justice

The ECJ has repeatedly held that the EC is based on the rule of law and that the principle of equality is one of the fundamental principles of Community law. However, in two recent equality cases it became clear that, as a Community concept, it has limitations.

I refer, of course, to the cases of *P* v. *S and Cornwall County Council*[47] and *Lisa Grant* v. *South West Trains*.[48] In both cases questions were raised in relation to the application of the general principle of equality in the Community legal order. The outcome was remarkable: the Court held that transsexuals should not be discriminated against, but that the protection against discrimination of homosexuals fell outside the Community's legal order.[49]

[46] That, in itself, creates a number of interesting problems in relation to the jurisdiction of the Luxembourg Court on the basis of Community (sex equality) law.

[47] Case C-13/94 [1996] ECR-I-2143; [1996] All ER (EC) 397.

[48] Case C-24/96 [1998] ECR I-621; [1998] All ER (EC) 193.

[49] It has been suggested that the reason for this difference in outcome is not so much influenced by legal principles as by the financial consequences of protecting homosexuals (a much larger group than transsexuals) against discriminations which would have dire financial consequences. See, e.g. Noreen Burrows, "Sex and Sexuality in the European Court", *International Journal for Comparative Labour Law and Industrial Relations* 153, at 158; Leo Flynn, annotation on the P. v. S. and Cornwall County Council case, 34 *Common Market Law Review* 1997, 367, at 381. In a more general sense, see Virginia Harrison, "Using EC Law to Challenge Sexual orientation Discrimination at Work" in Hervey and O'Keeffe, *op cit.* n. 7, 279.

The first case concerned the dismissal of a transsexual after he had become a woman. The core issues were (a) whether discrimination against a transsexual fell within the Community law concept of sex discrimination and (b) if that were the case with whom P should be compared. In both aspects, the Court helped itself out of the logical muddle by referring, not to the narrow concept of sex discrimination, but to the general principle of equality as a fundamental principle of Community law which the Court has the duty to observe.[50] The Court could not tolerate discrimination against transsexuals as that would be a failure to protect their dignity and freedom to which all individuals, including transsexuals, are entitled.

The judgment seems to indicate that the law must be applied justly to all persons. Although the Court did not entirely overlook the problem of finding a comparator,[51] thus considering a separate equal treatment (sex discrimination) test, the reference to the fundamental nature of the much wider principle of equality and the dignity and freedom of individuals seems to recognise that the equality principle is underlying the legal order and inherent in its substantive rules.

The just application of the rule is not necessarily brought about by the logic of treating (un)alike cases (un)alike. If, for example, due to the operations necessary in the course of a sex change, P's absence from work would have fallen within the terms of lawful redundancy because of extended sick-leave, it could be argued that it would be unjust to apply this rule in her case as it would lead to unjust results. On the other hand, it could have been argued that the dismissal was just, as there would be no reason for the employer to grant P a longer term of sick-leave than other employees. The point is that the equality discussion adds nothing to solve this; the decision of what is just or unjust in each individual case cannot be solved by referring to the concept of equality.

The importance of this case is that the Court recognises that the objective of the law is to safeguard the human dignity and freedom of the individual; to take employment away from transsexuals because of sex-change (defined as "gender reassignment") operations affects their freedom to be what they are which may seem an unjust application of a rule. The Court accepts the protection of the human dignity and freedom of transsexuals as its duty – which, as the *Grant* case shows, does not extend to homosexuals. It is submitted that the reason for this conceptual confusion is that the Court mixes up this objective of the law (protection of human dignity and freedom) with an equality argument.

The *Grant* case dealt with the unequal treatment of Lisa Grant and her homosexual partner vis à vis South West Trains' employees who had heterosexual partners. Whereas different sex couples received certain travel facilities these were denied to same sex couples. The question was whether discrimina-

[50] Case C-13/94, Para. 19.
[51] See Para. 21 of the Judgment.

tion based on sexual orientation fell within the Community concept of sex discrimination.[52] The Court concluded that this was not the case[53] so it referred, again, to the wider principle of equality.

As in the previously discussed case, in Lisa Grant the Court also referred to the ECHR case law to find inspiration for its judgment. In Lisa Grant's case, it thus found support for the opinion that discrimination against homosexuals did not fall within the concept of equality. It pointed to the Strasbourg Commission/Court case law which did not consider "differential treatment" of homosexuals to fall within the scope of the Convention. Whereas this case law was used to support denial of equal treatment of homosexuals, case law which was used to support equal treatment, was rejected: the Court accepted Article 26 ICCPR as a guiding principle in Community law, but it did not accept the UN Human Rights Committee's conclusion[54] that this provision included sexual orientation as a prohibited ground of discrimination to be applicable in Community law. The Court held that the Human Rights Committee is not a "judicial institution" and its findings have no binding force in law.[55] These arguments are not necessarily convincing. Strictly speaking, the Strasbourg Court's opinions are not legally binding upon the ECJ either. It would be difficult to deny the Strasbourg case law effect in Community law, as the EU Member States are bound by it, but the ECJ itself has denied any formal link between the case law of the two courts, until the Treaties are formally amended to that effect.[56] Like the Strasbourg Court, the Human Rights Committee consists of highly qualified, independent, experts in the protection of human rights; the latter cannot be dismissed solely because it is, indeed, not a judicial body.[57] In particular the ECJ's conclusion that the Human Rights Committee did not reflect popular opinion in the world is rather unconvincing.[58]

[52] See on this issue Robert Wintemute, "Recognising New Kinds of Direct Sex Discrimination: Transsexualism, Sexual Orientation and Dress Codes" 60 *Modern Law Review* (1997), 334.

[53] An incorrect conclusion, according to John McInnes in an annotation on the *Grant* case, 36 *Common Market Law Review* 1999, 1043 at 1049. For a comment on this case, see also Laurence R Helfer, "International Decisions" (1998) *American Journal of International Law* Vol. 93, 200.

[54] UN Human Rights Committee, *Toonen* v. *Australia*, Communication No. 488/1992, UN Doc. CCPR/C/50/D/488/1992 (1994).

[55] Case C-249/96 Para. 46.

[56] Opinion 2/94.

[57] On the composition of the Human Rights Committee, see, e.g., A H Robertson, "The Implementation System: International Measures" in L Henkin (ed.), *The International Bill of Human Rights: The Covenant on Civil and Political Rights* (New York, Columbia University Press, 1981), p. 332 and P R Ghandi, *The Human Rights Committee and the Rights of Individual Communication* (Aldershot, Ashgate Dartmouth, 1998).

[58] The Court stated that, in spite of the Human Rights Committee's opinion, discrimination of homosexuals was not universally accepted to fall within the forbidden grounds for discrimination. One can only say that discrimination on the basis of sex is not universally considered unacceptable either. This is confusing factual statements with normative arguments. The fact that discrimination on whatever ground is not universally accepted does not mean that it should be condoned.

The conclusion from these two cases must be that, whereas recognition of the "wider" concept of equality as a general principle of law means that the dignity and freedom of transsexuals has to be protected, this is not the case for homosexuals.[59] The Court's use of an impressive range of formal arguments to come to this conclusion cannot hide the impression that the recognition of the general principle of equality in Community law does not necessarily mean the same to all categories of persons.

These two cases show that using the equality argument does not solve the problem of how to achieve justice and fairness; that depends to a large extent on the interpretation of the judiciary of the available rules and principles. It also demonstrates – like the two ECHR cases examined above – that equality arguments obscure the objective of substantive rules. The travel facilities in the *Grant* case were given to South West Trains employees and their partners in either a married or "steady relationship".[60] What can be an objective reason not to apply the latter to same-sex couples, unless one wants to deny that homosexuals cannot have steady relationships? Does this not, ultimately, deny them the freedom to have such relationships? Is this not the kind of freedom the Court vowed to respect in the *P* v. *S and Cornwall County Council* case?

The Court suggested that the outcome could have been different if the new anti-discrimination provision (now Art 13 TEC) had had force of law at the time of its judgment. Article 13 is not, however, a legally enforceable right,[61] so, until the Community legislature has created legislation to that effect, the Court can still make use of the evasive argument that, because the Community legislature has not acted upon Article 13 and created law expressly prohibiting discrimination against homosexuals, this does not fall within the concept of equality as accepted by society.[62] Would it be different if a legally enforceable right were incorporated, explicitly prohibiting discrimination on the basis of sexual orientation? Surely it would; it would no longer be primarily a case of interpreting but of applying the rule. The Court's arguments in the *Grant* case point very much into the direction of a (newly found?) reluctance to step ahead of the legislature in accepting sexual orientation as a status which may not be subject to discrimination. But, again, the main function of such an explicit pro-

[59] This is reminiscent of the *Bowers* v. *Hardwick* case, where the American Supreme Court held that "there is no fundamental right to homosexual sodomy (under the Due Process Clause)" which was interpreted by the lower courts as meaning that state endorsement of discrimination against homosexuals is not "constitutionally infirm". See Courtney G Joslin, "Equal Protection and Anti-Gay legislation: Dismantling the Legacy of Bowers v. Hardwick – Romer v. Evans" 116 S.Ct. 1620 (1996) *Harvard Civil Rights-Civil Liberties Review*, Vol. 32, No. 1, 1997, 225.

[60] I leave aside here the questionability of the assumption that a two days young marriage is steadier than an unmarried relationship of, for instance, two years.

[61] On the possibility that Article 13 might offer the ECJ an opportunity to expand the general principle of equality, see Lisa Waddington "Testing the Limits of the EC Treaty on Non-discrimination" (1999) *Industrial Law Journal*, 133.

[62] It has been suggested that even though Article 13 TEC is not legally enforceable, it might provide "interpretive guidance" for the ECJ. Richard Whittle, "Disability discrimination and the Amsterdam Treaty", 23 *European Law Review* (1998) 50, at 54.

hibition of discrimination against homosexuals would be political, rather than legal. It would raise the awareness that discrimination of homosexuals should be abandoned; as a legal argument it would add very little. As argued above, the travel facilities rule should have been applied to everybody. There was no justification to exclude Lisa Grant and her partner; that Grant's lawyer was forced to treat this as an equality argument weakened, rather than strengthened Grant's position.

Although I would accept Westen's submission that no separate equality test is necessary to apply rules equally to everyone, unless there are justifiable reasons for not doing so, this does not solve a number of crucial questions of justice and fairness. At the same time, one can argue that applying the principle of equality to one category of persons, while denying to another category when accepting that the objective is the protection of human dignity and freedom of individuals may perhaps not signify that the principle of equality is empty, but that it is volatile and entirely dependent on the interpretation of the judiciary. This is not to say that the blame for this apparent injustice should be put entirely on the judiciary. The ECJ's argument in *Grant* that it cannot single handedly expand the scope of Community law by incorporating the non-existent principle of equal treatment of homosexuals, is a valid one.[63] It is up to the legislature to do so. What is strange, however, is that this argument has not stopped the Court before.[64] The principle of equal treatment of transsexuals (whether disguised as a sex discrimination argument or not) does not form part of the Community legal order either. If the confusion by the equality arguments is removed, then what the Court really submitted is that the human dignity and freedom of transsexuals should be protected whereas that is not the case for homosexuals. Equality may not be an entirely empty vessel, it does indeed confuse the argument.

4. CONCLUSION

The above examined cases demonstrate how the focus on an equality argument can obscure the true objective of a rule. Although there is much objection to Westen's empty vessel theory,[65] it does bring home the point that a rule should be applied to everyone unless this would lead to an injustice. There is no objective reason to limit the freedom of speech on the basis of race, gender or creed etc. There may be another reason to limit the freedom of speech, for instance, for state security reasons. That limitation of the rule is not solved by referring

[63] Case C-249-96, Para. 47.

[64] See, for example, Hjalte Rasmussen, *On Law and Policy in the European Court of Justice; A Comparative Study in Judicial Policy Making* (Dordrecht, Martinus Nijhoff, 1986) and, by the same author, "Between Self-Restraint and Activism: A Judicial Policy for the European Court" 19 *European Law Review* (1988), 28.

[65] See n. 25 *supra*.

to an equality argument. The legislature or judiciary have to come up with very sound reasons to justify the limitation. The second paragraphs of the provisions in the European Convention acknowledge that limitations to fundamental rights may be justified for a number of well defined reasons such as the protection of public safety, public order, morals, safety and health, the rights and freedoms of others, etc. which have little to do with equality.

The new autonomous equality provisions in European law could have an important function in raising the awareness of the evil nature of discrimination of people because of what they are. In the multiracial, multireligious and multicultural societies of European countries that may be more important than ever.[66] It may be "morally necessary because it compels us to care about how people are treated in relation to one another".[67]

It is quite a different question whether the new provisions will indicate a new way of dealing with the persisting inequalities in (European) society. The Aristotelian concept that like cases should be treated alike and unalike cases unalike has been applied in European law for the best part of the last five decades. In spite of that, the recently revealed data about the gender payment gap in Great Britain, thirty years after the adoption of the Equal Pay Act[68] are only the tip of the proverbial iceberg.[69] It suggests that the law has its limitations as an instrument to bring about change in that situation. Above I have suggested that focusing on the equality discussion confuses the underlying objective of a rule and may, thus, prove to be counterproductive. In particular the above examined ECHR cases show that this is something of which the European judiciary ought to be well aware.

[66] Recent research in The Netherlands, a country famous (or infamous, depending on one's view) for its tolerance of "other life styles", has shown that 25 per cent of national (secondary) schoolchildren had difficulty with accepting homosexuality; of the non-national children that percentage was 75.

[67] Chemerinsky, *loc cit.* n. 25, at 576. It's rhetorically necessary – because it is "a powerful symbol that helps to persuade people to safeguard rights that would otherwise go unprotected" – remains doubtful as does the analytical necessity – "because it creates the presumption that people should be treated alike and puts the burden of proof on the discriminator". *(Ibid.)*

[68] A recent study by the Women's Unit and Department of Social Security revealed a pattern of striking differences between the payment of men and women workers in Britain, nearly thirty years after the Equal Pay Act became law. The study shows that, although the gender pay gap has been narrowed by one per cent in 1999, the real earnings gap is still nearly fifty per cent, setting women's average income at half that of their male counterparts. (*New Statesman*, 1 November 1999, 5) Although one has to be careful with arguments based on statistics there is little disagreement about persisting inequalities, not only in pay but also in treatment and opportunities.

[69] See also, for instance, Galbraith who writes that the gap between the rich and the poor has only widened in the last decades. J K Galbraith, *The Culture of Contentment* (Boston, Houghton Mifflin, 1992). See also the new edition of Galbraith's *The Affluent Society* (London, Hamish Hamilton, 1999).

7

The Rule of Law in the Legal Order of the European Community

PAUL LASOK QC

1. INTRODUCTION

The rule of law is a fundamental value in two senses. First, respect for the rule of law is an objective to which modern legal systems aspire and for whose the attainment there exists the panoply of rights, remedies, procedures and court systems found in modern systems. Secondly, the "rule" or dominance of law has at its core the principle that no person or body is above the law. The European Community is founded upon the rule of law and therefore that fundamental value is incorporated in the system set up under the Treaties.[1] Viewed from a historical perspective, the major landmarks in the case law of the Court of Justice of the European Communities[2] have been instances in which the Court has sought to develop or improve the mechanisms for securing respect for the rule of law, or even put in place appropriate mechanisms where they were previously lacking. For example: the development of the concepts of the primacy and direct applicability or direct effect of Community law;[3] the evolution of the concept of rights under Community law so as to encompass the right to reparation from Member States in respect of damage caused by a breach of Community law;[4] the creation of new remedies[5] or the extension of existing remedies.[6] That

[1] *Cf.* Opinion 1/91 [1991] ECR I-6079, paragraph 21 of the judgment: "the EEC Treaty, albeit concluded in the form of an international agreement, none the less constitutes the constitutional charter of a Community based on the rule of law".

[2] Hereafter "the Court of Justice" (ECJ). The jurisdiction of the Court of Justice is, of course, divided between it and the Court of First Instance (CFI) of the E uropean Communities. For the sake of simplicity, references to "the Court of Justice" are to be understood as encompassing both courts save where the context indicates otherwise.

[3] For example, Case 26/62 *Van Gend en Loos* v. *Nederlandse Administratie der Belastingen* [1963] ECR 1.

[4] For example, Cases C-6 and C-9/90 *Francovich* v. *Italy* [1991] ECR I-5357.

[5] For example, Case C-2/88 Imm. *Zwartfeld* [1990] ECR I-3365.

process indicates the fundamental nature of the rule of law as a value to which the Community aspires.

To assert that the rule of law is a fundamental value in the Community's legal order is therefore to assert a truism. However, no doubt because it is a truism, it is all too easy to take the rule of law for granted, to fail to consider what it really means and where its limits lie. The basic question about the rule of law in the Community is, just how fundamental a value in the Community's legal order is it? That question can be approached from three different perspectives. The first involves discussion of the difference between "EC law" and what is often described as "EU law", namely, the difference between those parts of the system set up by the Treaties that are subject to judicial control by the Court of Justice and those parts (introduced, or expanded, for the most part by the Treaty on European Union, as amended by the Amsterdam Treaty) that are not (apparently) subject to such judicial control. The second involves discussion of the apparent exceptions to the operation of the rule of law *within* that part of EC (or EU) law that is generally regarded as founded upon the rule of law. The most important example of such apparent exceptions, and the one that will be considered here, is the relatively limited degree of judicial control of the exercise of legislative and (albeit to a lesser degree) admin-istrative discretion. The third concerns the effectiveness of the mechanisms within the EC legal system for ensuring respect for the rule of law: to what extent does the Community's legal order lack appropriate mech-anisms and how strong or effective is the pressure to remedy those deficiencies?

Investigation of the last aspect of the question would necessitate an historico-legal discussion that could not be accommodated within the confines of this paper.[7] Accordingly, after an exploration of what is meant by the rule of law, attention will turn to the first two aspects of the question referred to above.

2. THE MEANING OF "THE RULE OF LAW"

In English, the phrase "the rule of law" has no technical legal meaning. It is not to be found in the main dictionaries of legal terms. In ordinary language, particularly in the non-technical discourse of lawyers, "the rule of law" is used in different ways but, generally speaking, those different ways reflect the same basic meaning of the expression.

To an English lawyer, the starting point for an examination of what is meant by "the rule of law" is the view expressed by Dicey.[8] He considered that "the

[6] For example, Case 294/83 *Parti Ecologiste "Les Verts"* v. *European Parliament* [1986] ECR 1339; Case C-70/88 *Parliament* v. *Council* [1990] ECR I-2041.

[7] See for example, Mackenzie Stuart, *The European Communities and the Rule of Law* (London, Stevens, 1977).

[8] A V Dicey, *An Introduction to the Study of the Law of the Constitution* (10th ed., London, Macmillan, 1960), pp. 187–203.

rule of law" had at least three distinct conceptions: (i) no man is punishable or can be lawfully made to suffer in body or goods except for a distinct breach of law established in the ordinary legal manner before the ordinary courts of the land; (ii) no man is above the law and every man, whatever his rank or condition, is subject to the ordinary law of the realm and amenable to the jurisdiction of the ordinary tribunals; and (iii) the general principles of the constitution are the result of judicial decisions determining the rights of private persons in particular cases brought before the courts, in contrast to states where rights of individuals result from the general principles of the constitution. He refined those three conceptions as follows: (i) the absolute supremacy or predominance of regular law as opposed to the influence of arbitrary power; (ii) equality before the law, being the ordinary law of the land;[9] and (iii) "rule of law" expresses the fact that, in England, the law of the constitution is not the source but the consequence of the rights of individuals.[10]

Dicey's approach was an attempt at a description of what "the rule of law" meant in the particular context of English law. His first conception expresses a protective principle: a person's position cannot be adversely affected otherwise than pursuant to law. In the way Dicey put it, that protective principle implies a basic, or default, position that is a state of liberty. That state cannot be limited otherwise than by law. The second conception is nothing more nor less than a principle of equality before the law and can be regarded as a general principle not peculiar to the situation in England. However, it too has a particular English aspect to it: the idea that all persons in society are subject to the *same* rules of law. Thus, the idea that public bodies should be subject to law – but to a different body of rules than those applicable to private persons – is inconsistent with Dicey's concept.[11] The third conception appears to be entirely English. It seems to be based on the idea that the rule of law is immanent in the *English* system and not required by written law (by contrast with the position, as Dicey perceived it, in other European states).

In many respects, the most interesting feature of Dicey's approach concerns his first conception and its relationship with the third. The first conception is strongly linked to the third because it proceeds on the assumption that individual rights are not conferred by law (or at least by written law). Rights are, instead, the expression in law of something that the citizen already possesses. Dicey's first conception is also something that has rather more relevance to the

[9] See in particular p. 184, where he cites Year Books, XIX Henry VI: "par la ley il meme [that is, the king] et toutes ses sujets sont rules".

[10] *Ibid.*, pp. 202–03.

[11] In *The New Despotism* (reprint, London, E Benn Ltd, 1945), Lord Hewart put it as follows: "Between the 'Rule of Law' and what is called 'administrative law' (happily there is no English name for it) there is the sharpest possible contrast. One is substantially the opposite of the other" (p. 37). The point of criticism is not that "administrative law" provides a cloak to cover the fact that the State and its servants are more or less above the law but that the position of the State and its officials is to be determined by reference to principles of law that differ from those applicable to the ordinary citizen (see pp. 39–40).

exercise of public powers than to relationships between private persons. In that respect, Dicey's first conception has both a general and a particular aspect. The general aspect is the notion of the rule of law as a state of affairs in which the individual's position is determined by law rather than arbitrarily. The particular aspect is the implicit assumption of a state of liberty, which may be regarded as a peculiarity of the situation in England as Dicey saw it.[12] The assumption of a pre-existing state of liberty that can be limited only by law (and, typically, by express provision or by necessary implication but not otherwise) is often said to be a feature of English law (or of the common law) that distinguishes it from other systems of law, in which the rights and liberties of the individual are said to be the creation of the law. However, it would be going too far to elevate the pre-existing state of liberty into the equivalent of a charter of inalienable human rights.

As Lord Hewart put it:

> The right of personal liberty is the right not to be arrested or detained or otherwise subjected to physical restraint except in accordance with the law. . . . The right of freedom of speech, again, is simply the right which everyone has to say, write, or publish what he pleases so long as he does not commit a breach of the law. . . . The liberty of the press is similarly a mere application of the principle that no one is liable to be punished or condemned in damages except for a breach of the law. . . . In like manner, there is not in the British Constitution any such thing recognised as a definite right of public meeting. The right is the result of individual rights of personal liberty and freedom of speech, which are themselves the result of an application of the principle of the Rule of Law. In other words, the right of a number of people to assemble together in a lawful manner for public discussion or other lawful purposes is simply an aggregation of the rights of each of the members of the assembly to go where he pleases so long as he does not break the law. . . .[13]

Thus, the pre-existing state of liberty is just that: a precarious freedom that is resistant only to those encroachments that lack legal power. Nonetheless, the rule of law, as so understood, expresses a very fundamental principle: that the pre-existing state of liberty may not be invaded in the absence of lawfully constituted authority. The Diceyan concept of the protection of liberty ultimately turns upon there being a general level of tolerance in society and a corresponding degree of restraint on the part of the legislature (in a democratic society, of course, the two march hand in hand because, in theory at least, a tolerant public will not tolerate an intolerant legislature). Further, the reason why the Diceyan concept is antagonistic towards the subjection of the State and

[12] It is not as peculiar to the situation in England as all that, although it may be regarded as a particular feature of the common law tradition. A colloquium held in Chicago in 1957 produced a number of general statements about the rule of law, one of which was: "The rule of law is based upon the liberty of the individual and has as its object the harmonising of the opposing notions of individual liberty and public order" (see Wade's introduction to Dicey's work n. 6 *supra* at p. cix).

[13] *Op. cit.*, pp. 27–32.

its servants to a system or branch of the law ("administrative law") different from that applicable to the ordinary citizen is that such a development would make it possible for the State to constitute its lawful authority to encroach upon that pre-existing state of liberty in such a way as to escape the constraints that apply to other members of society and, thus, gain for itself and its servants a privileged position.[14]

In that connection, the Diceyan emphasis on the role of the courts is explained by two things. The first is a feature peculiar to the common law: the development of the law and of legal concepts by the courts. The second is something more general: the desire to subject the State and its servants to the same conditions in all respects as those to which ordinary citizens are subject. If the State and its servants were subjected to the same law as ordinary citizens but had their disputes (and, in particular, their liabilities to the ordinary citizen) settled by special tribunals, there would at once be created a difference of treatment between the State and the citizen and, if not the possibility of there being divergences, and a fragmentation, in the future development of the law, then at least the appearance that the State and its servants occupy a place above the ordinary citizen.

However, "the Rule of Law is not a Law of Nature, constant and invariable at all times and in all circumstances. It is not necessarily and for ever what Dicey conceived it to be and still less what Lord Hewart conceived it to be".[15]

More modern views of the rule of law, as expressed by English commentators, eschew the particularly English viewpoint held by Dicey and attempt to identify features or meanings that can be expressed in more universal terms. One, for example, retains a threefold concept (like Dicey) but expresses it in rather different terms as comprising: (i) a preference for law and order in society; (ii) the principle that government must be conducted according to law; and (iii) a body of political opinion as to what the law should contain.[16] Another view identifies four significant meanings of "the rule of law": (i) as applied to the power of government, the concept requires that every government author-

[14] The fear that that was taking place in the English legal system prompted Lord Hewart's diatribe in *The New Despotism*. It should not be thought that Lord Hewart was a lonely eccentric in his views. The problems posed by developments in administrative law in the common law systems was not unique to England. In the United States, in *Administrative Justice and the Supremacy of Law* (Cambridge, Harvard University Press, published in 1927, two years before the publication of *The New Despotism*), Dickinson had set out an extensive critique of regulation by government and regulation by law.

[15] Allen, *Law and Orders* (3rd ed., London, Stevens, 1965), p. 23. In many respects, the Diceyan view, in particular as enunciated by Lord Hewart, was based upon a simple view of the intervention of the State in the life of the ordinary citizen. Since Lord Hewart's time, views about the role of the State in society have ebbed and flowed. The view prevailing since at least the early 1980s, that the role of the State should be reduced, has not taken the role of the State back to what was regarded as acceptable to libertarians such as Dicey and Lord Hewart (that is, to proponents of the *laissez-faire* form of liberalism); and it does not appear to be possible to achieve that under modern conditions.

[16] E C S Wade and A W Bradley, *Constitutional and Administrative Law* (11th ed., London, Longman, 1993), pp. 101–03.

ity which does some act that would otherwise be a wrong or that infringes a person's liberty must be able to justify its action as authorised by law (the principle of legality); (ii) government should be conducted within a framework of recognised rules and principles that restrict discretionary power; (iii) disputes as to the legality of acts of government are to be decided by judges who are independent of the executive (separation of powers); and (iv) the law should be even-handed between government and citizen (equality before the law).[17]

One of the significant features of those different attempts to define what "the rule of law" means is the emphasis on the role of the rule of law in determining the relationship between the State itself, or State authorities, and the individual. That emerges with particular force in the last view summarised above: the exponents of that view recognise that the principle of legality is, in itself, insufficient to explain what is meant by the rule of law because it must be supplemented by a second principle (to which a third is added – judicial review by courts independent of the executive) that is concerned with the control of discretionary powers held by the State and State authorities. As the authors put it, the rule of law demands more than the legality of the conduct of government "since otherwise it [the rule of law] would be satisfied by giving the government unrestricted discretionary powers, so that everything that they did was within the law. *Quod principi placuit legis habet vigorem* (the sovereign's will has the force of law) is a perfectly legal principle, but it expresses rule by arbitrary power rather than rule according to ascertainable law".

In short, the concept expressed in the phrase "the rule of law" is not, to English lawyers, a closed concept. It has acquired no fixed meaning since Dicey's attempt to define it. That state of affairs opens up the opportunity to look again at the concept; and I will attempt to do that by making some rather basic points about the concept.

"The" rule of law is quite different from "a" rule of law: the latter is a specific provision or rule that forms part of "the law" as opposed to some other body of rules, such as some social or moral code, that is not "law"; the former does not refer to any particular part of "the law" but to a general concept concerning the role of law in society, or a particular society. In other words, in the phrase "the rule of law", the word "rule" describes what "the law" does, or what its effect is, rather than seeking to identify a discrete part of "the law". Equally, the word "law" in the phrase "the rule of law" does not qualify the word "rule", whereas it does in the phrases "a rule of law" or "rules of law". Thus, the phrases "a rule of law" or "rules of law" can without difficulty or change of meaning be replaced by "legal rule" or "legal rules". In "the rule of

[17] H W R Wade and C F Forsyth, *Administrative Law* (7th ed., Oxford, OUP, 1994), pp. 24–7. The authors go on to say that "the rule of law" has other meanings outside the sphere of public administration. They cite by way of illustration the principle that no one should be punished except for some legally defined crime, which appears to be one aspect of the first meaning that they give to "the rule of law" (the principle of legality).

law", no such transposition is possible. The word "law" in that phrase connotes the entire body of rules having the particular character of being "law". However, in that sense at least, the expression "the rule of law" appears to be a tautology: if "law" did not "rule", how could it be "law" (if one defines "law" as a body of rules emanating from the sovereign in society and backed up by sanctions that override in their consequences the sanctions arising from breach of other norms, such as customary norms or the norms of fashion)?

It is no misuse of language to say of rules other than rules of law that they "rule". Social rules, rules of fashion, moral rules, "rule" or prevail over or dictate right conduct to society or portions of society for a greater or lesser period of time. Does the expression "rule of law" mean no more than that the claims of law, or of legal rules, have the same force and effect as other, non-legal, rules that can be said to "rule" at any one time? To put it another way, in order to avoid the tautology apparent in the expression "the rule of law", does the word "rule" describe a state of affairs, of acquiescence in the requirements of legal rules, or of their performance, that is quite distinct from the nature or the *intended* effect of law? What about that other expression – "respect for the rule of law" – that is frequently encountered? Is that, too, a tautology (or rather a triple tautology, if such exists) because "respect" for the "rule" of "law" can mean only one thing: that law is law, or that law has an effect?

In ordinary language, the phrases "the rule of law" and "respect for the rule of law" are very often used to describe a state of affairs: the fact that rules of law are generally observed in practice, by (unspoken) contrast with a state of affairs in which observance of the law is, or is perceived to be, the exception rather than the norm. For example, a state of anarchy, in which the public authorities are, or seem to be, powerless to enforce the law, would not in ordinary language be described as a state in which there was "respect for the rule of law" or, indeed, "the rule of law". However, the anarchic behaviour of individual members of society, in or around a football stadium, a public house or an area of social housing, is perhaps too localised and exceptional to be described in ordinary language as an instance of the absence of "the rule of law" (even though it may be described as an (aberrant) instance of the absence of "respect for the rule of law"). Even the failure of a particular rule of law to be observed as a matter of fact by significant numbers of members of society from all walks of life and different social and economic backgrounds (such as rules requiring road vehicles not to exceed a maximum speed) is not indicative of the absence of "the rule of law" (although, again, it may indicate absence of respect for it), at least where there is active enforcement of the rule and (perhaps more importantly) where there is positive recognition in society that the rule is a rule of law and that it therefore demands compliance. When faced with a particular instance of lack of respect for the law, courts may invoke "the rule of law" in order to justify action to repress the unlawful conduct in question; but that is usually done in order to show that exceptions to proper observance of the law cannot be created because to do so would bring about a more generalised failure of the legal system.[18]

In ordinary language, therefore, the concept embodied in the phrase "the rule of law" is concerned not so much with the behaviour of individual members of society or particular social groups as with the all-encompassing nature of law. By that I do not mean that law is perceived to embrace all forms of behaviour in society.[19] Rather it is that law is perceived to apply to all persons and bodies within society. Hence the fact that, in ordinary language, a breakdown in "the rule of law" is generally understood to mean a situation in which the public powers fail, for whatever reason, to secure observance of the law on a sufficiently wide scale. That focus on the role of public authorities is important because the notion of "the rule of law" is not really concerned with the idea that law commands obedience from members of society. That idea is readily understood in a practical (as opposed to philosophical) sense because laws in practice operate, and are perceived as operating, as commands backed up by sanctions of various sorts. It is also apparent to members of society in a practical (as opposed to philosophical) sense that there can be such a thing as "the rule of law" and even "respect for the rule of law" even though laws are not observed in practice. It is common experience to find that individuals who break particular legal rules (for example, exceeding a mandatory speed limit or breaking a contract) do retain a concept of the rule of law (and are no less concerned that others should respect it). Instead, the notion of "the rule of law" is best explained by going back to the idea of what it is to "rule".

"The rule of law", in ordinary language, expresses the idea of law as a sovereign or ruler. It prevails over other prescriptive forms, such as moral, customary or behavioural codes. But even sovereigns may from time to time encounter a certain lack of respect, or downright disobedience, from their subjects; and so it is with the law. As long as such incidents remain the exception rather than the rule, the sovereign can still be said to rule, and to rule effectively; and so it is with the law. The expression "the rule of law" is therefore different in meaning from "respect for the rule of law" or, indeed, "respect for the law". Further, there is no tautology in the expression because the true meaning of "the rule of law" lies in the sovereignty of law rather than in the nature of law as law.

[18] Thus, in *R* v. *Chief Constable of the Devon and Cornwall Constabulary, ex parte Central Electricity Generating Board* [1982] QB 458 at 471, a case concerning non-violent protests against the surveying of land with a view to the construction of a power station, Lord Denning MR said of the protest: "if there was here no breach of the peace or apprehension of it, it would give a licence to every obstructor and every passive resister in the land. He would be able to cock a snook at the law as these groups have done. Public works of the greatest national importance could be held up indefinitely. This cannot be. The rule of law must prevail".

[19] It is not necessary in this context to go into the question of the "complete" nature of law, which leads into the attempts to find a basic legal rule to the effect either that all things that are not prohibited are permitted or that all things that are not permitted are prohibited. It is not unknown to find *lacunae* in legal systems: see generally, *Le Probleme des Lacunes en Droit*, ed. Ch. Perelman (Brussels, Bruglant, 1968).

In what can be described as pre-modern times, the law was not sovereign. The monarch was sovereign and the fount of justice and law. Law as a system of rules commanding obedience certainly existed; but the sovereign was above the law and escaped judicial control. In contrast, in most modern legal systems, the relationships between members of society and between them and the different arms of the State, and the powers of the different arms of the State, are regulated by law. It is because the law disposes of those matters that the law, and not the monarch or modern head of state, is sovereign and, thus, "rules".[20]

Even in the United Kingdom, which has no written constitution (and, arguably, no constitutional "law" as such), the sovereignty of the law in that sense is recognised. As Lord Denning MR put it in *Gouriet* v. *Union of Postal Workers*,[21] "To every subject in this land, no matter how powerful, I would use Thomas Fuller's words over 300 years ago: 'Be you ever so high, the law is above you'". Although those words were directed at the possibility that a "powerful subject" might disregard the law with impunity if the Attorney-General refused his consent to the enforcement of the criminal law, the real target of the remark was the argument advanced in that case by the Attorney-General that he was "the final arbiter as to whether the law should be enforced or not".[22] The Court of Justice has put the same thought in more prosaic terms:

> . . . the European Economic Community is a Community based on the rule of law, inasmuch as neither its Member States nor its institutions can avoid a review of the question whether the measures adopted by them are in conformity with the basic constitutional charter, the Treaty. In particular, in Articles 173 and 184, on the one hand, and in Article 177, on the other, [now Articles 230, 241 and 234, respectively] the Treaty established a complete system of legal remedies and procedures designed to permit the Court of Justice to review the legality of measures adopted by the institutions. . . .[23]

[20] The supremacy of the rule of law has also been derived from the concept of the rule of law as the mechanism for achieving social solidarity. In that context, not only is the State subject to the rule of law but "from the rule of law . . . there is imposed upon the State the obligation to assure to each and all its citizens the means to enable them to contribute all it is in them to give to the fullest realisation of social solidarity. It is because of this obligation that the State is entitled to use force for the achievement of its end": see H J Laski, "M. Duguit's Conception of the State" in I Jennings (ed.), *Modern Theories of Law*, (London, Oxford University Press 1933), p. 54.

[21] [1977] QB 729 at 761H–762A.

[22] *Ibid.* at 761C. Earlier in the judgment, Lord Denning had said: "The Attorney-General tells us that when he refuses his consent his refusal is final. It cannot be overridden by the courts. He is answerable to Parliament, and to Parliament alone. He declines even to give reasons for his refusal. This is, to my mind, a direct challenge to the rule of law" (p. 758G). In the event, the decision of the Court of Appeal was reversed by the House of Lords ([1978] AC 435), essentially because private persons cannot sue on behalf of the public in order to prevent public wrongs (unless the person concerned would suffer injury as a result of the wrong). A later commentator has said: "The issue of the direct reviewability of the Attorney-General's decision ultimately fell away, though Lord Denning's observations on it in the Court of Appeal, which prompted strong adverse comment in the House of Lords at the time, may one day be accepted as the law": Mr. Justice Richards, "Public powers – preventing misuse" *JSB Journal* 2000, issue 9, p. 4 at p. 7.

[23] Case 294/83 *Les Verts* v. *Parliament* [1986] ECR 1339, paragraph 23.

The law's claim to "rule" over all members of society without exception can be explained in two ways. In one sense, it is an aspect of the effect of law: unless the law controls the conduct of all members of society, in particular those charged with government and the administration of the law, the law can be deprived of its effectiveness because it may not be enforced (the problem of concern in the *Gouriet* case) or because any perceived flouting of the law by those responsible for administering it – or even their perceived immunity from legal control – gives a pernicious example that other members of society are likely to follow. The claim of the law to obedience (its effect) therefore drives it to extend as far as is possible the personal scope of the law and to limit as far as is possible inconsistent claims (typically, and most importantly, claims to act in an arbitrary manner falling outside the control of the courts – that is, the exercise of discretion by public bodies). In another sense, the law's claim to universal control in society is driven by the balance between individual members of society and between them and the State. Individuals may well accept the constraints placed upon their conduct by the law in the knowledge that human frailty may lead to a certain degree of lack of observance of the requirements of the law on the part of other individuals. However, one element of individual consent to the constraints imposed by law is the expectation that proper steps will be taken by the responsible authorities to enforce the law; and that what is expected of – and given by – individual members of society is expected in equal measure of – and given by – the authorities of the State.

The two aspects of the sovereignty of law, its supervening claim to observance and its application throughout society, including agents of the State, come together in *R* v. *Horseferry Road Magistrates' Court, ex parte Bennett*, a case in which a New Zealand citizen alleged to have committed criminal offences in England was traced to South Africa and forcibly brought from there back to England by the English police, in disregard of the available extradition process and in breach of international and South African law. Lord Bridge said: "There is, I think, no principle more basic to any proper system of law than the maintenance of the rule of law itself. When it is shown that the law enforcement agency responsible for bringing a prosecution has only been enabled to do so by participating in violations of international law and of the laws of another state in order to secure the presence of the accused within the territorial jurisdiction of the court, I think that respect for the rule of law demands that the court take cognisance of that circumstance".[24] A particular feature of that case is the sense that, just as individual members of society are not entitled to "take the law into their own hands" in order to remedy a perceived defect in the application or enforcement of the law, or to achieve a *result* that may be regarded as just or as in accord with the law (there, the bringing of a person to justice),

[24] [1994] 1 AC 42 at 67.

State authorities are also required to comply with the law and are not entitled to break one rule in order to achieve the object of another.[25]

3. THE EXTENT OF THE RULE OF LAW IN THE EUROPEAN COMMUNITY

3.1. EC law and EU law

Although "EU law" is now often used to describe the "law" of the European Union, the structure created by the EU Treaty actually comprises two quite di ferent things. The first is the system of law commonly known as "EC law", which is set out in and derived from the founding Treaties (and the EU and Amsterdam Treaties).[26] The second is a system of political co-operation in various areas.

In relation to the first element, the EC, ECSC and EAEC Treaties all provide that "the Court of Justice shall ensure that in the interpretation and application of this Treaty the law is observed".[27] In so providing, the Treaties necessarily imply that the Treaties, and the system of law engendered by each of them, incorporate the rule of law. As noted above, the Court of Justice concluded that the Community was based on the rule of law inasmuch as the Community institutions and the Member States were subject to the control of the courts (specifically, the Court of Justice itself). The control exercised by the Court of Justice nonetheless varies considerably from certain (exceptional) forms of action in which its role is to achieve an accommodation between national interests and the general interests of the Community,[28] through forms of action in which the Court has unlimited jurisdiction and can substitute itself for the administration,[29] to what could be described as more conventional types of judicial review, in which the Court's function is limited to ensuring compliance with the law and in which the Court does not have power to substitute itself for the administration.[30] That variation does not affect the principle that

[25] It is also worth noting that the law infringed in that case was not the internal law of the State but international law and the law of another country. The acceptance of other laws as forming part of "the rule of law" is not novel: see Wade's introduction to Dicey's *Introduction to the Study of the Law of the Constitution*, p. xcvii.

[26] When the United Kingdom acceded to the Communities, the prevailing term was "common market law". That was widely supplanted by "EC law", or "European Community law" in the late 1970s. The latter expression was more accurate because "EC law" covered more things than the law of the common market did.

[27] EC Treaty, Article 220 (ex 164); EAEC Treaty, Article 136; ECSC Treaty (which is worded slightly differently, but not in any respect that is here relevant), Article 31.

[28] For example, ECSC Treaty, Article 37, as explained in Cases 2 and 3/60 *Niederrheinische Bergwerks AG* v. *High Authority* [1961] ECR 133 at 145–7.

[29] For example, EC Treaty, Article 229 (ex 172).

[30] For example, ECSC Treaty, Article 33 (where the limit on the Court of Justice's powers of review is express); EC Treaty, Article 230 (ex 173) (where the limit is not stated expressly but can be found in the case law): see further below.

the Member States and the Community institutions are subject to judicial control.

The first breach in the general principle that the system of law in and created by the Treaties is subject to the rule of law (in the sense that the Community institutions and the Member States are subject to judicial control) appeared in Article 31 of the Single European Act, which provided: "The provisions of [the EC, ECSC and EAEC Treaties] concerning the powers of the Court of Justice of the European Communities and the exercise of those powers shall apply only to the provisions of Title II and to Article 32 [of the Single European Act] . . .". Thus, the common provisions in the Single European Act and the provisions dealing with European co-operation in the sphere of foreign policy were excluded from the jurisdiction of the Court of Justice.

The next step was taken in Article 46 (ex Article L) of the EU Treaty (the Maastricht Treaty), as amended by the Amsterdam Treaty. That provisions excludes the operation of the Court of Justice's jurisdiction and powers in relation to the common provisions of the EU Treaty (Title I – Articles 1–7, ex A–F.1)[31] and the provisions on a common foreign and security policy (Title V – Articles 11–28, ex J.1–J.18). The jurisdiction and powers of the Court of Justice apply to the EU Treaty provisions on police and judicial co-operation in criminal matters (Title VI – Articles 29–42, ex K.1–K.14) but only under the conditions laid down in Article 35. Those conditions effectively limit the jurisdiction of the Court of Justice to: (i) giving preliminary rulings, where and to the extent that a Member State has accepted such jurisdiction; (ii) reviewing the legality of framework decisions and decisions in actions brought by a Member State or the Commission; (iii) ruling on disputes between Member States regarding the interpretation or application of acts of the Council adopted under Article 34(2); and (iv) ruling on disputes between Member States and the Commission regarding the interpretation or application of conventions established by the Council under Article 34(2)(d). The jurisdiction and powers of the Court of Justice apply to the provisions on closer co-operation between Member States (Title VII – Articles 43–45, ex K.15–K.17) under the conditions provided for by Article 11 (ex 5a) of the EC Treaty and Article 40 (ex K.12) of the EU Treaty. Of those two Articles, the only relevant provision seems to be that contained in Article 40(4) of the EU Treaty, which provides that the powers of the Court of Justice extend to Articles 40(1)–(3).

As a result of those provisions, there is now, as previously there was not, a clear line between those matters that fall within the jurisdiction and powers of the Court of Justice and those that do not. In relation to the latter ("the excluded areas"), the Court of Justice has no jurisdiction to review the legality of

[31] Article 6(2), which provides that the Union shall respect fundamental rights, is within the jurisdiction and powers of the ECJ so far as it relates to acts of the Community institutions and insofar as the ECJ otherwise has jurisdiction: see Article 46(d) of the EU Treaty.

measures falling within them and no power to annul such measures.[32] The rule of law, as it is and has been understood in the context of the founding Treaties, therefore does not apply in those excluded areas. Nonetheless, the borderline between those two areas is still policed by the Court of Justice because it retains jurisdiction to construe Article 47 (ex Article N) of the EU Treaty. That Article provides that, apart from the amendments made by it to the ECSC, EC and EAEC Treaties and the final provisions, "nothing in this Treaty [that is, the EU Treaty] shall affect the Treaties establishing the European Communities or the subsequent Treaties and Acts modifying or supplementing them".

The true scope of Article 47 of the EU Treaty has not been explored judicially. At this stage, it appears to establish a paradox. Article 46 denies the jurisdiction and powers of the Court of Justice over matters falling within the provisions dealing with the excluded areas. On the other hand, Article 46 also provides that the Court of Justice *does* have jurisdiction in relation (*inter alia*) to Article 47; and Article 47 clearly states the intention of the Member States that the excluded areas should *not* entrench upon the founding Treaties and the Treaties and Acts modifying or supplementing them. If the exclusion of jurisdiction effected by Article 46 were regarded as complete, Article 47 would be rendered meaningless, or at least ineffective as a *legal* provision, because nothing other than political self-restraint would be capable of preventing acts adopted within the scope of the excluded areas from having effects inconsistent with the intention expressed in Article 47. Yet, if Article 47 were intended to be a provision expressing only a political, and not a legal, responsibility, it would have been included among the provisions excluded from the Court of Justice's control.

The fact that Article 47 is a provision to which the jurisdiction and powers of the Court of Justice extend indicates that the Court of Justice does have jurisdiction over the excluded areas, albeit only for the purpose of ascertaining whether or not Article 47 has been respected. Nonetheless, that means that the Court of Justice may construe acts adopted within the excluded areas and determine their lawfulness, in the sense of their compatibility with the founding Treaties and the Treaties and Acts modifying or supplementing them. It remains a matter of debate whether, if the Court of Justice finds that such an Act is incompatible with Article 47 of the EU Treaty, it may annul the Act (or that part of it containing the incompatibility) or may only declare the Act to be incompatible, leaving it to the Member States and the other Community institutions to discharge their political responsibility by removing the conflict and, in particular, leaving it to the author of the Act to withdraw or amend it. In the latter event, a failure by the Member States or, as the case may be, the Community institution concerned to rectify the problem could potentially be actionable under the EC Treaty because a failure to eliminate the problem would

[32] Case T-174/95 *Svenska Journalistforbundet* v. *Council* [1998] ECR II-2289, paragraph 85 of the judgment.

constitute an actionable breach of Article 10 (ex 5) of the EC Treaty (if one or more Member States were responsible) or would otherwise be actionable under Articles 230 or 232 (ex 173 and 175) (if a Community institution were to be responsible). Hence, in one way or another, whether directly or indirectly, respect for the rule of law, as it operates in the context of the founding Treaties, could be restored.[33] If the Court of Justice did not have that jurisdiction and power, a very serious inroad would have been made into the rule of law.[34]

Passing now to the excluded areas themselves, which comprise the second element of the system created under the Treaties – political co-operation, the fact that the jurisdiction and the powers of the Court of Justice are excluded does not necessarily mean that they constitute a "lawless Alsatia" (with the connotations of licentious behaviour that that phrase implies). The excluded areas remain matters upon which the Member States have reached basic agreement as to what they propose to do. As such, they can be dealt with in accordance with the principles of public international law. Further, where the action taken requires the Member States to take measures that are effective within their own jurisdictions, those measures come within the jurisdiction of the national courts. However, two points should be made about that state of affairs. The first is that the possibility of judicial control, and therefore of securing respect for the rule of law, is limited because the excluded areas are concerned essentially with international co-operation. Secondly, to the extent that there is judicial control and respect for the rule of law, that takes place outside the scope of the system of law created by the founding Treaties and of the rule of law as it is known in that context.

The distinguishing feature of the excluded areas is the political and non-legal nature of the obligations accepted by the Member States in conjunction with the Community institutions involved in the system of co-operation.[35] The excluded areas operate essentially at the level of international co-operation (between states and international organisations). It is a moot question whether or not they are properly described as "law" at all. To the extent that "law" is

[33] The problems referred to here are rather different from those considered by the Court of First Instance in the *Svenska Journalistforbundet* case (above) and in Case T-14/98 *Hautala* v. *Council*, 19 July 1999 (see paragraphs 41–2 of the judgment in that case). The fact that documents drawn up in application of provisions falling within Titles V or VI of the EU Treaty are covered by Decision 93/731 on public access to documents held by the Council (OJ 1993 No. L340/43) is a matter of interpretation of that Decision. As the Court of First Instance pointed out (paragraphs 71–2 of the judgment in *Hautala*), when deciding whether or not to disclose such documents, the Council must take account of its political responsibilities under Title V; and the Court must also recognise and take account of them when exercising its powers of review, which operate within the legal context of the EC Treaty because the Decision was adopted under Article 207(3) (ex 151(3)) of that Treaty.

[34] The judgment of the Court of First Instance in the *Svenska Journalistforbundet* case (above) suggests that the Court of Justice has no power at all to review the legality of measures falling within the excluded areas. That is true as a general proposition. However, the Court of First Instance was not considering the effect of Article 47 on the Court's jurisdiction.

[35] Not all the Community institutions are involved. As has been seen, the Court of Justice is largely excluded.

involved, it is public international law, not "EU law" or "EC law". When the system of co-operation in the excluded areas generates "law", the correct description of that law depends upon its precise nature. It may take the form of domestic legal measures adopted by Member States individually in order to give effect to some point on which the system of co-operation has settled. In that event, the "law" so produced is domestic law, not public international law, "EU law" or "EC law"; and that "law" forms part of, and is subject to, the rule of law as it is known in each state. The system of co-operation in the excluded areas would produce something capable of being described as "EU law" or "EC law" only if the legal measures adopted pursuant to the product of that co-operation were adopted within the scope of the system of law set up by the founding Treaties (in which case, those legal measures would have ceased to be within the excluded areas).[36] In that event, an exploration of the meaning or validity of such measures would probably lead the Court of Justice back into the excluded areas in the same (limited) way in which it has recourse to public international law for the same purpose.[37]

In the result, "EU law" either means nothing more than "EC law" or else it is a misnomer because it refers to something more than "EC law" (namely, the structure of law *and* political co-operation set up by the EU Treaty) or something other than "EC law" (namely, the system of political co-operation in the areas excluded from "EC law" in the true sense). Although a linguistic point, it is not a lawyer's quibble. If one is talking about the same thing, it is a mere fad to use "EU law" instead of "EC law", or *vice versa*. If, on the other hand, "EU law" is supposed to mean something different from "EC law", it is necessary to be sure about what that something else is and whether or not it really is "EU law". The implication of using a phrase such as "EU law" to describe, or encompass, the system of political co-operation envisaged in the EU Treaty risks creating the impression that it is "EU law" in the real sense – which, for the reasons given above, it is not. Further, by using the expression "EU law", the expectation is created that the rule of law does, or ought to, apply to "EU law".

However, properly understood, the system of political co-operation in the excluded areas is not subject to the rule of law, as understood in the context of "EC law"; nor should it be. The exclusion of judicial control by the Court of Justice is not a defect in the system of law in the European Union but an inevitable consequence of the nature of political co-operation, which is that it operates, and can operate successfully, only in an extra-legal environment. The rule of law comes into play in two respects. The first is where the product of political co-operation threatens to affect EC law (a consequence that would be incompatible with Article 47 of the EU Treaty). The second is where the product

[36] That appears to be what the EU Treaty envisages in relation to measures adopted in the sphere of police and judicial co-operation and closer co-operation between Member States.

[37] See, for example, Case C-53/96 *Hermes International* v. *FHT Marketing Choice BV* [1998] ECR I-3603 and Case C-162/96 *A. Racke GmbH & Co.* v. *Hauptzollamt Mainz* [1998] ECR I-3655.

of political co-operation affects in some other manner the legal position of individuals. Respect for the rule of law necessitates that, in the first situation, the Court of Justice has the means to rectify the position. As pointed out above, on one interpretation of Article 47, the Court of Justice has the necessary means. Respect for the rule of law would count against the adoption of any other interpretation of Article 47. Respect for the rule of law necessitates that, in the second situation referred to above, the product of political co-operation cannot affect the legal position of individuals otherwise than by properly enacted laws or other measures whose compatibility with the superior rules of law recognised in the state concerned or, as the case may be, the European Community, and the legality of whose implementation is subject to independent judicial control. Again, as pointed out above, there seems to be no reason to fear that political co-operation will result in measures affecting the legal position of individuals that escape such control.

3.2. The limits to judicial review

"In any attempt to discern the meaning of 'rule of law' or 'stato di diritto' at any given time, one of the central problems, perhaps *the* central problem, is judicial control of administrative discretion".[38] More generally, the central problem can be said to be judicial control of the discretion of the different organs of the State, in particular, the legislature as much as the executive or the administration. It is not necessary to look far for the reason: although respect for the rule of law is an injunction directed at all persons within society, the core problem with which the rule of law is concerned is the relationship between the individual, on the one hand, and the State and its servants, on the other.

The mechanisms available under EC law for securing respect for the rule of law are well known and do not need exhaustive description here. They operate at two levels: that of the Court of Justice and that of the courts of the Member States. At the first level, they centre on the actions for annulment and in respect of a failure to act (which concern the acts and defaults of the Community institutions),[39] on the liability in damages of the Community,[40] and on the actions that can be brought against a Member State in respect of its failure to fulfil its EC law obligations.[41] At the second level, the mechanisms use the principles of the direct applicability and direct effect of EC law in the Member States in combination with the remedies and procedures available for securing respect for the rule of law in each State. By that combination, individuals have recourse against

[38] G Grotannelli de' Santi, "An Italian looks at English Administrative Law" [1985] *Public Law* 115 (original emphasis).

[39] For example, EC Treaty, Articles 230–3 (ex 173–6).

[40] For example, EC Treaty, Articles 235 and 288 (ex 178 and 215).

[41] For example, EC Treaty, Articles 226–8 (ex 169–71).

measures adopted by the Community institutions that they could not attack directly before the Court of Justice,[42] measures adopted by the Member States in contravention of EC law, most notably legislative measures,[43] and may seek reparation from the State and its organs in respect of damage resulting from their breach of EC law.[44] The domestic procedures and remedies apply subject to the principles of equivalence and effectiveness. The principle of equivalence requires the protection given by domestic law to rights under EC law to be no less than the protection afforded to equivalent domestic rights. The principle of effectiveness excludes the operation of domestic rules that would render the exercise of rights conferred by EC law virtually impossible or excessively difficult.[45]

As noted above, the control exercised by the Court of Justice varies considerably from certain (exceptional) forms of action in which its role is to achieve an accommodation between national interests and the general interests of the Community, through forms of action in which the Court has unlimited jurisdiction and can substitute itself for the administration, to what could be described as more conventional types of judicial review, in which the Court's function is limited to ensuring compliance with the law and in which the Court does not have power to substitute itself for the institution whose measure is under review. The type of control which can be described as properly representative of the scope of the Court of Justice's powers of review is the third (that reflects the general position in the Member States);[46] and it is to be found in the most frequently encountered action by which the Court of Justice reviews acts of the other Community institutions, the action for annulment.

In actions for annulment brought under Article 33 of the ECSC Treaty, the ECJ and the CFI "may not, however, examine the evaluation of the situation, resulting from economic facts or circumstances, in the light of which the [Commission] took its decisions or made its recommendations, save where the [Commission] is alleged to have misused its powers or to have manifestly failed to observe the provisions of this Treaty or any rule of law relating to its

[42] For example, by means of references for a preliminary ruling under EC Treaty Article 234 (ex 177).

[43] For example, Case C-213/89 *R* v. *Secretary of State for Transport, ex parte Factortame Ltd.* [1990] ECR I-2433 (interim relief against the operation of an impugned domestic statute).

[44] For example, Cases C-46/93 and C-48/93 *Brasserie du Pecheur SA* v. *Germany and R* v. *Secretary of State for Transport, ex parte Factortame Ltd.* [1996] ECR I-1029.

[45] For example, Case C-228/96 *Aprile* v. *Amministrazione delle Finanze dello Stato* [1998] ECR I-7141, paragraphs 18–21 of the judgment. In Case C-90/94 *Haahr Petroleum* v. *Abenra Havn* [1997] ECR I-4085, Advocate General Jacobs pointed out that the phrase "virtually impossible" should really be read as meaning "impossible in practice" (see paragraph 172 of his Opinion, at p. 4137).

[46] *Cf.* Lagasse, *L'Erreur Manifeste d'Appreciation en Droit Administratif* (Brussels, Editions Ciaco, 1986); Schwarze, *European Administrative Law* (London, Sweet & Maxwell, 1992).

application".[47] No such provision appears in the corresponding Articles of the EC and EAEC Treaties.[48] Nonetheless, a similar limitation is to be found in the case law. Thus, in Case C-225/91 *Matra SA* v. *Commission*,[49] the ECJ held that "in the context of an action challenging legality, the Court's function is solely to ascertain whether the contested decision is vitiated by one of the grounds of unlawfulness set out in Article 173 of the treaty [now Article 230], and the Court cannot substitute its own assessment of the facts, especially in the economic sphere, for that of the author of the decision". The ECJ went on to hold that, in a "review of legality" of an administrative decision adopted in a sphere in which the Commission enjoys a wide discretion, the exercise of which involves assessments of an economic and social nature, "the Court must therefore restrict itself to determining whether the Commission has exceeded the scope of its discretion by a distortion or manifest error of assessment of the facts or by misuse of powers or abuse of process".[50]

The principle that emerges is that it is inherent in the Community law concept of judicial review of the lawfulness of conduct that judicial intervention cannot, and does not, extend to a complete review of all the factors taken into account by the institution in relation to the challenged conduct: the principle is inherent in the concept because, in order to limit the scope of judicial review, it is not actually necessary to have a Treaty provision that uses the same words as those used in Article 33 of the ECSC Treaty for that purpose. It is implicit in the Treaty, but rarely stated expressly in the case law, that there is complete review of matters of law.[51] The need to draw lines of demarcation arises once the Court of Justice is engaged in the task of reviewing aspects of the conduct of the institutions that do not turn on the meaning and effect of a rule of Community law but concern matters of fact and judgment. Express words are required in order to extend the powers of the Court of Justice beyond that limited form of review.

[47] For an explanation of the origin of Article 33, see H G Schermers and D Waelbroeck, *Judicial Protection in the European Communities* (5th ed., London, Kluwer Law and Taxation, 1992), paragraph 310. The reference in Article 33 to a "manifest" failure to observe the Treaty or any rule of law relating to its application does not imply that there is some discretion regarding the interpretation of the Treaty or a rule of law; it refers to the ability of the Commission to err in its evaluation of relevant facts when applying the Treaty (or other rule of law) properly construed: see Case 6/54 *Netherlands* v. *High Authority* [1954–1956] ECR 103 at 115.

[48] Articles 230 (ex 173) and 146, respectively. For a brief discussion of the reasons for that omission, see G Bebr, *Development of Judicial Control of the European Communities* (The Hague, Mingham Ma, 1981), pages 126–127.

[49] [1993] ECR I-3203, see paragraphs 23–5.

[50] In the French version of the judgment: "la Cour doit, des lors, se limiter a examiner si la Commission n'a pas excede les limites inherentes a son pouvoir d'appreciation par une denaturation ou une erreur manifeste d'appreciation des faits ou par un detournement de pouvoir ou de procedure".

[51] For one of the few judicial pronouncements, see Case 14/61 *Hoogovens* v. *High Authority* [1962] ECR 253 at 268: "to recognise the High Authority's power of appraisal is not to deny the jurisdiction of the Court of Justice to see whether the Decision of the High Authority rests on a correct application of the Treaty, of the basic Decisions and of the rules recognised by the *SNUPAT* judgment, and whether it is accordingly justified in law".

In contrast to the position at Community level, the view was taken in a number of quarters in the United Kingdom that the limited form of judicial review available in the United Kingdom could no longer stand where EC rights were in issue. The case usually cited for the proposition that the courts of the United Kingdom had to abandon the customary approach in judicial review cases was *R* v. *Ministry of Agriculture, Fisheries and Food, ex parte Bell Lines Ltd.*[52] The argument had certain obvious weaknesses, notably in the fact that it failed to take into account the limited nature of judicial review in other jurisdictions and the reasons why such limited forms exist. In Case C-120/97 *Upjohn Ltd.* v. *The Licensing Authority established by the Medicines Act 1968 and others*,[53] the Court of Justice held that national courts must be in a position to apply the relevant principles and rules of Community law effectively when reviewing the legality of measures taken by domestic State bodies; but it rejected the view that Community law requires national courts to substitute their assessments for those of the author of the measure under review. In so concluding, the Court of Justice dismissed the argument that such limited forms of judicial review render ineffective the protection afforded to rights under EC law.

How does that approach square with respect for the rule of law; or, in other words, is it right that the more extensive forms of judicial review are limited to exceptional cases, the general approach to judicial review of administrative and legislative acts being one of limited judicial interference?

The phenomenon of the (generally) limited nature of judicial review of acts of the State and State bodies is not inconsistent with the rule of law. Instead, it is an inherent part of the rule of law and reflects an important principle of modern constitutional law: the separation of powers between legislature, executive and judiciary. In short, the role of the courts in reviewing the acts of the State and of State bodies does not empower the courts to substitute themselves for those bodies. The principle of the separation of powers requires the courts to remain within the functions ascribed to them (which are, broadly speaking, to ensure that the law is observed) and not to descend into areas of activity attributed to the executive and the legislature.[54] That is entirely consistent with the concept of the rule of law. "The rule of law" means just that, not "the rule of the courts". The courts cannot go further than the limits set by the law itself. Where the law allocates to another body the function of making factual and judgmental evaluations, the role of the courts is necessarily limited.

The basic rule in Community law is that the judiciary controls the lawfulness of the exercise by the other institutions of the powers conferred on them; and it is only in a few defined and exceptional cases that the separation of

[52] [1984] 2 CMLR 502.

[53] [1999] ECR I-223, paragraphs 27–37 of the judgment (see also paragraphs 37–59 of the Advocate General's Opinion).

[54] For a discussion of the role of the courts in reviewing administrative acts, see Lagasse, *op. cit.*, preliminary chapter.

powers is removed and the power to make factual and judgmental evaluations disappears as an area preserved from judicial intervention. Having said that, the *absolute* immunity of that power from judicial intervention is not a feature of the judiciary's "normal" jurisdiction – the review of the legality of the conduct of the institutions. Consistently with general trends within the Community, the Court of Justice has made use of different devices (such as the principle of proportionality) in order to extend judicial control into the areas of factual and judgmental evaluation left to the other institutions.[55]

The case law generally shows that the legislature benefits from an area preserved from judicial intervention that covers all aspects of the exercise of a discretionary power (with the exception of the purely legal limits to the power). The judiciary may interfere only to the extent that the exercise of the discretion can be said to be "manifestly", "clearly" or "obviously" wrong. Accordingly, if the judiciary considers that the exercise of the discretion is or may be wrong in its factual or judgmental elements (as opposed to, for example, in the view taken by the legislature of the legal rule conferring on it the power to act), that does not, in itself, justify judicial interference. A few examples will suffice to illustrate the point.

Case 138/79 *Roquette* v. *Council*[56] concerned the exercise of a legislative power so as to introduce a quota system for isoglucose producers modelled on that applied to sugar producers after the Court of Justice had annulled part of the isoglucose regime.[57] It was contested, *inter alia*, on the ground that it infringed the principle of equal treatment. The Court of Justice rejected the challenge, holding:

> When the implementation by the Council of the agricultural policy of the Community involves the need to evaluate a complex economic situation, the discretion which it has does not apply exclusively to the nature and scope of the measures to be taken but also [applies] to some extent to the finding of the basic facts inasmuch as, in particular, it is open to the Council to rely if necessary on general findings. In reviewing the exercise of such a power the Court must confine itself to examining whether it contains a manifest error or constitutes a misuse of power or whether the authority in question did not clearly exceed the bounds of its discretion.[58]

That *dictum* was repeated in Case C-4/96 *NIFPO and Northern Ireland Fishermen's Federation* v. *Department of Agriculture for Northern*

[55] A more detailed analysis of the case law than is possible here would reveal a certain ebb and flow in judicial intervention over the years that appears to have been influenced by three principal factors: the personality of the judges; the subject-matter of judicial review in particular cases; and changes in the case load of the Court of Justice.

[56] [1980] ECR 3333. The action was admissible because it was directed against that part of the contested regulation that provided for the fixing of production quotas for individual undertakings. However, the focus of the challenge was on the policy decision to introduce a quota system.

[57] See Cases 103 and 145/77 *Royal Scholten-Honig* v. *Intervention Board for Agricultural Produce* [1978] ECR 2037, paragraphs 38–84. In that case, the Court of Justice was able to detect the errors vitiating the relevant part of the regime without difficulty.

[58] *Roquette*, n. 56 *supra*, paragraph 25 of the judgment.

Ireland,[59] which concerned the allocation of fishing quotas. The Court of Justice rejected arguments based on the principles of proportionality and non-discrimination by again emphasising the discretionary nature of the power that had been exercised and the need in such a case for a challenge to be based upon the disputed measure's "patent" unsuitability for achieving its objectives, its "arbitrary" nature or "manifest inappropriateness".[60]

In Case C-122/94 *Commission* v. *Council*,[61] the Commission unsuccessfully challenged two Council decisions authorising the grant of state aid under the third subparagraph of what is now Article 88(2) of the EC Treaty (ex Article 93(2)). The Council had power to act if there were "exceptional circumstances". The Court of Justice pointed out that the Council had to decide whether or not there were such circumstances and, in doing so, it necessarily had to carry out an assessment of a complex economic situation. The Court of Justice regarded the Council's discretion as extending to finding basic facts (in that it could rely upon general findings) because the exercise of its power required such an assessment to be carried out. Even though the Commission (obviously a particularly well-informed critic) thought that, on the facts of the case, the Council was wrong, that was not the point. The question was whether or not the Council had made a manifest error in its assessment of the facts and in its assessment of the correct policy choice to make. No such error was apparent.[62]

The same applies in the case of administrative decisions that involve the exercise of a discretion. In Case T-203/96 *Embassy Limousines and Services* v. *Parliament*,[63] the European Parliament had issued an invitation to tender for a contract for the provision of chauffeur-driven transport. The contract was to be awarded in accordance with Directive 92/50,[64] which governs the award of public service contracts. The criterion for determining the person to whom the contract should be awarded was the economically most advantageous tender, taking account of price and technical merits. After the contract award procedure had progressed for some time, the Parliament decided to halt it and start all over again on the ground that none of the tenders had proved satisfactory. Embassy Limousines & Services, which had been led to believe that it would get the contract, brought an action for damages, claiming that the Parliament had acted unlawfully.[65] It was held that, because the Parliament had a broad discretion in assessing the factors to be taken into account for the purpose of deciding on the award of the contract, "the Court's review should be limited to

[59] [1998] ECR I-681, paragraph 42. See also Case C-179/95 *Spain* v. *Council*, 5 October 1999, paragraphs 28–9.

[60] The *NIFPO* case, n. 59 *supra* paragraphs 57 and 62.

[61] [1996] ECR I-881.

[62] Paragraphs 18–25 of the judgment. The Commission did not assert misuse of power.

[63] [1998] ECR II-4239.

[64] OJ 1992 No. L209/1.

[65] The abbreviated description of the facts given above does not do full justice to the sense of grievance that Embassy Limousines & Services must have felt about the conduct of the Parliament.

checking that there has been no serious and manifest error" or a "grave and manifest error".[66]

On the other hand, in those instances in which the exercise of a power depends upon the existence of certain facts (as in the case of Commission decisions in application of Articles 81, 82 and 87 – ex 85, 86 and 92 – of the EC Treaty), it is usually said that judicial review extends to simple error of fact, the Court being able to take its own view of primary facts. For example, in Case C-83/98P *France* v. *Commission*,[67] it was claimed that a court reviewing a Commission decision concerning the application of the state aid rules in the EC Treaty was limited to satisfying itself whether or not there had been a manifest error. The Court of Justice rejected that argument, saying: "State aid, as defined in the Treaty, is a legal concept which must be interpreted on the basis of objective factors. For that reason, the Community courts must in principle, having regard both to the specific features of the case before them and to the technical or complex nature of the Commission's assessments, carry out a comprehensive review as to whether a measure falls within the scope of Article 92(1) [now 87(1)] of the Treaty".[68]

However, some care needs to be taken over the meaning to be given to "comprehensive review". That expression certainly means that, in principle, all parts of the decision under review fall within the scope of judicial review. Nonetheless, it does not follow that all parts of the decision can be reviewed in exactly the same way. For example, in Case T-65/96 *Kish Glass & Co. Ltd.* v. *Commission*,[69] a case concerning Article 82 (ex Article 86) of the EC Treaty, it was held: "although as a general rule the Community judicature undertakes a comprehensive review of the question whether or not the conditions for the application of the competition rules are met, its review of complex economic appraisals made by the Commission is necessarily limited to verifying whether the relevant rules on procedure and on stating reasons have been complied with, whether the facts have been accurately stated and whether there has been any manifest error of assessment or a misuse of powers". In that case, the "complex economic appraisal" in question was the definition of the relevant market. The position is similar in the case of Commission decisions adopted under the Merger Control Regulation,[70] albeit that, under Articles 81 and 82 (and, very often, under the State aid rules), the Commission is engaged in what is essentially an historical investigation (unless it is deciding whether or not to give a negative clearance or an exemption in respect of a notified agreement that has not yet taken effect). The function of the Commission under the Merger Control

[66] Paragraphs 56 and 60 of the judgment.
[67] 16 May 2000, paragraphs 24–5 of the judgment.
[68] Other aspects of the state aid rules are more obviously judgmental: see, for example, Cases T-132/96 and T-143/96 *Freistaat Sachsen and Volkswagen AG* v. *Commission* 15 December 1999, paragraphs 169 and 244 of the judgment.
[69] 30 March 2000, paragraphs 64 and 69 of the judgment.
[70] Council Regulation No. 4064/89 (OJ 1989 No. L395/1), as amended.

Regulation is to decide whether or not something that has not yet taken place or taken effect (the merger under examination) will, in the future, result in the creation or strengthening of a dominant position as a result of which effective competition would be significantly impeded in the common market or a substantial part of it.[71] In order to do that, the Commission must make an educated guess on the basis of known facts. It is therefore involved in a judgmental exercise. That part of its assessment that involves a prognostication about the future can in principle be attacked only on the basis of manifest error.[72] On the other hand, if the basic facts concerning the past that are used by the Commission to make its assessment of the future are irrelevant or wrong, or if relevant facts are left out of account, the Commission's assessment can be attacked (to the extent that they are undermined by the error).[73]

When examination shifts from judicial review by the Court of Justice of the acts of the Community institution to judicial review of acts of the Member States and their organs, the position becomes slightly complicated. As noted above, the Court of Justice accepted in the *Upjohn* case that limited forms of judicial review (similar in nature to the type of judicial review generally available under the Treaties) are consistent with the requirements of Community law. However, in an earlier case, Case 182/84 *Miro*,[74] the Court of Justice appears to have taken a different view.

That case concerned a Dutch legislative provision that limited the use of certain appellations (indicating that the product was jenever) to beverages that, so far as is here relevant, had a minimum alcohol content of 35 per cent. Miro (which ran a chain of off-licences in The Netherlands) imported and sold bottles of jenever from Belgium. The bottles bore one of the appellations in question but the contents had an alcohol content of 30 per cent. Miro was prosecuted for infringing the Dutch legislation. The question of its compatibility with Community law was raised and the matter was referred to the Court of Justice for a preliminary ruling. Before the Court of Justice, the German Government argued that the question whether or not a ban on using the appellation "jenever" was necessary for products that did not satisfy certain requirements depended upon the commercial view prevailing in the country concerned. The national authorities were in the best position to judge the facts. It was therefore for them and not for the Court of Justice to reach a decision on the facts. The national legislature was competent to take such a decision. Once it had done so, the matter was settled and the national courts were bound by the legislature's

[71] *Ibid.*, Article 2(2) and (3).

[72] Cases C-68/94 and C-30/95 *France and others* v. *Commission* [1998] ECR I-1375, paragraphs 220–5 of the judgment; Case T-102/96 *Gencor* v. *Commission* [1999] ECR II-753, paragraphs 162–5 and 245. Accordingly, in paragraph 208 of the judgment in *Gencor* it was held (in effect) that there was sufficient evidence to support the Commission's conclusion; in paragraph 210 it was held that the Commission could "reasonably" assess the effects of the proposed merger; similar remarks appear elsewhere (such as paragraph 222).

[73] Contrast *France and others* v. *Commission* and *Gencor* v. *Commission*, n. 72 *supra*.

[74] [1985] ECR 3731, paragraphs 13–14 of the judgment.

assessment. The German Government's argument divided into two parts. The first part, which provided the premise supporting the second part, was the assertion that the lawfulness of a ban on the use of a particular appellation depends upon the commercial view prevailing in the country concerned. Most of the judgment is devoted to disposing of that part of the argument. However, the Court of Justice started off by rejecting the second part of the German Government's argument (to the effect that assessments of the national legislature are final) in these terms:

> When in order to satisfy mandatory requirements recognised by Community law national legislation creates obstacles to the fundamental principle of the free movement of goods, it must observe the limits laid down by Community law. It is for the Court, which interprets Community law in the final instance, and for the national courts, which reach their decisions on the basis of that interpretation, to ensure that those limits are observed. In the final analysis the German Government's argument amounts to a repudiation of review by the Court and therefore runs counter to the uniformity and effectiveness of Community law. It must therefore be rejected.

Two things should be noted about that passage. The first is the predictable rejection of an argument tending to exclude in its entirety judicial review of the acts of the domestic legislature. The second is the assertion that it is a judicial function to ensure that the limits laid down by Community law are observed. That assertion implies that the role of the courts may be more extensive than the normal, limited form of judicial review would suggest; and, in a later case, Case C-145/88 *Torfaen Borough Council* v. *B&Q plc*,[75] the Court of Justice held that "the question whether the effects of specific national rules do in fact remain within that limit [that is, the limit set by Community law] is a question of fact to be determined by the national court".[76] In order to determine whether or not that is the case, it is necessary to examine the legal context in which the Court of Justice made the assertion.

When considering the case law of the Court of Justice concerning judicial review of the acts of the Community institutions, it should be borne in mind that the cases concern the exercise of powers that the Treaties have conferred upon the institutions. The function of the Court of Justice, in securing respect for the rule of law, is to ensure that those powers have been exercised within the limits set by the power conferring provision. The legal context of the judicial review of acts of the Member States (and their organs) by reference to the requirements of Community law is rather different. In some instances, the Member States are governed by power conferring provisions of Community law. For example, directives can be classified as power conferring provisions in that they require the Member States to act so as to achieve the result specified in the

[75] [1989] ECR I-3851, paragraph 16 of the judgment.

[76] Another illustration of the same point can be found more recently, in Case C-176/96 *Jyri Lehonten and another* v. *Federation Royale Belge des Societes de Basket-ball*, 13 April 2000, paragraph 59 of the judgment.

directive. Directives, by definition, leave the Member States some discretion as to how the intended result is to be achieved.[77] The power therefore encompasses a duty coupled with a discretion. The function of the courts is to ensure that, in implementing a directive, the Member States do not exceed the margin of appreciation that is left to them.[78] The extent of judicial control is therefore the usual, limited form. Another example is the *Upjohn* case itself, which concerned a directive regulating the way in which the national bodies responsible for authorising pharmaceuticals were to exercise their powers.

However, the Member States are also the subject of prohibitions. Rules that are prohibitory in form cannot be approached in quite the same way as power conferring provisions. The normal application of a prohibitory provision is that the prohibition applies when the relevant facts or circumstances defined in the provision exist. A court called upon to decide whether or not the prohibition applies must itself decide whether or not those facts or circumstances exist. There is no room for some area, allocated to the person or body whose act is under review by the court, that escapes judicial control.

In the Treaties (specifically the EC Treaty), prohibitions are often accompanied by exceptions or derogations. Thus, in the context of the free movement of goods rules in the EC Treaty, the prohibition of quantitative restrictions and measures having equivalent effect on imports is mitigated by what is occasionally described as the "*Cassis de Dijon* rule" and by Article 30 (ex Article 36) of the EC Treaty. Such exceptions or derogations are not power conferring provisions; but in many respects they operate in a manner similar to a power conferring provision. Member States are not obliged to take advantage of an exception or derogation. If they do, they must act within the limits of the exception or derogation; and that was the point at issue in the *Miro* case.

There are three characteristic features of the operation of such exceptions and derogations: first, the burden lies on the author of the impugned measure to prove that the measure falls within the exception or derogation in question; secondly, the measure must be necessary in order to achieve an objective permitted by the exception or derogation; thirdly, the measure must be proportionate.

The first feature is a procedural matter. Its significance lies in the fact that the shift in the burden of proof subtly alters the role of the court. When a measure is attacked because the author of the measure was not empowered by law to adopt it, the burden of proving the illegality of the measure lies on the person challenging it. The role of the court is to determine whether the challenge has been made good. The focus in the case lies on the strength of the challenge; and, in theory at least, the author of the challenged measure may simply

[77] EC Treaty, Article 249 (ex 189), third paragraph.

[78] For example, case C-435/97 *World Wildlife Fund* v. *Autonome Provinz Bozen* [1999] ECR I-5613, paragraphs 36–49 and 68–71 of the judgment.

take a negative stance and put the challenger to proof of the assertions supporting the challenge. When, as in the case of reliance upon exceptions and derogations, the burden shifts to the author of the challenged measure, the role of the court is actually to examine the claim made by the author of the challenged measure that the exception or derogation in question applies. The author of the measure cannot take a negative stance. It must make out a positive case.

The second feature is one that typically involves the court that is reviewing the measure in question in making its own assessment of the factual basis for the claim that the measure has its justification in the exception or derogation relied upon.[79] That is not always the case. For example, in a series of cases, the Court of Justice has held that, where there are uncertainties in the prevailing state of scientific research, it is for the Member States to decide what degree of protection of the health and life of humans they intend to assure, having regard to the requirements of the free movement of goods (and always assuming that there has been no harmonisation at Community level). In consequence, Member States are entitled to take a view as to the extent to which, for example, certain additives can be used in foodstuffs. As long as the choice made by the State falls within the range of acceptable possibilities having regard to the prevailing state of scientific research (and always assuming that there are no other, less burdensome alternatives to the action taken by the State – such as by providing consumers with sufficient information to make an informed choice), there is no basis for judicial intervention in the choice made by the State.[80] The effectiveness of judicial control in such cases is strengthened by the requirement that the State (or the State body whose act is in dispute) must prove that its action is justified.

The third feature typically involves a review of an assessment made by the author of the impugned measure; and it is at that point that the court's powers of review are inevitably limited. They are limited, however, by the nature and content of the principle of proportionality rather than by anything else.[81] In Case 181/84 *R* v. *Intervention Board for Agricultural Produce, ex parte E.D. & F. Man (Sugar) Ltd.*,[82] for example, the Court of Justice held that a legislative

[79] For example, in Case C-222/95 *Parodi* v. *Banque H. Albert de Bary* [1997] ECR I-3899, paragraphs 27–9 of the judgment, the Court of Justice envisaged that, when the national court scrutinised the extent to which domestic banking legislation satisfied the requirement of the equivalent of the "*Cassis de Dijon* rule" applicable in the context of the freedom to provide services, it would actually investigate the question whether or not the legislation was necessary for the protection of the different types of customers of banks.

[80] *Cf.* for example, Case 178/84 *Commission* v. *Germany* [1987] ECR 1227.

[81] A different view was expressed by Hoffmann J (as he then was) in *Stoke-on-Trent City Council* v. *B&Q plc* [1991] Ch. 48 at 69B-71C. For some reason, his view was not based upon the case law of the Court of Justice.

[82] [1985] ECR 2889.

provision prescribing the forfeiture in its entirety of a security given in respect of the export of sugar from the Community, when the time limit for submitting applications for export licences was not observed, was invalid as being inconsistent with the principle of proportionality. In that case, the applications had been submitted a matter of hours after the expiry of the time limit. In a subsequent case, Case 9/85 *Nordbutter* v. *Germany*,[83] a similar situation had arisen: financial aid was available if certain declarations were submitted in time but, in the event, the persons concerned delayed in submitting them. The relevant legislative provision did not provide that the aid would be withheld in its entirety if the time limit was not observed. Instead, it provided for a 10 per cent reduction in the amount of the aid where the delay in submitting the declarations did not exceed ten days. The entitlement to the aid was extinguished (in its entirety) only if the delay exceeded ten days. In the *Nordbutter* case, the time limit was exceeded by twelve or thirteen days and the entitlement to the aid was therefore lost in its entirety. The Court of Justice concluded that the legislation was not contrary to the principle of proportionality. It pointed out that, by providing for the reduction in the amount of the aid in the event of a delay of less than ten days, the legislation had taken into account the difficulties of a strict application of the time limit where it had been only slightly exceeded; and had related the reduction in the entitlement to the seriousness of the failure to observe it. The Court of Justice went on to say: "In those circumstances it is not for the Court to consider whether the legislative bodies of the Community should have provided that time-limits were 'only slightly exceeded' where they were exceeded by 12 or 13 days rather than 10 days".[84] Similarly, in Case C-233/94 *Germany* v. *Parliament and Council*,[85] it was argued that what was known as an "export prohibition" in Article 4(1) of Directive 94/19,[86] which required Member States to set up deposit-guarantee schemes for the banking sector, was disproportionate. The Court of Justice rejected the submission, holding that:

> In assessing the need for the measure in question, it should be emphasised that the Community legislature was seeking to regulate an economically complex situation. Before the adoption of the Directive, deposit-guarantee schemes did not exist in all the Member States; moreover, most of them did not cover depositors with branches set up by credit institutions authorised in other Member States. The Community legislature therefore needed to assess the future, uncertain effects of its action. In so doing, it could choose between the general prevention of a risk and the establishment of a system of specific protection. In such a situation the Court cannot substitute its own assessment for that of the Community legislature. It could, at most, find fault with its legislative choice only if it appeared manifestly incorrect or if the resultant

[83] [1986] ECR 2831, followed in Case C-345/88 *Butterabsatz Osnabruck-Emsland* [1990] ECR I-159.

[84] Paragraph 17 of the judgment.

[85] [1997] ECR I-2405, paragraphs 54–6 of the judgment.

[86] OJ 1994 No. L135/5.

disadvantages for certain economic operators were wholly disproportionate to the advantages otherwise offered.

In so concluding in the *Nordbutter* case and *Germany* v. *Parliament and Council*, the Court of Justice was accepting that, in the circumstances of those cases, the legislator had a margin of appreciation in relation to the determination of the proportionality of the challenged measure that fell outside the scope of the Court of Justice's powers of review. In the *E.D. & F. Man* case, the Court of Justice had not encountered the problem because the circumstances of the case were different. In that case, the critical factor was that the security was forfeited in its entirety for an infringement of the rules that was significantly less serious than any infringement of the primary obligation that the security was intended to guarantee. The topsy-turvy nature of the legislation (imposing a more serious sanction for a less important infringement) provided a reliable basis on which to conclude that the principle of proportionality had been infringed. In *Nordbutter*, on the other hand, the application of the principle of proportionality could not provide a simple yes/no answer. There were obviously various ways in which delays in submitting declarations could be dealt with. The way selected in that case was to impose a 10 per cent reduction in the entitlement for delays of up to ten days and a 100 per cent reduction for longer delays. Other ways were conceivable. For example: 10 per cent for five days, 20 per cent for the next five days, 30 per cent for the next five days again and so on. Or: 10 per cent for ten days; 50 per cent for the next ten days; 100 per cent thereafter. Essentially the same problem had arisen in *Germany* v. *Parliament and Council*.

Although those cases are drawn from the case law concerning the judicial review of acts of the Community institutions, they are reliable indications of the nature and scope of the principle of proportionality. They show that the obligation flowing from that principle was (and is) really capable only of requiring the author of the contested measure to direct its mind to the proportionality of the measure to be taken and to avoid a manifest lack of proportionality. In the context of the reliance by a Member State upon an exception to, or derogation from, a prohibition imposed by Community law, the result is that, as long as the State can demonstrate that its choice falls within the range of possible proportionate options, the Court cannot interfere. Whether or not a Member State can do that depends upon the circumstances of the case and, more particularly, upon the nature and complexity of the problem that the challenged measure is intended to resolve.

There is no blanket rule that, when applying the principle of proportionality, it is not the function of the Court "to carry out the balancing exercise or to form [its] own view on whether the legislative objectives could be achieved by other means. These questions involve compromises between competing interests which in a democratic society must be resolved by the legislature. The duty of the court is only to enquire whether the compromise adopted by the . . .

Parliament, so far as it affects community trade, is one which a reasonable legislature could have reached".[87] In contrast, the Court of Justice has stated that it *does* weigh different interests (*in casu*, the risk of misleading consumers and the requirements of the free movement of goods) and form its own view, a task that also falls to national courts, which may have recourse to various forms of evidence in order to reach a conclusion. In the case in point, however, which concerned rules governing the marketing of cosmetics, the Court of Justice pointed out that the weighing exercise operates where there is no risk to public health.[88] That simply indicates that there are some areas in which the principle of proportionality can be applied by a court in order to produce a result and other areas in which the complex and policy-driven nature of the exercise makes the principle of proportionality too crude an instrument to be used by a court save in clear cases.

Accordingly, while it is for the courts to decide whether or not a measure can escape from the prohibition imposed by Community law through reliance upon some exception or derogation, the courts' decision-making function reaches its limits when the exception or derogation permits the State or State body in question a discretion.

4. CONCLUSIONS

The rule of law can be seen working as a fundamental value in EC law in the various developments of EC law made by the Court of Justice over the years. The characteristic features of those developments, which indicate the nature of the rule of law in the Community's legal order, are the claims of Community law to supremacy over other norms and to the observance of Community law by all sections of society, including the Member States (and their organs) and the Community institutions. Those claims are secured by the principle of judicial control. However, there is now a clearly marked division between those aspects of the activity of the European Union that are subject to the rule of law and those that are not. Further, the rule of law has its limits as a fundamental value. It is not capable of providing all the answers to all the questions that arise in a sophisticated, modern legal system. In particular, the rule of law does not provide a complete answer to the problem of the control of legislative and

[87] Hoffmann J (as he then was) in the *Stoke-on-Trent* case, n. 81 *supra*, at 69D–E. He went on to say: "The function of the court is to review the acts of the legislature but not to substitute its own policies or values". That is consistent with the Court of Justice's case law; but it misses the real point, which is that the balance between different values is already set by Community law. Some values, or the means required to protect them, are, however, absolute whereas others are relative. The application of the principle of proportionality can provide a yes/no answer in relation to the former but not always in relation to the latter.

[88] Case C-220/98 *Estee Lauder Cosmetics GmbH & Co. OHG* v. *Lancaster Group GmbH*, 13 January 2000, paragraphs 27–31 of the judgment.

administrative discretion. That suggests a weakness in the rule of law as a fundamental value, a weakness that can be removed only by acceptance of a catalogue of fundamental human rights by means of which the courts can overcome the inherent limitations of the rule of law.

8

Legal Subjectivity as a Fundamental Value: the Emergence of Non-State Actors in Europe

CHRISTOPHER HARDING

1. INTRODUCTION: RECONFIGURING PARTICIPATION IN INTERNATIONAL ACTIVITIES

It is axiomatic that participation in legal activity requires some kind of recognition or status as a legal "person" and in that sense the process according to which legal "personality" or "subjectivity" is decided upon entails dealing with one of the most fundamental legal values, that of entitlement to exist and act in the legal domain. At the level of national legal orders, this issue of participation has been worked out for the most part in a positivist manner, employing rules laid down in basic constitutional and legislative provisions. However, in international and European legal contexts, the whole business of subjectivity and participation, of determining who may act legally and to what extent, necessarily has a more empirical and problematical character. Indeed, it is an issue which goes some way towards defining the very nature, role and purpose of "international" and "supranational" orders. To explore the values underlying notions of international or European legal subjectivity is therefore to explore also the values underpinning that type of legal order: why and for whom do such legal systems exist?

The discussion here explores this issue of subjectivity and legal identity by examining the impact of the emergence of the EC and more recently the EU on both perceptions and the actuality of legal personality and participation in legal and political activity at the international level. The argument is informed by a sense of significant late twentieth century transformation as regards the issue of participation in international legal activity. In the middle part of the twentieth century, at the time of the Community's inception, international legal life was very much dominated by an orthodox state-centred perspective,[1] which

[1] There were exceptions to this view; see e.g. H Lauterpacht, *International Law and Human Rights* (Stevens, 1950).

presented sovereign states as both key and controlling actors, the primary subjects and also the dominant law-making entities on the international scene. Indeed many works on international law continue to open their discussion with this presentation of the nature of the international legal order. The shorthand way of expressing this model of legal and political organisation is to say that states are, within this scheme, the *original* persons who through their controlling and juridically authoritative position may decide, as an act of sovereign will, to bequeath a *derivative* personality on other entities (typically organisations and individuals), to act *for certain defined purposes* at the international legal level. In the European context there have been some notable examples of this kind of award of "derivative" legal personality: for instance, the founding Community Treaties establishing the distinct personality of the Communities, Community and Union; or the European Convention on Human Rights giving to individuals a procedural capacity to pursue claims against states at an international level by petitioning the European Commission (and now the Court) of Human Rights. Both these examples have also been commonly cited to show how the role of non-state actors at the international level has expanded over the last fifty years, while acknowledging however that this has happened by the leave of the European sovereign states. Orthodox theory still presents these non-state actors as subsidiary persons.

The present discussion will seek to reinterpret these events and tendencies and in particular to suggest that there is, within the totality of this process, a dynamic which has transformed the nature of participation at the international (or, it may be better to say supranational) level. The main line of argument may be summarised as follows. An analysis of the evolution of the EC and the EU will show that this "institutional" actor began its life, in conventional legal terms, as a derivative entity, a creature of the sovereign will of its Member States. But it is possible to trace successive stages of political and legal emancipation. Firstly, the Community asserted the distinctive nature of its own legal order and the primacy of its own law over that of Member States and supplied a new status to individuals as holders of supranational rights and as key players in assuring the effectiveness of the new European legal order. Later, by developing such concepts as European citizenship and promoting a regional (i.e. non-state) identity within the European context, such new entities as the European citizen and the region have been used as a basis for asserting the EU's own distinct *legitimacy* as an international actor. In one sense, this may be seen as an emancipation, a "coming of age", or the new entity "trumping" its begetters, the "old" sovereign states. But in another, and more explanatory sense, this process reflects an underlying shift in political organisation and power relations: a seepage of power and legitimacy from the sovereign states to other entities who are at once more diverse and also representative of different kinds of interest. Ultimately, it is a story of evolving participation, moving from a relatively straightforward world of sovereign state actors to a more diverse and complex landscape of newer individual, group, regional and institutional actors, sometimes overlapping with each other and also jostling with the older state and governmental players. Moreover, it is a transition which is still in process: a paradigm under construction but not yet completed.

Before embarking upon a more detailed analysis, a word of caution about terminology may be helpful. This is of course a discussion of a political and legal order and the nature of its participants. Traditionally that order has been described by the term "international" and this has implied a set of relations between a number of entities, themselves fairly easily identified in juridical terms as sovereign states. In other words (and perhaps more accurately as a matter of legal analysis), "international" has meant "inter-sovereign state". But, if there is a new paradigm which includes a number of other entities distinct from the sovereign state, may the term "international" still safely be used to describe such phenomena? In fact, the gist of the argument is that what has previously been referred to as the international plane is now a domain of diverse actors (it is "inter-various") so that what now most easily identifies this plane of activity is its distinction from the national or "municipal" paradigm of legal and political organisation. Through this more negative process of identification, perhaps a more appropriate (though still not entirely satisfactory) description would be to use the term "supranational". The latter term has at least the virtue of moving away from connotations of intergovernmental activity and suggests the business of actors representing distinct non-national, non-state interests. A radical aspect of this argument is therefore the suggestion of a major shift from a system of inter-national to supra-national law and ordering.[2]

2. EARLY CHAPTERS: THE EMERGENCE OF THE EUROPEAN COMMUNITIES

In juristic terms, the European Communities – the Coal and Steel Community (ECSC) in 1951 and the Economic (EEC) and Atomic Energy (Euratom) Communities in 1957 – derive their existence from a collective act of sovereign will on the part of the original Member States. The founding treaties as the acts of equal sovereigns are familiar instruments of classical international law and in those very first moments the power, authority and legal personality of the Communities depended upon the willingness of the Member States to award such capacities. But the necessity of initiating legal developments by means of familiar contractual acts of international law did not inhibit a sense of novelty as to what might be happening once the Communities, and especially the EEC, had been established. This sense of something different becomes increasingly

[2] See also on this point C Harding and C L Lim, "The Significance of Westphalia: an Archaeology of the International Legal Order", ch. 1 in C Harding and C L Lim, *Renegotiating Westphalia: Essays and Commentary on the European and Conceptual Foundations of Modern International Law* (Nijhoff, 1999).

apparent in legal commentary during the 1960s and the later passage of time. For instance, Edward Wall, writing in the late 1960s, noted:

> . . . the three community treaties were arrangements not merely for *collaboration*, even if under the direction of a single institution, but for positive *integration* . . . from the moment of its establishment, each Community, like a ship leaving harbour, is propelled by the exercise of the pooled sovereignty thus conferred upon it, and enjoys, in law, a wholly independent existence.[3]

Similarly, Lasok and Bridge, in one of the earliest general British works on EC law, compared what had taken place with the more familiar modes of federation and confederation: "the [EEC] Treaty is not a mere contractual compact, it is an institutional stage of European unity".[4] This illustrated the early search for analogies. In reviewing the earlier literature on the character of the Communities' legal order, Mann observed that some writers proceeded from the "traditional international law view", others from a "federal-like view", but most eventually arriving at some concept of "supranational organisation".[5] And indeed, the European Court of Justice itself in due course, in developing a jurisprudence of integration, discovered a *sui generis* aspect of the Community's legal order, notably of course in its landmark *Van Gend en Loos* ruling.[6] It is worthwhile for present purposes to recall some of the vocabulary and suggestive argument employed by the Court in that ruling: the Treaty being "more than an agreement which merely creates mutual obligations between the contracting states"; its preamble referring "not only to governments but to peoples"; the "establishment of institutions endowed with sovereign rights"; the idea of the Member States being called upon "to cooperate in the functioning of the Community" via the Parliament and the Economic and Social Committee; and individuals deriving rights from Community law which "become part of their legal heritage".[7]

All of this, and many other statements, reveal during the 1960s and 1970s an epistemic rhetoric, promoting the idea of a new kind of political and legal ordering. The landscape suggested by this argument and literature is not always clearly delineated – there is a jumble of institutional, governmental and human actors in an evolving structure of transferred sovereignty and emerging "legal heritage". From the present vantage point, however, it is possible to detect a dynamic at work, enabling a group of different actors to explore possible new forms. The initial treaty-based transfer of powers was a legally conventional act which simply triggered much of this later activity and the outcome and the more mature forms could not easily be predicted in those earlier days. But a key

[3] Edward Wall, *Europe, Unification and Law* (Penguin, 1969), pp. 34–5.

[4] D Lasok and J W Bridge, *Law and Institutions of the European Communities* (Butterworths, 1st ed., 1973), p. 23.

[5] C J Mann, *The Function of Judicial Decision in European Economic Integration* (Nijhoff, 1972), p. 4.

[6] Case 26/62, *Van Gend en Loos v. Nederlandse Tariefcommissie* [1963] ECR 1.

[7] [1963] ECR, at p. 12.

element was nonetheless sensed at that stage – that if the Community was to be described as an international institution, it was different from most other entities characterised in that way, since it was a vehicle for an evolutionary process with radical longer-term implications for international ordering.

The remaining part of this discussion will seek to identify some of the crucial aspects in this process over the past twenty or thirty years. The major topics to be addressed in this way comprise: (a) the conventional international legal personality of the Communities; (b) the role of individual human and corporate actors; (c) the emergence of supranational popular legitimacy in the European context; and (d) novel local and regional configurations of power and representation.

3. THE INTERNATIONAL LEGAL PERSONALITY OF THE COMMUNITY AND UNION: THE EVOLVING IDENTITY OF THE EUROPEAN ENTITY

From the earliest days, the European Coal and Steel Community (ECSC) was straightaway a new legal person on the international plane – Article 6 of the ECSC Treaty accorded the Community the conventional international legal personality of an organisation ("in international relations, the Community shall enjoy the legal capacity it requires to perform its functions and attain its objectives" – paragraph 2 of Article 6). The Economic Community's personality was provided for in simple and much broader terms (just that it "shall have legal personality", in Article 210 of the original EC Treaty) but there was never any doubt that this extended to what was necessary for the Community to carry out its functions at the international level. What was necessary in this respect followed from the tasks enumerated in the Treaty itself, originally, it is true, by the Member States but subject also to the view of the European Court of Justice as to the extent and more precise nature of such activities which may require international action. Once the capacity to act as an international legal person was established, the crucial question concerned the extent of that capacity and in particular the extent to which the Community replaced Member States in certain areas of international activity. Within the broad outlines of activity laid down in the Treaty, it was ultimately for the Court of Justice to determine such questions, as the Court itself made clear in 1970:

> To determine in a particular case the Community's authority to enter into international agreements, regard must be had to the whole scheme of the Treaty no less than to its substantive provisions.
>
> Such authority arises not only from an express conferment by the Treaty . . . but may equally flow from other provisions of the Treaty and from measures adopted . . . by the Community institutions.[8]

[8] Case 22/70, *Commission v. Council, re ERTA* [1971] ECR, 263, 274.

This approach opened the door to the possibility of the Community's own interpretation of its internal powers which in turn determined the extent of its external powers (*in foro interno, in foro externo*).[9] The significance of this development may be gauged from the instances of Member State opposition to the adoption of certain EC measures which might imply the exercise of a Community treaty making power in relation to the same subject matter.[10] Stein has gone so far as to argue that the influence of the Court of Justice in the expansion of the external competence of the Community is a distinctive characteristic of Community law unique in the history of national and international legal orders.[11]

While on the one hand, therefore, there has been a development of the scope of international personality *from within*, exercising legal personality on the international plane also depends of course on the actual degree of engagement with other established international legal actors. In many contexts this has proven to be unproblematic for the Community as may be seen in particular from the range of agreements entered into with third states and other organisations and from its body of diplomatic activity. But there have been some obstacles and some resistance at the international level. For instance, during their era of socialist governance, the COMECON countries refused to deal with the Community as a distinct legal entity; while they were unwilling to accord COMECON an autonomous legal identity they similarly (until 1985) refused to do likewise with the Community, so that the Member States of both organisations had to deal with each other bilaterally.[12] Similarly, not being a member of the ILO, the Community had to act through its Member States in respect of ILO conventions, although it did possess some capacity in relation to meetings involving the ILO, through an observer status and ability to join negotiations.[13] What should be noted about such external limits, however, is that they are not fixed; depending on political circumstances, the Community may be thought of as being in a continuous process of negotiating its acceptance by other international actors (as for instance the COMECON problem was eventually resolved and is now of mainly historical significance). Ultimately, it is political and other non-legal forces which determine both the "internal" scope of Community powers (the expanding list within Article 3 of the EC Treaty) and also

[9] See for example, P Pescatore, "External Relations in the Case-Law of the Court of Justice of the European Communities" 16 (1979) *Common Market Law Review* 615; N Emiliou, "Towards a clearer demarcation line?" 19 (1994) *European Law Review* 76.

[10] See for example, the UK House of Lords Select Committee on the European Communities, 16th Report, *External Competence of the European Communities*, 1985.

[11] E Stein, "External Relations of the European Community: Structure and Process" in *Collected Courses of the Academy of European Law*, Vol. 1, Book 1 (Nijhoff, 1990), pp. 127–8.

[12] The problem was resolved eventually by the Warsaw Convention of 27 June 1985 on the Legal Capacities, Privileges and Immunities of COMECON.

[13] See Opinion 2/91, on Convention No. 170 of the ILO [1993] ECR 1–1061, [1993] 3 CMLR 800; and also the note by Emiliou, n. 9 *supra*.

the extent to which it may be accepted as a person by other actors at the international level. And its role as a legal person has expanded significantly in this way over the last forty years.

This developing role is also very much in evidence in the broader non-economic sphere of foreign relations. Even before the Single European Act and the Maastricht Treaty accorded the Community and Union a formal role in "foreign and security policy", the EC had been flexing its muscles in this domain on the basis of its traditional economic policy powers. For instance, the Community had in 1982 imposed sanctions against Argentina during the Falkland Islands dispute: a response to Argentina's military action in the Falkland Islands, but technically having its legal basis in Article 113 of the EC Treaty as a measure of common commercial policy.[14] Much more in the way of foreign and security policy action has followed of course on the basis of the Single European Act (Article 30) and the second pillar of the Treaty on European Union Article 11 *et seq* (ex Article J). While there has been an understandable tendency to downplay the extent of progress in this field – initiatives are typically seen as modest, basically still inter-governmental in character and sometimes confused and ineffectual in their conception and outcome[15] – some recognition ought to be given to its incremental and generative character. For instance, the 1991 Declaration on Guidelines on Recognition of New States in Eastern Europe and the Soviet Union[16] may be open to criticism on a number of grounds, yet does represent the crossing of a threshold, whereby a hitherto state-centred activity was being subjected to a process of common evolution and first steps were taken towards the expression of "European" values (e.g. respect for the position of minorities, and for human rights) as components in the practice of recognising new states. The dynamic which is contained within the framework of Common Foreign and Security Policy (CFSP) activities is identified for instance by Soetendorp in terms of the incremental psychological impact of simply acting within a culture of co-operation:

> The institutionalization of co-ordination and co-operation with respect to foreign policy matters has created a habit of co-operation. . . . This repeated practice, which has been coined by observers of the EPC as a "co-ordination reflex", is an illustration of how actors involved in joint decision-making change from self-interested actors into joint problem-solvers and from self-maximizers into joint-maximizers.[17]

[14] Council Regulation 887/82, OJ 1982, L 102/1; Pieter Jan Kuyper, "Community Sanctions against Argentina" in D O'Keeffe and H G Schermers (eds.), *Essays in European Law and Integration* (Kluwer, 1982).

[15] See for instance the concluding comments by Steve Peers to his report on Common Foreign and Security Policy in 1995–6, in 16 (1996) *Yearbook of European Law*, 611–44, referring to the limited achievement during the period under review.

[16] (1993) 4 *European Journal of International Law* 72.

[17] Ben Soetendorp, "The Evolution of the EC/EU as a Single Foreign Policy Actor" in W Carlsnaes and S Smith (eds.), *European Foreign Policy* (Sage, 1994), p. 118.

Moreover, Ifestos also points to the existence of an opaque normative element within the practice of CFSP, quoting a "former policy maker":

> A kind of unwritten law has developed among the Member States. There are no penalties attached, of course, but there is tacit recognition of a rule which may be broken from time to time, but which nevertheless exists.[18]

What kind of international legal actor (or actors) has the EC/EU therefore become? In strictly legal terms the picture has been and remains complicated. On the one hand, the EC has in some respects the conventional legal personality of an international organisation, but one with a significant internal dynamic for its own development. The personality of the EU, on the other hand, has been very much more obscure. Prior to the Amsterdam amendments, Lenaerts and De Smijter argued:

> The EU Treaty does not expressly confer legal personality on the European Union and neither its competences nor the means conferred on it in respect of those competences reveal any such intention on the side of the Contracting Parties. It may therefore be concluded that the European Union has no legal personality and therefore cannot as such enter into legal relations, internal or external.[19]

Yet at the same time Article 2 (ex Article B) of the European Union Treaty (EUT) refers to an assertion of its identity on the international scene as an objective of the Union, and it is difficult to deny that the Union has acted on the international plane in ways which are legally consequential even if it did not, like the Community, enter into specific agreements with other legal persons. Moreover, a complete legal separation of Community and Union is not possible, in view of the participation of common institutions, personnel, not to mention Member States, and also the general obligation under Article 3 (ex Article C) of the EUT to ensure that EC and EU external policies are consistent with each other. The crucial question was put by McGoldrick: what would be the position if the Union sought to make international agreements and its capacity to do so was accepted by other international actors?[20] A further conundrum had been presented by the issue of European citizenship (which will itself be discussed further below). Article 20 of the EC Treaty provides that "every citizen of the Union shall, in the territory of a third country in which the Member State of which he

[18] P Ifestos, *European Political Cooperation: Towards a Framework of Supranational Diplomacy* (Avebury, 1987), p. 272. For a more detailed account of the development of the CFSP and its EC antecedents, see: Soetendorp, n. 16 *supra*; Geoffrey Edwards, "European Political Co-operation" 12 [1992] *Yearbook of European Law* 643; *ibid.*, "Common Foreign and Security Policy" 13 [1993] *Yearbook of European Law* 497; *ibid.*, "Common Foreign and Security Policy" 14 [1994] *Yearbook of European Law* 541; Steve Peers, n. 15 *supra*.

[19] 16 [1996] *Yearbook of European Law*, pp. 5–6. See also R Eaton, "Common Foreign and Security Policy" in D O'Keeffe and P Twomey (eds.), *Legal Issues of the Maastricht Treaty* (Wiley, 1994), for the same view. This was also the official position of the UK Government and implicitly that of the Commission and the European Parliament (which in its submissions to the 1996 IGC called for the Union to be given international legal personality).

[20] D McGoldrick, *International Relations Law of the EU* (Longman, 1997), p. 37.

is a national is not represented, be entitled to protection by the diplomatic and consular authorities of any Member State, on the same conditions as nationals of that State". This *European Union* citizenship gives rise to a right of legal protection, vis-à-vis non-EU countries and which can be invoked from any Member State in a position to provide such protection. As McGoldrick has remarked, it would be strange for non-EU states to be presented with an assertion of citizenship, to be internationally recognised, pertaining to an entity which is said not to have international legal personality.[21] It is worth referring to this debate since it illustrates the legal dynamic of evolving personality (for instance the contestation between the British Government's position and that of the European Parliament and Commission). At the same time the long-term direction of development was signalled by the agenda for the 1996 IGC which included, as an area to be addressed, the issue of giving to the Union a greater capacity for external action. The matter has now been further resolved by Article 24 of the consolidated (Amsterdam) version of the Treaty on European Union, which will enable the Union to conclude international agreements under both the CFSP and as regards police and judicial co-operation in criminal matters.

In summary, then, the EC has a significant and the EU an evolving personality and presence on the international plane and the two entities are in any case closely inter-related as international actors. The essential point to note for present purposes is the dynamic and distinctive nature of the EC/EU participation in international activity. But the EC/EU's role as an international actor remains different from that of the conventional state actor and it is misleading to think in terms of the European integration process as leading towards the establishment of a new European "super state". Contrary to the earlier "realist" interpretations of European integration – for instance, Bull's view that the resulting European entity would simply be the nation state "writ large"[22] – more recent commentary and analysis has tended to view this European entity as a *new form* of political domination and integration.[23] This distinctive character of the new European (EC/EU) entity should also be viewed in terms of its relationship with individuals (a matter to be addressed further below), in that power and authority can be seen as co-existing in a number of layers and the individual – for instance, as a European citizen – may be able to identify simultaneously with more than one of these layers of authority (for instance: local or regional governance, national or state governance, European governance; in practical terms, for example, as an elector).[24] This significant but also novel and distinctive legal identity of the evolving European entity should be borne in mind during the later stages of the discussion.

[21] *Ibid.*, at p. 180.

[22] Hedley Bull, *The Anarchical Society: A Study of Order in World Politics* (Macmillan, 1977), p. 266.

[23] See for example, P C Schmitter, *The European Community as an Emergent and Novel Form of Political Domination*, Working Paper 1991/26, Centre for Advanced Study in the Social Sciences of the Juan March Institute, Madrid, 1991.

[24] See for instance, Derek Heater, *Citizenship* (Longman, 1990), p. 320 et seq.

4. THE ROLE OF THE INDIVIDUAL: EMPOWERMENT AND "NEW" CITIZENSHIP

There are a number of respects in which the role of the individual (meaning both natural and corporate persons) has been enhanced and become more distinctive in the European context. Taken together their impact is significant for purposes of assessing the issue of participation at a supranational or international level.

Perhaps the most obvious way in which the individual's position has been enhanced is in relation to procedural opportunities. The access of individuals to the European Court of Justice and the Court of First Instance may in some respects be limited[25] but nonetheless a legal nexus had been established under (the original) Article 173 of the EC Treaty, enabling individuals to challenge certain categories of Community action before a supranational tribunal (so paralleling the right of petition against governmental action provided by the European Convention on Human Rights). In terms of legal principle, this was a big jump: challenging a supranational body before a supranational jurisdiction, so contributing to an extension of the individual's conventional international legal personality. As Helfer and Slaughter have recently written: "The provisions for such jurisdiction . . . provide a point of departure for penetrating the surface of the state, allowing the tribunals to interact directly with the principal players in the national legal systems".[26] After some decades of legal activity and a huge case law, it is perhaps easy to take this jurisdiction for granted, but it was certainly regarded as exceptional when it was first established.[27] But individual access to the European Courts is just part of what is now a wider process of European petitioning activity, including in particular also the right to petition the European Parliament's Committee on Petitions (Article 194 (ex Article 189c) of the EC Treaty) and complaints to the European Ombudsman (Article 195 (ex Article 189e) of the EC Treaty), discussed further below.

There is another procedural context in which the individual has become an important European player. The European Court of Justice has of course used the concept of direct effect of Community rules to enable individuals to take legal action before national courts in order to enforce Community measures, thus at one and the same time asserting their own substantive rights and inter-

[25] Especially in the context of "direct" claims under Article 230 (ex Article 173) of the EC Treaty. There is a substantial literature on this question but see in Particular the discussion by Carol Harlow, "Towards a Theory of Access for the European Court of Justice" 12 (1992) *Yearbook of European Law* 213.

[26] Laurence L Helfer and Anne-Marie Slaughter, "Toward a Theory of Effective Supranational Adjudication" 107 (1997) *Yale Law Journal* 273, 277.

[27] See for example, Eric Stein and G Joseph Vining, "Citizen Access to Judicial Review of Administrative Action in a Transnational and Federal Context" in F G Jacobs (ed.), *European Law and the Individual* (North Holland Publishing, 1976), p. 113.

ests and also policing the implementation of Community law and contributing to its effectiveness.[28] At first sight the role of the individual here appears conventional, simply litigating before national courts; but the cumulative contribution of a large number of such individual claims to the effectiveness, vitality and psychological dominance of the Community enterprise has been considerable. It has not only enhanced day-to-day implementation, but also allowed individuals to identify with a supranational activity, often in opposition to the interests and position of national governments.

A related point concerns the substantive rights which may be asserted in this way, which originate as rights given to individuals by the Community rather than by Member State governments. In the earlier days of the Community's operation these comprised for the most part trading rights and opportunities, but increasingly the Community has concerned itself with the promotion of social rights, sometimes giving more to individuals than their own governments would have been willing to provide. The Community and Union have been increasingly *protective* of individuals: for instance, new Article 29 of the TEU states that the Union's objective is to provide citizens with "a high level of safety within an area of freedom, security and justice"; new Articles 12 and 13 prohibit and control discrimination. New Article 127 of the ECT states that the Community shall contribute to a high level of employment; new Article 136 of that Treaty refers to improved living and working conditions as an objective; new Article 149 to the "development of quality education"; new Article 151 to the "flowering of cultures"; new Article 152 to a "high level of human health protection"; new Article 153 to a "higher level of consumer protection"; new Article 174 to "preserving, protecting and improving the quality of the environment". Moreover, in the Preamble to the Community Charter of the Fundamental Social Rights for Workers (the so-called "Social Charter"), the State parties stress the priority to be given to job creation, the importance of social consensus as a factor in economic development and the rejection of all forms of discrimination and exclusion. All of this may be seen as comprising a European *welfare citizenship regime*.[29] In strict legal terms the EC and EU act as guarantors of welfare citizenship – in practice, a body of economic and social rights and opportunities to be granted by the Member States – and does this by empowering individuals to act at the supranational level to enforce state obligations (for instance, invoking the support of the Court of Justice via direct effect, or triggering Commission enforcement, or through parliamentary pressure). The enforcement of such "European" rights is also reinforced by the Community law doctrine of supremacy over any countervailing provision in national law.[30] As individuals, EU nationals (or European citizens) have an increasing

[28] Case 26/62, *Van Gend en Loos* v. *Nederlandse Administratie der Belastingen* [1963] ECR 1, and resulting case law and literature.

[29] P Taylor-Gooby, "Welfare State Regimes and Welfare Citizenship" (1991) *Journal of European Social Policy* 96.

[30] Case 6/64, *Costa* v. *ENEL* [1964] ECR 585, and following case law.

number of rights and the kind of opportunity to enforce such rights which is not normally available to individuals located outside the EU. In so far as these rights are defined and applied through supranational processes they enhance the individual's participation in supranational legal life. As Close comments:

> The occurrence of supra-national citizenship within the Union will mean that any individual who enjoys the citizenship rights entailed will have a direct, internally-oriented relationship with the supra-national, granting (and ultimately guaranteeing or enforcing) body; and therefore a relationship which by-passes and supersedes the authority and sovereignty of the Member States.[31]

The impact of these developments is psychological as much as legal and political since the individual is increasingly emancipated in terms of legal personality, political ability and self-identity from the paradigm of nationality and exclusive state authority. This is particularly so since European citizenship is a device intended, not so much to control and exploit (which is arguably often the function of nationality), but to empower and elevate. Norbert Reich has cast this perception in the following terms:

> The Union 'Charter of Rights' is directed at the Member States, who may be said to be the monarchies of modern Europe; crowned heads who refuse to abandon any of their power either 'upwards' to the Union or 'downwards' in favour of the individual citizen.[32]

In other words, the European citizen actor is in many respects a different kind of person compared with the state national: a freemoving, highly entitled and supranationally assertive actor. For the individual human persons concerned, the role has great novelty in political and legal terms, but also involves a mixed identity, overlapping with that same human person's national *persona*.

5. SUPRANATIONAL POPULAR LEGITIMACY IN THE EUROPEAN CONTEXT

A crucial basis for the claim of (or for) sovereign states to be regarded as primary and "original" legal actors at the international level is not only the fact of territorial control, but also the state's representation of the peoples within its territorial sovereignty in the international arena. For practical reasons alone, it is clearly impossible for millions of human actors to represent their own interests individually at a global level, and this indeed is a reason for the existence of political structures such as the State. But what is really at issue is the sovereign state's claim to be immutably the natural or most appropriate and effective representative of individual or even group interests in an international

[31] Paul Close, *Citizenship, Europe and Change* (Macmillan, 1995), p. 266.

[32] Norbert Reich, "A European Constitution for Citizens: Reflections on the rethinking of Union and Community Law" (1997) 3 *European Law Journal* 131, at 164.

setting. This claim is an essential component of sovereignty and is often also a distinguishing feature of the "international" role traditionally assumed by federal governments but not by states or political units within federations. Moreover, it is a claim which *in some respects* appears to have been strengthened by the emergence of representative democracy as a major global ideology and aspiration in the late twentieth century. As Hirst and Thompson argue:

> Non-democratic regimes are now signs of political failure and chronic economic backwardness. . . . Democratic elections legitimated the sovereign powers of state institutions, and thus provided a better foundation for a state viewed as the organ of a self-governing territorial community than did the will of a prince.[33]

Thus the late twentieth century sovereign state might appear at first sight to have impeccable credentials for purposes of claiming primacy as an international actor: not only the fact of actual control over territory and populations, but also to have a moral legitimacy in that role via processes of representative democratic governance.

However, the historical shift towards representative as distinct from elite governance also contains the seeds of the demise of state sovereignty, simply by virtue of the fact that "popular" sovereignty need not always coincide with "state" sovereignty. For it is a logical possibility that a genuine exercise of popular will might include making a choice between governing structures,[34] including alternatives to the sovereign state paradigm, and it is arguable that this process has been at work in the case of the evolution of the EC/EU. The sovereign state has been able to maintain a credible claim to be the primary international actor for so long as it could present itself as the most effective vehicle for representing popular interests at a supranational level. To a large extent this was a question of the existence of credible alternatives to the state in performing such a role. While it is clear that many international organisations, by reason of their functions, have not been equipped nor would seek to play a representative role, the EC/EU, as an organisation dedicated to the promotion of a wide range of individual and group interests, naturally does perform such a role and also one which has increasingly competed with that of states. And, as already noted, the EC/EU's promotion of positive social and environmental values has rendered it more politically attractive in comparison with states which (again according to their nature) continue to carry a number of repressive and controlling functions in relation to individuals. The relationship between the European entity and its Member States thus takes on an intriguing aspect of competing values, whereby the former, in the eyes of individuals, begins to represent the "better life", which is guaranteed, more

33 P Hirst and G Thompson, *Globalization in Question* (Polity Press, 1996), pp. 173–4.

34 The exercise of such a choice is also inherent in the right of self-determination, which has also gained steadily in political and legal vigour during the second half of the twentieth century.

concretely, by processes such as the Article 234 reference procedure to the Court of Justice and the right of petition to the Parliament.

On the other hand, care should be taken not to push the above argument too far too fast. In relation to some areas of policy no doubt the informed European citizen will perceive the EC/EU as a friend and protector. But popular resistance to some aspects of European integration and the replacement of the national by the European polity still exists, sometimes in a dramatic form (most notably in the case of referenda which have prevented accession to the EC, or cast serious doubt on the degree of popular support for certain EC/EU policies). An underlying concern is identified by Weiler in the following terms:

> . . . the European electorate (in most Member States) only grudgingly accepts the notion that crucial areas of public life should be governed by a decisional process in which their *national* voice becomes a minority which can be overridden by a majority of representatives from other European countries. In theoretical terms there is, arguably, still no legitimacy to the notion that the boundaries within which a minority will accept as democratically legitimate a majority decision are now European instead of national.[35]

Nonetheless, this is not a fixed position or feeling. It would be surprising if national electorates had very quickly acquired a new sense of identity as a European electorate. But, over time, as a new generation of electors become accustomed to the idea of and perceive some of the benefits of being European rather than national citizens, this reluctance may recede and the locus of allegiance may shift.

Such a shift in citizen identity and allegiance is likely to be stimulated by the EC's stronger claim to legitimacy as the "democratic deficit" in European level decision-making is gradually eroded.[36] The deficit has of course been addressed in stages: firstly, with the advent of direct elections to the European Parliament in 1979; and then via the successive extension of the Parliament's participation in the Community's legislative process under the Single European Act and the Maastricht and Amsterdam Treaties.[37] Through this extension of the formal democratic basis of Community legislation, the judicial doctrines of direct effect and supremacy of Community law have acquired a greater constitutional legitimacy, which in turn reinforces the substantive appeal of Community measures. Moreover, this process addresses the concern identified by Weiler – the informed and determined European citizen, who may have previously feared the consequences of transferring sovereign powers to distantly accountable Com-

[35] J H H Weiler, "The Transformation of Europe" (1991) *Yale Law Journal* 2472–3.

[36] See the discussion by Jean-Claude Piris: "After Maastricht, are the Community Institutions More Efficacious, more Democratic and More Transparent?" 19 (1994) *European Law Review* 449, at 462 et seq.

[37] For a critique of the democratic element within EC rule-making, see P P Craig, "Democracy and Rule-making within the EC: An Empirical and Normative Assessment" (1997) 3 *European Law Journal* 105.

munity institutions, may now have a voice in the composition of the European Parliament, an increasingly significant partner in the European law-making process.

In addition to the Parliament's role in the democratisation and hence legitimation of EC policy and rules, the Parliament itself has also established closer legal and political relations with the European populace: through the access of electors and pressure groups to MEPs, through the traditional and, since 1992, treaty-based right of petition, and, also since 1992, through the procedure of complaints to the European (Parliament-based) Ombudsman. As a result, there has sometimes been a significant dialogue between important interest groups and the Parliament (a notable example was the mass petition, signed by more than two and a half million people, on the testing of cosmetics on animals, which was presented to the Parliament's Committee on Petitions).[38] The outcome of these developments is a new supranational dimension to the process of policy formation and legal change, via the route of public pressure > European Parliament > European legislation > changes to the national legal position. The European Parliament, the Commission and the Court of Justice all have a mediating role in the evolution of new norms which are eventually applicable at the national level.

A further component of this emerging legitimacy on the part of the EC/EU comprises a number of more specialised representative bodies which have been established at the European level. In addition to the Economic and Social Committee (established under the original ECT: see Article 257, ex Article 193), which represents broadly employers, trade unions and "other interests" (for instance, professional groups and self-employed persons), the Maastricht Treaty established the Committee of the Regions (see Article 263 (ex Article 198a) of the ECT), which has two hundred and twenty-two representatives of regional and local bodies. There are also cognate organisations, such as the Association of European Border Regions (founded in 1971 and representing areas which straddle Member State borders and possess common economic interests, for instance the Franco-German-Swiss region between the Vosges, the Black Forest and the Jura), and the Conference of Peripheral Maritime Regions in the European Community (set up in 1973 and representing the interests of the coastal regions).

But it has also begun to be argued that issues of representation and legitimacy should not be viewed only through the familiar, conventional prism of state-like processes (typically, for example, the Western model of parliamentary, majoritarian democracy). Some commentators have more recently urged that different criteria of accountability and legitimacy should be applied to European policies and institutions since the nature of the European enterprise is in

[38] See Epaminondas Marias, "The Right to Petition the European Parliament after Maastricht" (1994) 19 *European Law Review* 169; Carol Harlow, "A Community of Interests: Making the Most of European Law" 55 (1992) *Modern Law Review* 331, 341.

a number of ways different from that of the soveriegn state. Majone, for instance, has put forward the view that:

> . . . the process of European integration is inherently non-majoritarian, and the relevant standards of legitimacy and accountability should reflect this basic fact. . . . The key question. . . . Is whether it is realistic and methodologically correct to assess the legitimacy of present institutions and policy-making processes with reference to norms that are largely irrelevant today and may not become relevant in the future.[39]

On this view, the criteria appropriate for assessing the legitimacy of European Community policy, at least, are not so much or only the "democratic" tests of popular or majority support and approval, but perhaps also the more outcome-oriented factors of "expertise, procedural rationality, transparency and accountability by results".[40] In a similar vein, Christiansen[41] has cautioned against a wholesale rush towards direct democratisation without considering the need for alternative bases of legitimacy. It is not inconceivable that some aspects of the democratic deficit have worked to the benefit of individuals as "Euopean citizens" (again, in terms of effective outcomes). As Christiansen puts the argument:

> both intergovernmental bargaining and administrative networking are generally regarded as normatively discredited because of the limits they impose on transparency and public participation. Yet a closer look at the integration process thus far demonstrates that substantial advances have been due to non-transparent bargaining and élite networks. Sacrificing élite consensus for greater openness and citizen involvement, while desirable from the perspective of democratic theory, is likely to come at a cost in terms of systemic output.[42]

Thus, while not asserting that participatory democracy should be wholly put aside as a legitimating goal of the European entity, it may be argued that it should not occupy an exclusive role in this respect. The significance of this kind of argument for present purposes is that it reinforces the perception of the distinctive nature of the EC/EU as an entity with a role and identity which is different in particular from that of the sovereign state.

Altogether, therefore, what may be detected is a shift in the processes of representation and so also a relocation of political and legal identity, away from the traditional locus of both within the political framework of sovereign states. In one sense, representation has become more fragmented and complex, but the common factor is that most of this activity takes place in a supranational space and occurs under the aegis of the EC and EU. In this way, the European entity,

[39] Giandomenico Majone, "Europe's 'Democratic Deficit': The Question of Standards" (1998) 4 *European Law Journal* 5, at 7 and 27.

[40] *Ibid.*, p. 28.

[41] Thomas Christiansen, "The Limits of Legitimating European Integration" (1997) 8 *Irish Studies in International Affairs* 35.

[42] *Ibid.*, pp. 47–8.

as a provider and facilitator of alternative forms of representation and avenues of aspiration, has begun to compete significantly with the older established states as a "manager" of individual and group interests in both the international and also to some extent more incursively in national domains.

6. NEW LOCAL AND REGIONAL CONFIGURATIONS OF POWER AND REPRESENTATION

In discussing the late twentieth century fragmentation of the power and authority of sovereign states,[43] it should be noted that the outcomes of such a process are not necessarily uniform or predictable. Sometimes there is a relocation of power and authority "upwards" to a supranational level as in the case of the EC/EU, but this is in fact only one model of possible international or supra-national organisation and governance. There may also be a process of relocation "downwards", to "sub-state entities" or "smaller" political units. Furthermore, the latter downward shift in power and authority may manifest itself very differently in different regional contexts – comparing, for instance, recent tendencies in Western and Eastern Europe. In the case of the former, in the context of the EU, devolution has resulted in a stronger "regional" identity, either adding to or correlating to existing sub-national political units such as the German Länder. In Eastern Europe, however, the trend during the 1980s and 1990s has been a fragmentation along classical statist and nationalist lines, often inspired by minority fears and producing a larger number of smaller new sovereign states.[44] Such a comparison lends force to the argument that the EC/EU experience is stimulating new forms of governance and supranational participation, in that "regionalism"[45] in Western Europe in the closing years of the twentieth century has been something novel in those respects.

During the 1990s the devolution of power and authority to sub-state regional or local structures of governance in Western Europe has been articulated in particular by means of the concept of subsidiarity, itself formally enunciated in the post-Maastricht (Article 3b) and post-Amsterdam (Article 5) EC Treaty. As Constantinesco argues:

[43] See generally: Liesbet Hooghe and Gary Marks, "Contending Models of Governance in the European Union", ch. 1 in Alun W Cafruny and Carl Lankowski (eds.), *Europe's Ambiguous Identity: Conflict and Consensus in the Post-Maastricht Era* (Lynne Reiner, 1997); Karl-Heinz Ladeur, "Towards a Legal Theory of Supranationality – The Viability of the Network Concept" (1997) 3 *European Law Journal* 33; Inger-Johanne Sand, "Understanding the New Forms of Goverenance: Mutually Interdependent, Reflexive, Destablised and Competing Institutions" (1998) 4 *European Law Journal* 271.

[44] See James Mayall and Hugh Miall, "Towards a Redefinition of European Order", ch. 16 in Hugh Miall (ed.), *Redefining Europe* (Pinter, 1994), pp. 264–5.

[45] Care must be taken in using terminology. A distinction is often drawn between "regionalism", indicating a "bottom-up" process of regional development, and "regionalisation", signifying a "top-down" process. See e.g. the discussion in Thomas Christiansen, "Reconstructing European Space: From Territorial Politics to Multilevel Governance" *EUI Working Papers*, RSC No. 96/53 (EUI Florence, 1996).

> . . . subsidiarity has an obvious part to play in the move towards rationalizing the management of public affairs because with it we may be able to give a clear answer to the question who does what as between the central State, its regions or entities, and the Community.[46]

Subsidiarity then becomes an organising principle of multi-layered governance. The advantages of this reconfiguration of governance are further explained by Weale in the following terms:

> . . . instead of the view that individuals have one basic political identity from which all the others are derivative, we might suppose that individuals can have multiple identities, ranging through the neighbourhood, through the city and region to the nation-state and continental level, and perhaps even to the global level. Of course the concerns expressed and attended to at these levels will be different, but they may certainly be complementary and even inter-related (as when people are concerned about public transport in their city because they are worried about global climate change).[47]

However, the implications of devolution and subsidiarity are still in the process of being worked out, especially at the European sub-state level, at which regions and other local entities are as yet only at an early stage of exploring and forming their role and identity (as in the case of the current UK devolution). Any discussion of the participation of such actors at a supranational level must therefore remain tentative at present, although the establishment of the EC Committee of the Regions (ex Article 198a-c, new Articles 263–5 of the EC Treaty) has provided elements of formal representation and advisory status in the Community context. It is also important to note the EC/EU encouragement of regional and local identity. As Laffan comments:

> What is striking about regionalist movements is the extent to which they see European integration as providing a roof or a home within which to assert "regional/national identities" that had been undervalued or trapped within existing national states. The integration project, by disturbing existing political spaces, created new political arenas.[48]

What, then, constitutes more specific evidence of a developing supra- or trans-national presence on the part of regions and other local actors at the present time? One significant move was that by the German Länder, following ratification of the Single European Act and intended to compensate for a diminution of representation within the German Federation at the European level; the Länder subsequently persuaded the German Government to enhance

[46] Vlad Constantinesco, "Who's Afraid of Subsidiarity?" (1991) 11 *Yearbook of European Law* 33, at 36.

[47] Albert Weale, "Majority Rule, Political Identity and European Union", ch. 8 in Percy B Lehning and Albert Weale (eds.), *Citizenship, Democracy and Justice in the New Europe* (Routledge, 1997), p. 138.

[48] Brigid Laffan, "The Politics of Identity and Political Order in Europe" (1996) 34 *Journal of Common Market Studies* 81, p. 90.

their involvement in the preparation of the German negotiating position in the EC Council.[49] Brussels "presence" and transnational linkages have also developed since the 1980s: regional offices in Brussels increased from two in 1985 to fifty in 1994, and bodies such as the Association of European Regions, the Council of European Municipalities and the Euro-Cities Association provide a focus for trans-European networking. Regional actors are not only grouping together but also entering into agreements which imitate the international treaties engaged in by sovereign states. For instance, the group of regions known as the "Four Motors" – Baden-Württemberg, Cataluna, Lombardia and Rhône-Alpes and described by Harvie as a "type of inter-regional cartel" able to "control the dissemination of high-tech industries, negotiate as an equal with multi-nationals, and diffuse the benefits down to regional *entrepreneurs*"[50] – in March 1990 entered into an agreement with another "region", Wales, concerning economic co-operation and technology transfer, the sharing of environmental information and research results, and student and cultural exchanges.[51] Such regional networking, assertion of interests and supranational representation are the manifestations of a political process of identity-building and reconfiguration, actively encouraged by the Commission,[52] and contributing to the displacement of the older sovereign states as the primary locus of authority and representation. Considered individually, the above examples may not appear at present to be so very significant but they are the early steps towards achieving the vision of a "Europe of Regions" and their eventual cumulative impact may bring about an important transformation in political and juridical structure.[53]

What is important to note for purposes of the present discussion is the momentum now existing in a European context towards "sub-state" governance with a supranational political and legal dimension. This momentum derives legitimacy both from a growing identification on the part of individuals with regions as much as with states, and from the political and moral claims inherent in the concept of subsidiarity. But the dynamics of this process are undoubtedly complex. To some extent, what is happening may be seen as a process of (bottom-up) "regionalism", particularly for instance in so far as the dynamic has been triggered or encouraged by a long-established sense of distinct nationhood (as in the case, for example, of Scotland, Wales, Cataluna or Flanders). Equally, EC/EU fostered (top-down) "regionalisation" has played its part,

[49] Laffan, *ibid*., at p. 91; Juliane Kokott, "Federal States in Federal Europe: the German Länder and Problems of European Integration" (1997) 3 *European Public Law* 607.

[50] C Harvie, "Yes Minister-President!" (1992) 82 *Planet* 45.

[51] *Ibid*., pp. 44–7.

[52] For instance, regional policy now comprises the second largest element in the Community budget.

[53] Christiansen remarks: ". . . the expectation must be that regional politics will use the avenues which are opened up by European integration, and consequently that changes which currently are 'only' symbolic will result in substantial changes – that is, changes of public policy and institutional reform – in the future": Christiansen, n. 45 *supra*, at pp. 15–16.

especially in the construction of geographically dispersed new "regions", such as the "Four Motors". As already noted, the outcome of this momentum towards "sub-state" governance is far from predictable. Yet, just as the EC/EU has now taken on a representative role at a supranational level, so too are regional and other sub-state actors with a role in public governance.

7. RECONFIGURATION BEYOND THE NATION STATE, BEYOND THE MEMBER STATE

The argument presented here is that the European enterprise of the second half of the twentieth century, most obviously manifested in the emergence and organisational consolidation of the EC and EU, represents a catalytic phenomenon which is now producing a new international – or, better, supranational – configuration of power, authority, representation and participation. Such developments are already well recognised in the literature and debate on multi-level governance and post-statist political organisation and this aspect of the subject requires no further rehearsal. The focus of the discussion here has been rather the implications for juridical perceptions and legal organisation: new modes of participation on the supranational plane suggest the need to re-think conventional wisdom regarding legal personality (i.e. the primacy of the sovereign state and the concomitant derivative status of institutions, individuals and other actors). Serious attention ought to be given to the claim that the EC/EU now functions as an independent legal actor (in "old" terminology, may be seen as possessing its own sovereignty), while other non-state actors – individuals (natural and corporate), sub-state bodies exercising functions of public governance, and various types of NGO – are discovering for themselves new modes of participation and thus juridical identity. Much of this catalytic process appears to be linked to shifts in modes of representation (and the demise of the sovereign state's exclusive role in this respect), and so in claims to legitimacy and authority as international or supranational actors.

One reason for describing these developments in terms of a "catalytic phenomenon" is to emphasise the interdependent mutual reaction of these actors occurring in such a way as to produce, at a critical point, a self-sustaining web of relations. Within such a process new actors may also emerge. In a somewhat different context Robert Axelrod has described[54] the way in which states enter into alliances and the alliances themselves may then emerge as new actors (it may be said, for instance, that NATO is now a significant actor in its own right, as, if not more, significant than some of its individual members; the EC/EU is another obvious example of such a process). Thus, the European arena may be perceived as a political, economic, cultural and also legal space within which

[54] Robert Axelrod, *The Evolution of Cooperation* (Basic Books, 1984).

the earlier "stability" or "steady state" condition of single-level governance by sovereign states has given way to a more fractured, less predictable but no less dynamic complex of legal and political relations, one manifestation of which is a more varied and variable participation not only in political but also in legal life.

In summary, some basic points may be made in description of this emergent legal landscape of "international" European activity. First, in structural terms, it is less hierarchical, more horizontal than vertical, as regards the location of authority. This of course is characteristic of multi-level governance and implies the disappearance of autonomous competence and exclusive decision-making.[55] For jurists of the positivist school, however, this represents a challenge, since it recognises a dispersal of authority among a number of actors, supported by novel claims to legitimacy. Secondly, it confronts the very notion of the "international" by questioning the dynamics of participation at that level of ordering which exists beyond the territorially-based framework of authority and representation emanating from the community of sovereign states. In this sense, the network of European actors described above comprises a reconfiguration of the "international" community as a locus for "international" law. Thirdly, it suggests questions about the dynamic of continuity and discontinuity in legal orders. How does such a juridical re-ordering come about, and in particular to what extent may it be seen in human terms as an "élite" or "mass" activity (arguably the "Westphalian" international order was fashioned by an élite), and to what extent is it driven by non-human phenomena such as environmental or technological change? For some readers, such argument will confirm a sense of inhabiting a "postmodern" legal realm. It will certainly recall the assertion made by Santos, over a decade ago, that:

> We live in a time of porous legality or of legal porosity, of multiple networks of legal orders forcing us to constant transitions and trespassings. Our legal life is constituted by an intersection of different legal orders. . . .[56]

Finally, what does all this suggest about the *value* of personality, subjectivity and identity? The principal conclusion would appear to be that human needs in the legal domain should be served by constructions of legal identity which are dynamic and adaptable and not static. This is especially true of the configuration of non-human, "corporate" actors, which for long has been dominated

[55] As Carter and Scott comment, in envisaging the "Europeanised" role of the individual as "at the same time a Scot, a Briton and a European" – "No single role takes precedent over any other in the hierarchical sense. Instead there are different perspectives and viewpoints that coexist in identical space. Mutual support from contemporaneous interaction is as likely a consequence as mutual antagonism": Caitríona Carter and Andrew Scott, "Legitimacy and Governance Beyond the European Nation State: Conceptualising Governance in the European Union" (1998) 4 *European Law Journal* 429, at 442.

[56] Boaventura De Sousa Santos, "Law: A Map of Misreading: Towards a Postmodern Conception of Law" (1987) 14 *Journal of Law and Society* 297, at 298.

by the conventional forms of the company and the state. Values of horizontal and interactive (more "democratic") participation, of legitimacy and of representativeness may be seen as driving the processes and developments described above. These are likely to result in changes not only in the legal landscape of the near future but also in its "personal" composition.

9

Towards Reconciling Free Trade and Environment

INDIRA CARR

1. INTRODUCTION

Free trade among nations is seen as the key to economic growth, peace and better standards of living leading to a happier state of human existence at a global level.[1] The General Agreement on Tariffs and Trade (GATT)[2] established in 1947, following the destruction caused by the Second World War, promoted free trade vigorously through the principles of non-discrimination (Most Favoured Nation obligation) and elimination of quantitative restrictions.[3] The principle of non-discrimination is found in Articles I and III. Article I requires that a contracting party should treat all contracting parties alike so that where a trade advantage has been granted by one contracting party to another that advantage should be granted equally to all the other contracting parties. Article

+ This paper was born out of seminars to LL.M. (International Business Legal Studies) students at the University of Exeter between 1993 and 1997. As ever, I am indebted to my students for providing a stimulating environment for engaging in a fruitful debate.

[1] There are trade theorists who think that free trade does not provide the best solution in economic terms. Protectionism and unfair trade practice are seen as providing greater economic benefit to a country (see P R Krugman, "Increasing Returns, Monopolistic Competition and International Trade" 1979 9(4) *Journal of International Economics* 467; "A Model of Innovation, Technology Transfer and the World Distribution of Income" 1979 87(2) *Journal of Political Economy* 253). Regardless of this theory, the general consensus seems to be that free trade is worthy of pursuit in economic terms. Free trade owes much to the work of Adam Smith, *An Inquiry Into the Nature and Causes of the Wealth of Nations* (London, W Stahn & T Caldwell, 1776) and David Ricardo, *On the Principles of Political Economy and Taxation* (London, John Murray, 1817).

[2] It came into effect on 1 January, 1948. The GATT 1947 in no longer in force. Many of its key provisions have been carried over into GATT 1994. The GATT 1994 is set out in Annex 1A to the (W)orld (T)rading (O)rganisation Agreement.

[3] Article XI in part reads:

(1) No prohibitions or restrictions other than duties, taxes or others charges, whether made effective through quotas, import or export licences other measures, shall be instituted or maintained by a contracting party on the importation of any product of the territory of any other contracting party or on the exportation or sale for export of any product destined for the territory of any other contracting party.

III requires that no discrimination be made between imported products and domestically produced like products.[4] Along with global economic growth came over, and at times random, exploitation of natural resources, depletion of wildlife, and a lowering of the quality of the natural environment we live in. Though the degradation of the human environment through industrial activity was known in the nineteenth century,[5] it was the publication of Rachel Carson's book *The Silent Spring* in 1962 that highlighted the devastating effects of pesticides on the environment and triggered a greater "public awareness and understanding of environmental issues".[6] This book, now a classic, was momentous in harnessing money for research into the after effects of human activity on the environment and the formation of a dedicated group of intellectuals and enthusiasts who undertook to ensure that the world was not overrun by a wild mob of free trade nightmares. Since the 1960s there has been a legendary growth in the number of environment-oriented legislation with the United States a major player. Though environmental concerns caught the attention and imagination of scientists, politicians, legislators and the public it was not until the much publicised United States – Restrictions on Import of Tuna (popularly known as the tuna/dolphin dispute)[7] that the conflict between the free trade camp and the environmentalists' camp came to the fore. The conflict between these two camps

[4] Article I in part reads:

> (1) With respect to customs duties and charges of any kind imposed on or in connection with importation or exportation or imposed on the international transfer of payments for imports or exports, and with respect to the method of levying such duties and charges, and with respect to all rules and formalities in connection with importation and exportation, and with respect to all matters referred to in paragraphs 2 and 4 of Article III, any advantage, favour, privilege or immunity granted by any contracting party to any product originating in or destined for any other country shall be accorded immediately and unconditionally to the like product originating in or destined for the territories of all the other contracting parties.

Article III in part reads:

> (1) The contracting parties recognise that internal taxes and other internal charges, and laws, and regulations and requirements affecting the internal sale, offering for sale, purchase, transportation, distribution or use of products, and internal quantitative regulations requiring the mixture, processing or use of products in specified amounts or proportions, should not be applied to imported or domestic products so as to afford protection to domestic production . . .
>
> (4) The products of the territory of any contracting party imported into the territory of any other contracting party shall be accorded treatment no less favourable than that accorded to like products of national origin in respect of all laws, regulations affecting their internal sale, offering for sale, purchase, transportation, distribution or use.

Other than the above the GATT also imposes obligations to adhere to the schedules of tariff concession negotiated during trade rounds (Article II) and to administer trade regulations uniformly and impartially (Article X).

[5] See G P Marsh, *The Earth as Modified by Human Action* (New York, Schreibner Armstrong, 1874).

[6] 1987 Sen Mitchell, United States Senate, 8.3.1987, A resolution to express the sense of the Senate that Rachel Carson is recognised on the twenty fifth anniversary of her book "Silent Spring" for her outstanding contributions to public awareness and understanding of environmental issues.

[7] BISD 39S/155, September 1991 (reproduced in 1991, 30 *International Legal Materials* 1594). This report was not adopted.

continues to this day with the World Trade Organisation (WTO)[8] fielding disputes in respect of trade related environment measures (TREMS) as made apparent in the following sections. The recent disruption of the WTO Ministerial Meeting at Seattle (November 30, 1999–December 3, 1999)[9] by environmental interests among others highlights this tension. It is often said that the co-operation or partnership between environmentalists and free trade promoters, if attainable, will be an uneasy one since they enshrine different and, in all likelihood, opposing values.[10] Simply expressed, international trade by its very nature promotes exploitation and environmental concerns conservation. Perhaps there is some truth in the view that free trade is exploitation oriented due to its interest in generating money and extra effort has to be expended to accommodate environment concerns since the Preamble to the GATT 1947 in part read:

> . . . Recognising that their relations in the field of trade and economic endeavour should be conducted with a view to raising standards of living, ensuring full employment and a large and steadily growing volume of real income and effective demand, *developing the full use of the resources of the world and expanding the production and exchange of goods . . .*
>
> (Italics added)

Equally one could add that the GATT 1947 did not rule out the importance of human/social values altogether since they are reflected in the Article XX exceptions in respect (reproduced below), conservation measures, human and animal health, and plant life.[11] That these values were initially recognised in 1947 by the GATT find support in Canada – Measures Affecting Exports of Unprocessed Herring and Salmon[12] where the panel stated:

[8] As of 8 September 2000 the WTO had 138 members of which approximately 80 percent were developing, least developed, or transition economies.

[9] The negotiations at Seattle were suspended as a result of the disruptions. This is not the first time that ministerial talks have been suspended. Previous examples of ministerial talks suspended are The Uruguay Round Mid-Term Review, Montreal, December 1989 and The Brussels Ministerial Meeting, December 1990 (see WTO Press Release 160 available on *http://www/wto/org/wto/seattle/english/press_e/press160.htm*). See D Brack "Trade and Environment after Seattle," (The Royal Institute of International Affairs, Briefing Paper New Series No. 13, April 2000) for an appraisal of the current status on the trade/environment debate.

[10] See B Weiss, "Environment and Trade as Partners in Sustainable Development: A Commentary" 1992 86(4) *American Journal of International Law* 728; J Cameron, "The GATT and the Environment" in P Sands (ed.), *Greening International Law* (London, Earthscan 1993).

[11] See S Charnovitz, "Exploring the Environmental Exceptions in GATT Article XX" 1991 25(5) *Journal of World Trade* 37 who suggests that Article XX exceptions are designed to include environmental measures [at p. 55]; D C Esty, "GATTing the Greens Not Just Greening the GATT" 1993 72(5) *Foreign Affairs* 32; "Greening the GATT: Trade, Environment and the Future" (Washington DC: Institute for International Economics, 1994); T J Schoenbaum, "Free International Trade and Protection of the Environment: Irreconcilable Conflict?" 1992 86(4) *American Journal of International Law* 700.

[12] BISD 355/98 (adopted 22 March, 1988).

> as the preamble of Article XX indicates, the purpose of including Article XX(g) in the General Agreement was not to widen the scope for measures serving trade policy purposes but merely to ensure that the commitments under the General Agreement do not hinder the pursuit of policies aimed at the conservation of natural resources.[13]

The establishing of the WTO and the adoption of the GATT 1994 however has not done away with the conflict between the environmentalists and the promoters of free trade. The purpose of this paper is to make apparent that whatever differences or conflicts there may be based on political and economic grounds between the environmentalists and the promoters of free trade they exist only at the surface level, and that at a deeper level they both share a common goal such that the issue is no longer reduced to a matter of choosing either environmental goals or free trade. Recognition of this common goal, this paper suggests, will be instrumental in bringing about a true reconciliation between the two camps thus facilitating a move from mere rhetoric to active and perceivable co-operation among the different factions. Before embarking on a voyage of discovery of what it is they have in common, this paper will examine, in brief, some of the disputes that have come before the GATT and the WTO panels to highlight and appreciate the ongoing debate between the two camps, developing nations, their woes and the various suggestions and steps taken (at the surface level) to arrive at an acceptable solution.

2. RECENT TREMS DISPUTES BEFORE THE GATT AND THE WTO

As stated earlier the tuna/dolphin dispute[14] made worldwide impact. Policy makers, politicians, economists, lawyers and the fishing industry paid close attention to the events in the GATT. It is difficult to say why this particular case caught the public eye since environment centred disputes had been considered previously by GATT panels.[15] It is possible that extensive leaking of the panel findings and the panel's intention to set rules for future interpretation of certain provisions of the GATT may have concentrated the interest. Due to its role in attracting widespread attention on the free trade *versus* environmental law debate it makes sense to begin this section with an examination of the tuna/dolphin dispute.

[13] Para. 4.6.

[14] Subsequent to the tuna/dolphin dispute initiated by Mexico the (E)uropean (E)conomic (C)ommunity and The Netherlands complained about the secondary embargo on third countries' tuna products under the MMPA provisions. The Panel held that the Article XX exceptions were inapplicable. United States – Restrictions in Imports of Tuna DS 29/R, June 1994. This was not adopted.

[15] See United States – Prohibition of Imports on Tuna and Tuna Products from Canada, GATT, BISD, 29th Supp. 91 (1983); Canada – Unprocessed Salmon and Herring, GATT, BISD, 35th Supp. 98 (1989).

2.1. United States – restrictions on import of tuna

In 1990, the United States (US) imposed an embargo on the import of commercial yellowfin tuna and yellowfin tuna products caught using the purse seine method from the Eastern Tropical Pacific under the Marine Mammal Protection Act of 1972 (as revised in 1988 and 1990). For our purposes the relevant sections are ss.101(a)(2) and 102(a)(2)(b) of the Marine Mammal Protection Act (hereinafter MMPA). Section 101(a)(2) prohibits the importation of fish or products from fish which have been caught with commercial fishing technology that results in the incidental kill or incidental serious injury of ocean mammals in excess of the US standards. Section 102(a)(2)(b) prohibits the importation of yellowfin tuna fish and yellowfin tuna fish products using the purse seine method unless the government of the exporting country has regulations that control the incidental taking rate of mammals comparable with those of the US. Mexico, one of the countries affected, approached GATT to establish a panel after its consultations to resolve the problem with the US failed. Mexico claimed that the embargo was a quantitative restriction and therefore a breach of Article XI of GATT. The US defended the embargo using Articles III(4), XX(b) and XX(g).

2.1.1. Article III(4)

The US argued that the measure, an internal one, enforced at the time or point of importation, fell within the ambit of Article III(4).[16] The treatment accorded to Mexican tuna was no less favourable than that accorded to like products of national origin in respect of all laws, regulations and requirements affecting their internal sale, offering for sale, purchase, transportation, distribution or use. The panel, after a close scrutiny of Article III,[17] concluded that it focused

[16] See n. 4 *supra* for text of Article III(4).

[17] Paras. 5.11 and 5.12. which read:

> The text of Article III:1 refers to the application to imported or domestic *products* of "laws, regulations and requirements affecting the internal sale . . . of products" and "internal quantitative regulations and requiring the mixture, processing or use of *products*"; it sets forth the principle that such regulations on *products* not be applied so as to afford protection to domestic production. Article III:4 refers solely to laws, regulations and requirements affecting the internal sale etc. of *products*. This suggests that Article III covers only measures affecting products as such. Furthermore, the text of the Note Ad Article III refers to a measue "which applies to an imported *product* and the like domestic *product* and is collected or enforced in the case of the imported *product* at the time or point of importation". This suggests that this Note covers only measures applied to imported products that are of the same nature as those applied to the domestic products. such as prohibition on importation of a product which enforces at the border an internal sales prohibition applied to both imported and like domestic products.
>
> A previous panel had found that Article III:2, first sentence, obliges contracting parties to establish certain competitive conditions for imported *products* in relation to domestic *products*. Another panel had found that the words "treatment no less favourable" in Article III:4 call for effective equality of opportunities for imported *products* in respect of the application of laws,

on the characteristics of products and not on the method of production. Article III(4) "calls for the comparison of tuna *as a product* with that of domestic tuna *as a product*".[18] The panel could not see how tuna as a product could be affected by the incidental taking of dolphins. The US was therefore obliged "to accord treatment to Mexican tuna no less favourable than that accorded to United States tuna, whether or not the incidental taking of dolphins by Mexican vessels corresponds to that of the United States vessels".[19]

2.1.2. Article XX(b) and Article XX(g)

The US also relied on the environmental exceptions contained in Article XX, in particular paras (b) and (g) of the GATT which state:

> Subject to the requirement that such measures are not applied in a manner which would constitute a means of arbitrary or unjustifiable discrimination between countries where the same conditions prevail, or a disguised restriction on international trade, nothing in this Agreement shall be construed to prevent the adoption or enforcement by any contracting party of measures:
>
> (b) necessary to protect human, animal or plant life or health; . . .
> (g) relating to the conservation of exhaustible natural resources if such measures are made effective in conjunction with restrictions on domestic production or consumption; . . .

Using Article XX(b), the US argued that the embargo was justifiable since the legislation was aimed at the preservation of animal life. Other than the MMPA, they had no other measure at their disposal for the preservation of dolphins. The US argued that the GATT exception should be read in a manner that would endorse the ban on importation of products caught in a dolphin unfriendly manner outside their territorial waters. Article XX(b) however is silent about its geographic scope; it does not indicate whether it could be used to protect animal life outside the jurisdiction. The ambiguity led the panel to consider the provision's drafting history.[20] They traced it to the New York Draft of the ITO (International Trade Organisation) where the article had been amended to read:

> For the purposes of protecting human, animal or plant life or health, *if corresponding domestic safeguards under similar conditions exist in the importing country.*
>
> (italics added)

regulations or requirements affecting the sale, offering for sale, purchase, transportation, distribution or use of *products*. It was apparent to the Panel that the comparison implied was necessarily one between the measures applied to imported products and the measures applied to like domestic products.

[18] Para. 5.15.
[19] *Ibid.*
[20] Para. 5.25.

The proviso, according to the records, had been added to reflect concerns about abuse of sanitary conditions. On the basis of this evidence the panel stated that Article XX(b) was not intended to have extrajurisdictional effect.[21] Concern was also expressed about the long-term effects on trade of a wide interpretation of Article XX. It was felt that it could restrict trade to contracting parties who had identical internal regulations thus attracting retaliatory action from those who did not have the same internal regulations. A wide reading of Article XX could result in trade war – the very situation that the GATT was meant to avoid.

The US also, according to the panel, did not adequately demonstrate that their measure was *necessary* for dolphin protection.[22] There was no indication whether other options such as international co-operative arrangements consistent with the GATT had been pursued.[23]

The US also claimed that the Restrictions under the MMPA were aimed primarily to (i) protect dolphins, applying the interpretation given to "relating to the conservation of exhaustible natural resources" in the context of Article XX(g) in Canada – Measures Affecting Exports of Unprocessed Herring and Salmon,[24] and (ii) render effective restrictions on domestic production or consumption of dolphins.[25]

The panel could not see how the measure was primarily aimed at conservation of dolphins. It was impossible for Mexico to tell with certainty whether her conservation policies met the US standards during a given period since the tolerance level during a specific period was to be calculated in terms of the US incidental dolphin taking recorded during the same period. According to the panel:

> [they] did not consider that the United States measures, even if Article XX(g) could be applied extrajurisdictionally, would meet the conditions set out in that provision. A previous panel found that a measure could be considered as "relating to the conservation of exhaustible natural resources" within the meaning of Article XX(g) only if it was primarily aimed at such conservation. The panel recalled that the United States linked the maximum incidental dolphin-taking rate which Mexico had to meet during a particular period in order to be able to export tuna to the United States to the taking rate actually recorded for United States fishermen during the same period. Consequently, the Mexican authorities could not know whether, at a given point in time, their conservation policies conformed to the United States conservation standards. The panel considered that a limitation on trade based on such unpredictable conditions could not be regarded as being primarily aimed at the conservation of dolphins.[26]

[21] Para. 5.26.

[22] CITES (Convention on International Trade in Endangered Species of Wild Fauna and Flora) was of no use to the US since the dolphins they sought to protect was not cited in Appendix I listing of species in danger.

[23] Para. 5.28.

[24] Adopted 22 March, 1988, BISD 35S/98, 114, para. 4.6.

[25] Para. 5.30.

[26] Para. 5.33.

As for the second reason given by the US, the panel found, basing on earlier interpretations, that "a country can effectively control the production or consumption of an exhaustible natural resource only to the extent that the consumption or production is under its jurisdiction".[27] Article XX(g) did not have extrajurisdictional effect. The panel was not willing to give an extrajurisdictional interpretation to Article XX(g) since it felt "each contracting party could unilaterally determine the conservation policies from which other contracting parties could not deviate without jeopardising their rights under the General Agreement".[28]

Regardless of the conclusion, the message emanating from the findings seems to be that had the US exhibited serious intentions at finding a bilateral/international solution to incidental dolphin taking prior to the embargo and also announced an incidental dolphin-taking rate that the Mexicans could work with, the panel may well have found for the US.

2.1.3. Criticisms of the panel findings

A number of criticisms can be made if the panel findings are viewed from an environmental perspective. It is a truism to say that good and effective law is one that keeps pace with social changes and reflects changing attitudes. By the 1990s environmental concerns were firmly rooted in social, political and legal agenda world-wide. If the GATT panel had taken the opportunity in the tuna/dolphin dispute to weave environmental issues into the fabric of the GATT by interpreting Article XX widely it would not have caused a major surprise. Indeed, it would have endorsed the concerted effort that was taking shape at the international level such as multilateral agreements and debt-for-nature swaps (discussed below) to help developing nations meet environment objectives. Indeed, many of the environmental groups felt that the tuna/dolphin decision may have undone the good they had done.

The product/process distinction used in relation to Article III(4) is also fraught with difficulties. Conceptually the distinction is given to some degree of fuzziness. Is it always the case that the means of production do not contribute to the characteristics of the product? Characteristics, arguably, could include other than the physical attributes,[29] the aesthetic/psychological/moral reactions or the physical sensations the product conveys. For instance, it is often said that the taste of courgettes grown organically differs markedly from

[27] Para. 5.32.

[28] *Ibid.*

[29] Like product, for the purposes of the GATT, seems only to refer to the physical characteristics, end uses and tariff classification of the produce. See Spain – Tariff Treatment of Unroasted Coffee, BISD 28S/102 (1982) Adopted 11 June, 1981. In United States – Standards for Reformulated and Conventional Gasoline, WT/DS2/9 (adopted May 1996) the WTO Panel construed a "like" product as having the same physical characteristics, end uses and tariff classification (para. 6.9).

courgettes grown using modern farming techniques even though they may look the same shape-wise and size-wise. The process in this case appears to contribute to the characteristics, albeit at the physical sensation level.[30]

The suggestion that the US should have explored other avenues like international co-operation is perhaps naïve in administrative and political terms since some environmental issues may require immediate action – for example where near extinction is imminent. Co-operative efforts, though desirable, by nature, are slow and need not conclude satisfactorily. Not allowing a country's internal regulation to have extrajurisdictional effect especially when it comes to environmental issues seems nonsensical since the environment is shared by all. Since talk of boundaries in this context appears meaningless it seems reasonable to expect legislation aimed genuinely at environmental preservation to apply extrajurisidictionally.[31]

Persuasive from an environmental perspective, the panel's lack of interest in instituting changes is defensible policy wise. The GATT is primarily a multilateral trade instrument where the principle of non-discrimination is sacrosanct. As such, to allow what may seemingly appear to be sound environmental measures within an importing country to have extrajurisdictional effect would change the focus of the GATT and undermine its role in facilitating free trade. As the panel stated:

> . . . Article XX(b) allows each contracting party to set its human, animal or plant life or health standards. The conditions set out in Article XX(b) which limit resort to this exception namely that the measure taken must be "necessary" and not "constitute a means of arbitrary and unjustifiable discrimination or disguised restriction on international trade", refer to the trade measure requiring justification under Article XX(b), not however to the life or health standard chosen by the contracting party . . . if the broad interpretation suggested by the United States were accepted . . . [t]he General Agreement would then no longer constitute a multilateral framework for trade among all contracting parties but would provide legal security only in respect of trade between a limited number of contracting parties with identical internal regulations.[32]

[30] Perhaps one can draw a distinction like John Locke (1632–1704 CE) between primary and secondary qualities: *Essay Concerning Human Understanding* (Oxford, Clarendon Press 1975). Primary qualities are qualities like size, shape, number, weight which are measurable in physical terminology. Secondary qualities are qualities produced by way of sensation such as taste, colour, and one could perhaps add aesthetic qualities. Notwithstanding Locke's distinction based upon properties dealt with in the physical sciences and properties that fall outside of the remit of the physical sciences, Bishop Berkeley (1685–1753 CE) in his *Three Dialogues between Hylas and Philonous* (in Ayer M (ed.), *Philosophical Works* (London, Dent, 1975)) (Hylas means Substance or Matter and Philonous Lover of Mind) raised considerable problems concerning the legitimacy of such a distinction. It continues to be a problem in contemporary philosophy. See for instance J L Mackie, *Problems from Locke* (Oxford, Clarendon Press, 1976).

[31] For an excellent collection of papers that analyse the tuna/dolphin panel report closely see J Cameron, P Demaret, P and D Geradin (eds.), *Trade & the Environment: The Search for Balance Volume I* (London, Cameron May, 1994).

[32] Para. 5.27.

2.1.4. *Aftermath*

Given the publicity caused by the tuna/dolphin panel report, and that at a time when the Uruguay Round[33] was in progress, it is surprising that environmental issues were not immediately addressed through suitable amendments to relevant provisions. For instance, Article III with its emphasis on product could have been amended[34] to accommodate methods of production such that where the production method is objectively established as resulting in an unacceptable level of environmental harm, the product would not be treated as a like product. Alternatively, Article XX (b) and XX(g) could also have been amended to allow an internal regulation promoting environmental ends to have extrajurisdictional effect in prescribed circumstances – for instance, where urgent action to protect the environment is necessary, or where there are no multilateral environmental agreements providing the necessary protection and the species is close to extinction. The Uruguay Round could have also used ancillary agreements modelled for instance on the GATT Agreement on Technical Barriers to Trade adopted in the Tokyo Round, 1972.[35]

The objections raised by the environmentalists however had some impact. Policy makers realised that the conflict between the two camps could not be swept under the carpet and some reference to the environment was required. The Preamble of the Agreement establishing the WTO makes specific reference to environmental protection. The relevant part of the Preamble now reads:

> . . . relations in the field of trade and economic endeavour should be conducted with a view to raising standards of living, ensuring full employment and a large and steadily growing volume of real income and effective demand, and expanding the production of trade in goods and services, while allowing the optimal use of the world's resources in accordance with the objective of sustainable development, seeking both to protect and preserve the environment and to enhance the means for doing so in a manner consistent with the needs and concerns at different levels of economic development . . .[36]

The emphasis on environmental objectives, it was felt, may have heralded a new era. This optimism was short-lived. The first dispute to be heard by the WTO after its formation centred around a trade-environment issue: United States –

[33] The Round lasted from 1986–94. The other GATT Conferences comprise the Conference of Annecy, France (1949), Conference of Torquay (1950), Conference of Geneva (1956), Dillon Round (1962), Kennedy Round (1964–7) and the Tokyo Rounds (1973–9).

[34] A consensus of two thirds of the members would have been required to amend Article III.

[35] This agreement deals with issues relating to product standards so that they are not used as a form of discrimination.

[36] See Introduction above for the wording of the preamble to GATT 1947. In United States – Standards for Reformulated and Conventional Gasoline (citation n. 37) the Appellate Body did note that the language of the preamble did add colour, texture and shading to the interpretation of the agreements annexed to the WTO Agreement.

Standards for Reformulated and Conventional Gasoline.[37] Under the Clean Air Act 1963 (as amended in 1990) the US Environmental Protection Agency promulgated a Gasoline Rule which allowed only gasoline of specified cleanliness to be sold to consumers in high pollution areas in the country. The Agency assigned a statutory baseline which affected importers of gasoline. Venezuela and Brazil complained that the Gasoline Rule violated Article III. The US argued that there was no violation of Article III and that the Rule could be justified under the Article XX exceptions. The panel concluded that the statutory baseline was discriminatory since the importer would be required to provide gasoline of a higher quality than that provided by a domestic producer who used an individual refinery baseline.[38] The reasoning of the panel was not unlike that of the tuna/dolphin panel.

Does it follow that environmental issues will continue to be disregarded under WTO despite the wording in the Preamble? No doubt the panel's conclusions can be criticised along the same lines as the tuna/dolphin decision. It must be said yet again that the US was proposing a unilateral action that could have resulted in retaliatory action. Unilateral action may have played a primary role in the evolution of international environmental law, but its usefulness now is questionable since the importance of environmental protection is openly and positively acknowledged by the international community. The many multilateral environment agreements bear witness to this. Against this sympathetic backdrop it makes better sense to include environmental objectives as an integral part of a free trade treaty through consensus. It would only be fair at this juncture to say that the Appellate Body, while recognising the importance of co-ordinating policies on trade and environment as enshrined in the preamble to the WTO, were in no way questioning a state's authority to pursue environmental objectives. They said:

> [i]t is of some importance that the Appellate Body point out what this does *not* mean. It does not mean or imply that the ability of any WTO Member to take measures to control air pollution or, more generally, to protect the environment is at issue. This would be to ignore the fact that Article XX of the *General Agreement* contains provisions designed to permit important state interests – including the protection of human health, as well as the conservation of exhaustible natural resources – to find expression. The provisions of Article XX were not changed as a result of the Uruguay Round of Multilateral Trade Negotiations. Indeed, in the preamble to the WTO Agreement and in the *Decision on Trade and Environment* [adopted by Ministers at the Meeting of the Trade Negotiations Committee in Marrakesh on April 14, 1994], there is specific acknowledgement to be found about the importance of coordinating policies on trade and the environment. WTO members have a large measure of

[37] Panel Report: WT/DS2/R January 1996; Report of the Appellate Body WT/DS2/AB/R, April 1996. Both the Reports are available on the website of the WTO. Address of website *http://www.wto.org/*.

[38] United States – Standards for Reformulated and Conventional Gasoline (January 1996); Appellate Body Report (April 1996) WT/DS2/AB/R.

> autonomy to determine their own policies on the environment (including its relationship with trade), their environmental objectives and the environmental legislation they enact and they implement. So far as concerns the WTO, that autonomy is circumscribed only by the need to respect the requirements of the *General Agreement* and the other covered agreements.[39]

The importance of environment issues was endorsed in the more recent case of United States – Import Prohibitions of Certain Shrimp and Shrimp Products (a.k.a. shrimp/turtle dispute).[40] The complainants in this case were India, Malaysia, Pakistan and Thailand who, as exporters of shrimp and shrimp products were affected by the prohibition on the import of shrimp and shrimp products imposed under s. 609 of Public Law 101–162 16 United States Code § 1537. Section 609(b)(1) banned the import of shrimp and shrimp products that were harvested using technology that would adversely affect sea turtles. The US trawlers used approved (T)urtle (E)xcluder (D)evice(s) in order to harvest shrimp. Section 609(b)(2) provided that the import ban would not apply where a harvesting nation had a certificate from the US Department of State.[41] Certificates were granted to governments of harvesting nations who fell in one of the following categories where:

(1) there were no relevant species of sea turtles in waters subject to its jurisdictions;
(2) shrimp was harvested by methods (such as artisanal methods) that did not pose a threat to sea turtles;
(3) commercial shrimp trawling operations takes place exclusively in waters subject to its jurisdiction in which sea turtles do not occur;
(4) there was documentary evidence of the adoption of a programme governing the incidental taking of sea turtles in the course of shrimp trawling that was comparable with the US programme and where the average rate of incidental taking of sea turtles was comparable with the US vessels.[42] The regulatory programme of a harvesting nation was assessed on the basis of whether (1) the harvesting nation required the use of TEDs; (2) they were as effective as the devices used in the US; and (3) credible efforts were made to ensure that trawlers were complying with the regulations and appropriate sanctions imposed on those in breach of the requirements.[43]

[39] Last paragaraph of Section V.
[40] WT/DS58/R, May 1998 (Report of the Panel). The Panel concluded that the US measure was inconsistent with Article XI:1 of the GATT 1994 and the measures could not be justified under Article XX (para. 8.1). The US appealed on a number of grounds – the Panel had erred in not considering unsolicited information from non-governmental organisations, in finding s.609 was outside the scope of the chapeau to Article XX. The Appellate Body Report was published in October 1998 (WT/DS58/AB/R). The references in this article are to the Report of the Appellate Body.
[41] Details of the regulatory guidelines for certificates were provided in Regulatory Guidelines 1991 (56 Federal Register 1051, 10 January, 1991) 1993 (58 Federal Register 9015, 18 February, 1993) and 1996 (61 Federal Register 17342, 19 April, 1996).
[42] Section 609(b)(2)(A) & (B).
[43] See Guidelines 1996, p. 17344.

The complainants argued that the US embargo contravened Article XI[44] of the GATT which prohibited quantitative restrictions which are not duties, taxes or charges. Since the shrimp harvested by other methods were no different from shrimps harvested using TEDs, they were like products. By allowing shrimps with TEDs certificates to be imported and excluding those that did not, the US was discriminating between like products. The US relied on the Article XX exceptions and argued that the sea turtles, exhaustible natural resources, were threatened with extinction and the use of TEDs was essential to arrest the process. They also argued that the measure was not arbitrary discrimination since the criteria for certification is sympathetic to the conditions of each shrimp-exporting country. Moreover, there was international consensus in respect of the need to conserve sea turtles[45] and the usefulness of TEDs in aiding that effort was well recognised.

During the course of the hearing a number of points emerged:

(1) the US excluded the import of shrimp harvested with TEDs that were caught in the waters of non-certified countries;[46]

(2) the US had not engaged in serious negotiations to conclude bilateral or multilateral agreement for the preservation of sea turtles;[47]

(3) the US, when expecting other countries to adopt the US regulatory framework, did not take into account the different conditions occurring in those countries;[48]

(4) there was evidence of differential treatment between the countries – for instance, in the effort made by the US in transferring TED technology to various countries;[49] and

(5) there was no transparency or procedural fairness in the certification process. No formal procedures for a country applying for certification to be heard, or for that matter respond to any arguments made against them during the certification process existed. The applicants were denied basic fairness and due process; the minimum standards for transparency and procedural fairness in the trade negotiations as set out by Article X(3)[50] were not met.[51]

[44] See n. *supra* 3 for text of Article XI.

[45] The sea turtles that the US measure sought to protect are included in the list of endangered species in Appendix I of the Convention on International Trade in Endangered Species.

[46] Report of Appellate Body, WT/DS58/AB/R, para. 165.

[47] Paras 166–72.

[48] Para. 164.

[49] Paras 163–75.

[50] Article X(3) in part reads:

(a) Each Member shall administer in a uniform, impartial and reasonable manner all its laws, regulations, decisions and rulings of the kind described in paragraph 1 of this Article.

(b) Each Member shall maintain, or institute as soon as practicable, judicial, arbitral or administrative tribunals or procedures for the purpose, inter alia, of the prompt review and correction of administrative action relating to customs manners . . .

[51] Paras 180–3.

The Appellate Body found that even though the measures served an environmental objective recognised as legitimate under Article XX(g), the US measure as applied amounted to unjustifiable discrimination and arbitrary discrimination contrary to the requirements of Article XX chapeau.

The Appellate Body however went to some length to reassert the view expressed earlier in United States – Standards for Reformulated and Conventional Gasoline. In finding the US measure had been applied in a manner that amounted to unjustifiable discrimination and arbitrary discrimination contrary to the requirements of chapeau of Article XX they did not hold that environmental issues were unimportant. In their words:

> . . . we wish to underscore what we have not decided in this appeal. We have not decided that the protection and the preservation of the environment is of no significance to the Members of the WTO. Clearly, it is. We have not decided that the sovereign nations that are Member States of the WTO cannot adopt effective measures to protect endangered species, such as sea turtles. Clearly, they can and should. And we have not decided that sovereign states should not act together bilaterally, plurilaterally or multilaterally, either within the WTO or in other international fora, to protect endangered species or to otherwise protect the environment. Clearly, they should and do.
>
> What we have decided in this appeal is simply this: although the measure of the United States in dispute in this appeal serves an environmental objective recognised as legitimate under paragraph (g) of article XX of the GATT 1994, this measure has been applied by the United States in a manner which constitutes an arbitrary and unjustifiable discrimination between Members of the WTO, contrary to the requirements of the chapeau of Article XX, For all of the specific reasons outlined in this Report, this measure does not qualify for the exemption that Article XX of the GATT 1994 affords to measures which serve certain recognised, legitimate environmental purposes, but which, at the same time are not applied in a manner that constitutes a means of disguised restriction on international trade. As we emphasised in United States – Gasoline, WTO members are free to adopt their own policies aimed at protecting the environment as long as, in so doing, they fulfill their obligations and respect the rights of other Member States under the WTO Agreement.[52]

Compared with the tuna/dolphin dispute, there is a definite shift in favour of the environment in the shrimp/turtle dispute. It acknowledges that the measure was justifiable, provisionally, under Article XX (g). Secondly, the shortcomings of the US (listed above) indicate what a country should do in order not to fall foul of the WTO provisions. It must, for instance, make sure that it meets the minimum standards for procedural fairness, does not treat countries differentially and that serious effort is made in procuring a bilateral or multilateral agreement. As to what constitutes serious effort, for example, remains open to further interpretation. In procedural terms also, the shrimp/turtle is perhaps a landmark decision. As noted earlier (in n. 40), the US had also appealed on the grounds that the panel had erred in not considering unsolicited information

[52] Paragraphs preceding Findings and Conclusions.

from the (N)on (G)overnment (O)rganisations. The Appellate Body ruled that the NGOs could submit briefs to the WTO directly.[53]

3. DEVELOPING NATIONS, ENVIRONMENTAL CONCERNS AND SOLUTIONS

The decisions in the three cases cited in this article reinforced the confidence of the developing nations in the GATT/WTO since free trade continues to remain the primary objective of the WTO agenda. Developing countries have a reputation for being the worst offenders in environmental terms. Environmental regulations and standards of developing nations are not always comparable with those of the developed nations for a number of reasons. Manufacturing industries tend to use outdated machinery and equipment in environmental terms. Replacing existing technology with environment-friendly technology requires investment which is likely to push up production costs and affect the competitiveness of goods made in these countries in the global marketplace. The governments of these countries are ill-placed to subsidise the industries due to other commitments such as education, health and defence (in some parts of the world). Inhabitants of the developing nations also contribute to the erosion of environmental quality due to ignorance and poverty. The cutting down of trees for firewood by the poor in India is one illustration. Ignorance also plays a role in the wanton exploitation of natural resources. Removing ignorance and igniting environmental awareness requires access to scarce public funds. Population explosion and the associated pressures on the natural resources is another endemic problem in developing nations. It is not that the leaders of these nations are unaware of the degradation of environmental quality, both nationally and globally. However, lacking the economic/social infrastructure, the task of regulating environmental degradation is an uphill one. Add to this the Third World debt and there is every reason for a government to exploit natural resources, rather than protect it, to service the debts.[54] The effect of the developing countries' external debt on environmental damage is well argued in the Brundtland Report which called for urgent action to alleviate these debts.[55] Further, developing countries view developed nations as the worst offenders in producing pollutants and find the moral tone adopted by the rich nations highly objectionable.

[53] See para. (a) Findings and Conclusion. See also T Cottier "The WTO and Environmental Law: Some Issues and Ideas" available on *http://www.itd.org/issues/essay1.htm*, J Cameron and S J Orava, "WTO Opens Disputes to Private Voices" *National Law Journal*, 7 December, 1998.

[54] See J W Sanders, "Global Ecology and World Economy; Collision Course or Sustainable Future" December 1990 24(1) *Bulletin of Peace Proposals* 395; J G Speth, "Towards a North-South Compact for the Environment" June 1990 32(5) *Environment* 16. See also Case Studies Conducted in the framework of the UNCTAD/UNDP project on "Reconciliation of Trade and Environment Policies" available http://www.unctad.org/trade.env/.

[55] World Commission on Environment and Development, Our Common Future (Oxford, OUP, 1987).

Various possibilities of easing a developing nation's progress to adopting environment-friendly measures have been mooted over the years – though not always with success. Transfer of technology aimed at waste management, efficient use of energy, pollution emission and control at subsidised rates is one way to ensure that the manufacturing industries in the Third World use environment-friendly technology.[56] Removing such technology from the sphere of intellectual property protection is another way of reducing the cost of such technology. Such suggestions are greeted with dismay by the nations with the technology since they fear that they would be sowing the seeds for a dependency culture in the developing nations. There is also the fear that free availability, or availability of technology at subsidised rates, would stifle much needed research and development by commercial organisations who hold the patents for such technology. There is a lot of truth in the view that private companies are motivated by financial incentives rather than philanthropic concerns. A world where vital discoveries and inventions are free of patents remains an ideal and it seems we still have a long way to go.

Financial aid to developing countries for environmental purposes is another suggestion but there are concerns. It is felt that aid would only promote corruption, neo-colonialism[57] and dependency,[58] and give an opportunity for the developed nations to ignore examining environmental issues – such as, consumption practices – at their doorstep.[59]

Another idea that has met with limited success[60] is the debt-for-nature swaps.[61] The idea was first proposed by Thomas Lovejoy in 1984 when he was Vice President of the World Wildlife Fund. Though debt-for-nature swaps can

[56] M Townsend, "The International Transfer of Technology" April 1993 23(2) *Environmental Policy and Law* 66; I M Carr, "Environment and International Trade – An Uneasy Partnership" (Exeter Papers in European Law, No.2, University of Exeter, Centre for European Legal Studies, 1997).

[57] See W Wayne Nafziger, *The Economics of Developing Countries*, 2nd ed. (Cliffs NJ, Prentice Hall, 1990).

[58] See P McCully, "The Case Against Climate Aid" November 1991 21(6) *The Ecologist* 244.

[59] See P Chatterjee and M Finger, *The Earth Brokers* (London, Routledge, 1994).

[60] The first instance of debt-for-nature swap is that of Conservation International with Bolivia where $650,000 was bought by Conservation International for $100,000 in return for Bolivia's agreement to provide an endowment fund for $250,000 in local currency for managing the Beni Biosphere Reserve. Since then there have been a number of swaps, involving debtor countries such as Poland (Paris Club debt-for-nature swap (anti-pollution measures), 1991), Colombia (Canada debt-for-nature swap, 1993), and the Philippines (Germany debt-for-nature swap (Community Forestry Project, 1996).

[61] For further information on this see: D Logsdon, "Debt-for-Nature Evolves: The Enterprise for the Americas Initiative" 1992 3 *Colorado Journal for International Environmental Law & Policy* 635; M S Sher, "Can Lawyers Save the Rainforest? Enforcing the Second Generation Debt-for-Nature Swaps" 1993 17 *Harvard Environmental Law Review* 151; M L Minzi, "The Pied-Piper of Debt-for-Nature Swaps" 1993 14 *University of Pennsylvania Journal of International Business Law* 37; A Lewis, "The Evolving Process of Swapping Debt for Nature" 1999 10 *Colorado Journal for International Environmental Law & Policy* 431; A Patterson, "Debt-for-Nature Swaps and the Need for Alternatives" 1990 32(10) *Environment* 5; R Mahony, "Debt-for-Nature Swaps: Who Really Benefits?" May 1992 22(3) *The Ecologist* 53.

take a variety of forms,[62] the object of a debt-for-nature swap is to lower a debtor country's external debt in return for an agreement that the country will utilise a percentage of the debt to fund (in local currency) conservation activities. The debt (normally bought by a NGO which in turn becomes a creditor) is swapped for environment-oriented activities in the debtor country. Despite the attractions the scheme has attracted criticisms. The most obvious is in terms of sovereignty since it restrains the debtor country's right to exploit its resources as it wishes by imparting the NGO with control over the use/exploitation of the resources. Swaps also do not take into account the lifestyles and interests of the indigenous people whose land is subject to control. Further, in the absence of enforcement provisions there is no way of ensuring that the debtor country does in fact honour its obligations under the agreement. Nevertheless, the debt-for-nature swaps have the potential to play an important role in promoting the environment. The criticisms can be overcome with suitable clauses such as sovereignty clauses and enforcement clauses in the agreement, and by inviting the views of the indigenous people who are affected. The inclusion of an enforcement clause in the agreement when The Netherlands in 1993 purchased Costa Rica's commercial debt to the tune of US $30 million to fund reforestation provides an illustration. Fears about sovereignty can also be allayed by involving a local NGO. For instance, in 1992 The Nature Conservation bought US $2.2 billion of Brazilian debt and donated it to a local NGO, Fundacao Pro-Naturezo, in return for environmental government bonds. Despite these innovative measures and a rising tide of pro-environment sympathies, environmental issues continue to vex politicians, economists, lawyers and international organisations. More is expected of the WTO to weave environment issues into the very fabric of the philosophy of free trade. Even though the decisions in the disputes cited in this paper may be viewed as ignoring the opportunity to put matters right, it must be stressed that environmental issues are firmly embedded in the WTO agenda. Since its creation, the WTO has taken a number of steps to ensure greater communication between the conservationists and free trade promoters. It established a permanent Committee on Trade and Environment (CTE) to carry on the work carried out by the GATT Working Group on Environmental Measures and International Trade. Unlike the GATT Working Group, which was largely inactive, the CTE has been very active since its inception in 1995. The regularity with which the CTE issues Trade and Environment Bulletins[63] bears witness to the importance given by the WTO to environment concerns. It has discussed a number of issues ranging from export of domestically prohibited goods,[64] eco-labelling and packaging,[65] border

[62] See Conservation International Foundation (1991 Supplement) "The Debt – For-Nature Exchange: A Tool for International Conservation" for the different forms.

[63] All the Bulletins can be accessed from the WTO website *http://www.wto.org/wto/environ/bul letin.htm*.

[64] See WTO Trade and Environment Bulletins 1, 5, 7, 10 and 11.

[65] See WTO Trade and Environment Bulletins 6, 8, 9, 17, 23 and 28.

tax adjustment,[66] environmental policies and intellectual property agreements,[67] to trade measures in multilateral environment agreements,[68] as well as holding seminars on trade and environment for developing countries.[69] Disappointingly, the Committee, apart from exhibiting the complexity of the issues and demonstrating the need for further analysis and discussion of the issues, has not come up with anything more concrete. It remains at the level of rhetoric and oratorial flourishes, and the quest for a better ordered world where the protagonists of the environment and the promoters of free trade support each other continues. The CTE has also not addressed issues such as technology transfer and debt relief which are of central concern to developing countries.[70] It therefore comes as no surprise when it is said that environment and trade issues would fare better in the hands of another organisation. Professor T N Srinivasan,[71] for instance, suggests that the CTE should be wound up and environment tackled by the (U)nited (N)ations (E)nvironment (P)rogramme. Despite the gathering clouds of WTO scepticism it must be pointed out that there is a way out of the trade/environment conundrum. What is required is a return to the grass roots of trade and environment policy, a deep level enquiry of the central concerns of these two camps.

4. TRADE, ENVIRONMENT AND THE DEEP LEVEL

Free trade is intended to promote economic growth. Economic growth in recent times has unfortunately come to be associated with savings rates of a country, deficit-to-GDP[72] ratio, current account deficit and interest rates. Growth seen purely in monetary terms has tended to promote individualism, self-interest, opportunism and gain at the expense of others. More recently, globalisation has brought with it powerful transnational corporations, downsizing and unemployment. Issues with social dimensions – e.g. environmental issues, use of child labour, and the welfare of future generations – are seen in negative terms, as detractions from the twin goals of profit and greater returns for investment. In this scheme social and moral values are anathema. As to whether this is the goal that the GATT initially promoted in 1947 in adopting the notion of free trade is highly debatable. Some sense of the goal of the GATT may be gained by considering it in its original setting. The GATT was born out of the cornucopia of horrors that the world witnessed in the 1930s and 1940s. Acts of ferocity that

[66] See WTO Trade and Environment Bulletin 17.

[67] WTO Trade and the Environment WT/CTE/W/8 June 8, 1995.

[68] See WTO Trade and Environment Bulletins 6, 8, 10, 11 and 15.

[69] See WTO Trade and Environment Bulletin 24.

[70] See India's observation in the Discussion part of International Institute for Sustainable Report on the WTO's High-Level Symposium on Trade and Development, 17–18 March 1999. Available on *http://www.wto.org/wto/hlms.sumhldev.htm.*

[71] See Keynote Addresses *http://www.wto.org/wto/hlms.sumhldev.htm*. See the opening remarks of Director-General Mike Moore to CTE's Information Session on Multilateral Environment Agreements October 24, 2000 available http://www.wto.org/english/news_e/spmm_e/spmm_38e.htm

[72] Gross Domestic Product.

questioned man's rationality and undermined social and moral values, values that humanity held dear and set them apart from the animals, made the world shudder. Free trade as enshrined in the GATT 1947 was intended to bring communities and nations together, to improve standards of living globally, and to promote peace and harmony among people and nations. The aim of the GATT 1947 was the welfare (or prosperity) of human beings at large – that is, not the welfare of human beings in a particular state or a particular time. It is intended to include all. It is meant to be universal and intergenerational. Viewed in this manner economic growth was not profiteering at the cost of human happiness. It was not opportunism or self-interest. Economic growth, against the backdrop of the GATT 1947, was meant to promote and aid the development of a better future where human worth, human dignity and human prosperity are equally recognised and respected. In such a world order, the notion of economic growth includes development – development towards providing a better all-round living environment for all. The GATT 1947 was essentially public spirited. And, in a public spirited world order there was no room for greed, self-interest, or disregard of the interests and rights of others. It is possible that sight of this public spirited enterprise of the GATT 1947 may have been lost due to the unclear wording of the Preamble where the emphasis seems to be on expansion and ensuring a volume of real income. It must be stressed that there was no suggestion in the Preamble that the real income of the few (the developed as opposed to developing, the one as opposed to the many) was the aim of the GATT 1947, since it talked in general terms about raising the standard of living; obviously in the absence of qualification the standard of living of all. The quality of life surely cannot be enhanced where social elements such as healthcare, education and the environment are ignored, or dignity and mutual respect are lacking. The prosperity that the GATT 1947 had in mind could not simply have meant economic gain, though economic gain (regardless of the time) is vital to the building of an infrastructure aimed at the welfare of human beings. Economic gain was simply the means and not the end.[73]

The notion that economic growth embodies development is perhaps better expressed in the Preamble to the WTO where it says that:

> relations in the field of trade and economic endeavour should be conducted with a view to raising standards of living . . . expanding the production of trade in goods and services, while allowing the optimal use of the world's resources in accordance with the objective of sustainable development, seeking both to protect and preserve the environment and to enhance the means for doing so in a manner consistent with the needs and concerns at different levels of economic development.

The economic growth which free trade is meant to foster is thus not an end in itself. It is a means to an end. It is aimed at human prosperity and is

[73] This view may be compared to what Aristotle says about economic prosperity in his Politics (A Sinclair (tr.), (Harmondsworth, Penguin, 1962) where he views the end of economics as meeting the needs of social life, not the wealth it may generate (1.9 1258a8–14).

cognisant of social values, the needs and concerns at different levels of economic development. That this is not far fetched is confirmed by the recent Press Release 143[74] from the WTO. In a statement to the General Council on developments in the international trading environment the Director-General Mike Moore said:

> [globalization] holds benefits for us all and we need to take steps to ensure that the prosperity that flows from globalisation is accessible to all.
>
> . . . trade is good for the consumer and like the tide, it can raise all boats. But there are adjustment costs and there are those who perceive inequities in globalization. Clearly, appropriate social policies need to accompany liberalisation . . .
>
> . . . I urge you to remember that trade is not the end: it is a means to progress, a tried and trusted vehicle for advancement, prosperity and a safer, better world for us all.[75]

Lacking an economic shroud, the rationale guiding environmental concerns is perhaps more obvious in that it is directed at human welfare and is also intergenerational.[76] Justifications for saving the environment have been sought in ethical terms ranging from utilitarianism[77] to value ethics.[78] Debates are equally raging round the question of whether environmental concerns are man-centred (anthropocentric) or nature centred (bio-centric).[79] Regardless of these debates, at the very least, environmental concerns are aimed at the welfare of human beings and are also aimed at future generations.[80] The goal of sustainable development, a cornerstone of environmental concerns, is to meet the current generation's needs without compromising those of future generations.[81]

From the above paragraphs, it is apparent that both the free trade promoters and environmentalists converge in having a common goal – the welfare of

[74] 3 November, 1999.

[75] Available on *http://www.wto.org/wto/new/pres143.htm.*

[76] See A D'Amato, "Do We Owe a Duty to Future Generations to Preserve the Global Environment?" 1990 84 *American Journal of International Law* 190.

[77] See for example, I M Carr, "Saving the Environment – Does Utilitarianism Provide a Justification?" 1992, 12 *Legal Studies* 92, R Routley and V Routley, "Against the Inevitability of Human Chauvinism," R Elliot (ed.) *Environmental Ethics* (Oxford: OUP, 1995).

[78] See for example, T Regan (ed.), *Matters of Life and Death* (New York, Random House, 1986).

[79] See for example, P S Elder, "Legal Rights for Nature: The Wrong Answer to the Right(s) Question" 1984 22 *Osgoode Hall Law Journal* 285; A Emmenegger and A Tschentscher, "Taking Nature's Rights Seriously: The Long Way to Biocentrism in Environmental Law" 1994 6 *Georgetown International Environmental Law Review* 545, J Passmore, "Attitudes to Nature," in *Environmental Ethics* (Oxford, OUP, 1995). Also see T Hill Jr, "Ideals of Human Excellence and Presuming Natural Environments" (1983) 5 *Environmental Ethics* 211 for a framework from the viewpoint of virtue ethics.

[80] G Pinchot, *The Fight for Conservation*, (Seattle, University of Washington Press, 1990) for a feminist viewpoint see V Plumwood, "Nature, Self and Gender: Feminist Environmental Philosophy and the Critique of Rationalism" in R Eliott (ed.) *Environmental Ethics* (Oxford, OUP, 1995).

[81] See J Pasek, "Obligations to Future Generations: A Philosophical Note" 1992 *World Development* 513; D van De-Veer and C Pierce (eds.) *The Environmental Ethics and Policy Book: Philosophy, Ecology, Economics* (Belmont, Calif. Wadsworth, 1994), R Sylvan, *Universal Purpose, Terrestrial Greenhouse and Biological Evolution* (Canberra, Research School of Social Sciences, Australian National University Press, 1990).

humanity across space and time. They share a common goal. So, what does this commonality of goal mean in positive terms for the free trade and environment debate?

The foremost and obvious answer is that trade and environment should no longer be seen as contradictory forces but as forces working side-by-side to promote values fundamental to human existence – human welfare and better standards of living. Once the two camps are seen as complementary forces it inevitably paves and eases the way for concrete developments. Co-operation and arriving at common decisions will no longer be forced affairs but become part of the natural course of events. And Mike Moore, the Director-General of the WTO, does not have to imprint the environment on the free trade conscience by periodically emphasising that "trade and environment need not be contradictory but can indeed be complementary"[82] in his addresses. It provides the basis, the foundation, for meaningful action. For instance:

- A future panel when considering a TREMs dispute should find it easier to lay down guidelines that any government has to follow for a unilateral action to fall within the Article XX exceptions of the GATT 1994. The Appellate Body in the shrimp/turtle dispute did list the actions that the US did not take.[83] However, in the absence of any indication, its relevance at a general level is open to debate. The free trade camp does not have to fight shy of environmental concerns and can play an active role in exhibiting the common purpose of free trade and environmental concerns.
- The WTO could also set up a special advisory body comprising of members drawn from the WTO, other regional groupings such as the NAFTA,[84] ASEAN,[85] and the EU,[86] and environmental organisations on trade related environment measures with the objective of advising members on the legitimacy of any measures (e.g. embargoes) they may be considering. The advisory body could also be provided with powers to initiate fast-track bilateral or multilateral negotiations where scientific opinion, for instance, foresees real threat or irreversible environmental harm.
- Given the liberalisation of investment, a special body, under the auspices of the WTO and consisting of members from industry, international agencies and NGOs, could also be set up to ensure that multinationals do not trade off the environment when investing abroad.
- In procedural terms, the task of making suitable amendments to provisions, such as Article III in the GATT 1994, to combat environmental harm should be easier. It would make sense to amend Article III in a

[82] See Press Release, "Trade Liberalisation Reinforces the Need for Environmental Co-operation" dated 8 October, 1999 available *http://www.wto.org/wto/new/pres140.htm*.

[83] See "Recent TREMS disputes before the GATT and the WTO" above.

[84] North American Free Trade Association.

[85] Association of Southeast Asian Nations.

[86] European Union.

manner to ensure that "like product" status is not given to products produced in a manner that results in environmental harm.[87]

- More sense can be made of the demands of developing nations to make environment-friendly technologies available at subsidies or at no cost.[88] It should be possible to persuade countries with the technology to think of alternative ways (e.g. public recognition, special titles, prizes) of rewarding the inventors (be they individuals or companies). It may also force a reassessment of the current approach to the legal protection of intellectual property rights.
- The WTO could also actively seek the co-operation of governments world wide to provide special incentives to industries/manufacturing/harvesting processes which seek reduction in environmental harm. This could also result in increased policy co-ordination among the governments.
- It will help developing nations to see themselves as equal partners in the quest for a better world for all instead of seeing themselves as the victims of the developed nations, and as the exploited in the race to economic prosperity. This should bring about all round environmental awareness, be it at the political, legal, social and individual level within a developing nation.

5. CONCLUSION

The view put forward in this essay is that both the environmentalists and free trade promoters at the deep level share the goal of welfare of humanity, and that this should aid co-operation. It cannot be denied that the sharing of a common purpose can provide a useful tool in bringing people together – be they policy makers, legislators, politicians or individuals, and likely to evince a degree of collaboration that will produce concrete results. The common goal will facilitate the breaking of barriers, such that issues ranging from transfer of environment-friendly technology to stronger environment oriented provisions by making suitable amendments to the GATT 1994 need no longer remain an abstract futuristic ideal but can take centre stage. It will provide the momentum necessary to convert mere rhetoric into action.

[87] See "Criticisms of the Panel Findings" under "Recent TREMS disputes before the GATT and the WTO" above.

[88] See "Developing Nations, Environmental Concerns and Solutions" above.

10

Free Trade As A Fundamental Value in the European Union

ERIKA SZYSZCZAK

> "To prohibit a great people . . . from making all that they can of every part of their own product, or from employing their stock and industry in the way that they judge most advantageous to themselves, is a manifest violation of the most sacred rights of mankind".[1]

The development of the concept of free trade as a fundamental value in the international economic arena is associated with the writings of Adam Smith. Traditionally Smith's work is seen as paving the way for the formulation of the Ricardian theory of comparative advantage which provided a justification for trade specialism between countries. Central to Smith's work is the emphasis on the value of international trade for the welfare of *citizens* rather than the previous mercantilist focus upon the accumulation of wealth for sovereigns.[2]

Since Adam Smith's day the development of a nation state has brought with it demands for new roles for the State to play in maximising the welfare of its citizens. Within the modern European context the State has addressed issues of consumer protection, environmental concerns, redistribution of wealth as well as developing, to different degrees, attachments to human rights/fundamental rights standards. This in turn has brought with it a need to re-appraise fundamental values in the light of potential conflicts between free trade principles and other values within a Member State.

One of the central questions of *world* trade law, that of managing interdependence of nation states, has, in principle, been resolved within the European Union in an institutional framework which not only has secured the dismantling of trade barriers between Member States but has also used law to address overt changes in policy. Economic integration has used the device of

[1] R H Campbell, A S Skinner and W B Todd (eds.), *Adam Smith An Inquiry into the Nature and Causes of the Wealth of Nations* (1776) (Oxford, Clarendon Press, 1976).

[2] However, Smith was not above justifying restrictions on trade on grounds of *national* interest: See D Landes, *The Wealth and Poverty of Nations* (London, Abacus, 1998).

"free trade" as a tool for co-ordinating economic and fiscal systems. It has also been utilised to tackle the pervasive non-tariff barriers to trade which continue to be formulated and re-formulated at a national level in response to changes in economic structure and infrastructure at the national level.

One of the greatest challenges facing the EU has been to build a structure and maintain a dynamic within that structure that can contain the multi-layered competencies and tensions that exist in the EU. The competencies are shared between the EU and the big players, the Member States, but also contain tensions between central, federal and transnational authorities and the role of private actors. The process of European integration, utilising law as an essential tool to reach certain ends, has thrown down a gauntlet. It is argued that in order to appreciate, understand and comment upon law's role in the EU we need a new constitutionalism.[3] In this essay the focus is upon the attempts to manage, restrain and contain the clash of fundamental values which exist between the shared competencies and competing tensions of the European Union.

1. FREE TRADE IN THE EC TREATY

The EC Treaty does not contain a list or set of fundamental values. Indeed the fundamental values which are now enumerated in the new Treaty are the classic international law triad of democracy, human rights and the rule of law. There is no list of fundamental economic rights beyond the four freedoms but, as Bridge points out, the original Treaty did provide, in general terms, two main categories of fundamental rights: those which create fundamental Community rights and those which safeguard certain existing rights of the Member States.[4]

Free trade is not easily located in the EC Treaty as a fundamental value in a literal sense: the whole Treaty resonates with the mantra of dismantling barriers to trade. Free trade has a special resonance as a value in the sense that strong justifications have to be made in order for a Member State to depart from this value. The statements in the Preamble see the aim of European Union as "balanced trade and fair competition". The founders of the Treaty implied that a number of positive by-products would emerge as a result of free trade: economic and social progress, constant improvements of the living and working conditions of their people. The commitment to free trade is specific in Article 14 (2) EC:

[3] J Weiler, "Does Europe Need A Constitution? Demos, Telos and the German Maastricht Decision" (1995) 1 *European Law Journal* 219.

[4] J Bridge, "Fundamental Rights in the European Economic Community" in J Bridge, *et al* (eds.), *Fundamental Rights, A volume of essays to commemorate the fiftieth anniversary of the founding of the Law School in Exeter 1923–1973* (London, Sweet and Maxwell, 1973).

> The internal market shall comprise an area without internal frontiers in which the free movement of goods, persons, services and capital is ensured in accordance with the provisions of this Treaty.

Free trade as a fundamental value is therefore an implicit concept which has been articulated in legal terms by the link between the non-discrimination principle and notions of fairness. In consequence the Court of Justice has upheld the principle of free trade as a fundamental right.[5] Harden argues that the rules relating to the "four freedoms" in the EC Treaty set constitutional boundaries to public/state action "affecting the conditions under which private economic actors participate in markets".[6] The Court has attempted to develop similar principles across the fundamental freedoms although trade in goods and services, has to date, been the principle focus of the litigation creating the opportunities for this development. As the Court has discovered the free trade provisions do not necessarily lend themselves to consistent horizontal principles.

The focus of the free movement provisions has been very much upon *access* to the market not market creation or securing a competitive market. As we shall see this has created tensions since the competition rules of Articles 81 and 82 EC are directed at private undertakings. The Court has stated that the rules (or values) of competition also bind the State[7] but the extension of the competition rules to state activity is still tentative in some areas. An example of the limited approach in applying the free movement provisions is seen in *Sodemare SA et al* v. *Lombardia*.[8] Here the Court refused to apply Article 43 EC to non-discriminatory restrictions on the *pursuit* of an economic activity. A Luxembourg company established a capital company governed by Italian law which ran a number of companies providing sheltered accommodation for elderly people. These companies were not allowed to enter into contracts with public authorities which would have provided for the reimbursement for healthcare services they provided since under the Italian law such contracts could only be negotiated with non-profit-making bodies. Sodemare argued these rules were trade barriers affecting its ability to run its business. The Court was not sympathetic. In its view Sodemare was not at a disadvantage when compared with the position of similar profit making undertakings in Italy. The Court allowed a discretion to the Italian State to organise its social welfare system.

Applying analogies with the free movement of goods case law the reasoning here is rather like the marketing rule of *Keck*.[9] Access to the market in services is not denied and the Member State has a measure of discretion as to how to organise the way the service is sold. Arguably, if we applied a "free trade at all

[5] Case C-44/89 *Von Deetzen* v. *Hauptzollamt Oldenburg* [1991] ECR I-5119.

[6] I Harden, "The Constitution of the European Union" (1994) *Public Law*, 609, 619.

[7] The starting point can be traced back to Case 229/83 *Leclerc* v. *Au Blé Vert* [1985] ECR 1.

[8] Case C-70/95 [1997] ECR I-3395.

[9] Joined Cases C-267 and C-268/91 *Keck and Mithouard* [1993] ECR I-6097.

costs" approach the alleged trade barrier at issue in *Sodemare* could be seen as a "compositional rule": a service provider has to re-package the service if he/she wants to compete on the host market and unless he/she does re-package the service she cannot compete on the same competitive terms in the host state. This ruling might be compared with the rulings in *Decker*[10] and *Kohll*.[11] Here the Court did find an infringement of the right to trade, where national rules imposed stricter conditions (requiring specific prior authorisation) on the reimbursement by the social security system of medical products acquired or hospital treatment provided in another Member State. Such cases make intrusions into Member States' welfare/social security systems and the fundamental values contained within them. The Court accepted in *Decker* that in principle, there might be aims of an economic character[12] capable of justifying the restriction on trade: the need to guarantee the balance of the social security system. An even more sensitive issue was presented to the Court where a challenge was made to The Netherlands' regulation of pension provision using the device of the competition rules and Article 86(1) EC.[13] Here the Court recognised the concept of social solidarity as a Community value to protect national systems of welfare provision.

2. FUNDAMENTAL VALUES AND THE ROLE OF THE COURT

Article 6 of the TEU includes respect for the fundamental principles of the EU as a precondition for membership[14] and a rule of continuing membership of the EU.[15] The Union therefore acts as guarantor and arbiter of fundamental values but these are addressed in the conventional language of civic and political rights rather than economic rights.[16]

The absence of a clear fundamental rights/values text has catapulted the Court of Justice into a central role in developing fundamental values of the Community. When dealing with *Community legislation* designed to build a

[10] Case C-120/95 [1998] ECR I-1831.

[11] Case C-158/96 [1998] ECR I-1931.

[12] A justification not accepted previously by the Court: Case 72/83 *Campus Oil Ltd* v. *Minister for Industry and Energy* [1984] ECR 2727.

[13] Case C-67/96 *Albany International BV* v. *Stichting Bedrijfspensioenfonds Tetielindustrie*, judgment of 21 September 1999. See also Joined Cases C-180–184/98 *Pavlov* pending. See T Hervey, "'Social Solidarity': A Buttress Against Internal Market Law?" in J Shaw (ed.), *Social Law and Policy in An Evolving European Union* (Oxford, Hart Publishing, 2000).

[14] Article 49 TEU.

[15] Article 7 TEU.

[16] Article 6 TEU 1. states that "The Union is founded on the principles of liberty, democracy, respect for human rights and fundamental freedoms, and the rule of law, principles which are common to the member states". Paragraph 2 states further: "The Union shall respect fundamental rights, as guaranteed by the European Convention for the Protection of Human Rights and Fundamental freedoms signed in Rome on 4 November 1950 and as they result from the constitutional traditions common to the Member States, as general principle of Community law".

market the Court has been unwilling to find a breach of Community fundamental rights.[17] This led to the conclusion by Coppell and O'Neil[18] that the Court has not taken fundamental rights seriously. Their argument is that whenever there is a conflict between the principles of market integration and fundamental rights or values,[19] market integration takes precedence.

The Court has attempted to diffuse the stark "sovereignty versus supremacy" conflict which fundamental values cases create. One device has to been to refocus the legal discourse from a hierarchical to a pluralist notion of a Community legal order. This has utilised a neutral device: the concept of "Community interest". Recent analytical work has focused upon this notion. In the context of the free trade value Poiares Maduro, in a major contribution to the constitutional debate, has focused upon the Court's choices and constraints to describe the normative application of Article 28 EC. He has argued for review of national regulatory processes where there is a suspicion of representative malfunction in the national political process with regard to nationals of other Member States.[20] The core of Poiares Maduro's thesis is that the political rights of participation and representation of European citizens in national political processes can be protected by asking the Court to review Member State measures which have effectively excluded them from these processes. This essay explores some aspects of this thesis in the light of recent case law and the litigation emerging in relation to the regulation of state activity in the market.

3. COMMUNITY INTEREST AS A NEUTRAL VALUE

Until recently, the analysis of the role of law in European integration seemed almost a set piece for piano practice: easy tasks are set for the Court of Justice, progressing on to the hard pieces. The same old tune was being hammered out, occasionally there was the note that jarred, but the tune was fundamentally familiar. Dismantling pervasive trade barriers *was a good thing*; a fundamental value of the Common/Internal Market. Free trade or dismantling trade barriers in order to create the conditions for free trade has become a mantra for the European integration project with little analysis of what it is as a fundamental value. One explanation for this is the use of law as a seemingly neutral tool:

[17] See for example, Case 44/79 *Hauer* v. *Land Rheinland-Pfalz* [1979] ECR 3727.

[18] J Coppel and A O'Neill, "The Court of Justice: Taking Rights Seriously?" (1992) 29 *Common Market Law Review* 669.

[19] A similar argument can be made in relation to the notion of "imperative requirements". For example in Case C-341/95 *Gianni Bettati* v. *Safety Hi-Tech Srl* [1998] ECR I-4355 the Court states that the protection of the environment is already considered by the Court to be one of the essential objectives of the Community, an imperative requirement which may limit the application of Article 28 EC, but is reluctant to find such a breach in relation to the Community legislation at issue.

[20] *We. The Court* (Oxford, Hart Publishing, 1998).

law has become a technical, almost serviant tool in the European integration project. The Court of Justice, which has played a central role in the direction of the European integration project, has enhanced this role for law and fostered the neutrality of the integration project by its own appeal to free trade as a fundamental value in European law as well as free trade being an essential constituent to the logic of market integration.

The Court has also appealed to lawyers and politicians as to the impartiality of judicial reasoning by resort to the device of the rule of law. The ruling in *Les Verts*[21] is repeated like a mantra by students of EU law but also by politicians willing to hand over disputes over trade issues to the independent arbiters of the Internal Market – the Commission and the Court. Thus the constitution built by the Court provides an appealing image of neutrality. The function of the constitution is merely to construct procedures and institutions to facilitate market integration whereby all actors are subject to the same rules.

4. ALTERING THE 1957 CONTRACT

The appeal of the neutrality of law in European integration – as well as the role of the two prime "independent" institutions which administer it, the Commission and the Court, can be explained by a simple functionalist argument. The contract struck in 1957 reflected in the Preambular statements and provisions of the Treaty of Rome 1957 contain a simple term: Member States calculate that the gains to be derived from creating a Common/Internal Market exceed the costs. By creating the neutral arbiters of the Commission and the Court the strength of the credibility of the Member States' commitment to the Common/Internal Market is assured.[22]

The 1957 bargain has been altered in a number of ways. First, by the Court's interpretation of the fundamental freedoms as fundamental *values* of the European integration project. Secondly, by limiting the role of defences/justifications as *derogations* which must be interpreted restrictively and in accordance with the principle of proportionality. The original Treaty envisaged conflicts to arise over Member States' fundamental values and for Member States to retain some autonomy in sensitive areas. A major weakness of the Treaty derogations is that they have not been revised *at the Treaty level* since 1957. This has led to manipulation by the Court[23] and the extension of the permissible derogations through

[21] Case 294/83 *Parti Ecologiste "Les Verts"* v. *European Parliament* [1986] ECR 1339.

[22] See for example, A Moravcsik, "Preferences and Power in the European Community: A Liberal Intergovernmentalist Approach" (1993) 31 *Journal of Common Market Studies* 473.

[23] For example, by finding that formal discriminatory measures are not caught by Community law by reason of the mandatory requirement interests they pursue: See Case 113/80 *Commission* v. *Ireland* [1982] ECR 1625, paras. 9ff.; Case C-2/90 *Commission* v. *Ireland* [1992] ECR I-4433. See M Poiares Maduro, "The Saga of Article 30: To Be Continued" (1998) 5 *Maastricht Journal* 298, 311.

case law, seen in the development of the "mandatory requirements doctrine" developed from *Dassonville*[24] and *Cassis*[25] in the area of free movement of goods and applied to other areas of free movement, most notably services. We are beginning to see a blurring of the distinctions between distinctly applicable and indistinctly applicable trade barriers and the appropriate justifications which may be raised by a Member State.[26]

The Court has relied upon the principle of proportionality to justify the free trade value and has added Community fundamental values to the set of criteria by which a Member State's trade restriction must be justified.[27] Poiares Maduro welcomes this development :

> The granting of broad discretionary powers by the European Court of Justice to national courts in reviewing national breaches of Community fundamental rights is laudable and may serve as an example of co-operation with national courts to be extended to other areas.[28]

But, by casting fundamental values which a Member State wants to uphold as *derogations*, the value of free trade as the norm cannot be questioned. According to Paul:

> The assumption of market normalcy is implicit in the European Court of Justice's landmark judgment in *Dassonville*. The Court's treated the market as the normal state which exists prior to the distortion of national laws.[29]

A third way in which this bargain has been altered is the *policing* of the Common/Internal Market. Arguably the 1957 deal allowed the Member States to take a gamble and to choose to ignore decisions of the Commission/Court they felt threatened by. Collectively they could re-interpret or reverse adverse decisions by Treaty amendment. This unspoken understanding was shattered by the Court using the concepts of direct effect and supremacy and their more penetrative effects to invade the defences of the domestic sphere of competence in the domain of remedies. The Court has not been able to pierce this defence totally but the principle has been made. At Maastricht the Member States themselves also placed greater emphasis on realising the Internal Market project in Article 238 EC by introducing the concept of fining a recalcitrant Member State for failing to obey a Court ruling. This, combined with the threat of *Francovich*[30] type actions where a Court ruling may be *prima facie* evidence of a

[24] Case 8/74 [1974] ECR 837.

[25] Case 120/78 [1979] ECR 649.

[26] See Case C-34–36/95 *De Agostini* [1997] ECR I-3843; Case C-120/95 *Decker* [1998] ECR I-1831; Case C-158/96 *Kohll* [1998] ECR I-1931.

[27] Case C-260/89 *ERT* v. *Dimotki Etairia Pliroforissis and Sotirius Kouvelas* [1991] ECR I-2925; Case C-368/95 *Vereinigte Familiapress* v. *Heinrich Baur Verlag* [1997] ECR I-3689.

[28] *Supra* n. 20, at p. 314. See J Weiler, "The Constitution of the Common Market Place" in P Craig and G De Búrca (eds.), *The Evolution of EU Law* (Oxford, OUP, 1999), p. 371.

[29] J Paul, "Free Trade, Regulatory Competition and the Autonomous Market Fallacy" (1994/5) 1 *Columbia Journal of European Law* 29, 39.

[30] Case C-6 &9/90 [1991] ECR I-5357.

Member State's culpability, has raised the stakes of membership of the original free trade club.

The neutral arbiters of the 1957 project have also changed the discourse of European integration. The original Treaty suggested that the Commission should play a pivotal role in the policing of European law between the Member States. The Court, in collusion with the Commission, has encouraged the use of preliminary rulings (Article 234 EC) from the national courts at the expense of the more confrontational infringement action of Article 226 EC. Preliminary rulings are ingenious devices.[31] They create a Community of European Courts, ostensibly seeking two (neutral) aims: to seek a proper interpretation of Community law and to apply the rule of (Community) law through national processes. Hidden behind this smokescreen of neutrality the Court of Justice is able to control the legal agenda. To control not only the Court's own jurisdiction but also the jurisdiction or reach of Community law. Examples of this process are seen in the discussions over the limits of Article 28 EC and the debate over whether the issue of "reverse discrimination" should be tackled in the Internal Market.

5. CONFLICTS OF VALUES AND THE REGULATION OF THE INTERNAL MARKET

The conflict over values and competences within the Common/Internal Market has occurred throughout the history of Community law but has become more problematic in recent years over the necessity to maintain the dynamic of the Internal Market programme. The Commission has sought to diffuse the clash over fundamental values by appeals to technocratic and bureaucratic regulation or management of the Internal Market.[32] A more aggressive side is seen, for example, in the "name and shame" policy in developing the Internal Market scoreboard and the Commission's repeated threats – which have been put into practice – to initiate more infringement actions against the Member States in the period after 1992.

The regulation or management of the Internal Market has now entered new territory. Regulation 2679/98[33] increased the Commission's powers, and the Member States' *duty*, to ensure free trade in the Internal Market. The

[31] See G F Mancini, "The Making of a Constitution for Europe" (1989) 26 *Common Market Law Review* 595. Contrast the criticisms of the Court's tougher approach to admissibility: D O'Keeffe, "Is the Spirit of Article 177 [234] under Attack? Preliminary References and Admissibility" (1998) 23 *European Law Review* 509.

[32] See for example, *Action Plan for the Single Market* CSE (97)1 final; Decision 3052/95/EC on the exchange of information on national measures derogating from the principle of free movement of goods, OJ 1995 L 321/1. Directive 83/189/EEC, OJ 1983 L109/8 is an earlier example of the Commission's "management" strategy.

[33] Of 7 December 1998 on the functioning of the internal market in relation to the free movement of goods among the Member States OJ 1998 L 337/8, 12 December 1998.

background to the Regulation lies in an infringement action taken against France.[34] For several years the Commission had warned France that she was in breach of her obligations under the Treaty of Rome for failing to take action against farmers and other interest groups who had interfered with the free movement of goods by blockades, strikes and other forms of political/industrial action. The Court upheld the Commission's complaint stating that France's efforts to intervene in such disputes were manifestly inadequate to ensure freedom of intra-Community trade. France was in breach of Articles 10 and 28 EC by failing to take appropriate action to ensure the free movement of goods.

Very quickly after this ruling the Commission published a proposal for a Regulation "creating a mechanism whereby the Commission can intervene in order to remove certain obstacles to trade".[35] The final version of the Regulation defines an obstacle to the free movement of goods as one which leads to a serious disruption of the free movement of goods "by physically or otherwise preventing, delaying or diverting, export, import or transport into, from or across a Member State, causes serious loss to individuals affected and requires immediate action in order to prevent, increase or intensify the disruption or loss in question".[36] The Member State must inform the Commission when an obstacle to free trade occurs (or even the threat of such an obstacle), the Commission will then facilitate an exchange of information between the Member States of the threat, or perceived threat, to free trade and of the measures taken by the Member State to counteract it.[37] Article 4 sets out the duty upon Member States to "take all necessary and proportionate measures" so that the free movement of goods is assured. Details of the action should be transmitted to the Commission which will disseminate it around the Member States. Where a Member State fails to appreciate that an obstacle to trade has occurred it will inform the Member State concerned and request the Member State ". . . to take all necessary and proportionate measures to remove the said obstacle" to free trade.[38]

An obvious fundamental clash of values here is the balance of the principle of free trade over the fundamental rights of freedom to strike, or to take other forms of action. In some Member States this is a guaranteed fundamental right.[39] The Regulation recognises this clash of fundamental values in its Preamble and also in Article 2:

> This Regulation may not be interpreted as affecting in any way the exercise of fundamental rights as recognised in member states, including the right or freedom to

[34] Case C-325/91 *Commission* v. *France* [1997] ECR I-6959.
[35] OJ 1998 C 10/14 , 15 January 1998.
[36] Article 1.
[37] Article 3.
[38] Article 5.
[39] Collective labour law rights in terms of freedom of association and associated rights attached

strike. These rights may also include the right or freedom to strike. These rights may also include the right or freedom to take other actions covered by the specific industrial relations systems in Member States.

The ruling in *Commission* v. *France*[40] and the new Regulation raise the prospect of a Member State being liable for damages for breach of Community law. This in itself raises fundamental value issues of whether the State should be liable for acts of third parties. Even more contentious, as *R* v. *Chief Constable of Sussex, ex parte International Traders Ferry Ltd*[41] has revealed, is that the Community courts will "become even more entangled in policy debates concerning budgetary appropriations, the allocation of scarce resources and public order measures which affect the free movement of goods or another fundamental Community right."[42]

6. CONFLICTS OF VALUES AND THE MAINTENANCE OF THE INTERNAL MARKET

The conflict of values has occurred in the Court's aggressive interpretation of the fundamental freedoms necessary to maintain an Internal Market. The analysis of perceived and alleged barriers to free trade has drawn the neutrality of the Commission and the Court into the political and constitutional arena, particularly where the expansion of the fundamental freedoms has challenged the social, cultural and political values of the Member States. The Court's appeal to neutrality and the presentation of an image of impartiality by constructing an image of the "market" weaves an impregnable defence around the Court: it provides a defence against allegations of a Supreme Court.[43] By appealing to free trade and within that concept a freedom *to trade* as an (economic) fundamental value the Court avoids conflicts over fundamental values which may be held in the Member States.[44]

to trade union activity may also be part of the fundamental values recognised in Community law as a result of either the constitutional traditions common to the Member States or international obligations. See for example, the ILO Declaration of 1998 on fundamental principles and rights. The Court has ruled that all international human rights treaties which are signed by the Member States or even those on which they have collaborated can provide guidelines which should be followed in Community law: Case 4/73 *Nold* v. *Commission* [1974] ECR 491. This would bring the ILO and the Social Charter into the framework of Community law fundamental rights principles. For an application of this approach see the Opinion of Advocate General Jacobs in Case C- 67/96 *Albany International*, *28* January 1999.

[40] *Supra* n. 34.

[41] [1999] 1 All ER 129.

[42] K Muylle, "Angry Farmers and Passive Policemen: Private Conduct and the Free Movement of Goods" (1998) 23 *European Law Review* 467, 474.

[43] For a discussion of the Court's formal reasoning see M Poiares Maduro, *We. The Court op.cit.* ch.1.

[44] The classic case in this respect is Case C-159/90 *SPUC* v. *Grogan* [1991] ECR I-4685. See S O'Leary, "The Court of Justice as a Reluctant Constitutional Adjudicator" (1992) 17 *European Law Review* 138. *Cf.* Case 379/87 *Groener* v. *Minister for Education* [1989] ECR 3967.

Two cases show the haphazard way choices can be made in determining free trade values at the expense of other fundamental values. In *Compassion in World Farming Limited*[45] an action was brought by Compassion in World Farming Limited challenging a decision by the Minister to refuse to restrict, on the basis of Article 30 EC (the protection of animal health) the export of veal calves from the United Kingdom to other Member States. Council Directive 78/923/EEC[46] had been adopted implementing The European Convention on the Protection of Animals Kept for Farming Purposes which had been adopted within the framework of the Council of Europe. It was alleged by CWF that some Member States did not implement the European Convention correctly.

The Court applied a well-established principle that where the matter was governed by Community rules they must be applied, and that where the export of goods was concerned the principle of mutual trust required reliance on other Member States to ensure that necessary checks and procedures were followed.[47] CWF also argued that other heads of Article 30 EC might be used by the UK. They argued that a section of national public opinion believed that the system put in place by the Directive did not adequately protect animal health. The Court countered this argument with:

> . . . so in reality, public policy and public morality are not being invoked as a separate justification but are an aspect of the justification relating to the protection of animal health, which is the subject of the harmonising Directive.[48]

The Court stated that in any event a Member State cannot rely upon the views and behaviour of a section of national public opinion in order to unilaterally change a harmonising measure adopted by the Community Institutions. The real reason[49] for the ruling is found in paragraph 44:

> . . . a ban on the export of calves would, as the United Kingdom has pointed out, affect the structure of the market and, in particular, would have a considerable impact on the formation of market prices, which would interfere with the proper functioning of the common organisation of the market.

This ruling might be compared with that in *Ditlev Bluhme*.[50] A Danish law provides that only Læso Brown bees may be kept on the island of Læso and certain neighbouring islands. The legislation also prohibits the importation of live domestic bees (or reproductive material from them) on to these islands. Bluhme was prosecuted for keeping bees on Læso other than the permitted

45 Case C-1/96 [1998] ECR I- 1251.

46 OJ 1978 L323/12.

47 Case C-5/94 *The Queen* v. *MAFF, ex parte Hedley Lomas* [1996] ECR I-2553.

48 Para. 66.

49 Another, unarticulated reason, for the outcome of this case is the Court's reluctance to encourage the use of Article 234 EC to circumvent the standing and time limits in the judicial review clauses of the Treaty.

50 Case C-67/97 [1998] ECR I-8033.

variety. Bluhme argued that the measure was a restriction/hindrance of trade and contrary to Article 28 EC. The Court agreed. But in the absence of harmonising measures at the Community level national law could continue to apply. The national law was defended by the Court. It was designed to preserve an indigenous animal population with distinct characteristics and contributed to the maintenance of biodiversity by ensuring the survival of the population of bees concerned.

The measure was deemed to be proportionate since the Læso bee was in danger of disappearing as a result of cross-breeding with the Golden Bee. The establishment of the protection area was an appropriate aim. Applying Poiares Maduro's thesis we see the weakness in its application beyond a purely normative tool. Foreign traders in competing goods were totally excluded from the Danish market and were given few rights to participate in the democratic processes on reviewing the proportionality of the measures taken. It was a pragmatic economic judgment taken by the Court, and by the nature of Article 234 EC, the discourse over participatory rights was controlled by a dialogue between judges and the lawyers of the Member States and the Commission.

It is trite to compare the two cases in this way. The comparison is made deliberately to make the point that Article 234 EC and Article 226 EC procedures, in their current form, are not the most appropriate vehicles to conduct the conception of "new forms of constitutional relationships between public power and the economy".[51] If the question was asked differently, as a question about fundamental values: what is a fundamental value for European society, the protection of an endangered species or the protection of veal calves on their way to slaughter? Surely the majority of European citizens would reply "both"? For many people neither are *competing* values which can or *should* be traded against another value – that of free trade. In *Bluhme* the protection of Læso bees could be salvaged because the creation of a Community market was not necessary and the Community interest was managed by the Court. In *CWF* veal calves could not be saved from degrading treatment because the matter had been handled by the Community "constitutional" process. This suggests that there is more to the constitutional debate than admitting excluded voices to market access. It may require courts to make value judgments about the way the *Community interest* intervenes in the market through non-democratic processes.

7. THE ROLE OF NON-STATE ACTORS IN THE NEW CONSTITUTIONALISM

A distinctive feature of the Community system is the harnessing of non-state actors into the enforcement arm of the Community. One issue which needs to

[51] Poiares Maduro, *We. The Court*, *op. cit.*, p. 175.

be addressed in developing a new constitutionalism is the multi-level composition of the European polity whereby the power of the most powerful actors on the EU plane can co-exist with the critical role played by non-state actors. In the shaping of the notion of "free trade" as a fundamental value of Community law non-state actors have wittingly been influential in developing the discourse. From the earliest of cases the Court sent out a message about a fundamental value inherent within the Treaty system. The use of the concepts of direct effect, and later indirect effect and state liability actions have been viewed as empowering *economic* actors to challenge the legitimacy of national laws within the Community legal order often in situations which would not be legally feasible in the national arena.[52]

Until recently, critical attention has not been addressed to the process whereby Community law has used individual economic actors in an instrumental way. Most of the literature tends to focus upon the way litigants use Community law for their own ends.[53] Poiares Maduro's work makes the link between litigation and the developing constitution:

> . . . as formal constitutions are mainly a product of the representation and participation in the political process, so too is the European Constitution, to a large extent, a result of participation and representation in the European judicial process.[54]

The use of individual economic actors is seen as empowering Community law with its own special magic. The magic worked *in Van Gend en Loos* [55] has been spun and re-spun. From 1962 onwards the use of direct effect, in conjunction with preliminary references, was the preferred approach endorsed by the Commission and a judicial willingness to forego a hierarchical relationship with national courts but to create a "gentleman's club atmosphere" of mutual understanding, goodwill and spirit of co-operation.[56] Article 226 EC was confrontational. The Commission, given its limited resources, had to make choices about which infringement actions were worth pursuing. The Court had a limited choice. A Member State was either in breach of Community law or it was

[52] See Case C-213/89 *R* v. *Secretary of State for Transport, ex parte Factortame* [1990] ECR I-2433; *Factortame Ltd* v. *Secretary of State For Transport* (No.2) [1991] 1 AC 603.

[53] See for example, A-M Burley and W Mattli, "Europe Before the Court: A Political Theory of Legal Integration" (1993) 47 *International Organisation* 41; C Harlow, "A Community of Interests? Making the Most of European Law" (1992) 55 *MLR* 331; R Rawlings, "The Eurolaw Game: Some Deductions From a Saga" (1993) 20 *Journal of Law and Society* 309; M Poiares Maduro, *We. The Court, op.cit.*, p. 29.

[54] *We. The Court, op. cit.*, p. 28.

[55] Case 26/62 [1963] ECR 1.

[56] It is easy to describe the process of judicial accommodation; much harder to explain its legitimacy. See the work carried out by K Alter, "Explaining National Court Acceptance of European Court Jurisprudence: A Critical Evaluation of Theories of Legal Integration" in A-M Slaughter, A Stone Sweet and J Weiler (eds.), *The European Courts and National Courts: Doctrine and Jurisprudence: Legal Change in its Social Context* (Oxford, Hart Publishing, 1998); D Chalmers, "Judicial Preferences and The Community Legal Order" (1997) 60 *Modern Law Review* 165.

not.[57] In contrast, Article 234 EC offers a breathing space; a chance to diffuse a clash of fundamental values often by resort to the principle of proportionality, leaving this principle to the national court to apply. It has also become the vehicle by which the Court has been able to create a discourse about the nature of the Community legal order and drive home messages about Community fundamental values.[58]

This use of the vigilance of individual actors to constrain the behaviour of the Member States has also had the effect of strengthening the enforcement of Community law at the national level. This process has been re-spun in the era of the development of an Internal Market by developing ideas of the availability of remedies against Member States for failing to comply with Community law.

The use of private actors in this way is problematic. We see that cases come before the Court in distinctive ways. Some litigation is random; other cases are part of a "repeat player" concerted action to use Community law to re-shape national (democratic) processes. Such repeat players are not neutral actors but players with political interests and resources. The classic example is, of course, the most fundamental free trade case of all, *Cassis de Dijon*.[59] Using the legal process to promote self-interest against fundamental values of the Member States raises questions which need to be addressed in the development of a new constitutionalism if this is to offer an alternative form of legitimacy for European law and its relationship with national law and democracy.[60]

In relation to Article 28 EC the floodgates of litigation were blown open by the rulings in *Dassonville*[61] and *Cassis*.[62] The ensuing litigation was often contradictory in terms of reasoning and outcomes. This provoked a crisis in the role of law and Courts to promote market integration. The use of private actors has, therefore, been analysed in a positive light to promote integration from below or negative integration.[63] But the corresponding reflex is a process of deregulation at the Member State level. This in turn creates regulatory gaps and has disintegrative effects when the paternalist/protectionist role played by the

[57] The Court can and does take a more nuanced approach. In the greater use made of Article 226 EC since 1992 the Court may find a breach of Community law in principle but may decide that the Commission has not offered up enough facts to prove the case. See for example, the utilities infringement action: Case C-157/94 *Commission* v. *Netherlands* [1997] ECR I-5699.

[58] See T de la Mare, "Article 177 in Social and Political Context" in Craig and De Búrca (eds.), *op. cit.* (1999).

[59] See Alter and Meunier-Aitsahalia's work arguing that Cassis was selected as a test case to provoke harmonisation of the alchohol industry: "Judicial Politics in the European Community – European Integration and the Pathbreaking Cassis de Dijon Decision" (1994) 26 *Comparative Political Studies* 535.

[60] Poiares Maduro, *op. cit.*

[61] Case 8/74 *Procureur du Roi* v. *Benoit and Dassonville* [1974] ECR 837.

[62] Case 120/78 *Rewe-Zentrale AG* v. *Budesmonopolverwaltung für Branntwein* [1979] ECR 649.

[63] The extreme version is the Ordoliberal view of the economic constitution which would rely upon market actors to define the rules of operation of the market without further interference from the State: See M E Streit and W Mussler, "The Economic *Constitution* of the European Community: From 'Rome' to Maastricht" (1995) 1 *European Law Journal* 5.

modern nation state in relation to fundamental national values such as consumer protection, environmental concerns, protection of certain groups within society, is not replaced by Community standards.[64] The idea of "home state control" which emerged from *Cassis* may have disintegrative effects when Community law replaces Member States' fundamental values.

The use of private actor enforcement can be disintegrative of fundamental values in other ways. The unity of a fundamental value in Community law can be lost in the disunity of national remedies. Leaving the application of the justification for the trade barrier and principle of proportionality to the national courts to apply may result in different outcomes. Direct effect re-creates the problem it seeks to resolve.

Disintegration can also occur in the use of litigation to challenge national laws in the name of free trade. By cherry-picking at individual instances of a trade barrier, rulings of the Court may destroy the coherence and balance of national policies particularly where judgments have been made on the balance between fundamental values and economic policy. An example of this is in *TV-Shop I Sverige AB and De Agostini*[65] where fundamental values shared in Swedish society, of protecting consumers and the interests of young children, were challenged by the free trade value. *TV Shop* concerned an action brought by the Swedish consumer ombudsman over misleading advertising. De Agostini, a Swedish company belonging to an Italian group, Istituto Geografico De Agostini, whose main economic activity was publishing magazines, advertised on the Swedish TV channels a magazine it published called "Everything About Dinosaurs!". This magazine had been sold and marketed in all the Member States since 1993 but it offended Swedish values in its marketing tactics; children were encouraged to buy the magazine on a bi-weekly basis in order to collect the constituent parts of a model dinosaur and ultimately to build up an encyclopaedic knowledge of dinosaurs. The situation was governed by a Community Directive on broadcasting which set out home state control principles.[66] A Member State could only suspend the re-transmission of television broadcasts under a limited set of circumstances enumerated in the Directive. The reaction to the issue by the Court was the classic distaste for placing double burdens on providers of services:

> If provisions of the receiving state regulating the content of television broadcasts for reasons relating to the protection of minors against advertising were applied to broadcasts from other Member States, this would add a secondary control to the control which the broadcasting Member State must exercise under the Directive.[67]

[64] F Scharpf, "Negative and Positive Integration in the Political Economy of European Welfare States" in G Marks (ed.), *Governance in the European Union* (London, Sage, 1996).

[65] Joined Cases C-34/95, C-35/95 and C-36/95, *Konsummentombudsmannen (KO) and De Agostini (Svenska) Förlag AB* [1997] ECR I-3843.

[66] Directive 89/552/EEC, OJ 1989 L 298/23.

[67] Para. 61.

The Court did state that a Member State could protect consumers against misleading advertising provided that the measures did not prevent the re-transmission in its territory of broadcasts coming from other Member States. A Member State may justify restrictions on advertising provided that they meet overriding requirements of public interest or one of the aims set out in either Article 30 EC or 46 EC and are proportionate and could not be achieved by other means which were less restrictive of trade. These factors, or justifications, should be applied by the national court. However, the Court ruled that Directive 89/552/EEC precluded a domestic law restricting advertising from applying to broadcasts from other Member States. Now there is an incentive for advertisers to advertise on broadcasts from another Member State, most notably the United Kingdom and Denmark, where similar rules do not exist. Short of banning their children from watching such programmes there is little that Swedish parents can do to protect a value which was regarded as fundamental in Swedish society.

A second case from Sweden goes to the very heart of Nordic values. It was also the subject of private action, a provoked prosecution. In *Franzén*[68] the system of regulation of the production and consumption of alcohol in Sweden was at stake. Under a law, which had been adapted to comply with Sweden's accession to the EU, the production and marketing of alcohol could only take place under a licence provided by an Alcohol inspectorate. A special state company, Systembolaget, wholly owned by the Swedish State was responsible for the retail of alcohol. Franzén was prosecuted for intentionally selling, without a licence, wine purchased from the Systembolaget or imported from Denmark. In defence he pleaded that the Swedish system was contrary to Articles 28 and 31 EC.

In relation to the jurisprudence on the free movement of goods the Swedish rules were indistinctly applicable, *Cassis de Dijon* type rules, which applied to *exports* and imports of alcohol in the Swedish market. They were not compositional rules and, on an application of *Keck*,[69] would not necessarily fall within the scope of Article 28 EC. Advocate General Elmer[70] argued that the Swedish rules were caught by Articles 28 and 31 EC and that these rules may be applied concurrently. The Advocate General found that the Swedish alcohol monopoly discriminated against traders and made market access difficult for foreign products from other Member States. It could not be justified under Article 30 EC since it did not satisfy tests of proportionality and necessity. The Court, in contrast, differentiated between Articles 28 and 31 EC. The monopoly was compatible with the Treaty under Article 31 EC. It found that it was uncontested that the Swedish alcohol monopoly pursued a public interest aim

[68] Case C-189/95 [1997] ECR I-5909.

[69] *Supra* n. 9.

[70] The intervening Governments of France, Finland, Norway – as well as the Commission were of the opinion that *Keck* did apply.

and that it was organised in such a way as to comply with the provisions of Article 31 EC.

The perspective of the Court is that of a competition perspective:

> . . . Article 31 EC requires that the organisation and operation of the monopoly be arranged so as to exclude any discrimination between nationals of member states as regards conditions of supply and outlets, so that trade in goods from other member states is not put at an disadvantage, in law or in fact, in relation to that in domestic goods and that competition between the economies of the member states is not distorted.[71]

It would have been difficult to strike down the alcohol monopoly under Article 31 EC since it had been the subject of political negotiation before Sweden's accession and to dismantle it would have distorted trade between the Nordic countries. What is striking is the Court's willingness to follow the Advocate General and find that the monopoly infringed the rules on free trade notwithstanding that the rules were *marketing* rules. Even more far-reaching is the effect of this finding, unarticulated in the case, that the Court was applying the principles of *Cassis* to the *internal production and marketing of products* in the home state, thus destroying one of the fundamental pillars for the application of *Cassis*: home state control. The Court spent very little time analysing Article 30 EC merely stating that the Swedish Government had not proven the proportionality principle.

Franzén is an example of how Poiares Maduro's thesis may work. Foreign competitors and traders were virtually closed out of the Swedish system. In order to comply with the ruling of the Court the Swedish Government has maintained the licensing system but made it easier to obtain licences by reducing the amount of the licence. Thus freedom to trade has been vindicated and a fundamental value of Swedish society remains intact.

8. FREE TRADE AS A MANTRA FOR ECONOMIC DUE PROCESS

We have begun to see how the use of private actors in the creation of a discourse about free trade as a fundamental value of the EU can be disintegrative of national fundamental values. The Court has found itself overwhelmed by the plurality of voices repeating its own mantra but creating conflicting values. The constitutional dilemma facing the Court is explained by Advocate General Tesauro in *Hünermund*:

> Is Article [28] of the Treaty a provision intended to liberalise intra-Community trade or is it intended more generally to encourage the unhindered pursuit of commerce in individual Member States?

[71] Para. 40.

Poiares Maduro discusses the difference between the two values. The first provides a dynamic whereby the subtle and pervasive non-tariff barriers to trade may be constantly assessed and re-assessed. The second goes further. According to Poiares Maduro it transforms Article 28 EC into an "economic due process clause". It is formulated around a particular conception of the Economic Constitution of the EU based upon the free market, open competition and a particular view of the kinds of regulation that are acceptable.[72] The latter assumes a role for law in the Internal Market which can assess state intervention in the market.

The development of an economic due process approach is seen in a shift from a focus upon litigation around the four freedoms where the Court is arguably restricting its own role – but not the role of law – to a rule of reason approach leaving the application of the proportionality defence to national courts. Now we see the application of the fundamental principles of the Internal Market in a more open confrontation with the regulation of state activity in competitive markets. The agnosticism of Article 295 EC[73] has been challenged fundamentally and as Sauter and Devroe have argued it is not only constraints that have been placed upon Member State action but also the promotion, *through law* and *legal processes*, of the fundamental values of liberalisation, deregulation and privatisation.[74]

Since 1987 the Internal Market project directed by the Commission has focused upon the abolition of the pervasive non-tariff barriers to trade which are exercised at the discretion of the Member States. There has been an increased willingness on the part of the Commission and the Court to subject state activity to competitive market principles. This is seen in the interest in improving the effectiveness of the procurement rules, tougher monitoring of state aid and the use of Article 31 EC and 86 EC to scrutinise state involvement in the market. We see a similar combination of Commission enforcement and encouragement of private actors to make the application of Community law effective with the Court taking a more aggressive approach to free trade using the fundamental values of the Internal Market project as well as the competition rules to regulate state intervention in the market.[75] The original Treaty provisions were agnostic about the public/private mix of the national economies. This agnosticism has been challenged by the Court's use of Community law, particularly the use of Article 86 EC, to challenge the operation of state

[72] *We. The Court, op cit* at p. 60.

[73] Article 295 states: "The Treaty shall in no way prejudice the rules in the Member States governing the system of property ownership".

[74] W Sauter, "Universal Service Obligations and the Emergence of Citizens' Rights in European Telecommunications Liberalisation" in M Freedland and S Sciarra (eds.), *Public Services and Citizenship in European Law* (Oxford, Clarendon Press, 1998); W Devroe, "Privatizations and Community Law: Neutrality versus Policy" (1997) 34 *Common Market Law Review* 267.

[75] See U Neergaard, *Competition & Competences, The Tensions between European Competition Law and Anti-Competitive Measures by the* Member *States* (Copenhagen, DJØF Publishing, 1998).

monopolies. This in turn has brought about a fundamental change in the economic regulation and values of the supply of public goods in the market. Petretto has argued:

> Entry to the European Union automatically implies acceptance of the concept lying at the roots of its "economic constitution": the developing of competition by means of widespread liberalisation processes in the industrial sectors. The aim of this process is the gaining of the advantages associated with free competition between agents – in terms of innovation, cost minimization, price containment, and a high level of quality – independently of the private or public ownership of the enterprises operating in single markets. This therefore means liberalisation, with or without privatization, above all in the basic sectors producing public-utility services such as telecommunications, energy, transport, and water supply.[76]

In *Centre d'insemination de la Crespelle* v. *Cooperative de la mayenne*[77] the Court of Justice upheld the principle that the mere creation of a dominant position by the grant of exclusive rights will not normally infringe Articles 86(1) and 81 EC, but stated that these Articles may be *exceptionally* infringed if in merely exercising the exclusive right granted to it, the undertaking in question could not avoid abusing its dominant position. The case law is difficult to classify. Edwards and Hoskins[78] have suggested that there are four different categories into which the judicial control of public monopolies can be allocated. These are first, the absolute sovereignty approach; second, the limited sovereignty approach; third, the absolute competition approach and fourth, the limited competition approach. They suggest that it is ultimately for the European Courts to determine how the balance should be made between the competing interests of market integration and national sovereignty.

Support for the limited sovereignty test and the limited competition test can be found in the Court's case law. Advocate General Jacobs, in his Opinion in *Albany*,[79] has classified the case law on Article 86 EC into three distinctive groups. In a series of cases the Court has subsequently found that exclusive rights have led inevitably to the undertaking abusing its dominant position.[80] In a different set of cases the Court has found that in situations where the State has done nothing more than grant exclusive rights the specific economic context and the nature of the services involved the undertaking placed in a dominant

[76] A Petretto, "The Liberalization and Privatization of Public Utilities and the Protection of Users' Rights: The Perspective of Economic Theory" in M Freedland and S Sciarra (eds.), *Public Services and Citizenship in European Law* (Oxford, OUP, 1997).

[77] Case C-323/93 [1994] ECR I-5077.

[78] "Competition Law Implications of Deregulation and Privatisation" (1995) 32 *Common Market Law Review* 157.

[79] *Supra* n. 39.

[80] Case C-260/89 *ERT* [1991] ECR I-2925; Case C-163/96 *Raso* [1998] ECR I-533; Case C-179/90 *Merci Convenzionali Porto di Genova* [1991] ECR I-5889. In *Raso* the Commission has suggested that the abuse does not have to be committed; the legislative framework may even hypothetically lead the undertakings to commit such abuses.

position could not avoid abusing that position.[81] In a third set of cases the Court has not identified exactly what particular features of the State's public monopoly/exclusive rights system infringed Article 86(1). Instead it automatically applied Article 86 (2) EC arguing that paragraphs (1) and (2) of Article 86 EC should be read together and a balancing process started on the justification of the scope of the monopoly.[82] Arguably there is no indication that an absolute sovereignty approach can be acceptable in Community law. The Court is consistent in ruling that the creation of public monopolies must always be balanced against the principles of Community competition law.[83] Equally the absolute competition approach cannot be acceptable since it is inconsistent with the presence of Article 86(2) EC.[84]

Despite the difficulties of classification the case law heralds a new era towards a more market-oriented public economy. In the face of this case law the Member States defended their positions, a reflex to market-orientated principles, in the new Article 16 of the Treaty and the Declaration in the Treaty[85] stating:

> . . . given the place occupied by services of general economic interest in the shared values of the Union as well as their role in promoting social and territorial cohesion, the Community and the Member States . . . shall take care that such services operate on the basis of principles and conditions which enable them to fulfil their missions.

This is a compromise text revealing that "There is no more stark exposure in the Treaty of the division . . . between those who wish to protect public utilities and those who wish to make them competitive".[86]

In Article 16 EC of the Treaty there is the reference to the *Community* interest and that of the Member States suggesting that there is scope for a *Community interest* to develop in the field of public goods.[87] In terms of respect for fundamental values the focus of attention is then again upon the defence or

[81] Case C-41/90 *Höfner and Elser* [1991] ECR I-1979; Case C-55/96 *Job Centre* [1997] ECR I-7119.

[82] Case C-320/91 *Corbeau* [1993] ECR I-2533; Case C-266/96 *Corsica Ferries France* [1998] ECR I-3949; Opinion of Advocate General Reischl Case 155/73 *Sacchi* [1974] ECR 409.

[83] See Case 202/88 *France* v. *Commission* [1990] ECR I-1223.

[84] For a fuller discussion of the case law see: L Hancher, "Community, State, and Market" in P Craig and G De Búrca (eds.), *op. cit.* (1999).

[85] The Declaration states that "The provisions of Article 16 . . . on public services shall be implemented with full respect for the jurisprudence of the Court of Justice, *inter alia* , as regards the principles of equality of treatment, quality and continuity of such services". There are further Declarations on Public Credit Institutions in Germany, Austria and Luxembourg. The French proposed a Declaration to protect gas and electricity and also to re-write Article 86 (2) EC to allow for positive discrimination in favour of the public sector. This was dropped.

[86] A Duff, *The Treaty of Amsterdam. Text and Commentary* (Federal Trust, London, 1997). See L Flynn, "Competition Policy and Public Services in EC law After the Maastricht and Amsterdam Treaties" in D O'Keeffe and P Twomey (eds.), *Legal Issues of the Amsterdam Treaty* (Oxford, Hart Publishing, 1999).

[87] See M Ross, "Article 16 EC and Services of General Interest: From Derogation to Obligation?" (2000) 25 *European Law Review* 22.

justification to a finding that a public monopoly may be infringing the Community rules. Member States' fundamental values may then be subject to Community fundamental values. In *Albany* Advocate General Jacobs explained the role of Article 86(2) EC:

> Article 86(2) EC seeks to reconcile the Member States' interest in using certain undertakings as an instrument of economic or social policy with the Community's interest in ensuring compliance with the rules on competition and the internal market. Since it is a provision permitting derogation from the Treaty rules it must be interpreted strictly.[88]

In the "guidelines" or factors offered to the national courts by Advocate General Jacobs in *Albany* he suggests that the national courts should be aware that the question of applying Article 86(2) EC is one of degree involving complex issues of economic and social choices. The national court's review is limited to systems which are manifestly inadequate but this is not where bad management or investment policy is involved. If this is taken as a generalised rule it suggests that Article 86(1) and (2) may not be as intrusive upon national autonomy as Article 28 EC has appeared to be in the past.[89]

9. CONCLUSION

As an emerging polity the European Union and the process of political, economic and monetary union has become a contested terrain. This essay has focused upon one fundamental value within this terrain: the fundamental value of free trade. It has been argued that free trade is projected by the Commission and the Court as a neutral fundamental value against which other values are measured and reviewed for their legality or compatibility with Community law. In its use of Article 86 EC we have seen the Court make a number of inroads into national fundamental values signalling the ability of Community law to invalidate national economic policies: Article 86 EC is capable of becoming an economic due process clause.

In relation to the fundamental freedoms, particularly goods and services, there is the potential for a similar normative development to occur but the "free trade at all costs" principle is tempered by an emerging rule of reason. Where a market has been closed down to foreign competition then the Court is demanding either a rigorous explanation for this barrier to free trade or expecting the Member State to open up *access* to its market to create a freedom to

[88] Case C-67/96 *Albany International BV* v. *Stichting Bedrijfspenensionenfonds Textielindustrie*, Opinion of 28 January 1999, para. 436.

[89] An alternative analysis of the *Albany* – type case is that the Court has developed a fourth derogation from the competition principle in the concept of social solidarity. See A Winterstein, "Nailing the Jellyfish: Social Security and Competition Law" (1999) *European Competition Law Review* 324.

trade. Cases such as *Keck*[90] and *Sodemare*[91] show that a Member State may command some regulatory autonomy on the host market. Advocate General Jacobs' Opinion in *Albany*[92] also suggests that the application of Article 86 EC may be tempered by a rule of reason. A similar analysis may be applied to the application of Article 31 EC in *Franzén.*[93]

Poiares Maduro's thesis offers us a useful normative understanding of the role of Article 28 EC – and how it could be applied to protect against national laws ". . . affecting interests not normally represented in national political process".[94] He argues that this test is a preferable test for *courts* to apply since it does not direct the court to review the degree of public intervention in the market. A court does not have to second guess national regulatory choices. This essay has explored issues which arise in considering fundamental values and their relationship with the wider meaning of free trade when it is taken as a fundamental value of the EU integration project. In so doing the essay has raised some points which require further thought and elaboration in the development of a new constitutionalism. The *CWF* case is part of a new set of problems which are emerging raising issues concerning possible restrictions on the right of exit from a Member State.[95] This is an area where easy solutions still remain elusive in the integration project. The logic of an Internal Market and free trade demands a certain degree of symmetry between market access and exit from the host and the home state. While both issues challenge Member State autonomy the Court has been reluctant, until *Franzén*, to make too many inroads into the regulation of the market within the home state. Poiares Maduro's thesis is not so easy to apply here since the exit cases tend to show the need to balance *national* rather than *Community* fundamental values against the right to free trade. *Franzén* is an example of how Poiares Maduro's thesis may cut across fundamental values of a Member State. It is argued that here we need a different approach if we want to salvage the principle of "home state control" or Member State autonomy over the production and marketing regulation of goods and services destined for the European Market. *Franzén* shows the extremes Poiares Maduro's thesis can take. *CWF* shows its limitations when applied to protecting non-market fundamental values.

[90] *Supra* n. 9.

[91] *Supra* n. 8.

[92] *Supra* n. 88.

[93] *Supra* n. 68. This is not necessarily the case in the rulings on gas and electricity utilities: Case C-157/94 *Commission* v. *Netherlands* [1997] ECR I-5699; Case C-158/94 *Commission* v. *Italy* [1997] ECR I-5699; Case C-159/94 *Commission* v. *France* [1997] ECR I-5789; Case C-160/94 *Commission* v. *Spain* [1997] ECR I-5851. Here the Court found infringements of Article 31 EC but not necessarily Article 86 EC. Article 31 EC provides no defence or justification.

[94] *We. The Court*, *op. cit.*, p. 173.

[95] See for example, Case C-415/93 *Bosman* [1995] ECR I-4921; Case C-275/92 *Schindler* [1994] ECR I-1039. In the national courts: *Attorney General* v. *X* [1992] CMLR 277; *R* v. *Human Fertilisation and Embryology Authority, ex parte Blood* [1997] 2 CMLR 591. Arguably the latter two cases pose greater problems in balancing free trade against fundamental values of a Member State. In both cases the national court did not make a reference to the Court of Justice.

CWF raises other issues. It shows how, when "Community interest" has taken hold, it becomes a fundamental value to be defended and it is difficult, if not impossible, for an individual trader or a pressure group (and here the pressure group had no economic interest to defend) to uphold conflicting fundamental values which may not even have any political attachment to a particular Member State's fundamental values but are regarded by some sections of society as shared values.

Finally, Poiares Maduro's thesis takes as given market access and the right to trade as a fundamental value. This in itself presumes equality of opportunity for all *market* citizens. Where the constitutional right is violated a court must then look to Article 30 EC and the other mandatory requirements justifications, as well as Community fundamental rights or Article 86(2) EC and now Article 16 EC to assess the fundamental values at stake. Increasingly the Court is asking national courts to fulfil this function through the tool of proportionality and relaxing the rigidity of the available justifications for a trade barrier by allowing for a wider range of Member States' fundamental values to be protected. But we see creeping into these justifications not just Member States' values but also *Community* values.[96] The formal mechanics of this process obscure the fact that value judgments are to be made on the political process through processes which are themselves inherently undemocratic.

Within the European Union citizens still look to governments as well as the courts to protect their interests and the interests of society but citizens are no longer assured that their interests will be respected in a market where the trader-citizen is sovereign.

[96] *Cf.* Case *C 368/95 Familiapress* [1997] ECR I-3689 and the new Article 16 EC discussed above with Case C-120/95 *Decker* [1997] ECR I-1831 and Case C-70/95 *Sodemare* [1997] ECR I-3395. The latter cases allow the Member States the autonomy to secure the financial balance of their social security systems and the organisation of welfare care provisions *over* the free trade value.

11

From Universal Sovereignty to Territorial Sovereignty- and Back? On the Flexibility of International Law as a Fundamental Value of the International Order

HARRY POST*

In what is usually assumed to be its original "raw" form sovereignty is taken to mean "summa potestas" or "summum imperium".[1] In seventeenth century international law, this supreme authority had already basically become translated into the omnipotence of the Prince and then, also, of the Prince's State as "sovereign" over a people and their resources. Problems arose as soon as more sophistication was asked for, notably in terms of the legitimacy of supreme authority. Sovereignty was supposed to be lodged either in the will of God, in the office of emperor or king, or, later again, it became located in the will of the people. Matters were further complicated when the role of international law as a universal system for order and justice was taken into account.

In sixteenth and seventeenth century Europe, when much of the foundations of international law as we know it now were formed, the medieval battle between the claims to supreme authority of pope and emperor, both vested in

* I am very grateful to Ige F Dekker for his invaluable comments on a first draft of this text.

[1] Notably in Grotius (cf. Hugo Grotius, *De iure belli ac pacis libri tres*, vol. ii, ch. 1. para. 16; from the 1646 ed. as reproduced in: *The Classics of International Law*, no. 3, Washington, 1913, vol. I, also Francis W Kelsey, *et al.*, A Translation of the Text, *ibid.*, volume II. Also: Arthur Nussbaum, *A Concise History of the Law of Nations*, rev. ed., New York 1962, p. 331, n. 134, who takes sovereignty as the prince's *imperium* and J K Oudendijk, *Status and extent of adjacent waters; a historical orientation*, Leyden 1970, p. 27). Compare, for an introduction to the terminology of sovereignty, *summa potestas*, *imperium* and *dominium* and their complex interrelations in the work of authors as Bodin, Grotius and Van Bynkershoek: Kinji Akashi, *Cornelius van Bynkershoek: his Contribution to the Development of International Law*, Utrecht 1996, pp. 66–73, and Marek St Korowicz, *Introduction to International Law*, The Hague 1964, chs. 1–3.

the shadowy past and whole- or halfheartedly derived from Christian Supremacy, was still not fully solved. However, serious competitors were already around: the Protestant, "liberation movements" whose national struggles eventually had culminated in the conclusion of the Eighty Years" (or Low Countries') War and, notably, of the Thirty Years" War by the (1648) Peace Treaties of Westphalia, in Münster and Osnabrück, respectively. Generally, it is held that a new configuration of power, the modern state system based on territorial sovereignty, which ever since has conquered the world, was then created. Although, for practical legal purposes territorial sovereignty was already in place, at least for some decades before 1648, from the more formal international legal point of view, the system can be said to have been founded by these treaties.

Albeit in a somewhat different form, international law itself is generally assumed to have been in existence, long before this transformation from universal to territorial sovereignty and from feudal to modern state, took place.[2] However, since the Renaissance, international law's capacity to accommodate has further, and even more deeply perhaps, been challenged by the rapid scientific, economic and other "grand scale" developments that have shaken the world. In the following pages the flexibility of this field of law within the new configuration of assumed supreme state power will be assessed. This review is undertaken both at the level of the "inherent" international legal qualities of that new configuration, as well as in view of an impression of its capacity to adapt to the practical "grand" developments.

1. THE NEW STATE SYSTEM

The (more or less) new state system of 1648 had a curious consequence for the notion of sovereignty: "supreme authority" had now become vested in many rather diverse political systems rather than in one, however diffuse the original universal source might have been. The growing number of separate supreme authorities had to function together, next to each other, including that, also physically, they had to be protected against each other. In such often violent and chaotic circumstances there was a clear need for normative, preferably legal order. However, in view of the vanishing spiritual and secular power of emperor and pope, who, or what, could provide legal order acceptable to all, including to religious curiosities like the United Kingdom, or recent religious revolutionaries like the new Protestant powers, notably the powerful Dutch Republic?

Gradually it became clear that international law might be the only force able to do that. It could, in principle at least, accomodate a system of *territorial* sov-

[2] See for example, Cornelis Van Vollenhoven, *Du Droit de Paix-De Iure Pacis*, The Hague 1932, p. 17 on differing views about the period of its emergence (in his view at least long before Grotius liftime; see also p. 25).

ereignty, separating, on a territorial basis, the legal orders called states. International law could also provide its own "secular" legitimacy for these independent legal state orders, a legitimacy which only much later than the seventeenth century really became established when Christian "eurocentrism" had to give way, in particular in the nineteenth and early twentieth century, or better, had been *battled* away, by Turk, Ethiopian and Japanese nations. For the time being, in the doctrine, state- or territorial sovereignty remained complementary to, and in competition with, the old concept of universal sovereignty.

Alberico Gentili (1552–1608) and Hugo De Groot, or Grotius (1583–1645), can be called the "founding fathers" of the framework for the new system of sovereignty which principles were elaborated upon by their major successors, like the Dutchman Cornelis van Bynkershoek (1673–1743) and, later, the Swiss Emmerich de Vattel (1714–67). Gradually and for a variety of religious, military, economic and, in the end, political reasons, this framework and its principles, in modified and adapted form, became generally accepted as the framework for the conduct of international relations.

The general acceptance of the innovating basic principles of the new framework was, of course, never a smooth process. These new rules tended to diminish the power of the old sovereigns or to show new and old sovereigns alike that they, first, had to sacrifice powers in order to benefit, in the longer run.

One of such new principles which eventually won in the practice of states was that the seas were not subject to territorial ownership but were "international" territory. Grotius proposed this had already in his early *Mare Liberum* of 1609.[3] However, it took well into the eighteenth century before the *mare clausum* theories, propagated by John Seldon (in his *Mare clausum sive de dominio maris* of 1635) and other English lawyers, had really lost the legal battle.[4] The latter viewpoint in fact still corresponded to quite some extent with one of the rules underlying the 1493 Bull *Inter Caetera Divinae*. In this Bull Pope Alexander VI Borgia, under the assumption of the validity of his universal sovereignty, had declared the title to vast land and ocean areas to Portugal and Spain.[5]

A *mare liberum* made the seas and oceans *res communis* and, what was in them, *res nullius*, in fact international territory and common resources. This

[3] See for example, Oudendijk, *op. cit.*, n. 1, pp. 22–3. In Grotius's view the maritime resources (at least fish) were *res nullius* (*ibidem*, p. 18 and 26), and the seas *res communis* (*ibidem*, p. 26).

[4] This was, of course, not a very smooth process (see Ernst Reibstein, *Völkerrecht; eine Geschichte seiner Ideen in Lehre und Praxis*, Munich 1957, pp. 423–6), and especially not as soon as the colonial domains of the main powers were concerned (*ibidem*, pp. 419–22).

[5] It is a matter of some interpretation whether or not, apart from the land territory, the Bull and the successive and related 1494 Treaty of Tordesillas, also granted the sea territory to Spain and Portugal. It seems the stronger view that it indeed intended to do so (cf. J Fisch who concludes: "Also das Meer als monopolisierbares Gebiet" ["Thus the sea as territory to be monopolised"]; in: *Die Europäische Expansion und das Völkerrecht* ["The European Expansion and International Law"], Stuttgart 1984, pp. 53/4; see, also Reibstein, *op. cit.*, n. 10, pp. 274–8).

new status then had found expression in the gradual acceptance of more sophisticated rules on the freedom of the high seas. Under the new rules all states could make use of this territory, navigate, fish and hunt. However, in their expeditions and ventures they were obliged to take the interests of other states into account, a process continuing to this day.[6]

In international state practice the co-existence of the two main sovereignty notions was much less important than it was in the doctrine. The state system consisting of independent legal orders existed in the practice of the international relations in Europe and gradually and slowly spread over the world. Eventually it also found its justification in the doctrine. If anywhere, the "summum imperium", the supreme legal authority, was now supposed to be located in this rather diffuse multiple state system, at times supposedly consisting of "Nation" States, but always of territorial (Nation) States.

This general recognition and acceptance of the phenomenon ànd of the international (legal) "construct" of state – or territorial sovereignty, also induced increasing interest in the scope of these new territorial powers. In that respect, now that the Roman Catholic faith and Church had largely lost its prevaling position in the normative centre, a religiously speaking "neutral" international law could be expected increasingly to assume such a role. After all, whatever its shortcomings – and not at all only in the area of enforcement – international law had become the sole remaining normative system of thought with anything coming close to a generally accepted claim as the "universal" source of legitimation of the new territorial state system.

2. UNLIMITED POWERS TO THE STATE?

What limits did this new international law authority impose on the State's legal powers or, in more appropriate legal language, on its jurisdiction? The gist of a state's sovereignty was now in fact no longer lodged in supreme authority at all, but in its *independence* from other states. In his famous 1928 Award in the *Island of Palmas Case* the single arbitrator, Max Huber, saw fit to define sovereignty as follows:

> Sovereignty in the relations between States signifies independence. Independence in regard to a portion of the globe is the right to exercise therein, to the exclusion of any other State, the functions of a State.[7]

It is not too difficult to imagine what sorts of problems this legal definition of sovereignty can cause, e.g. for a modern field like international environmental

[6] And a first example of the "erosion of State sovereignty", the subject of section C, *infra*.

[7] *Island of Palmas Case*, United States v. The Netherlands; in: *Repertory of International Arbitral Awards (RIAA)*, vol. II, p. 838. Compare: "The territory of the state in a narrower sense is that space within which in principle one state only, the state to which the territory belongs, is entitled to exercise its legal power, and especially to carry out coercive acts, a space from which all the other states are excluded"; in: Hans Kelsen, *Principles of International Law*, New York 1952, p. 213.

policy and law, if the territorial exclusivity of the state legal order is taken too strictly. The so-called "Harmon" doctrine provides an illustration. About one hundred years ago, in a conflict between the United States and Mexico, the US Attorney-General Judson Harmon tried to bring a strict notion of territorial sovereignty into practice when he argued:

> States enjoy *absolute sovereignty* over water within their territory and are free to do so as they please with those waters, including extracting as much as necessary, or altering their quality, regardless of the effects on other States.[8]

However, in the end Harmon's doctrine was not in all respects practically applied against Mexico, nor, at the time or nowadays, did it receive much support in (international) legal circles.[9] Thus, in 1929, in the Advisory Opinion in the *River Oder Case*, the Permanent Court of International Justice could declare that the riparian states of – at least – a navigable international river formed a "community of interest", which:

> . . . becomes the basis of a common legal right, the essential features of which are the perfect equality of all riparian States in the use of the whole course of the river and the exclusion of any preferential privilege of any one riparian State in relation to the others.[10]

A year before, in his 1928 Award in the *Island of Palmas Case*, just cited, Huber himself had already provided the more general argument for such a point of view. He had added the logical "corollary" to his notion of sovereignty:

> Territorial sovereignty, as has already been said, involves the exclusive right to display the activities of a State. This right has as corrolary a duty: the obligation to protect within the territory the rights of other States, in particular their right to integrity and inviolability in peace and in war, together with the rights which each State may claim for its nationals in foreign territory.[11]

3. LIMITS TO THE LEGAL POWERS OF THE STATE: THE PRACTICAL SPECTRUM

Still having sovereignty but less than supreme authority in the international order, can be seen as the logical price to pay for giving up the single feudal and Christian universal centre and replacing it with the states, the manifold of

[8] *Official Opinions of the Attorneys-General of the United States*, vol. XXI, 1898 Washington DC, p. 283.

[9] See the extensive discussion – although not of the text cited here- by Special Rapporteur Stephen McCaffrey of the International Law Commission (ILC) on the doctrine (in 1986 *Yearbook of the International Law Commission*, vol. II, Part One, pp. 105–10). He found good reason to reject the "doctrine" in international law, and also, otherwise, could not find much support for it in state practice (*ibidem*).

[10] *Case Relating to the Territorial Jurisdiction of the International Commission of the River Oder*, in: Permanent Court of International Justice (PCIJ), *Series A*, no. 23, p. 27.

[11] *RIAA*, vol.II, *op. cit.*, n. 3, p. 839.

"highest" authorities, co-existing and co-operating within their own, exclusive, separate realms.

In some areas the "absoluteness" of sovereignty had already eroded a long time ago. A good example is provided by the development of diplomatic law. In 1584 the Spanish Ambassador Bernardino de Mendoza appeared as one of the principal plotters to dethrone and kill Queen Elizabeth and to liberate the Catholic Queen Mary of Scotland. Before handing over the ambassador to the rather unpleasant English judiciary of the time, the Government decided to ask for some learned opinions. Both Gentili and the Frenchman Jean Hotman de Villiers advised expelling De Mendoza instead of bringing him to trial, and this advise was followed.[12] Notwithstanding the importance of the *Mendoza case* as a starting point for the development of diplomatic law, it took until well into the next century before the, at the time, unusual gesture in the *Mendoza case* had led to generally accepted rules resembling modern international rules on the immunity of diplomats from the penal law of the receiving state. In this century these rules were broadened to the current extensive international regime granting diplomats, consuls and other representatives immunity from most forms of law, as far down as modern traffic regulations.[13]

It took until the end of the nineteenth century, before normal aliens, apart from diplomats, by way of a minimum standard of treatment were also granted special, albeit much more limited, protection under international law. This international minimum standard granted better legal protection than generally was provided to the nationals of the guarantor state[14]. Not earlier than a decade after the Second World War, the international minimum standard, again gradually, became transformed into, and replaced by, international human rights protection laid down in treaties and other instruments. This modern human rights standard protects aliens present in the territory just as it protects the nationals of the States parties to those instruments, against the supreme authority of the State itself.

Less spectacular, although not to be underestimated in significance, standards for making treaties or for their interpretation or termination, gradually acquired general acceptance. As early as the end of the eighteenth century, this movement toward facilitating co-operation could be said, at least, to have given

[12] Although neither Gentili nor Hotman de Villiers advised to expel De Mendoza on grounds of diplomatic immunity (C G Roelofsen's conclusion on the basis of his study of the texts of their opinions; in A C G M Eyffinger (ed.), *Compendium Volkenrechtsgeschiedenis* ["Compendium of the History of International Law"], The Hague 1991, pp. 81–2).

[13] It is assumed that general recognition of immunity was achieved by the mid-seventeenth century. Grotius supported this development. He argued in favour of a state of *quasi-extra territorium* which also would exempt the ambassador from the criminal jurisdiction of the receiving State. He also pleaded to consider his movable property immune from civil jurisdiction (cf. Nussbaum, *op. cit.*, n. 1, p. 111, and Reibstein, *op. cit.*, n. 4, pp. 263–4).

[14] The so-called capitulations, from the thirteenth century on granted by Moslem rulers to Christian nations -and later, in particular, forced on to them- followed by the beginnings of consular practice, are a dubious predecessor to the international minimum standard (see, e.g. Nussbaum, *op. cit.*, n. 1, pp. 55–6).

ground for assuming, in the European nexus, the existence of order and legal security in a system of hundreds of treaties in a wide variety of fields like trade, shipping or diplomatic relations.

It was not before the end of the nineteenth century that the first limitations on the "sacred" practice of war, on the *ius in bello*, were eventually agreed upon (the so-called dum-dum bullet was prohibited, the prisoner of war appeared). In the aftermath of the Second World War much more substantial results in this area could be noted when on 21 October 1950 the Four Geneva Conventions, the four "Red Cross" Conventions, entered into force. In the same period the other related most sovereign of all areas of international law, the *ius ad bellum*, the law to wage war, was universally set limits to by the general prohibition of the threat or use of force, as formally laid down in Article 2(4) of the Charter of the United Nations.

In 1941 an international tribunal had decided that the use of a natural resource –air– within the sovereign territory was restricted if that use resulted in environmental damage in a neighbouring state. In its decision in the notorious *Trail Smelter* Arbitration between Canada and the United States, the case with a strong claim to being the first case in the field of international environmental law, the Arbitral Tribunal decided that:

> . . . under the principles of international law (. . .) no State has the right to use or permit the use of its territory in such a manner as to cause injury by fumes in or to the territory of another or the properties or persons therein, when the case is of serious consequence and the injury is established by clear and convincing evidence.[15]

However, it still took another thirty years before the rights and duties of states in respect to *transboundary* natural resources really substantially began to expand. Notably, the quality of shared water- and air resources became a matter of increasing international regulation thereby contributing, also from this angle, to the gradual erosion of the supreme authority of the State. Along this line: in still more recent times environmental concerns have even led to legal moves beyond the "transboundary" scope, into global natural resources. The state of the ozone layer, of biodiversity and even of the climate have become subjects of international regulation.

4. FROM TERRITORIAL BACK TO UNIVERSAL SOVEREIGNTY?

Lawyers tend to be quite specific and precise in their use of terms. The terminology, the meaning of terms, in international law is supposed to be a universal terminology expressing the rights and duties of all states in the world, as well as of other subjects which are much more limited in their rights and

[15] *Trail Smelter Case*, United States of America v. Canada; in: *RIAA*, vol. III, p. 1965.

duties.[16] How did this precise international legal doctrine account for the developments in practice just outlined?

In the early decades of this century, in particular in central Europe, several constitutional and international lawyers tried to show that the system of territorial sovereignty of states, in fact, fell victim to its own "contradictions". Perhaps most persuasively, this was done by the Austrian Hans Kelsen. He wrote, simplifying the issue to its ultimate limit: if sovereignty is taken in its original sense of a right to supreme authority, such a fundamental right cannot exist for states, because as subjects of international law, states are *subjected* to international law. In that sense, states as subjects of rights and duties are as little "sovereign" under international law as individuals are sovereign under municipal law. The authority of international law has, at some point, been established above the states and has become accepted by them. In that sense, international law, as are other systems of law, is in principle, a "vertical" system.[17]

Classical principles contributing to the preservation of the State's territorial sovereignty, like the duty of non-intervention, the right of legal equality of states, the principle of the territorial integrity of states and the right of self-defence, may be said to have survived quite intact, the onslaught of "grand scale" developments. However, as was illustrated in the previous section, increasingly international law can be shown as also including quite a wide variety of rights and duties limiting the territorial sovereignty of states.

The exclusivity of the State's legal order "in regard to a portion of the globe", to use Max Huber's terms again, must therefore be considered to be much less impenetrable now. In current international law it seems in fact quite legitimate to ask what useful purpose sovereignty (in the sense of state territorial sovereignty) still serves. Perhaps, it is more appropriate to ask what the state of the "fundamental hypothesis" of the state sovereignty system nowadays is, i.e., the hypothesis that the legal order of the State is supreme within the limits of its territory. Might it be so that the (legal) powers of the State have shrunk to such extent that the fundamental hypothesis should in fact be replaced by another one, one presuming the superiority of the international order? Or again differently phrased: does this development imply that a new kind of universal sovereignty has come to prevail again?

I do not believe so. International law has, primarily, proved over time to provide superiorly flexible norms and instruments. It has been able to accommodate the old order based on universal sovereignty and enabled the new system of state territorial sovereignty to function. It seems still able to support that

[16] Like governmental international organisations or individuals and their groups (international corporations, ngos, churches, etc.).

[17] Cf. notably, his *Principles of International Law*, *op. cit.*, n. 3, pp. 114 ff.

latter system notwithstanding the magnitude of changes states and peoples have faced and are still going through. Even now, in times of the web and other deep digging technological changes, or when challenged by the horrors of the Rwandan, Yugoslavian or Chechnyan disasters, the state system still seems the actual foundation for the international order, and also still holds the strongest claim to be the best available.

If it may be presumed then that, nowadays, perhaps against all odds, this territorial state system, supported by international law, has indeed maintained itself, does this not necessarily mean that it has hugely changed? Almost contrary to what was argued above on the prevailing "fundamental hypothesis", does more co-existence and co-operation induced by the grand practical developments, not automatically lead to strong international institutions with wide powers? I do not think so, although in the "classical" Austinian conception of legal order, such powers are easily presumed.

Of course, delegation to a relatively strong international institution has taken place, the European Union being the obvious example. However, such developments occur less frequently than is often presumed and, usually, result in institutions with somewhat less than striking powers. It can very well be imagined that in a flexible international legal order such powers are delegated by states, on an *ad hoc* basis. To take the most dramatic example, the actual military forces of states can be made use of, in one form or another, as the international instrument for enforcement. The 1991 Kuwait-Iraq crisis provided a dramatic example of such a transformation. When and under what circumstances, these military forces are fielded, is another question, its answer depending fundamentally on the political will of states to make use of the legal possibilities.

In modern times then, the opportunity for "Grotian" international law is still manifold. The sheer scope of the cobweb of rights and duties of states providing these opportunities, whether concluded in the past, explicitly by way of treaties or engaged "tacitly" in the form of international customary law, is immense. It is still easily possible to add new (binding) rules to them, and it happens on a daily basis. Without them much of the modernity and "global village" aspects of modern society would not have been possible and cannot operate: telecommunications, international data traffic, air traffic, monetary and financial relations, mass tourism, large scale exploitation of natural resources, etc. All such activities require co-operation and such is made possible by myriad international rules. International law, whatever the precise nature or source of sovereignty, apparently is still able to offer the necessary uniformity and, in particular, the legal security for this immensely complicated modern infrastructure to be constructed and to operate effectively. For the time being the states as their predominant subjects still largely determine its substance. In essence this means that the "fundamental hypothesis" of the territorial state system is still valid.

5. FLEXIBILITY AS A FUNDAMENTAL VALUE; SOME CONCLUDING OBSERVATIONS

At the end of the sixteenth, the beginning of the seventeenth century in Europe the notion of a multiple territorial sovereignty system was launched, mainly on the waves caused by the Protestant Reformation. By the middle of that century this new system of sovereignty can be said to have established itself as the new international order, normatively based on international law. This new international legal system based on the territorial sovereignty of states had replaced the old normative system based on universal sovereignty claimed by pope or emperor.

Political practice as expressed in international legal rules no longer allowed for "absolute" sovereignty: the multiple territorial sovereignty concept was much more relative than its centralist, universal predecessor. Although, theoretically speaking, the connotation of both concepts of sovereignty was the same, i.e. that legal power is supreme, in the new state system this supremacy appeared limited by international law. It was probably so from the outset in the sense that States were always under a duty to protect the rights of other states. However, supreme power continued to be limited, and increasingly so, due to further voluntary limitations states had to assume, driven as they were by the growing needs generated by the "grand scale" practical developments they went through. International law was offering the necessary *flexibility* for all this, primarily, by providing the instruments: treaties and international custom, in particular.

This is not to argue that flexibility, or adaptability mark the utmost fundamental quality of a legal system. There is, perhaps, even a danger of paying too much attention to it because fairness, equality, or justice easily tend to drift out of view. However, when the rule of (international) law collapses due to major and dramatic shifts of power (or grandiose scientific or economic developments, for that matter) all those involved are likely to lose out, those best-off no less than those worst-off. For that reason, the flexibility of international law, its capacity to adapt, is a matter of great concern, it might even rightly be labelled a "fundamental value" of that legal system. In my view, assessing its state and modalities is an important and highly justifiable academic activity which, unfortunately, tends to be somewhat underestimated.

Part 3

Fundamental Values in Public Law

12

Standards, Principles and Values in the Public Law of the United Kingdom

JOHN BRIDGE

1. INTRODUCTION

Future historians of the United Kingdom constitution will look back at the period spanning the end of the twentieth and the beginning of the twenty-first centuries as one of profound constitutional change. While constitutional reform has been a recurring theme in scholarly writing over the past thirty years,[1] the event which will doubtless be seen as a watershed will be the election of the Blair Government with a massive majority in May 1997. Four years earlier, as the Party's spokesman on home affairs, Tony Blair had presented a Labour Policy Commission Report entitled "A New Agenda for Democracy: Labour's Proposals for Constitutional Reform" to the 1993 Labour Party Conference.[2] That document, which ranged over human rights, regional and local government, freedom of information, reform of Parliament and reform of the judiciary, professed itself to be "the most radical package of democratic reform ever presented to the British people by a major political party".[3] Those themes were taken up by the Labour Party's 1997 Election Manifesto with the very important addition of proposals for devolution, the governance of London and the development of the English regions.[4] Once in power the new Labour Government, with the active support and participation of the Liberal Democrat Party, drew up a programme of constitutional reform.[5] By early 2000, a considerable part of that programme has been or is in the process of being implemented: the

[1] See for example, O Hood Phillips, *Reform of the Constitution* (London, Chatto & Windus, 1970); HWR Wade, *Constitutional Fundamentals* (London, Stevens, 1980); R Brazier, *Constitutional Reform* (Oxford, Clarendon Press, 1991); Lord Nolan and Sir Stephen Sedley, *The Making and Remaking of the British Constitution* (London, Blackstone Press, 1997).

[2] The text is substantially reproduced in R Blackburn and R Plant (eds.), *Constitutional Reform* (London, Longman, 1999), Appendix 1.

[3] *Idem* at 466.

[4] See *New Labour Because Britain Deserves Better* (London, Labour Party, 1997).

[5] See *Report of the Joint (Labour Party – Liberal Democrats) Consultative Committee on Constitutional Reform 1997*, reproduced *loc. cit., supra* n. 2, Appendix 2.

incorporation of the European Convention on Human Rights;[6] devolution in Scotland and Wales;[7] the restoration of provincial government in Northern Ireland;[8] a new mayor and system of government for London;[9] reform of the House of Lords;[10] freedom of information.[11]

This is a high profile, unprecedented and far-reaching programme of structural and substantive constitutional change. But, another highly significant change of a less obvious nature has also been taking place over a somewhat longer period of time in respect of the fundamental values underpinning the United Kingdom's constitution and system of public law. It is that process and the changes it has brought about which is the subject of this essay. Particular attention will be paid to the significance and impact of the "Seven Principles of Public Life" (the Nolan Principles), identified and elaborated by the Committee on Standards in Public Life in 1995.[12]

2. PRE-NOLAN VALUES

The constitutional and administrative law of the United Kingdom have long respected a number of values many of which are encapsulated in the concept of the rule of law:[13] checks against arbitrary power; democracy through universal suffrage and regular elections; representative and accountable government; individual freedom; fair procedures; and judicial independence. Within Parliament, one of the traditional roles of the Committee of Privileges of the House of Commons has been to maintain appropriate standards of conduct on the part of both Members and Officers.[14] In the same vein, from 1974 Members of Parliament were formally required to disclose and register personal financial interests subject to monitoring by the Select Committee on Members' Interests.[15] For many years prime ministers have issued their ministerial colleagues

[6] Human Rights Act 1998.

[7] Scotland Act 1998; Government of Wales Act 1998.

[8] Northern Ireland Act 1998.

[9] Greater London Authority Act 1999.

[10] House of Lords Act 1999.

[11] Freedom of Information Bill 1999. On the programme of reforms and its implementation, see A Barnett, *This Time: Our Constitutional Revolution* (London, Vintage, 1997); R Blackburn and R Plant (eds.), *Constitutional Reform* (London, Longman, 1999); R Hazell (ed.), *Constitutional Futures* (Oxford, Oxford University Press, 1999).

[12] See *First Report of the Committee on Standards in Public Life*, Cm. 2850-I, 1995, at 14. It is an assertion of this paper that there is a relationship between values, principles and standards in the sense that principles define conduct which is supported by standards and which together promote respect for values.

[13] See: J Raz, "The Rule of law and its Virtue" (1977) 93 *Law Quarterly Review* 195; I Harden and N Lewis, *The Noble Lie* (London, Hutchinson Education, 1986), Part One; C Harlow and R Rawlings, *Law and Administration* (London, Weidenfeld & Nicolson, 1984), ch. 1.

[14] See C J Boulton (ed.), *Erskine May's Treatise on the Law, Privileges, Proceedings and Usage of Parliament*, 21st ed., (London, Butterworths, 1989), especially chs. 5 and 9.

[15] *Idem*, 384–390.

with a statement governing their private financial interests entitled Questions of Procedure for Ministers.[16] There has also long been a concern to uphold integrity and counteract corruption and nepotism in public life.[17] The developing right to reasoned decisions and the revival of the tort of misfeasance in public office are advancing the causes of openness and accountability.[18] Values such as these have been traditionally underwritten by a combination of the law, constitutional conventions and professionalism in the public service.[19]

From time to time such an unstructured and to an extent informal set of arrangements inevitably has been found wanting. Such occasions have prompted investigation and remedial action. For example, a series of scandals in the 1970s and 1980s involving local government, civil servants, cabinet ministers and MPs called into question standards of behaviour in public life and resulted in recommendations designed to improve those standards, and thereby to enhance respect for the values they served. Over that period, two committees investigated conduct and the conduct of business in local government[20] and a royal commission inquired into "standards of conduct in central and local government and other public bodies".[21] The reports of those bodies all reflected common concerns about probity in public life. From the point of view of the theme of this essay, a significant outcome was the production of a National Code of Local Government Conduct, which constitutes "a frame of reference valuable to everyone serving in local government and especially to those doing so for the first time".[22] Observance of this Code was originally voluntary, but is now statutory.[23] Councillors are required to make a declaration to be bound by the Code and failure to observe it may be regarded as *prima facie* evidence of maladministration.

The National Code of Local Government Conduct currently in force[24] reminds councillors of their obligations to act within the law and standing

[16] See S de Smith and R Brazier, *Constitutional and Administrative Law*, 6th ed., (London, Penguin Books, 1989) at 181.

[17] For example, the long sequence of enactments, from the Corrupt Practices Act 1695 to the Representation of the People Act 1983, concerning the election offences of bribery, treating and undue influence.

[18] See de Smith. Woolf & Jowell's *Principles of Judicial Review* (London, Sweet & Maxwell, 1999), pp. 341–60 and 628–30 respectively.

[19] On common underlying values in public and private law, see D Oliver, "The Underlying Values of Public and Private Law" in M Taggart (ed.), *The Province of Administrative Law* (Oxford, Hart Publishing, 1997), p. 217.

[20] *Conduct in Local Government* (The Redcliffe-Maud Committee), Cmnd. 5636, 1974; *The Conduct of Local Authority Business* (The Widdicombe Committee), Cmnd. 9797, 1986.

[21] *Standards of Conduct in Public Life* (The Salmon Commission), Cmnd. 6524, 1976.

[22] *Conduct in Local Government*, Cmnd. 5636, para. 170. Also see *Standards of Conduct in Public Life*, Cmnd. 6524, ch. 12.

[23] Following the recommendations of the Widdicombe Committee: see *The Conduct of Local Authority Business: The Government Response to the Report of the Widdicombe Committee of Inquiry*, Cm. 433, 1988, ch. IV. See Local Government and Housing Act 1989, ss. 30 and 31.

[24] Set out in Joint Circular 8/90 (Department of the Environment), 23/90 (Welsh Office), 11/90 (Scottish Development Department). There is also a Code applicable in Northern Ireland; see *Re Dallas' Application* [1996] NI 276 at 294–5. A comparable Code applies to urban development

orders and of their responsibility to ensure that their personal conduct at all times complies with the requirements of the Code. The Code itself addresses the following issues: public duty and private interest; the disclosure of pecuniary[25] and other interests; the disclosure of dealings with councillors and council officers; the circumstances ruling out leadership, chairmanship or committee membership; the use of confidential and private information; the proper relationship between councillors and council officers; the acceptance of gifts and hospitality; the claiming of expenses and allowances; personal dealings with the council; the use of council facilities; representing the council on other bodies. While it may well be the case that "[c]odes of conduct and declarations of interest will have little impact on the dishonest, though they may dissuade the pliant",[26] it seems likely that the Code has contributed to an "awareness that high ethical standards are critical to maintain public confidence in local government".[27] Investigation of complaints of maladministration by the Commission for Local Administration in England based on allegations of infringement of the Code also clearly promotes that objective.[28]

Local government codes of conduct have also been considered judicially in both England and Northern Ireland. In two English cases they have been in issue in relation to allegations of bias based on personal interests in the consideration of applications for planning permission.[29] In the *Kirkstall* case Sedley J, as he then was, while questioning whether a Code of Conduct for an Urban Development Corporation met the requirements of the general law and puzzling over its precise meaning, nevertheless regarded it as having an advisory status and as such relevant to the issue of bias.[30] In the *Liverpool City Council* case, Hooper J held that a Local Commissioner for Administration was entitled to have regard to the National Code of Local Government Conduct and to make a finding of maladministration in respect of a breach of the Code.[31] In the case

corporations set up under the Local Government Planning and Land Act 1980; see *R* v. *S ecretary of State for the Environment, ex parte Kirkstall Valley Campaign Ltd* [1996] 3 All ER 304 at 309–11.

[25] Also see *The Pecuniary Interests of Members of Local Authorities*, Joint Circular 9/92 (Department of the Environment), 15/92 (Scottish Office Environment Department), 16/92 (Welsh Office).

[26] T Byrne, *Local Government in Britain*, 2nd ed. (London, Penguin Books, 1983), p. 145.

[27] Lord Nolan in a letter to the Prime Minister printed with *The Third Report of the Committee on Standards in Public Life*, Cm. 3702-I, 1997.

[28] See for example, Local Government Ombudsman, *Digest of Cases 1998*, section H 10–14. For the Local Government Commission's own Code of Practice and Code of Conduct, see its *Annual Report 1994/95* and *Annual Report 1995/96*, at Appendix 5 in each case.

[29] *R* v. *Secretary of State for the Environment, ex parte Kirkstall Valley Campaign Ltd* [1996] 3 All ER 304; *R* v. *Local Commissioner for Administration in North and North East England, ex parte Liverpool City Council* [1999] 3 All ER 85.

[30] *Loc. cit.* at 314, 329–30.

[31] *Loc. cit.* at 92–3. The judges differed in respect of the test of bias: Sedley J applied the "real danger" test laid down in *R* v. *Gough* [1993] AC 646; Hooper J applied a more stringent test based on the wording of the Code. The approach of Hooper J has recently been endorsed on appeal: see *R* v. *Local Commissioner for Administration in North and North East England, ex parte Liverpool City Council, The Times Law Report*, 3 March 2000 (CA). On this general issue, now see *R* v. *Bow*

from Northern Ireland,[32] Kerr J held that the Northern Ireland Code of Local Government Conduct for Councillors was "designed to promote certain standards of behaviour in public life because of the effect that a lapse in those standards might have in the minds of the public".[33] The council in question therefore acted reasonably in taking the Code into consideration when resolving to suspend the exercise of mayoral functions by one of its members.

Another device to set and monitor standards and thereby to enhance the delivery of public services is the Citizen's Charter.[34] This was introduced by the Conservative Government in 1991 as part of its market-oriented reforms of the public sector.[35] Within the framework of this so-called "new public management",[36] the Citizen's Charter established "The Principles of Public Service": the setting of published standards; openness promoting public scrutiny; information in plain language; consumer choice, wherever practicable, informed by consultation; non-discrimination in the provision of services; accessibility of services at the convenience of the customer; availability of a well-publicised machinery for audit, complaints and the redress of grievances.[37] The Charter was applied to all public services and to all public utilities provided by the private sector.[38] A series of charters was drawn up applying the above principles to a large number of individual public services, for example education, health, public transport, social services, postal services, revenue services and the police. While the Citizen's Charter mechanism initially attracted popular criticism and cynicism, informed commentators have generally taken it seriously. "There is no doubt that the *Citizen's Charter* suggests ideas which are rich in potential to improve service and it makes suggestions for customer consultation and grievance redress which appear to go substantially beyond tokenism".[39] The Citizen's Charter programme has been adopted and revamped by the Blair Government under the new name Service First.[40] The aim of this scheme is to "help

Street Magistrates, ex parte Pinochet Ugarte (No. 2) [1999] 1 All ER 577 (HL) and *Locabail (UK) Ltd* v. *Bayfield Properties Ltd, The Times Law Report*, 19 November 1999 (CA). The Standards Committee favours the "real danger" test; see its *Third Report*, Cm. 3702-I, at paras. 109–10.

[32] *Re Dallas' Application* [1996] NI 276.

[33] *Idem*, at 295–6.

[34] See generally C Willett (ed.), *Public Sector Reform and the Citizen's Charter* (London, Blackstone Press Ltd., 1996).

[35] See *The Citizen's Charter: Raising the Standard*, Cm. 1599, 1991.

[36] See E Ferlie, A Pettigrew, L Ashburner and L Fitzgerald, *The New Public Management in Action* (Oxford, Oxford University Press, 1996).

[37] *Citizen's Charter: Raising the Standard*, at 5.

[38] *Idem*, at 6. For the texts of the major national Charters, see the Cabinet Office web site: http://www.servicefirst.gov.uk/index/list.htm

[39] N Lewis and P Birkinshaw, *When Citizens Complain* (Buckingham, Open University Press, 1993), pp. 35–6. Also see A Barron and C Scott, "The Citizen's Charter Programme" (1992) 55 *Modern Law Review* 526; G Drewry, "Mr Major's Charter: Empowering the Customer" [1993] *Public Law* 248; D Cooper, "The Citizen's Charter and Radical Democracy" (1993) 2 *Social & Legal Studies* 149.

[40] See Cabinet Office (Office of Public Service), *Tough New Approach To Driving Up Quality Of Public Services* (CAB 156/98, 30 June 1998).

transform and modernise public services as part of the wider programme of Better Government".[41] It is supported by a web site which, *inter alia*, gives encouragement, information and practical advice on how to complain about public services.[42]

In these ways and against the background of traditional values, steps have been taken in recent years to articulate and clarify the principles and standards to be observed by those in public life so as to promote respect for fundamental values both in the interests of the public good and of individual citizens. This process has been given a fresh impetus and scope by the work of the Committee on Standards in Public Life (the Standards Committee).

3. THE NOLAN PRINCIPLES AND THEIR ACCEPTANCE

The background to the establishment of the Standards Committee in 1994 is well known. By that date there was widespread concern over departures from customary standards of public conduct. Instances of corruption, incompetence and partiality involving ministers, MPs, civil servants, and local government, collectively referred to as "sleaze", seemed commonplace. In announcing the establishment of the Committee, the Prime Minister, John Major, set out its terms of reference as follows:

> To examine current concerns about standards of conduct of all holders of public office, including arrangements relating to financial and commercial activities, and make recommendations as to any changes in present arrangements which might be required to ensure the highest standards of propriety in public life.[43]

The definition of "public life" was all embracing and includes ministers, civil servants and advisers, MPs and United Kingdom Members of the European Parliament, non-ministerial office holders, and members and senior officers of non-departmental public bodies,[44] National Health Service bodies, other bodies discharging publicly-funded functions and local authorities. The Committee's remit does not, however, extend to investigating individual allegations of misconduct.[45] The Committee was constituted as a standing committee.[46] In 1997

[41] *Idem*, at 1. For further information and comment, see C Scott, "Regulation inside government: re-badging the Citizen's Charter" [1999] *Public Law* 595.

[42] See http://www.servicefirst.gov.uk/1999/complaint/howtocmp.htm

[43] *Parliamentary Debates, House of Commons*, Sixth Series, Vol. 248, 1993/94, col. 758.

[44] *I.e.* bodies outside the framework of central government and created for specific policy objectives, sometimes known as quangos (quasi-autonomous non-governmental bodies). There are currently over one thousand such bodies; see The Stationery Office, *Public Bodies 1998*.

[45] *Loc. cit.*, in n. 43 *supra*, col. 759.

[46] Its first Chairman, Lord Nolan of Brasted, a Lord of Appeal in Ordinary, was succeeded by Lord Neill of Bladen, QC, former Warden of All Souls College, Oxford, in November 1997.

its terms of reference were extended to cover issues relating to the funding of political parties.[47]

In its *First Report*, the Standards Committee concentrated on a range of issues relating to MPs, ministers and civil servants and quangos and National Health Service bodies. Against the background of "well-publicised incidents indicating a certain slackness in the observance and enforcement of high standards by those concerned" and "a widespread suspicion that much more misconduct occurs than is revealed to the public gaze", the Committee made recommendations "designed to maintain, and where necessary restore the standards of conduct in public life".[48] The *First Report* made it very clear, however, that some of its conclusions and recommendations had general application across the entire public service.[49] Those general recommendations included the drawing up of codes of conduct, establishing systems of independent scrutiny and the provision of more guidance and training, all within the overarching framework of a restatement of "the general principles of conduct which underpin public life".[50]

The Committee's restatement took the form of identifying and defining "The Seven Principles of Public Life" in the following terms:[51]

"**Selflessness**: Holders of public office should take decisions solely in terms of the public interest. They should not do so in order to gain financial or other material benefits for themselves, their family, or their friends.

Integrity: Holders of public office should not place themselves under any financial or other obligation to outside individuals or organisations that might influence them in the performance of their official duties.

Objectivity: In carrying out public business, including making public appointments, awarding contracts, or recommending individuals for rewards and benefits, holders of public office should make choices on merit.

Accountability: Holders of public office are accountable for their decisions and actions to the public and must submit themselves to whatever scrutiny is appropriate to their office.

Openness: Holders of public office should be as open as possible about all the decisions and actions that they take. They should give reasons for their decisions and restrict information only when the wider public interest clearly demands.

Honesty: Holders of public office have a duty to declare any private interests relating to their public duties and to take steps to resolve any conflicts arising in a way that protects the public interest.

[47] *Parliamentary Debates, House of Commons*, Sixth Series, Vol. 300, 1997/98, cols. 899–900.

[48] Lord Nolan in a letter to the Prime Minister printed with the *First Report of the Committee on Standards in Public Life*, Cm. 2850-I, 1995.

[49] *Idem*, at 3.

[50] *Ibid*.

[51] *Idem*, at 14.

Leadership: Holders of public office should promote and support these principles by leadership and example".

The Standards Committee has confirmed the general applicability of the Nolan Principles by printing them and referring to them in each of its subsequent reports. Indeed, it has come to regard them as laying the "philosophical foundation" of its work.[52] In its *Second Report*, which was concerned with local public spending bodies,[53] it referred back to the general recommendations in its *First Report* which it called the "common threads" of public life.[54] The Committee's *Third Report*, which dealt with standards of conduct in local government, was even more explicit. In recommending new codes of conduct for local councillors, the Committee stated the general principles which should guide their conduct including the statement "If you are a local councillor . . . You should conduct yourself in compliance with the seven principles of public life set out below".[55] In its *Fifth Report*, which addressed the funding of political parties, the Committee again referred to the "Seven Principles" and identified three as especially relevant to the matter in hand: integrity, accountability and openness. It stated that it saw its role as trying to entrench those principles within the funding process.[56] A striking statement of the significance to which the Committee attaches to the Nolan Principles can be found in its invitation to submit evidence to assist its study of local government.[57] Under the heading "The Nolan Framework", the Committee referred to its first two reports as setting out "a common ethical framework which is in line with current thinking and good practice".[58] As for the Principles themselves, they were characterised as representing "the core values applicable in public life and public service of all kinds".[59] In its most recent report, *Reinforcing Standards*,[60] the Committee has stated that the Nolan Principles "inform every aspect of [its] thinking".[61]

In the words of an early commentator, "The Committee's 'strike rate' in getting its recommendations accepted in principle and for the most part promptly implemented has been remarkable".[62] The response of the Major Gov-

[52] *Review of the First Report of the Committee on Standards in Public Life*, 1999, para. 1.13; see http://www.public-standards.gov.uk/issues%20&%20questions/introd.htm

[53] A term used to cover further and higher education bodies (including universities), grant-maintained schools, training and enterprise councils and local enterprise companies, and registered housing associations.

[54] *Second Report of the Committee on Standards in Public Life*, Cm. 3270-I, 1996, at ii and 9.

[55] *Third Report of the Committee on Standards in Public Life*, Cm. 3702-I, 1997, at 20.

[56] *Fifth Report of the Committee on Standards in Public Life*, Cm. 4057-I, 1998, at 26–7.

[57] Committee on Standards in Public Life, *Aspects of Conduct in Local Government*, 1996.

[58] *Idem*, para. 14.

[59] *Idem*, para. 15.

[60] *Sixth Report of the Committee on Standards in Public Life*, Cm. 4557-I, 2000.

[61] *Idem*, para. 1.5.

[62] D Oliver, "Standards of conduct on public life – what standards?" [1995] *Public Law* 497 at 499, which also summarises the action taken by both the House of Commons and the Government.

ernment to the Committee's *First Report* made no explicit reference to the Nolan Principles as such.[63] That omission was remedied in a consultation paper published by the Government giving its preliminary view of the response to the Standards Committee's recommendation that the legal framework governing financial propriety and accountability and the arrangements for external audit should be reviewed.[64] That paper set out the Nolan Principles in full, prefaced by the following statement: "The Government endorses the Seven Principles of Public Life set out by the Nolan Committee for the benefit of all who serve the public in any way".[65] A further, explicit indication of the Major Government's acceptance of the Nolan Principles can be found in revised guidance on best practice for members of executive non-departmental public bodies[66] issued by the Cabinet Office (Office of Public Service).[67] There, not only is the Government's previous endorsement cited,[68] but there are specific references to and applications of the Nolan Principles to members of non-departmental public bodies. Thus the guidance states that "individual board members should be aware of their wider responsibilities as members of the board. Like others who serve the public, they should follow the Seven Principles of Public Life".[69] Elsewhere, it refers to the Principles of Integrity, Objectivity, Accountability and Openness.[70]

Further endorsements of the Nolan Principles have been given by the Blair Government. In its formal response to the Standards Committee's report on conduct in local government, it proposed "a new ethical framework" built on the Committee's recommendations and designed "to underpin standards of conduct in local government".[71] The "General Principles of Conduct" which local councillors are to be expected to observe include five of the Nolan Principles: selflessness, integrity, objectivity, accountability, and openness.[72] More recently in its response to the *Fifth Report*, on the funding of political parties, the Government not only welcomed the Committee's findings but also recorded its determination to implement its recommendations.[73]

[63] See *The Government's Response to the First Report of the Committee on Standards in Public Life*, Cm. 2931, 1995.

[64] *Spending Public Money: Governance and Audit Issues*, Cm. 3179, 1996.

[65] *Idem*, at 8.

[66] As to such bodies, see Cabinet Office (The Efficiency Unit), *Executive Non-Departmental Public Bodies 1997 Report*, Cm. 3712, 1997.

[67] *Guidance on Codes of Practice for Board Members of Public Bodies*, January 1997.

[68] *Idem*, at Appendix 1, which also reproduces the Nolan Principles.

[69] *Idem*, para. 12.

[70] *Idem*, paras. 2 and 29–32.

[71] Department of the Environment, Transport and the Regions, *Modern Local Government: In Touch with the People*, Cm. 4014, 1998, para. 6.2.

[72] *Idem*, para. 6.7.

[73] See *The Funding of Political Parties in the United Kingdom – The Government's proposals for legislation in response to the Fifth Report of then Committee on Standards in Public Life*, Cm. 4413, 1999.

4. THE IMPLEMENTATION OF THE NOLAN PRINCIPLES

The acceptance of the Nolan Principles as a desideratum is one thing; their practical implementation is quite another. To an extent the Principles reflect values long familiar to the constitutional and administrative law of the United Kingdom: democratic control, fairness, reasonableness and the absence of bias. But they are also at once wider and more pervasive. Novel values of merit based choices, protection of the public interest and leadership are included and their scope is the whole of public life. The Standards Committee itself, in reviewing the first four years of its work, has commented on the role and significance of the Nolan Principles in the following terms: "We have found these to be a useful touchstone against which to measure all aspects of work on public sector ethics. . . . It is gratifying to note that these principles have been widely adopted by organisations throughout the public sector and beyond".[74] This is reiterated in its *Sixth Report* in terms that the Nolan Principles "have come to be widely regarded as the touchstone for ethical standards in public life".[75] There is ample evidence to support that conclusion.

As far as Parliament is concerned the House of Commons, on the recommendation of its Committee on Standards and Privileges,[76] took a range of measures to implement the Standards Committee's *First Report*. A new officer of the House, the Parliamentary Commissioner for Standards, was appointed to receive and investigate complaints of improper conduct, to maintain a Register of Members' Interests and to advise Members on what to register. The old Committee of Privileges and Select Committee on Members' interests were replaced by the Committee on Standards and Privileges to oversee the work of the Commissioner and to consider matters relating to conduct referred to it by him. The rules for the Register and concerning payment to Members from outside individuals and bodies were strengthened and re-stated.[77] A Code of Conduct and a Guide to the Rules relating to the Conduct of Members were also drawn up.[78] The Code, in express terms, requires MPs to observe the Nolan Principles.[79] The Questions of Procedure for Ministers was also revised and reissued under the title Ministerial Code: A Code of Conduct and Guidance on Procedures for Ministers[80]. This new version clarifies the responsibilities of Ministers and their accountability to Parliament and gives guidance on business interests and activities, including the acceptance of appointments after leaving office. In

[74] Lord Neill of Bladen, in the Foreword to the *Annual Report for 1997/1998*; see http://www.public-standards.gov.uk/annreps/forewor.htm

[75] *Sixth Report of the Committee on Standards in Public Life*, Cm. 4557-I, para. 1.5.

[76] See *Third Report from the Committee on Standards and Privileges*, HC 604, (1995–6).

[77] *Parliamentary Debates, House of Commons*, Sixth Series, Vol. 265, cols. 608–61.

[78] HC 688 (1995–6).

[79] *Idem*, at 3.

[80] Issued by the Cabinet Office (Central Secretariat) in July 1997; see http://www.cabinet-office.gov.uk/central/1997/mcode.htm

commending it to his ministerial colleagues, and publishing it in the interests of openness and accountability, the Prime Minister has reminded them that "they can only remain in office for so long as they retain [his] confidence".[81] The Ministerial Code is complemented by the Civil Service Code[82] that requires civil servants to carry out their constitutional and practical duties "with integrity, honesty, impartiality and objectivity".[83] It also reminds them that they "owe their loyalty to the Administrations in which they serve" and of their accountability to their political masters.[84]

In respect of local government, building on current practice and responding to the Standards Committee's *Third Report*, the Government proposes "a new ethical framework"[85] which will promote "the new culture of openness and ready accountability".[86] Legislation is being introduced which will replace the existing National Code of Local Government Conduct. Instead each local council will be required to adopt its own Code of Conduct which must contain "General Principles of Conduct".[87] The "General Principles", which will be subject to parliamentary approval, have strong echoes of the Nolan Principles: leadership, selflessness, integrity, objectivity, accountability and openness.[88] They will be incorporated into a Model Code developed in partnership with local government bodies, approved by the Secretary of State and endorsed by Parliament.[89] Each council's Code must also contain rules relating to councillors' personal interests, whether pecuniary or otherwise.[90] Not only will all these arrangements have statutory backing but they will also involve new enforcement arrangements: each council will have a Standards Committee with power to reprimand.[91] In addition, independent Regional Standards Boards will be established with powers to give advice, receive and investigate individual complaints and impose penalties.[92] Conduct of council staff will similarly be subject to an Employees' Code which will form part of their terms and conditions of employment.[93]

The Nolan Principles have also clearly influenced the provisions of the Greater London Authority Act 1999, establishing a new form of governance for

[81] See the Foreword to and Section 1 of the Code.

[82] Operative from 1 January 1996 and revised on 13 May 1999; see http://www.cabinet-office.gov.uk/central/1999/cscode.htm

[83] *Idem*, para. 1.

[84] *Idem*, paras. 2 and 4.

[85] Department of the Environment, Transport and the Regions, *Modern Local Government: In Touch with the People*, Cm. 4014, 1998, ch. 6.

[86] *Idem*, para. 6.2.

[87] *Idem*, paras. 6.4–6.6.

[88] *Idem*, para. 6.7 and Figure 5.

[89] *Idem*, paras. 6.8 and 6.9.

[90] *Idem*, paras. 6.10–6.17.

[91] *Idem*, paras. 6.19–6.22.

[92] *Idem*, paras. 6.23–6.29 and Figure 6.

[93] *Idem*, paras. 6.4, 6.38 and 6.39. For the Government's proposals to implement these recommendations, see Local Government Bill, Part III, introduced into the House of Lords on 25 November 1999.

London, which deal with public accountability and ethical standards. In respect of the former, the Mayor will be required to submit a written report in advance of each meeting of the London Assembly and to answer questions thereon in person.[94] He will also be required to make an annual report on the exercise of his statutory functions and to organise an annual State of London Debate in consultation with the Assembly.[95] People's Question times will be held twice yearly to provide opportunities for members of the public to question the Mayor and members of the Assembly.[96] With regard to ethical standards, the Secretary of State may issue guidance to the Mayor, Assembly members, the Authority's staff and members of advisory and sub-committees of the Assembly. Such guidance may relate to the disclosure and registration of interests, conduct where an individual has an interest in an issue in question, the establishment of ethics committees and the prescription of model codes of conduct. Those subject to such guidance will be required to have regard to it in the exercise of their functions.[97]

In relation to regional devolution, provisions relating to Members' interests are to be found in both the Scotland Act 1998 and the Government of Wales Act 1998.[98] But the strongest statutory invocation of the Nolan Principles in this context is in the legislation to restore provincial government to Northern Ireland. Section 16 (4) of the Northern Ireland Act 1998 makes affirmation of "the pledge of office", of which a "code of conduct" forms part,[99] a condition precedent to the Northern Ireland First Minister and deputy First Minister taking up office. The "code of conduct" specifically requires Ministers at all times to "follow the seven principles of public life set out by the Committee on Standards in Public Life".[100] Such a statutory underpinning to the Nolan Principles may arguably lead to their direct enforcement by the Northern Ireland courts.[101]

5. THE NOLAN PRINCIPLES IN THE COURTS

The Standards Committee and its work, including the Nolan Principles, are indeed beginning to attract the attention of lawyers and the courts. In some cases this amounts to little more than background or context. *Porter et al.* v. *Magill*,[102] was an appeal against an auditor's finding of wilful misconduct after

[94] Greater London Authority Act 1999, s. 45.
[95] *Idem*, ss. 46 and 47.
[96] *Idem*, s. 48.
[97] *Idem*, s. 66.
[98] Section 39 and s. 72 respectively.
[99] *Idem*, s. 16 (10).
[100] *Idem*, Schedule 4.
[101] Cf. J Alder, *Constitutional and Administrative Law*, 3rd ed., (London, Macmillan, 1999), p. 121.
[102] (1998) 30 HLR 997.

examining accounts of Westminster City Council under the authority of the Audit Commission. In commenting on the auditor's roles of investigator, prosecutor and judge, the court referred to the reforms recommended by the Standards Committee.[103] Mentions are also to be found in two cases resulting from the "cash for questions" affair and concerned with parliamentary privilege. In each of these reference is made to the circumstances which led to the establishment of the office of Parliamentary Commissioner for Standards as recommended by the Standards Committee's *First Report*.[104] In another case, counsel drew the court's attention to the Committee's critique of the National Code of Local Government Conduct and its recommendations for reform.[105]

But in two other cases the Nolan Principles have been more central to the issues to be resolved. In *R.* v. *Housing Corporation, ex parte Rodgers*[106] allegations of a conflict of interest had been made arising out of a personal relationship between the applicant, the director of a co-operative housing society, and a partner in their principal solicitors. An officer of the respondent, exercising a regulatory function, commented adversely on the applicant's probity. The applicant then sought to challenge that "finding" by way of judicial review on the grounds of incompetence, unreasonableness and breach of the rules of natural justice. Although the judge held that there was no determination or decision susceptible to judicial review, he allowed himself to comment on the grounds. In respect of unreasonableness, and in the light of the respondent's adoption of a policy on standards of conduct and conflicts of interest, he observed: "Some may consider that the judgment of the Respondent on this issue was somewhat harsh. It is easy enough to impose 1996 (post Nolan) standards on those engaged in public life only a few years earlier. But the question is not whether the Respondent's judgment was harsh, but whether it was perverse. I am quite sure that it was not".[107]

In *Ward* v. *Chief Adjudication Officer*[108] the appellant had received a weekly attendance allowance in 1988 in his capacity as a local councillor. He claimed supplementary benefits for himself, his wife and his children. In assessing his claim the adjudication officer treated the attendance allowance as income and reduced the benefit accordingly. Mr Ward then launched on a sequence of appeals against that decision culminating in the Court of Appeal in 1998.[109] It

[103] *Idem*, at 1007.

[104] See: *R.* v. *Parliamentary Commissioner for Standards, ex parte Al Fayed* [1998] 1 All ER 83; *Hamilton* v. *Al Fayed*, Queen's Bench Division, Popplewell J, 31 July 1998, LEXIS file, ENGGEN library and [1999] 3 All ER 317 (Court of Appeal).

[105] *R* v. *Local Commissioner for Administration in North and North East England, ex parte Liverpool City Council* [1999] 3 All ER 85 at 92.

[106] Queen's Bench Division (Crown Office List), Dyson J, 11 May 1999, LEXIS file, ENGGEN library.

[107] *Idem*, at screen 15.

[108] Court of Appeal (Civil Division), Peter Gibson, Pill, Mummery LJJ, 16 October 1998, LEXIS file, ENGGEN library.

[109] The prolonged delay, which is not fully explained, seems to have been occasioned partly by administrative errors and partly by the appellant's illness.

was argued on behalf of the Chief Adjudication Officer that under the relevant Regulations[110] all forms of remuneration should be taken into account in assessing benefits unless expressly excluded, there being no exclusion in respect of an attendance allowance. In his response, Mr Ward relied, *inter alia*, on the Nolan Principle of "Selflessness" which requires holders of public office to act solely in the public interest and not so as to gain financial benefits for themselves or their families. He argued that by treating the attendance allowance as income a direct financial link was being established between service as a councillor and the private interests of councillors. The Court accepted that local authority councillors should act and behave selflessly. But, in dismissing the appeal, held that the Chief Adjudication Officer's interpretation of the Regulations was not at odds with that principle.[111]

6. CONCLUSION

Writing in 1999 in his Foreword to the Standards Committee's Report for the period 1994 to 1997, Lord Nolan said that it had been set up "not as a short-term solution to individual concerns, but, as the then Prime Minister, John Major put it, an 'ethical workshop' ".[112] The Nolan Principles are arguably the most important product from that workshop to date. In its recent detailed review of the implementation and impact of its *First Report*, the Standards Committee has found general agreement among both informed observers and politicians that there has been a marked improvement in standards over the past five years.[113] This is attributed to a clearer definition of the standards themselves, the introduction of beneficial structures and systems and a resulting lower incidence of problems.[114] This, coupled with the readiness with which the Nolan Principles have been accepted, suggests that the values they represent are in the process of becoming firmly and permanently entrenched within the public law system of the United Kingdom. From a broader standpoint, they have provided a catalyst for a new stage in the continuing process of rethinking the traditional structures and styles of the United Kingdom's constitution. What a leading member of the Blair Government has termed "pragmatism based on principle . . . reconciling mature demands for reform with the status quo in the most appropriate way".[115]

In terms of substance, the Nolan Principles are now operating in both legal and constitutional conventional modes. In their legal mode, they are part of the

[110] Supplementary Benefits (Resources) Regulations 1981, SI 1981, No. 1527.

[111] *Loc. cit.* in n. 108 at screens 10–12.

[112] See http://www.public-standards.gov.uk/annreps/forewor.htm

[113] *Sixth Report*, Cm. 4557-I, paras. 2.2–2.3 and references there cited.

[114] *Idem*, para. 2.4.

[115] Lord Irving of Lairg, in "Government's Programme of Constitutional Reform", a lecture delivered on 8 December 1998; see http://www.open.gov.uk/lcd/speeches/1998/lc-const.htm

law of Parliament, they feature prominently in legislation of constitutional significance and they are beginning to be cited in the courts. In respect of the latter, there is considerable potential for them to play a significant role in judicial review proceedings, particularly in challenges alleging bias or unreasonableness. They are perhaps on their way to becoming what has been called "a common currency to guide the courts and administrative decision-makers".[116] In their constitutional conventional mode, they are informing the conduct and delivery of public administration and public services at national, regional and local levels. They are strengthening the armoury of existing institutions such as the Commissioners for Local Administration as well as prompting the establishment of new institutions. As between their evolving legal and constitutional conventional modes, the current balance clearly favours convention rather than law. But, as an early commentator has suggested, the conscious choice of new conventions may well be "a preferred tool of constitutional development and a preferred means of achieving constitutional propriety".[117] There does now seem to be sufficient evidence to suggest that the Nolan Principles "are not simply sharpening the means of implementing old values, they are also making a knowing and positive contribution to the creation of new conventions, recommending new standards reflecting new values, with new institutions and procedures to give effect to them".[118]

There remains the question of monitoring and regulating the future observance of these new standards, principles and values. The standing role of the Standards Committee itself has an important part to play in this connection. As Lord Neill has put it: "The strength of this Committee is its ability to return to a subject and to review both progress in implementing recommendations and the effect of implementation".[119] But the Committee is clearly neither designed nor equipped for a task of scrutiny that is likely to become increasingly complex. It is equally not a role for the courts. There is now a developing, complex and multi-faceted construct for which the Nolan Principles provide a common substratum. But the construct as a whole has no single focal point capable of or responsible for monitoring activities and maintaining consistency. The diversity of the mechanisms employed is already considerable.[120] While

[116] J Alder, *Constitutional and Administrative Law*, 3rd ed., (London, Macmillan, 1999), p. 61.

[117] G Wilson, "Postscript: The Courts, Law and Convention" in Lord Nolan and Sir S Sedley, *The Making and Remaking of the British Constitution* (London, Blackstone Press, 1997), p. 124.

[118] *Ibid.*

[119] In a letter to the Prime Minister printed with the Committee's *Sixth Report*, Cm. 4557-I. Also see the Committee's earlier consultation paper *Review of the First Report of the Committee on Standards in Public Life*,
http://www.public-standards.gov.uk/issues%20&%20questions/ index.htm

[120] This is part of a larger phenomenon that has been termed "regulatory creep". A recent study has revealed a total of more than one hundred regulators employing more than ten thousand people full time. See C Hood, C Scott, O James, G Jones and T Travers, *Regulation inside Government: Waste-watchers, Quality Police and Sleaze-busters* (Oxford, Oxford University Press, 1999).

there is a case for diversity in the sense of "structures sensitive to place and people, not uniform structures imposed for uniformity's sake",[121] diversity itself requires a central point of reference in the interests of integrity and consistency. As Lord Nolan himself is quoted as observing: "I am not at all sure that Whitehall has fully recognised that diversity does increase the need for a strong central core".[122] That issue will be a crucial one for the next stage in the process to underwrite the fundamental values of the United Kingdom's constitution and system of public law.

[121] Lord Irving of Lairg, *loc. cit.* in n. 115 *supra*.
[122] Quoted in *The Financial Times*, 25 February 1997.

13

Fundamental Environmental Values and Public Law

JOHN ALDER

1. INTRODUCTION: CONFLICTS OF VALUE

Environmental ethics are concerned with why we should protect the environment and how we should rank competing interests.[1] Public law is concerned (*inter alia*) to ensure that decision makers take into account all relevant interests. As well as conflicts between environmental and economic interests, most obviously in the case of industrial pollution, there are conflicts between different kinds of environmental interest. For example, should we prefer the apparently friendly and intelligent dolphin to the rare species of turtle that might be threatened as a side-effect of our attempts to protect the dolphin? Windfarms raise conflicts between the environmental goods of energy saving, landscape quality, and wildlife protection.[2] Genetic engineering generates conflict between the integrity of the individual life-form, environmental concerns for ecological processes and human well-being.[3]

In a democracy, within the limits of survival and stability, disagreement between values is to be cherished as a safeguard for freedom and equality.[4] Reflecting the inevitability of such disagreement, statutory definitions of "environment" usually lack guidance as to the values involved[5] and international instruments, although less reticent in this respect, often contain multiple and

[1] See generally J Alder and D Wilkinson, *Environmental Law and Ethics* (Basingstoke, Macmillan, 1999) A Dobson, *Green Political Thought*, 2nd ed. (London, Routledge, 1995); J DesJardins, *Environmental Ethics*, 2nd ed. (Belmont, Wadsworth, 1997); J Passmore, *Man's Responsibility for Nature*, 2nd ed. (London, Duckworth, 1980).

[2] *North Devon DC* v. *West Coast Windfarms* [1996] JPL 767.

[3] See Dobson, "Biocentrism and Genetic Engineering" 4 *Environmental Values* 227.

[4] See J Waldron, *Law and Disagreement* (Oxford, OUP, 1998).

[5] See for example, Environmental Protection Act 1990 s. 1 (2), "all or any of the following media, namely the air, water and land". Compare the New Zealand Resource Management Act s. 2 (1) which refers, *inter alia*, to ecosystems and their constituent parts including people and communities, natural and physical resources, amenity values, social, economic, aesthetic and cultural conditions affecting the above, all sorts of plants and animals.

conflicting ethical pronouncements.[6] In particular the concept of pollution is value laden. Pollution is the introduction of an alien substance[7] but nothing in nature is entirely pure. Statutory definitions of pollution usually refer to "harm",[8] but the concept of environmental "harm" also reflects a diversity of values. For example, our pollution may be a wild animal's meal.

We might agree that harm includes threats to human life and health and that it also includes offence to our aesthetic sensibilities,[9] but what if a species of insect which we might never see is extinguished? Do we worry about nature conservation because we value nature in its own right or only because of nature's benefits to ourselves? We cannot help but depict nature through our own needs. However, nature is constantly changing over a very long time scale so that we cannot know whether the environmentalists' depiction of nature as balanced and harmonious is correct and if so whether this is good. For example, by preserving the traditional English countryside we may be producing an artifact analogous to a Disneyland under the illusion that we are protecting nature.[10]

Environmental values are incommensurable in the sense that there is no objective measure or scale which can be used to choose rationally between them. Human nature is inconsistent in the sense that the same person can hold conflicting values simultaneously without there being any overarching universal principle to reconcile them, and with good reasons to prefer either value. For example, I may have competing duties to tell the truth and to protect another person's reputation between which I am forced to choose.[11] Incommensurables can sometimes be combined in the sense that the application of different values may happen to produce the same outcome. For example, ensuring the survival of a scientifically important rare species may protect the well being of individual members of that species. However, where combinability is not possible we are faced with what Berlin called the "tragic choice" that we cannot give effect to one interest without sacrificing the other either wholly or in part.[12] For example, in order to sustain a species as a whole we might have to slaughter individual members of it.

Lawyers like to give the task of making tragic choices the appearance of objectivity by talking about the need to "balance" competing interests and referring grandly to "the public interest". However, these terms are misleading since

[6] See for example, Declaration of the UN Conference on the Human Environment, 1972 (Stockholm Declaration), World Charter for Nature 1982, Declaration of the UN Conference on Environment and Development 1992 (Rio Declaration), Biodiversity Convention 1992.

[7] See *Young* v. *Bankier Distillery* [1893] AC 691.

[8] See Environmental Protection Act 1990 s. 1 (2) 78A(4).

[9] *Ibid*, s. 1 (4).

[10] See Elliot (ed.), *Environmental Ethics* (Oxford, OUP, 1995), chs. 11, 12, cf. the case of farming which can be alternatively characterised as a polluting industry or as part of "nature" leading to different legal responses. See P Lowe *et al Moralising the Environment* (London, UCL Press, 1997); Town and Country Planning Act 1990 s. 55 (2)e.

[11] See B Barry, *Political Argument* (London, Harvester Wheatsheaf, 1990).

[12] I Berlin, *Two Concepts of Liberty* (Oxford, OUP, 1968); J Raz, *The Morality of Freedom* (Oxford, OUP, 1986).

nothing can be balanced without common scale and the notion of public interest is inadequate, even in its most plausible sense of a good common to all. For example, environmental protection which is a good common to all may benefit the relatively well-off at the expense of the poor by, for instance, concentrating polluting activities in places where property values are low or rationing house building in order to preserve the countryside.

In *Airdale Housing Trust* v. *Bland*[13] the House of Lords had to decide whether doctors should withdraw life support from a man who had been so severely injured in the Hillsborough stadium disaster that he was unlikely ever to regain consciousness. Lord Hoffmann regarded the issue as one of tragic choice between the principles of the sanctity of life and of respecting what the individual would have chosen himself. His Lordship criticised the Attorney-General's argument that these principles could be harmonised as empty rhetoric "intended to dull the pain of having to choose".

The best we can do is to provide an accommodation between incommensurables made in accordance with a decision-making process which we can respect as fair and open and which, by using concepts such as proportionality, tries to minimise the harm resulting from any tragic choice. Ideally every democratic accommodation should be provisional and reversible, hence the cherished principle that Parliament cannot bind its successors and our belief in the common law as a flexible mechanism to adjust the law to changing values in an orderly fashion. In the case of the environment there are however special problems. Environmental decisions and environmental damage may be irreversible and it is sometimes suggested that the threat to the environment is so great that it cannot be met without sacrificing democratic values.[14]

The concept of "sustainable development"[15] is intended to provide a democratic policy framework for combining the incommensurable interests of environmental protection, economic development and social justice. For example, waste can be reprocessed to produce energy, thus saving unrenewable resources and creating jobs albeit possibly at the cost of pollution and habitat damage. It could be argued that sustainable development is a political smokescreen designed to advance the interests of economic development[16] but the concept at least helps us to recognise that what appears at first sight to be a clash of values

[13] [1998] 1 All ER 821.

[14] See G Hardin, "The Tragedy of the Commons" 162 *Science* 1243; G Hardin, "Living in a Lifeboat" 24 *Bioscience* 561. The usual argument linking democracy with environmental concerns is that environmental degradation is alleged to be the outcome of exploitation by technocratic elites. See R Eckersley, *Environmentalism and Political Theory* (London, UCL Press, 1992), pp. 53–5, A Dobson, *Green Political Thought*, 2nd ed. (London, Routledge, 1992), ch. 1 and pp. 80–5, 126–33 M Sagoff, "Can Environmentalists be Liberals?" in Elliot (ed.), *supra* n. 10, cf. Principle 10, Rio Declaration 1992.

[15] Environment Act 1995 s. 4 (1), (3). Sustainable Development: the UK Strategy (Cmnd 2426 (London, HMSO, 1994), EC Treaty Article 6.

[16] See Jewell and Steele *infra* n. 37, Dobson, *supra* n. 1 ch. 3, M Redclift, *Sustainable Development: Exploring the Contradictions* (London, Macmillan, 1992).

may turn out to be merely a factual disagreement as to whether different objectives can be combined. For example, can a rare species of rhino be preserved without creating a nature reserve which would damage the interests of local farmers and might threaten humans with starvation?[17]

Sustainable development also recognises that it may be difficult to justify giving priority to the environment. In *Tennessee Valley* v. *Hill*[18] the US Supreme Court banned the completion of a federal project (the Tellico Dam) that would have brought huge economic benefits to an underdeveloped region, in favour of the preservation of the snail darter which is an obscure but endangered species without any known benefit to humanity whose habitat lay in the path of the work. This was because the language of the Endangered Species Act 1973 (which had been passed after the project commenced), was read as imposing an absolute obligation to preserve endangered species. This case led to an amendment to the Endangered Species Act first to allow protection to be overridden by a special committee (popularly known as the "god squad") and secondly to require an economic assessment before designating certain critical habitats.

UK legislation usually leaves the ranking of competing values and interests to executive discretion but occasionally ranks interests in priority. The Environment Act 1995 s. 61 requires national park authorities to give priority to conservation concerns over the interests of tourism and amenity but not over factors such as employment. The Habitats Directive 1992 attempts to rank interests by sometimes favouring species preservation over social and economic concerns in an hierarchical structure under which designation as a protected "European Site" must be based on environmental criteria alone. However, after designation, human social and economic interests sometimes justify interfering with the site but only where there is no alternative solution and compensatory measures are taken. In the case of sites which are host to "priority species" the only factors that can outweigh designation are those relating to human health, public safety, beneficial consequences of primary importance for the environment or imperative reasons of overriding public interest permitted by the Commission.[19]

The precautionary principle which, although not part of UK law is a prominent instrument of environmental policy, also attempts to give special weight to environmental concerns, in this case by requiring scientific uncertainty to be discounted where there is a risk of serious or irreversible environmental damage. However, the meaning and scope of the precautionary principle is controversial. Indeed the version applied in UK policy requires that environmental

[17] See R Attfield, "Saving Nature, Feeding People and The Foundations of Ethics" 7 *Environmental Values* 294; H Rolston, *ibid.* 349.

[18] 437 U.S. 153 (1978).

[19] EC 92/43. See Conservation (Natural Habitats) Regulation 1994 (SI 1994 no. 2716); *R* v. *Secretary of State for the Environment, ex parte RSPB* [1998] JEL 92 cf. *Commission* v. *Spain* [1883] ECR 1; *Commission* v. *Germany* [1991] ECR 1 883; A Nolkaemper, "Habitat Protection in European Community Law, Evolving Conceptions of a Balance of Interests" 9 *JEL* 271.

measures be cost effective, a proposition that is difficult to apply in a context of scientific uncertainty.[20]

2. DIFFERENT KINDS OF ENVIRONMENTAL VALUE

There is a wide spectrum of environmental values and it is sometimes urged that the need to protect the environment must generate a "new" ethic.[21] The problem for environmental ethics is how to identify and rank objects of value in nature without unjustifiably preferring our own human interests.

2.1. Instrumental, deontological and virtue ethics

Environmental values, in common with other values, are broadly of three kinds. First there are instrumental values which exist as a means to some other end. From this perspective, applied routinely in the form of cost-benefit analysis, we value the dolphin as an instrument of human well-being by virtue of the pleasure we get from observing dolphins or even from knowing that such creatures exist. The most widely used form of instrumentalism is utilitarianism according to which a "good" outcome is whatever satisfies the greatest number of preferences or interests although there is controversy as to how these are to be recognised. Are they actual demands or are they interests which the ruling elite think are good for us? J S Mill for example regarded some preferences, namely those representing our higher culture as inherently more valuable than others because they represent a more informed choice, ". . . it is better to be Socrates dissatisfied than a pig satisfied . . . and if the pig (is) of a different opinion it is because (it) only knows its own side of the case".[22] Utilitarianism raises the difficulty for environmentalism that it does not value nature as such. If we could create an artificial environment that reproduced the pleasure we obtain from animals and other natural features, from a utilitarian perspective this would arguably be as good as the real thing.[23]

Secondly, there are intrinsic values which we give to an object for its own sake irrespective of any benefits it might have. The idea of intrinsic value underpins "deontological" ethical perspectives which, following Kant (1724–1804) take the view that certain things are good in themselves and that it is wrong to treat

[20] See T O'Riorden and J Cameron (eds.), *Interpreting the Precautionary Principle* (London, Earthscan, 1994) and text above n. 88 *infra*.

[21] See J Rodman, "The Liberation of Nature?" 20 *Inquiry* 83; R Routley, "Is there a Need for a New, an Environmental Ethic?" in *Proceedings of the Fifteenth World Congress of Philosophy* (Sophia, Sophia Press, 1973) cf. T Regan, "The Nature and Possibility of an Environmental Ethic" 3 *Environmental Ethics* 19.

[22] *Utilitarianism*, (ed.) Warnock (London, Collins, 1962), p. 260.

[23] See L Tribe, "Ways Not to Think about Plastic Trees" 83 *Yale Law Review* 1315; M Sagoff, "On Preserving the Natural Environment" 84 *Yale Law Review* 205. Cf. n. 73 *infra*.

them as instruments. We would not for example make anyone a slave in order to benefit the majority although utilitarianism is capable of countenancing this.[24] Intrinsic value must be distinguished from "inherent" value or "existence" value. These expressions refer to the *instrumental* value which an object may have by virtue of its existence alone, for example an original painting or a beautiful landscape, and are contrasted with "use value". For example, tuna have use value whereas the dolphin has inherent value. Believers in intrinsic value might maintain that each has value irrespective of any human interest and some claim that value would exist even without human values.

Thirdly, there are "virtue ethics". Virtue ethics are not concerned with the outcomes of our actions as such but our motivation or what kind of people we are. Derived from the Aristotelian teleological idea that everything has an inherent nature or purpose,[25] virtue ethics focus upon what it means to be a good citizen, what sorts of attitudes we should have and how we should set about decision-making. It favours moderation, diversity, prudence and the avoidance of waste and thus may be attractive to environmentalists. In legal terms we would expect virtue ethics to be concerned with fair procedures, participatory rights and concepts such as proportionality which favour minimising the harm we do in pursuit of our legitimate aims. Given the wide range of competing interests that fall within the loose notion of environmental justice, a virtue ethics approach may well be the most realistic. Commentators on international law have emphasised the importance of procedural rights in relation to environmental protection.[26]

2.2. Anthropocentric perspectives

Environmental ethics can be broadly divided into anthropocentric and non-anthropocentric schools of thought. Anthropocentric perspectives regard human well-being as the exclusive object of environmental concern and regard the environment as a resource providing wealth, life support, aesthetic pleasure and other forms of entertainment. Anthropocentrists tend to have faith in human ingenuity in the form of science, economics and technology to resolve our environmental problems and may argue that the environmental movement exaggerates the problems.[27] This raises an important legal issue relating to how

[24] Utilitarianism has many problems among which, taken to extreme, it is conducive to serious injustices such as persecuting minorities. See e.g. J Smart and B Williams, *Utilitarianism For and Against* (Cambridge, Cambridge University Press, 1973).

[25] See R Rorty (ed.), *Essays on Aristotle's Ethics* (Berkeley, University of California, 1980).

[26] See Final Report of UN Special Rapporteur on Human Rights (Ksentini Report) (1994); A Boyle and M Anderson (eds.), *Human Rights Approaches to Environmental Protection* (Oxford, Clarendon Press, 1996).

[27] See for example, W Beckerman, *Small is Stupid: Blowing the Whistle on the Greens* (London, Duckworth, 1995); R North, *Life on a Modern Planet: A Manifesto for Progress* (Manchester, Manchester University Press, 1995).

far non-scientific notions of rationality must be taken into account by official decision-makers (*infra*).

Anthropocentric values are grounded in a synthesis of the Aristotelian and Christian traditions that nature exists for the benefit of humankind and that we have a right and indeed a duty to exploit nature in order to realise human potential.[28] This belief was the driving force of the Enlightenment and the Industrial Revolution and has influenced the common law.[29] It relates to the Kantian view that ethics depends on the participation of equal rational beings. From this it has been claimed, albeit fiercely contested,[30] that human beings can owe duties only to rational beings. Rawls, for example, claimed that non-humans cannot participate in a system of justice although he thought that we should be kind to animals anyway.[31] The traditional Kantian explanation is that being cruel to animals makes us morally insensitive to ourselves, a proposition that has been applied in English cases.[32]

Anthropocentrism includes the notion of moral duties to future generations. However, the idea that we can owe moral duties to future generations is controversial.[33] For example, large reductions in the future population might help to protect the environment. Can we justify sacrificing clear benefits for existing people in favour of uncertain benefits for hypothetical future generations who might be better off than ourselves or malevolent towards cultures such as our own? Indeed according to "Parfit's paradox" which is based upon the inevitability that whatever we do now changes the identity of those yet to be born, it is wrong to deny the possibility of life to any class of being for the sake of giving life to another class of being in a better environment.[34] It is arguable however that we owe duties to those of our descendants to whom we are able to relate, namely our children and grandchildren, and that maximising their environmental well-being creates a chain of responsibility down the generations.[35] For example, English land law particularly in the nineteenth century Settled Land Acts has been influenced by the tension between the desire to provide for the security of future generations and the needs of the market.

[28] See Passmore, *supra* n. 1, ch. 1.

[29] See for example, *Salvin* v. *North Brancepeth Coal Company* [1874] 9 Ch. App. 705 at 709–10; *Hole* v. *Barlow* (1858) LJCP 207; *Hunter* v. *Canary Wharf* [1997] 2 All ER 426. Blackstone, following Locke thought that man's duty to exploit nature was the foundation of private property: see C Rose, "Possession as the Origin of Property" 52 *University of Chicago Law Review* 73 (1985).

[30] See M Midgely, "Duties Concerning Islands" in Elliot, *supra* n. 10, ch. 5, cf. Passmore *supra* n. 1, ch. 7.

[31] See J Rawls, *A Theory of Justice* (Oxford, OUP, 1972), p. 512; see also R Frey, *Interests and Rights: The Case Against Animals* (Oxford, Clarendon Press, 1980).

[32] See *Re Wedgewood* [1915] 1 Ch. 113 at 122; *R* v. *Somerset County Council, ex parte Fewings* [1995] 3 All ER 20 at 31.

[33] See Alder and Wilkinson, *supra* n. 1, pp. 129–134.

[34] See D Parfit, "On Doing the Best for our Children" in M Bayles (ed.), *Ethics and Population* (Cambridge Ma, Schenkman, 1976) cf. Agora, "What Does One Generation Owe to the Next?" 84 *Am Jl Int Law* 190.

[35] See Passmore, *supra* n. 1, pp. 88–9.

The anthropocentric approach commonly uses money as a measure of value. For example, economic cost, benefit analysis is built into public environmental law as a general duty of the Environment Agency[36] and the contaminated land regime created by the Environment Act 1995 is driven by the notion of "fitness for use" in terms of the market as mediated by planning authorities rather than by the notion of a desirable state of the environment *per se*.[37] However, financial methods may not be appropriate to incommensurable goods in which there is no commercial market such as a rare species or a landscape. Indeed, the very reason why we value natural features may be because they are outside commercial concerns. For example, the "value" of a rare butterfly cannot be compared with that of a new motorway that threatens its habitat. Therefore, we cannot compare an environmentalist's assertion that the disappearance of the butterfly is too high a price to pay with the assertion of a developer that the benefits of the road outweigh its costs. If we value the butterfly for its own sake, the notion of a cost-benefit analysis is offensive in the same way that it is offensive deliberately to kill a human being in order to advance an economic goal.[38] Moreover, the benefits of a development such as a new road are easier to estimate than are its costs so that the dice are loaded against environmental interests.

There is a broader version of anthropocentrism known as "enlightened anthropocentrism". This is related to another Christian tradition, that of Stewardship.[39] Enlightened anthropocentrism argues that our well-being depends on co-operating with rather than exploiting nature. It looks beyond the material benefit we gain from exploiting nature and includes the spiritual benefits we obtain from our interdependence with nature, our admiration for and fear of nature and our feelings of sympathy for other living things.

The common law does not currently favour enlightened anthropocentrism. In particular property law is not well suited to protect the goods characteristically associated with enlightened anthropocentric values such as the beauty of nature since these are public goods not easily reducible to private interests. For

[36] Environment Act 1995 s. 4 (1), s. 39 (1). See also the BATNEEC requirement of the integrated pollution control and GMO regimes (Environmental Protection Act 1990 s. 7, s. 109 (3)). Compare environmental impact assessment requirements under EC Directive 85/337 (as amended by 97/11 EC) which sets out the nature of the factors to be taken into account but does not require any particular form of weighting.

[37] See Jewell and Steele, "UK Regulatory Reform and the pursuit of Sustainable Development" 8 *Journal of Environmental Law* 283.

[38] See D Pearce *et al*, *Blueprint for a Green Economy* (London, Earthscan, 1989); D Pearce, "Green Economics" 1 *Environmental Values* 3; C Rose, "Environmental Faust Succumbs to Temptations of Economic Mephistopholes" 87 *Michigan Law Review* 1361; M Sagoff, *The Economy of the Earth* (Cambridge, Cambridge University Press, 1988); M Sagoff, "Four Dogmas of Environmental Economics" 3 *Environmental Values* 285; M Prior, "Economic Valuation and Environmental Values" 7 *Environmental Values* 423. Cf. contingent valuation techniques: K Baker, "Consorting With Forests: Rethinking Our Relationship to Natural Resources and How We Should Value their Loss" 22 *Ecology Law Quarterly* 677.

[39] Passmore, *supra* n. 1, ch. 2.

example, nuisance law is restricted to the protection of proprietary rights, and natural amenities such as the right to a pleasant view are not protected.[40] If natural amenities were protected the private landowner would effectively be required to confer a public benefit without compensation[41] although it could be argued that the privilege of ownership which is made possible by the law carries social obligations.[42] However, even in the public law context of charitable trusts, the courts have held that interests such as wildlife conservation and animal welfare are worthy of protection only where they directly benefit humans. Thus, a wildlife sanctuary intended to protect animals from human interference was refused charitable status[43] as was the anti-vivisection movement on the ground that medical benefit to humans must always outweigh animal welfare.[44]

2.3. Individualistic non-anthropocentrism

Non-anthropocentric ethics argue that nature has moral value irrespective of human interests. The common law has not subscribed to a non-anthropocentric ethic as is illustrated by the law's attitude to wildlife which it treats only as potential property.[45] Non-anthropocentric ethics tries to avoid what is sometimes called "speciesism". It is argued that over the centuries increasing moral awareness has gradually overcome discrimination in the form for example of slavery, sex discrimination and racial discrimination and that the next logical step is to overcome species discrimination.[46]

[40] *Hunter* v. *Canary Wharf* [1997] 2 All ER 426; *Aldred's Case* (1610) 9 Co. Rep 57b. The law of nuisance is prepared to sacrifice environmental standards to developmental needs albeit, except in the case of property damage which is always actionable, environmental harm is evaluated according to a crude zoning technique based on the "normal" character of the neighbourhood in question *St Helens Smelting Co Ltd* v. *Tipping* 1865 11 HLC 642.

[41] The equitable doctrine of restrictive covenants has been applied broadly to protect interests not capable of being quantified in money terms; *Wrotham Parks Estates Ltd* v. *Parkside Homes Ltd* [1974] 2 All ER 321.

[42] See K Gray, "Equitable Property" 47 *Current Legal Problems* 157 (1994); W Lucy and C Mitchell, "Replacing Private Property: The Case for Stewardship" 55 *Cambridge Law Journal* 566 (1996).

[43] *Re Grove-Grady* [1929] Ch. 557, cf. *AG for New South Wales* v. *Sawtell* [1978] 2 NSWLR 200 where a trust for wildlife conservation was held to be charitable on characteristically "enlightened anthropocentric" grounds including cultural values and biological diversity as well as narrower grounds of science, education and amenity.

[44] *National Anti-Vivisection Society* v. *IRC* [1948] AC 31 – anti-vivisection interests had no public benefit in relation to medical research and were also political objects.

[45] See *Blades* v. *Higgs* (1865), 11 HL Cas. 621; *AG for British Columbia* v. *AG for Canada* [1914] AC 153; (*Marquis of Granby* v. *Bakewell UDC* (1823) lxxxvii JP 105); cf. Trail Smelter Arbitration 33 *AJIL* (1939) 182; *Commonwealth of Puerto Rico* v. *SS Zoe Colocotroni* 456 Fed. Sup. 1327 (1978).

[46] See A Leopold, *A Sand County Almanack* (New York, OUP, 1949), ch. 1. R Eckersley, *supra* n. 14; M Midgely, *Animals and Why they Matter* (Athens GA, University of Georgia Press, 1983). Bentham seems to take a similar view, *Introduction to the Principles of Morals and Legislation*, ch. XVII, para. 4.

Non-anthropocentric ethics rejects the Kantian idea that we can owe moral duties only to rational beings as arbitrary, pointing out that rights and duties do not have to be reciprocal. Perhaps the strongest argument against the traditional view that rationality is the basis of moral value is that it degrades those humans who lack full rational capacity such as the very young or the mentally impaired.

There are different degrees of non-anthropocentrism depending on what qualities each proponent finds morally attractive. At the conservative end of the spectrum are individualistic animal welfare ethics. According to Peter Singer who takes a utilitarian approach,[47] we have an obligation to avoid causing suffering to any sentient creature although we might have to weigh different kinds of suffering so as to choose the least harmful solution. Where an animal has a greater capacity to suffer than a human, for example in the case of a very young child, Singer's rationale leads to conclusions which are likely to offend many people.

Tom Regan takes a deontological stance which gives animals moral value. Regan asserts that some creatures are the "subject of a life" and therefore entitled to be left alone to pursue their own goals. To be the subject of a life is to have "beliefs and desires, perception, memory and a sense of the future".[48] As a working hypothesis Regan limits moral considerability to mentally normal mammals of at least one-year old. Regan's favoured beings therefore extend less far into the natural world than Singer's although Regan would give some protection for example to battery chickens on the Kantian ground that cruelty to them lays open the way to cruelty to higher creatures.

Regan and Singer are not concerned with environmental protection as such. Their approaches sometimes happen to be combinable with environmental protection but neither would give moral weight to whether a creature is a member of a rare species and neither would permit interference with creatures in the interests of environmental enhancement. It has often been suggested that Singer and Regan remain essentially racist in spirit being patronisingly prepared to admit into the moral club only creatures who are sufficiently like ourselves.[49] This is one response to the problem of the tuna/dolphin dispute in the United States, where, in order to protect both commercial interests in tuna fishing and the welfare of dolphins, the interests of endangered species of turtle were put at risk.[50]

UK law has not seriously embraced either of these perspectives. Animal welfare legislation seems to be animated primarily by a human centred form of virtue ethics in the sense that we try to minimise the suffering of animals but without too much inconvenience to ourselves. The law has developed pragmatically, mainly as the result of lobbying by pressure groups such as the RSPB and RSPCA set against lobbies for human interests notably in agriculture and

[47] P Singer, *Animal Liberation*, 2nd ed. (London, Cape, 1995).
[48] T Regan, *The Case for Animal Rights* (London, Routledge, 1988).
[49] J Rodman, "The Liberation of Nature" 20 *Enquiry* 194.
[50] See Alder and Wilkinson, *supra* n. 1 ch. 11 by Ilona Cheyne.

hunting. The law's main concern is to prevent the infliction of suffering solely for entertainment or other than for purposes of economic value. For example, vivisection for scientific purposes is controlled by a licensing system.[51] There is a proportionality requirement that the research to be undertaken cannot be done by other means and that the minimum possible suffering is caused.

The law is strongest in relation to creatures that we regard as useful, attractive or similar to us.[52] Rare or endangered species are also strongly protected and there are overrides for a wide range of socially acceptable human concerns. There is a weak proportionality principle in some statutes that exempts "unavoidable" injury incidental to "lawful" human activities.[53] However, this does not provide for an evaluation of the importance of the human interest in question and would not therefore satisfy a non-anthropocentric ethic. For example, the measure of cruelty to farm animals is that of normal practices of good husbandry.[54] The Wild Mammals (Protection) Act 1996 is perhaps the most radical legislation. However, the original Bill was watered down by a deal between the animal welfare and hunting lobbies. The Act applies only to the intentional infliction of "unnecessary" suffering by specified acts of cruelty. It contains exemptions for poisoning, hunting and sporting and has dropped the Bill's original use of the broader terms "torture and mistreat".

Moving further away from the human model, the "biocentric" approach developed by Paul Taylor extends moral considerability to all living things whether sensate or not. The rationale for this is "respect for life". Life has the capacity to flourish and to achieve a natural goal as where an acorn grows into an oak. According to Taylor this gives all life "a good of its own" with which it is wrong to interfere. Life is not hierarchical with humans at the top but all life forms are *prima facie* equal, each one having interests and purposes as a "teleological centre of a life". It is irrelevant, according to Taylor whether or not the life form is aware of its purpose.[55] However, a purpose of which one cannot be aware could be regarded as a contradiction.

Apart from difficulties in deciding what counts as life[56] this is a recipe for strange conflicts, for example between myself and the weeds in my garden. Taylor proposes elaborate criteria to resolve such conflicts. All life forms are equal in value but the *content* of the bundle of entitlements of each life form

[51] Animals (Scientific Procedures) Act 1983. Experiments on the higher animals are completely banned.

[52] For example, Protection of Animals Act 1911 – animals in captivity; Wildlife and Countryside Act 1981 – wild birds and rare species; Badgers (Protection) Act 1992. See HL Deb. Vol. 857 col. 1692 (1973), *ibid.* vol. 864 col. 22 (1973), *ibid.* vol. 867 col. 43 (1973).

[53] For example, Wildlife and Countryside Act 1981 s. 4 (2)c; Badgers (Protection) Act 1992 s. 8 (2).

[54] See *Ford* v. *Wiley* (1889) 23 QBD 203; *Roberts* v. *Ruggiero* (Unreported, 3 April 1985, QBD); *Hall and Anor* v. *RSPCA* (Unreported, 1993).

[55] P Taylor *Respect for Nature* (Princeton, Princeton University Press, 1986); R Nash, "The Case for Biotic Rights" 18 *Yale Journal of International Law* 235 (1993); J Sterba, "A Biocentrist Strikes Back" 20 *Environmental Ethics* 361.

[56] See N Agar, "Biocentrism and the Concept of Life" 108 *Ethics* 147–68.

differs according to the *telos* or purpose of that particular life form. Thus, even the basic interests of lower life forms might be sacrificed to important cultural interests of ourselves. However, we must be guided by principles of minimum harm and proportionality and where we cause harm we must provide compensation.[57] Taylor's approach may be considered one of virtue ethics and is congenial to the lawyer's concern with fair process as opposed to particular outcomes.

2.4. Ecocentric perspectives

A further conceptual jump is made by proponents of the "ecocentric" perspective. They value collective entities such as species, habitats, or ecosystems, treating individuals merely as components of a larger "whole" depicted as a community, such as a city or even as a collective organism. Ecocentrists, like communitarian political theorists in the human sphere, argue that the individual is instrumental to the group or even that the individual is unreal apart from the group.[58]

Perhaps the most influential ecocentric ethic is the "land ethic" promoted by the American game warden Aldo Leopold. According to Leopold "all ethics so far evolved rests upon a single premise: that the individual is a member of a community of interdependent parts. . . . The land ethic simply enlarges that community to include soils, waters, plants and animals, or collectively: the land"; and "a thing is right when it tends to preserve the integrity, stability and beauty of the biotic community. It is wrong when it tends otherwise".[59] To some extent the land ethic fits the enlightened anthropocentric approach by emphasising the relationship of interdependence between nature and ourselves. The land ethic does not give humans or individual animals any special status in the biotic community. Nor does the land ethic value rare or endangered species unless they contribute to the functioning of the system as a whole.

The land ethic has been called totalitarian and "environmental fascism".[60] However, it has been argued that if the whole is to flourish, its component parts must also flourish so that "the land ethic leaves our traditional human morality quite intact".[61] Nevertheless, under the land ethic a tragic choice

[57] See also D Van De Veer, "Interspecific Justice" 22 *Inquiry* 55 (1979) who produces a similar weighting system from a utilitarian perspective.

[58] See R Eckersley, *supra* n. 14. Whatever the scientific validity of this, any complex entity has discrete components which may conflict.

[59] A Leopold, *A Sand County Almanac* (Oxford, OUP, 1995); B Callicott, *In Defence of the Land Ethic* (Albany, State University of New York, 1989). See H Rolston, "Value in Nature and the Nature of Value" in R Attfield and A Belsay (eds.), *Philosophy and the Natural Environment* (Cambridge, Cambridge University Press, 1994).

[60] T Regan, *supra* n. 48 p. 362. See M Kheel, "The Liberation of Nature, A Circular Affair" 7 *Environmental Ethics* 135.

[61] Eckersley, *supra* n. 14 at 62; D Marietta, "Environmental Holism and Individuals" 10 *Environmental Ethics* 251.

between the individual and the larger whole cannot always be avoided. For example, an ecocentric approach might have to sacrifice human beings by culling "excessive" populations or saving the life of a rare reptile at the expense of a human life.

Ecocentrism has conceptual advantages in relation to environmental liability in that it rejects traditional ideas of legal responsibility based on individual autonomy which seek to track causation to blameworthy individuals and find difficulty with strict and corporate liabilities.[62] Environmental degradation often has multiple causes which are not easily separable as when a polluted river has many different sources or where pollution or a loss of a habitat is caused by a combination of different factors each innocent in itself. Thus the "polluter pays" principle which is a feature of both international and domestic environmental policy[63] is difficult to apply. For example, the polluter arguably includes all who benefit from the pollution such as the users of a product made by a polluting industry. This is one reason for the popularity of market mechanisms such as pollution charges as a means of spreading responsibility.[64]

It is sometimes suggested that international law is gradually broadening its ethical perspective towards biocentric or ecocentric ethics.[65] For example, since the Second World War the international whaling regime has shifted its emphasis towards preserving the whale for its own sake rather than protecting the whaling industry; the Habitats Directive 1992[66] prevents human social and economic considerations from being taken into account in deciding whether to designate a protected site; many international instruments claim that nature has intrinsic value irrespective of human concerns; and the Convention on International Trade in Endangered Species (1972) has a strong enforcement regime.

However, this view must be treated with caution. Anthropocentric and animal welfare perspectives also value collective entities such as species and ecosystems. Indeed the concept of sustainable development is strongly anthropocentric. From the anthropocentric perspective, for example, a species is a repository of genetic resources and a source of education or aesthetic pleasure.

[62] See *Empress Car Co (Abertillery)* v. *NRA* [1998] WLR 350. Where a company is sued as directly liable the law attempts to identify an individual as the "controlling mind" of the company. (See *Tesco Supermarkets* v. *Natrass* [1972] AC 153, but cf. *National Rivers Authority* v. *Alfred MacAlpine Homes East* [1994] 4 All ER 286 recommending a broader approach in environmental cases.

[63] See Rio Declaration 1992 Principle 16, EC Treaty Article 174.

[64] Thus the principle has different implications depending upon whether we regard it as enshrining legal values of fault or economic values of internalising costs. See Alder and Wilkinson, *supra* n. 1 p. 171 *et seq*., p. 211 *et seq*. G Teubner, L Farmer, D Murphy (eds.), *Environmental Law and Ecological Responsibility* (Chichester, Wiley, 1994).

[65] S Emmeneger and A Tschentscher, "Taking Nature's Rights Seriously: The Long Way to Biocentrism in International Law" 6 *Georgetown International Environmental Law Review* 545; A D Amato and S Chopra, "Whales: Their Emerging Right to Life" 85 *Am. Jl Int. Law* 21. See also A Boyle and M Anderson (eds.), *Human Rights Approaches to Environmental Protection* (Oxford, Clarendon Press, 1996).

[66] *Supra* n. 19.

Most of the international declarations take the form of preambles or soft law without binding force and there are relatively few enforcement mechanisms for non-human interests, as opposed for example to arrangements for protecting or exploiting resources.[67] The above examples can be explained in human terms particularly in the context of supposed duties to future generations and the enlightened anthropocentric ethic.

3. JUSTIFYING AND RANKING ENVIRONMENTAL INTERESTS

All ethical theories, but conspicuously those non-anthropocentric perspectives which claim that what is natural is right, face the problem of the is/ought distinction identified by the Enlightenment philosopher David Hume (1711–76)[68] and which has never been successfully refuted. According to the is/ought distinction, sometimes called the naturalistic fallacy or the fact/value distinction, we cannot logically derive normative values, i.e. standards of behaviour, from the existence of any factual state of affairs. We must interpose some system of moral belief between the two, the basis of which so far nobody has been able satisfactorily to rationalise.[69] Thus, no environmental ethic can depend solely on statements as to what nature is like whether beautiful, harmonious, or anything else. Moreover, environmentalists risk gliding between two unrelated meanings of "natural", the first being biological the second meaning "normal" with the implication of rightness. It also seems impossible to value nature independently of human concerns. For example, in the absence of a human element there is no reason to think that it is good for a tree to exist since existence in itself is not a value. Attempts to justify non-anthropocentric perspectives sometimes ignore the is/ought problem by claiming to "perceive self-evident truths" in nature.[70] Others stress the interdependence of humans and nature[71] or reason outward by a process of "reflective intuition" from widely held values about humans in an attempt to show that it is arbitrary "speciesism" to limit these to

[67] See for example, Biodiversity Convention 1992, World Charter for Nature 1982, Berne Convention on the Conservation of European Wildlife and Natural Habitats 1979, Bonn Convention on the Conservation of Migratory Species of Wild Animals 1979, Ramsar Convention on Wetlands of International Importance 1971.

[68] See D Hume, *An Enquiry Concerning the Principles of Morals, in Enquiries*, 2nd ed. (Oxford, OUP, 1975); Alder and Wilkinson, *supra* n. 1, at 46; M Macdonald, "Natural Rights" in Waldron (ed.), *Theories of Rights* (Oxford, OUP, 1984).

[69] Dobson, *supra* n. 1, 53–71, cf. E Pluhar, "The Justification of an Environmental Ethic" 5 *Environmental Ethics* 47; E Pluhar, *Beyond Prejudice: The Moral Significance of Human and Non-Human Animals* (Durham, Duke University Press, 1995).

[70] See H Rolston, "Value in Nature and the Nature of Value" in R Attfield and A Belsay (eds.), *Philosophy and the Natural Environment* (Cambridge, Cambridge University Press, 1994). It is not clear whether this literally means that nature would have value even if there were no human valuers or that nature has qualities which humans interpret as value. See also C Spretnak and F Capra, *Green Politics* (London, Paladin, 1985).

[71] See B Callicott, *In Defence of the Land Ethic* (Albany, NY University Press, 1989).

humans.[72] Another approach is to claim that humans harmonise with nature and that nature has aesthetic value akin to a work of art.[73] These in effect seem to return to an anthropocentric perspective.

Non-anthropocentric perspectives therefore face acute conflicts, not only between human interests and those of non-humans but also between non-human species, for example between animal liberation and the preservation of rare species by culling their predators. Non-humans have different needs from ourselves so that no one suggests that all nature's components be treated the same. Equality means treating like cases alike so that the problem for non-anthropocentrists is how to decide what counts as "like".

Most attempts to adjudicate favour a hierarchy of values based on the size or complexity of the interests involved and there is a tendency to equate moral value with self-awareness and rationality although some regard this as arbitrary. These qualities inevitably favour human beings because we have more to lose. As Dobson puts it, "it is striking how often these intrepid philosophical adventurers return in a pretty traditional way to home base".[74] For example, in a clash between a human life and that of a dog (or a thousand dogs), the human life is, even according to Regan,[75] worth more because of the human's greater capacity for experience. We are outranked only in as much as we are not an endangered species and Hardin is prepared to grasp this nettle and recommend reducing the human population.[76]

Bookchin divides nature into first and second classes, humans being in first.[77] Van DeVeer indirectly reaches a similar conclusion by privileging "serious" interests which relate to psychological complexity over "peripheral" interests.[78] In relation to these devices we are of course lawmakers, judges and executioners in our own case and have a clearer understanding of our own needs than we do those of others. For example, how would we compare the interest of a farmer in fencing land against that of a wild animal to roam?

A stricter approach is that of a species egalitarianism which would allocate rights to all species according to their needs and natures so that the rights of different species, although differing in content, would be equal in

[72] See Regan, *supra* n. 48; S Wenz, *Environmental Justice* (New York, NY University Press, 1988); Pluhar, *supra* n. 69.

[73] See Elliot, *supra* n. 10. E Hargrove, *Foundations of Environmental Ethics* (Englewood Cliffs, New Jersey, Prentice-Hall 1989); Y Saito, "Appreciating Nature on its Own Terms" 20 *Environmental Ethics* 135; J Appleton, "Nature as Honorary Art" 7 *Environmental Values* 255; R Hepburn, "Nature Humanised, Nature Respected" 7 *Environmental Values* 267. This surmounts the "plastic trees" problem (*supra* n. 23) since a genuine work of art is more valuable than even a perfect forgery.

[74] *Supra* n. 1 at 54. See also R Eckersley, "Beyond Human Reason" 7 *Environmental Values* 167; J Anderson, "Species, Equality and the Foundation of Moral Theory" 2 *Environmental Values* 347; F Matthews, *The Ecological Self* (London, Routledge, 1991), p. 123; V Plumwood, "Intentional Recognition and Reductive Rationality: A Reply to John Andrews" 7 *Environmental Values* 396.

[75] *Supra* n. 48, 286 *et seq*.

[76] "Living in a Lifeboat" 24 *Bioscience* 561.

[77] *Remaking Society* (Montreal, Black Rose, 1989).

[78] *Supra* n. 57.

value. Where equal interests conflict, for example the "rights to life and liberty" of self-aware species, we are not entitled to treat animals any differently from how we would treat a human being in the same circumstances.[79] For example, we can kill an animal where the alternative is the death of ourself or someone close to us and possibly as mercy killing but not for food nor for scientific experiments.

4. CONFLICTS OF VALUE IN PUBLIC LAW: DIFFERENT REGULATORY CULTURES

Ethical values have an internal and an external impact on the law. Internally they help to shape the law by influencing the way legislators frame laws, and how the courts and other officials interpret the law and exercise discretionary powers. Externally they provide a basis for criticising the law. They impact on public law most importantly in connection with the range of factors which an official decision-maker such as the Environment Agency (EA), a local planning authority or a minister is entitled or bound to take into account. Should a public authority take into account ethical perspectives based for example on public opinion or the views of groups or indeed derived from the ethical beliefs of its own members? Can a decision-maker ignore ethical views held by minorities?

English law tends to rely on executive discretion although statutes sometimes set out and occasionally prioritise the factors which the decision-maker must take into account.[80] The court can ensure that relevant factors are taken into account and irrelevant factors excluded but, except where a decision is "*Wednesbury* unreasonable", it cannot interfere with the weight which the decision-maker gives to the competing considerations.[81] In *R* v. *Secretary of State for the Environment ex parte Berkshire, Buckinghamshire and Oxfordshire Naturalists Trust*,[82] Sedley J appeared to regret this relative impotence in relation to environmental concerns. The Secretary of State for Transport proposed to build a road which conflicted with a proposal by English Nature that part of the area affected should be protected under the Habitats Directive 1992 as the home of the rare pulmonate snail. Sedley J held that it was no business of the court to choose between these competing interests but remarked that "one can appreciate the force of the view that if the protection of the natural environment keeps coming second we shall end by destroying our own habitat".

[79] See for example, Pluhar, *supra* n. 69.

[80] For example the Countryside Act 1968 requires environmental decision makers to take into account social and economic factors (s. 11) and all public authorities to take into account environmental factors, (s. 37). See also the duties of the Environment Agency in Environment Act 1995 Part 1 and text above n. 19.

[81] *Tesco Stores Plc* v. *Secretary of State* [1995] 1 WLR 759.

[82] [1997] Env. LR 80.

A regulatory culture is a shared set of values between those making legal decisions in a particular area. The variety of ethical values means that environmental agencies may be particularly vulnerable to competing values. Ethical conflicts may arise between different agencies, particularly between elected and non-elected bodies or between elected members of a body and their appointed officials. Different regulatory cultures may be adopted by different agencies and indeed by different persons within the same agency, particularly in the case of a multi-disciplinary body such as the Environment Agency which contains staff both from the natural and the social sciences with their sometimes contrasting cultures and attitudes to rationality.

In particular, there may be tensions between those who prefer instrumental, scientifically generated, cost-benefit principles and those who favour an aesthetic approach to environmental problems or between individualistic and ecocentric ethics. In deciding whether to permit the construction and operation of a waste disposal plant the Environment Agency may be guided primarily by the former, whereas a local planning authority may adopt a broader perspective including political and cultural attitudes to environmental risks and priorities. Where there is overlapping jurisdiction in relation to the same project, the local planning authority's duty is only to consider whether it is appropriate to rely on the expertise of the EA.[83] Indeed, it would be an unlawful fetter on discretion for a decision-maker to rely on a decision made by another body without an express or necessarily implied statutory mandate so to do.[84]

Environmental values may therefore clash with scientific conceptions and both may clash with democratic values in the shape of public opinion.[85] For example, scientific methods of risk assessment (based on the magnitude of the risk and the probability of it happening) may not be in line with ethical, political and cultural aspects of environmental risk. These take into account non-quantifiable factors such as public attitudes to scientists, familiarity with the nature of the risk, legal or moral notions of responsibility, the vulnerability of those exposed to the risk such as children, media attention, whether the danger is hidden or overt, social and economic consequences etc.[86] The long time scale involved with environmental problems also complicates scientific predictions and the scientific method of hypothesis, and experiment is not possible where

[83] *Gateshead Metropolitan Borough Council* v. *Secretary of State for the Environment* [1995] *Envir. Law Rep.* 37.

[84] *Lavender* v. *Minister of Housing* [1970] 3 All ER 871.

[85] See R Grove-White, "On 'Sound Science': The Environment and Political Authority" 8 *Environmental Values* 277; M Cohen, "Science and Society in Historical Perspective" *ibid.* 153; C Hill, "When Something has to Be Done: Proof of Environmental Harm and the Philosophical Tradition" *ibid.* 3; K Shrader-Frechette and E McCoy, "How the Tail Wags the Dog: How Value Judgements Determine Ecological Science" 3 *Environmental Values*, 107; L Caldwell, *Between Two Worlds: Science, the Environmental Movement and Policy Choice* (Cambridge, Cambridge University Press, 1996); O'Riorden, *Environmentalism* (London, Pion Press, 1981).

[86] See J Gillroy (ed.), *Environmental Risk, Fundamental Values and Political Choices* (Boulder CO, Westview Press, 1993) ch. 6; N Stanley, "Public Concern: the Decision Maker's Dilemma" [1998] *JPL* 919; U Beck, *Risk Society: Towards a New Modernity* (London, Sage, 1992).

controlled experiments cannot be carried out. A false hypothesis may cause irreversible harm, for example in relation to genetically modified organisms. Nevertheless, polluting firms may be reluctant to reduce their economic activity without proof of harm which in the nature of the scientific method is never possible.

Worries about the limits of science have led to the emergence of the precautionary principle as a widely accepted instrument of environmental policy.[87] The ethical dimension of the precautionary principle is that of prudence combined with responsibility. The precautionary principle requires us not to take risks with the environment even where the scientific evidence of harm is not conclusive. It requires the best scientific evidence to be taken into account but "where there are threats of serious or irreversible damage, lack of full scientific certainty shall not be used as a reason for postponing cost-effective measures to prevent environmental degradation".[88] The precautionary principle therefore calls upon the decision-maker to be responsible for an ethical judgement as to when a risk is worth taking which cannot hide behind a claim of scientific objectivity. Scientific orthodoxy remains, however, the dominant approach in the UK because the precautionary principle is not legally binding.[89]

In two cases involving pollution risks from proposed waste disposal plants the Court of Appeal has taken the view that planning authorities should take public opinion into account even where this is not founded on expert scientific evidence. In *Gateshead Metropolitan Borough Council* v. *Secretary of State*[90] Glidewell J thought that such opinion must be "justified" but did not explain what this means in relation to scientific standards. In *Newport Borough Council* v. *Secretary of State for Wales*[91] the Court of Appeal went further, holding that a genuine public fear, even if not founded on "objective" scientific evidence, must not only be taken into account but could justify a refusal of planning permission. These cases therefore raise the question whether ethical factors must be taken into account including unorthodox views such as those of "deep" ecologists. There is a distinction, illustrated by the *Fewings* case (*infra*), between factors which *must* be taken into account as essential to any application of the governing legislation and factors which an authority is *entitled* but not bound to take into account. Here the authority's decision would be reviewed according to *Wednesbury* principles of relevance and rationality. It could be argued

[87] See, EC Treaty Article 174; O McIntyre and T Mosedale, "The Precautionary Principle as a Norm of Customary International Law" 9 *Journal of Environmental Law* 221.

[88] Rio Declaration (1992) Principle 15. The precautionary principle has been regarded as too open-ended and contradictory to be of practical help. See T O'Riordan and A Jordan, "The Precautionary Principle in Contemporary Environmental Politics" 4 *Environmental Values* 190; D Bodansky, "Scientific Uncertainty and the Precautionary Principle" *Environment* (September 1991), 4–5, 43–4. See generally Alder and Wilkinson, *supra* n. 1 ch. 6.

[89] *R* v. *Secretary of State for Trade and Industry, ex parte Duddridge* [1995] *Env. Law Rep.* 151.

[90] [1995] *Envir. LR* 37. See also *Envirocor Waste Holdings* v. *Secretary of State for the Environment* [1995] *Envir. LR* 37.

[91] [1998] JPL 377.

that some non-anthropocentric ethical beliefs are on the borders of *Wednesbury* rationality. On the other hand even extreme perspectives are supported by substantial scholarly opinion. Moreover, attempts to exclude such views as irrational might fall foul of the Human Rights Act 1998 in as much as it protects freedom of expression, one purpose of which is to advance the interest of good political decision-making. The weight to be given to any particular factor is of course for the decision-maker. No particular ethical perspective has a right to prevail.

R. v. *Somerset County Council, ex parte Fewings*[92] inconclusively raised these issues. A local authority had resolved to ban deer hunting on moral grounds on land which it was required to manage for the "benefit, improvement or development of the area as a whole".[93] This was challenged on the basis that the authority should not have taken ethical factors into account but should have confined itself to economic land management factors. (One difficulty with this argument is that economic factors themselves rest on a particular ethical view of the world.) The judges were divided. Laws J held that the council had acted unlawfully in taking ethical considerations into account at all. He thought that, because hunting was a lawful activity, a public authority, even if democratically elected, was not entitled to take ethical values contrary to hunting into account unless the statute necessarily required it to do so. He took the view that it is not for subordinate public bodies such as local authorities to regulate morality.[94]

The Court of Appeal took a broader approach. The majority agreed with Laws J that the Council's decision was unlawful because the Council had failed to look at the matter through the framework of the statute. Their lordships were divided on the ethical issue. Lord Bingham MR thought that the ethical factors were relevant to the concerns of the legislation but left it open whether the authority should or merely could take them into account. Simon-Brown LJ thought that the authority was probably bound but certainly entitled to take ethical factors into account. He adopted an "enlightened anthropocentric" stance taking the view that the link with the statute was forged because "human well being for many will depend on their satisfaction as to animal welfare". Swinton Thomas LJ took the same approach as Laws J which can be characterised as traditional anthropocentrism. It was also argued that, as an elected body, the authority had a democratic basis for taking morality into account. Laws J regarded this as irrelevant but the views of Lord Bingham MR and Simon Brown LJ raise the question whether an *unelected* body such as the Environment Agency or English Nature is entitled to take ethical factors into account. One approach might be to agree with Laws J to the extent that an unelected body should only take such ethical values into account as are

[92] [1995] 1 All ER 513 (Laws J); [1995] 3 All ER 20 (CA).
[93] Local Government Act 1972 s. 120 (1).
[94] See *Calder and Hebble Navigation* v. *Pilling* (1845) 14 M and W 76.

expressed or necessarily implied in the governing statute and therefore reflect what the constitution regards as the wishes of the people. Given that ethical values are inseparable from environmental concerns this is tantamount to saying that elected local bodies should be entrusted with larger powers at the expense of quangos such as the Environment Agency.

It could be argued that an elected body should take into account any relevant ethical perspectives that its elected members wish to raise unless clearly excluded by statiste. According to traditional constitutional principles an elected member is not elected as a mouthpiece of the majority but as an agent to whom (subject to any specific commitments such as an election manifesto) his or her constituents pass the burden of judgment. It may be however that some ethical perspectives are so far outside the framework of conventional values that make society possible[95] that they can legitimately be ignored. This might include for example certain versions of "deep ecology" which aim to change human consciousness in favour of ecocentric values by means of unlawful direct action such as property damage.

The significance of different regulatory cultures is illustrated by the hedgerow conservation regime. Under the Environment Act 1995 s. 97 the Secretary of State can make regulations for the purpose of protecting hedgerows designated as "important" in accordance with criteria prescribed by regulations.[96] "Important" is of course an expression of value with no objective meaning. The regulations take a scientifically orientated, approach by relating importance to quantifiable factors such as the age of the hedgerow and to the number of rare species living in it. From the enlightened anthropocentric perspective that landscape is a cultural artefact reflected for example in literature, Holder[97] suggests an alternative approach based on local participation. The difficulties of such an approach are formidable. For example, if as seems likely local opinion is not unanimous, who is to decide what cultural orthodoxy shall be imposed, choosing for example between the Hardyesque view of nature as an impersonal force threatening human happiness or the romanticised images of Rupert Brooke? Local opinion as such has no necessary link with environmental values and is likely to favour the dominant elite.[98] An approach based upon literary percep-

[95] Cf. Dworkin's notion of "integrity." *Law's Empire* (London, Fontana, 1986).

[96] Hedgerows Regulations 1997, SI 1997 No. 1160.

[97] (1999) 62 MLR 100.

[98] Although participatory mechanisms might gradually shift the orthodoxy by ventilating different points of view. Another form of participation is based on individual market choice so that the "right" state of the environment is whatever the outcome of such choice happens to be provided that the market is not distorted. Hence market instruments such as pollution charges are a fashionable tool for environmental protection. See B Ackerman and R Stewart, "Reforming Environmental Law: the Democratic Case for Market Incentives" 13 *Columbia Journal of Environmental Law* 171 (1983); Pearce etc, *supra* n. 38. Both require public access to information which can be made available to a limited extent through mechanisms such as registers kept by regulators, environmental impact assessment requirements and access to information regimes. See S Ball and S Bell, *Environmental Law*, 2nd ed., pp. 162–71 (London, Butterworths, 1997); Directive 85/337 EEC; Directive 90/313 EEC; Environmental Information Regulations 1992 (SI 1992 no. 3240).

tions invites the objection that nature is valued only as a theme park for the intelligentsia. There are also libertarian objections to using the law to impose aesthetic values.

Clashes between regulatory cultures may also arise in relation to conservation policy. If the notion of nature having intrinsic value is adopted then conservation policy should favour leaving nature alone as far as possible. The traditional utilitarian perspective that entitles us to "enhance" natural beauty that features in much UK legislation might therefore be considered unethical, not only from this perspective but also from the perspective of those who envisage "genuine" nature as akin to a work of art the enhancement of which would be analogous to forgery.[99] Similarly, a planning agreement under which a developer promises to provide an environmental benefit in return for permission to despoil a natural feature, although almost certainly lawful, could be ethically questionable.[100]

5. ENVIRONMENTAL RIGHTS

To categorise a value or interest as a right is to give it stronger protection than merely an aspect of regulatory discretion. Although few rights, are absolute, a legal right enjoys *prima facie* protection in the sense that a strong reason expressed or implicit in statute must be given for overriding it. Environmental values might crystallise in the form of rights, although it is doubtful whether UK law recognises uniquely environmental rights as opposed to rights which happen to have environmental aspects such as health or property.[101] A value becomes a right where the holder or someone on the holder's behalf has the protection of legal machinery which confers a *prima facie* benefit on the holder giving effect to the value. Public law rights include representation embodied in *locus standi* requirements for challenging government action in the courts, rights to be consulted, access to information from government,[102] and the alleged human right to a decent environment.[103]

[99] See above n. 73. E.g. Environment Act 1995 s. 61 (1), s. 98; Town and Country Planning Act 1990 s. 12 (3A), s. 31 (3), s. 36 (3); Countryside Act 1968 s. 11; Wildlife and Countryside (Amendment) Act 1985 s. 4; Agriculture Act 1986 s. 17; Environment Act 1995 s. 61 (1). See Huxley Report, Conservation of Nature in England and Wales (cmnd 7122, (1947)), regarding conservation as akin to farming. Land management agreements between farmers and governmental agencies seem to represent a similar approach. See Wildlife and Countryside Act 1981 s. 39; Environment Act 1995 s. 98; Agriculture Act 1986 s. 18.

[100] The legal criteria for such agreements defer to the discretion of the executive by requiring only minimal thresholds of rational relationship and reasonableness. See *Tesco Stores Plc* v. *Secretary of State* [1995] 1 WLR 759.

[101] Cf. C Miller, *Environmental Rights: Critical Perspectives* (London, Routledge, 1998).

[102] There are an increasing number of consultation rights and rights to information mainly as a result of EU initiatives which the UK reluctantly implemented. See Alder and Wilkinson, *supra* n. 1, 370–3.

[103] See Alder and Wilkinson, *supra* n. 1 pp. 379–83; A Boyle and M Anderson (eds.), *Human Rights Approaches to Environmental Protection* (Oxford, Clarendon Press, 1996).

In English law *locus standi* is easily satisfied in relation to narrow anthropocentric interests since it is settled that a person with a particular interest in the matter has standing even without any legal right in the strict sense.[104] Enlightened anthropocentric interests are usually public or collective goods that cannot be reduced to individual rights. However, there is no reason in principle why an environmental pressure group should not represent enlightened anthropocentric and indeed non-anthropocentric values. In one case it was held that any member of the public can represent an environmental interest[105] and pressure groups have been given standing, at least in cases where they have a substantial prior involvement with the issue.[106]

As the law presently stands under the European Convention on Human Rights, environmental human rights are not free standing but must be subsumed under some other right, in particular the right to life (Article 2), which may include health but not quality of life, or privacy and respect for family life (Article 8). The European Convention on Human Rights, while treating certain rights as absolute,[107] in other cases, including those involving environmental rights, tries to accommodate deontological and instrumental values using notions such as proportionality and deference to democracy. In this respect the European Court seems to be liberal in allowing states to override environmental rights on economic grounds. It may only be prepared to protect an environmental interest if there is a reasonably convenient alternative way of achieving the economic goal in question.[108] This is why procedural rights such as rights to information and rights to ensure that an environmental impact assessment takes place are of particular importance.

Christopher Stone argues in favour of legal rights for natural objects such as trees and rivers.[109] This does not depend on a non-anthropocentric ethic as such. Just as artificial or fictitious entities such as companies have rights so can trees and this can be for human instrumental purposes as a means of focusing upon an environmental concern. Neither companies nor trees can of course assert their own rights in a court, but the law can designate human beings to do so

[104] *IRC* v. *National Federation for the Self Employed and Small Businesses* [1982] AC 617; *R* v. *Secretary of State for the Environment, ex parte Rose Theatre Trust* [1990] 1 QB 504; *R* v. *North Somerset DC, ex parte Garnett* [1998] JEL 161.

[105] *R* v. *Somerset County Council, ex parte Dixon* [1998] JEL 161.

[106] However in *R* v. *Pollution Inspectorate, ex parte Greenpeace* (No. 2) [1994] 4 All ER 329 Otton J seemed to require an accumulation of human interests.

[107] Article 3, Article 4 (1), Art 6 (part), Article 7.

[108] See *Lopes Ostra* v. *Spain*, Ser. A No. 303C (1994); *Guerra* v. *Italy* 1999 JEL 157 (right to information), *Powell and Rayner* v. *UK* 47 D and R (1986); R Desgagne, "Integrating Environmental Values into the European Convention on Human Rights" 89 *American Journal of International Law* 263. The right to property in Protocol 1 potentially limits public law environmental regulation although planning and other land use restrictions do not contravene Protocol 1 unless they are confiscatory; see *Fredin* v. *Sweden* (1991) ECHR 1–69, 327.

[109] "Should Trees Have Standing?" 45 *Southern California Law Review* 450; C *Stone, Should Trees Have Standing and Other Essays on Law, Morals and the Environment* (Dobbs Ferry, NY, Oceana, 1996).

on their behalf. In the case of natural objects, Stone suggests that a custodian or guardian might represent their interests as is the case with children, the mentally ill, and the very old. A limit fund would be created to satisfy claims.

As we have seen, a common objection to non-humans having rights is that they are not part of the rational community and that rights can apply only to creatures who are aware of them.[110] Indeed Waldron argues that we confer rights on human beings because we deserve them by virtue of our admirable qualities of rationality and self determination.[111] This suggests that a "right" is really a privilege which we can withhold from those whom we judge to be unworthy. However, there seems to be no logical or practical reason why rights should be limited to rational beings.[112] Only rational beings can have *duties* it is true but right holders need not have duties, a right being correlative only to a duty vested in another.

6. CONCLUSION

Environmental concerns embrace many different ethical perspectives some of which are uncombinable so that, in Lord Hoffmann's words, we cannot avoid the "pain of having to choose".[113] A certain amount of incoherence is the price we pay for democracy. The notion, beloved of lawyers and policy makers that conflicting interests can be "balanced" presupposes an objective method of weighing values which does not appear to exist. Similarly, as in the case of human rights litigation, the doctrine of proportionality which tells us to minimise harm and to try as far as possible to combine different values does not help us to assess the relative importance of conflicting values.

The extent to which any given value must be sacrificed is related to risk. Thus, the precautionary principle has a pivotal role. Ideally the law should provide procedural mechanisms that enable decision-makers to combine as many perspectives as possible When conflict is inevitable a subjective political choice must be made by an accountable body as a temporary accommodation in accordance with procedures that give the different perspectives a fair hearing. Unless we believe that the threat to the environment is so great and so immediate that a state of emergency overriding democracy is called for, it would not be appropriate to bind ourselves to any single ethical perspective.

[110] Passmore, *supra* n. 1, pp. 110–18, See also B Norton, "Environmental Ethics and Non-Human Rights" 4 *Environmental Ethics* 35.

[111] *Supra* n. 4.

[112] See M Midgely, *Duties Concerning Islands* in Elliot (ed.), *supra* n. 10. See also n. 74 above.

[113] *Supra* n. 13.

14

New Fundamentals – New Values? Change and Stability in South Africa[1]

MERVYN BENNUN

Kaliski talks about the legitimacy constructed in the past around these extreme forms of violence. The lawgivers made the laws, the lawyers executed them, and they were assisted by a whole lot of other professions. This creates a normative structure that legitimized the killings.

And the basis was not a fear of communism, Kaliski says. "We believed black people were not human; they were a threat, they were going to kill us all, and then waste away the country until it was nothing but another African disaster area".[2]

1. INTRODUCTION

The setting of the quotation above is the Truth and Reconciliation Commission (TRC) and the writer, Antjie Krog, was the leader of the South African Broadcasting Corporation's reporting team at its hearings. Trying to understand a group of police officers whom she had interviewed after they had given evidence in support of their amnesty applications, she took the tapes of the interviews to Dr Sean Kaliski at the Valkenberg Psychiatric Unit in Cape Town.

> One of the officers told her that he had resigned from the Dutch Reformed Church:
>
> I know what I did . . . and I don't want to burden the church. . . .
>
> When I drove back in the mornings after an operation, and people passed me on their way to work, I thought: "I did it for you and you. . . . You could sleep sound because I was doing my job . . ."

And he does not want to disclose where his sons work: "I don't want them to be identified as the sons of Jack Cronje".[3]

[1] I am grateful to many people for a great deal and in particular to Willy Hofmeyr MP, Johnny de Lange MP, and the ANC Study Group of the Justice Portfolio Committee in the South African Parliament who all gave me the chances, the experiences, and the ideas. This paper is dedicated to Antjie Krog, who, saying something to her fellow Afrikaners, has proved Evita Bezuidenhout to be wrong.

[2] Antjie Krog, *Country of My Skull* (Johannesburg, Random House, 1998), p. 93.

[3] Krog, *Country of My Skull*, p. 92.

What happened in South Africa happened to people, and it was because of what people did: it was not a natural disaster or visited on the country by aliens from another planet. There are many lessons and much understanding about law to be sought from it because, at a certain point, jurisprudence moves from an amiable discourse over common-room coffee or by students in a seminar, and becomes something one must live – something which one must go out and consciously *do*.

Sometimes the living and the doing are ugly; yet, if Cronje leaves nothing else that we would like to remember of him, then at least let this be said for him: what he told Antjie Krog teaches more jurisprudence than he probably realised. He and others in the security police were robbed of their humanity by the legal order they were caught up in and had to serve; they too are victims – of a sort – and we can legitimately feel pity – of a sort – for them. Krog comments:

> Every single gruesome detail, their hands did, their eyes saw, their brains sucked. Their testimony changed the debate among white South Africans. Whereas before people denied that atrocities happened, now they deny that they *knew* they were happening.[4]

One of the many striking features of the accounts of the evidence before the Truth and Reconciliation Commission is that those who defended the legal order of apartheid believed so passionately in what they were doing – that it was *right*. They doubtless resent the words of the strident political commentator Evita Bezuidenhout, one of the characters created by the satirist Pieter-Dirk Uys – sometimes in writing but usually with a wig, excruciating couture and a dab of lipstick in front of a packed audience at the satirical theatre founded by Uys in a converted railway station now called *Evita se Perron* ("Evita's Platform"). Referring to the TRC in one of "her" essays, "Ms" Bezuidenhout writes:

> Sorry: a horrible little word. Too little, always too late. But being an Afrikaner means never having to say: sorry![5]

The purpose of this paper, then, is to say something about the changes from the fundamental legal values which drove South African laws in the past, to those which led to the TRC. Perhaps there are lessons for the rest of the world for, in truth, apartheid created a unique laboratory in which legal theory could be tested to breaking-point.

The Truth and Reconciliation Commission, Chaired by Archbishop Desmond Tutu, had its origins in the Provisional or interim Constitution of

[4] Krog, *Country of My Skull*, pp. 91–2.

[5] Pieter-Dirk Uys, *The Essential Evita Bezuidenhout* (Claremont, South Africa, David Philip, 1997), p. 79.

1993. This was painfully negotiated as the apartheid State collapsed, and established a Constitutional Assembly[6] to draw up what, after the 1994 election, became today's final Constitution.[7]

The history of the idea for the TRC was set out by the Vice-Chair of the Commissioners, Dr Alexander Boraine, in a speech in Brussels in 1996. He recalled that the idea came first from the African National Congress (ANC) before the 1994 election. The ANC was accused of perpetrating human rights violations in some of its camps while in exile, and it responded by appointing an internal commission of inquiry. On publication, its report was criticised as lacking impartiality. A second independent commission was appointed; when its findings were presented to the national executive of the ANC their decision was that there were grounds for criticism but that:

> . . . these should be seen against the overall human rights violations which gripped South Africa over a very long period, and the way to resolve this was the appointment of a truth commission.[8]

This idea was taken to the National Assembly. The Provisional Constitution accordingly concluded with a remarkable passage entitled "National Unity and Reconciliation" which captures the tensions and emotions of the time:

> This Constitution provides a historic bridge between the past of a deeply divided society characterised by strife, conflict, untold suffering and injustice, and a future founded on the recognition of human rights, democracy and peaceful co-existence and development opportunities for all South Africans, irrespective of colour, race, class, belief or sex. The pursuit of national unity, the well-being of all South African citizens and peace require reconciliation between the people of South Africa and the reconstruction of society.
>
> The adoption of this Constitution lays the secure foundation for the people of South Africa to transcend the divisions and strife of the past, which generated gross violations of human rights, the transgression of humanitarian principles in violent conflicts and a legacy of hatred, fear, guilt and revenge.
>
> These can now be addressed on the basis that there is a need for understanding but not for vengeance, a need for reparation but not for retaliation, a need for ubuntu[9] but not for victimisation.

[6] Section 68.

[7] Constitution of the Republic of South Africa 1966.

[8] Alex Boraine, speaker, "Alternatives and Adjuncts to Criminal Prosecutions," paper presented at conference on "Justice in cataclysm: criminal tribunals in the wake of mass violence" (Brussels, 1996), \www.trc.org.za\reading\speech01.htm.

[9] ". . . A subtle and not easily translatable concept which means broadly that each individual's humanity is ideally expressed through his relationship with others and theirs in turn through a recognition of his humanity. "*Ubuntu ungamntu ngabanye abantu*" goes the Xhosa proverb – "People are people through other people. It is a saying that Archbishop Desmond Tutu likes to quote, and it never fails to bring sighs and nods of understanding from his black audiences". Allister Sparks, *The Mind of South Africa: The Rise and Fall of Apartheid* (London: (I) William Heinemann; (ii) Arrow Books, (i) 1990; (i) 1997), p. 14.

The concept is discussed at length by the TRC: Truth and Reconciliation Commission, *Report of the Truth and Reconciliation Commission*, Vol. 1 (1998), ch. 5, from para. 80.

> In order to advance such reconciliation and reconstruction, amnesty shall be granted in respect of acts, omissions and offences associated with political objectives and committed in the course of the conflicts of the past. To this end, Parliament under this Constitution shall adopt a law determining a firm cut-off date, which shall be a date after 8 October 1990 and before 6 December 1993, and providing for the mechanisms, criteria and procedures, including tribunals, if any, through which such amnesty shall be dealt with at any time after the law has been passed.
>
> With this Constitution and these commitments we, the people of South Africa, open a new chapter in the history of our country.
>
> Nkosi sikelel' iAfrika.
> God seën Suid-Afrika.
> Morena boloka sechaba sa heso.
> May God bless our country.
> Mudzimu fhatutshedza Afrika.
> Hosi katekisa Afrika.

As required by the fourth paragraph quoted above, Parliament duly enacted the Promotion of National Unity and Reconciliation Act, 1995.

The fundamental details of the Act were hammered out in protracted and tense negotiations with the collapsing apartheid regime. This is important, as the effect was to co-opt as many political forces as possible into the process. The story is fully set out in the TRC's Report.[10] One topic especially is worth mentioning at this stage: there was bitter discussion, and finally agreement, on how amnesties for political offences would be dealt with in the new democratic order which was being born. As the Report makes clear, two matters were settled relatively early: first, actions taken in terms of apartheid law would not merely for that reason be regarded as illegal; secondly, in respect of such acts legally committed in the course of implementing apartheid the "Nuremberg option" would not be chosen – there would be no trials for the many human rights violations if amnesties were sought on the basis of full disclosure and granted. We may well think that these matters lie at the heart of all that subsequently transpired.

It is also important to bear in mind that the final result is that an independent body sat and listened to, and reached conclusions about, the submissions made to it. The old South African Government was denied the opportunity to forgive itself.

A comparison with Chile is instructive. On April 19 1978, the Chilean Government announced that since Chile's "internal commotion" had subsided and a state of "peace and order" reigned, it had been decided to grant amnesty to all "authors, accomplices, or concealers" of politically connected crimes committed since the coup, including those condemned by military tribunals. The goal of the measure, officials claimed, was to "leave hatreds behind" and foment

[10] Truth and Reconciliation Commission, *Report, Vol. 1.*

national reunification.[11] The principal effect was to absolve military and police from responsibility for the death and abuse of thousands. "For thousands of victims, and their families, the need to know the truth, let alone see justice done, was flatly denied".[12]

Asmal, Asmal and Roberts note that in Chile the Truth Commission's findings were followed by an apology to the victims from President Alwyn. They describe as "inadequate, if not grotesque" anything analogous attempted by South Africa's new President, Nelson Mandela; it would be "less than half a loaf of reconciliation; in fact, it would defy comprehension. Apology is a task for [Mr F W de Klerk]".[13]

An account of the expiring apartheid government's efforts to achieve the same result is given by Berat. It legislated in November 1992 for amnesty hearings to be in secret and without the disclosure of the offences or the identities of the victims, and to bar subsequent civil or criminal proceedings. However, this legislation and its effects were in effect brushed aside by subsequent events.[14] This is a fundamental matter, for what replaced the apartheid government's secret self-pardoning was an open and public exercise. This was fully commented on, in due course, by the Truth and Reconciliation Commission:

> A distinctive feature of the Commission was its openness to public participation and scrutiny. This enabled it to reach out on a daily basis to large numbers of people inside and outside South Africa, and to confront them with vivid images on their television screens or on the front pages of their newspapers. People saw, for example, a former security police officer demonstrating his torture techniques. They saw weeping men and women asking for the truth about their missing loved ones. The media also helped generate public debate on central aspects of South Africa's past and to raise the level of historical awareness. The issues that emerged as a consequence helped the nation to focus on values central to a healthy democracy: transparency, public debate, public participation and criticism.[15]

2. THE TRUTH AND RECONCILIATION COMMISSION

Though it was set up by an Act of Parliament as the Constitution required, the TRC was bitterly resisted by some of the parties in the National Assembly and

[11] Pamela Constable and Arturo Valenzuela, *A Nation of Enemies: Chile Under Pinochet*, 1st ed. (New York and London, W.W. Norton & Co., 1991), p. 129.

[12] Constable and Valenzuela, *A Nation of Enemies: Chile Under Pinochet*, p. 130.

[13] Kader Asmal, Louise Asmal, and Ronal Suresh Roberts, *Reconciliation Through Truth: A Reckoning of Apartheid's Criminal Governance*, with a foreword by President Nelson Mandela (Bellville, Cape Town, Mayibuye Books, University of the Western Cape, David Philip (jointly), 1996), p. 31.

[14] Lynn Berat, "South Africa: Negotiating Change?" in Naomi Roht-Arriaza (ed.), *Impunity and Human Rights in International Law and Practice* (New York, Oxford University Press, 1995), p. 272.

[15] Truth and Reconciliation Commission, *Report, Vol. 1*, ch. 5, para. 5.

was given only grudging support by others. The debate on the Bill[16] reveals much about the atmosphere in which the TRC thereafter commenced its work.

The Inkatha Freedom Party opposed the Bill, one of its MPs comparing the TRC to the Holy Inquisition and what he called the "McCarthy Commission".[17] It was supported reluctantly by the National Party (NP)[18] – once the government, and now a minority party after the first democratic, non-racial election in the history of South Africa. The NP sought to equate the "mistakes" committed by the apartheid government and its agents with the conduct of the ANC.[19] One NP speaker pointed out that in its camps the ANC had been guilty of human rights violations also – a matter which the ANC in due course acknowledged and gave details of in its submission to the TRC.[20] The extreme right-wing Freedom Front opposed the Bill because the cut-off date for offences for which amnesties might be given had the effect that some Freedom Front members were excluded from the possibility of amnesties for crimes committed while the Provisional Constitution was being negotiated and under which the TRC was established.[21]

In a detailed speech on behalf of the Government, Kader Asmal, a senior Cabinet Minister, claimed that the ANC was unique in that it had accepted collective responsibility for the grave wrongs which had happened in the camps. He pointed out that there had, however, been no reciprocal gesture from the National Party for what had happened in South Africa from 1960 to 1993, which was the period on which the TRC was to focus.[22] His explanation of the purpose and context of the TRC is crucial to an understanding of its functioning. He listed eight reasons for establishing the TRC:

(1) it was necessary to recognise in the most meaningful way the illegitimacy of the system which had preceded the Government of National Unity;
(2) it was necessary to "make it impossible for those who were part of an evil past to present a sanitised, whitewashed version of the facts to future generations";
(3) it was necessary to ensure that there was no deliberate denial of history which would lead to resentment, revenge, and reversed racialism;

[16] Promotion of National Unity and Reconciliation Bill, No. 30 of 1995.

[17] M A Mzizi, MP, Inkatha Freedom Party, *Debates of the National Assembly (Hansard)* 5 ⟨Second session – first Parliament⟩ (17 May 1995): col. 1362.

[18] C L Fismer, MP, National Party, *Debates of the National Assembly (Hansard)* 5 ⟨Second session – first Parliament⟩ (17 May 1995): col. 1358.

[19] C L Fismer, MP, National Party, *Debates of the National Assembly (Hansard)* 5 ⟨Second session – first Parliament⟩ (17 May 1995): col. 1358.

[20] D P A Schutte, MP, National Party, *Debates of the National Assembly (Hansard)* 5 ⟨Second session – first Parliament⟩ (17 May 1995): col. 1377.

[21] C P Mulder, MP, Freedom Front, *Debates of the National Assembly (Hansard)* 5 ⟨Second session – first Parliament⟩ (17 May 1995): cols. 1372–3.

[22] Kader Asmal, Minister of Water Affairs and Forestry, ANC, *Debates of the National Assembly (Hansard)* 5 ⟨Second session – first Parliament⟩ (17 May 1995): col. 1378.

(4) it would enable the roots of violence in South Africa to be confronted if they were to be eradicated;
(5) provision had to be made for "a cathartic release of emotion, but without the excess of violent disruption";
(6) it was needed as it would encourage the revival of a moral conscience "to fuel a democratic, caring future";
(7) it was necessary not only to put in place new structures but also a new value system which would overcome the old "master-servant, overlord-victim" assumptions; and
(8) the fundamental objectives of the TRC were civil reconciliation and unity, and to achieve these it was necessary deliberately to avoid trials and the victimisation and scape-goating which would go with them.[23]

The Truth and Reconciliation Commission itself recognised severe limitations on its work. It understood that the focus of its enquiries was limited to:

> gross violations of human rights defined as the "killing, abduction, torture or severe ill-treatment" and the "attempt, conspiracy, incitement, instigation, command or procurement to commit" such acts. In essence, therefore, the Commission was restricted to examining only a fraction of the totality of human rights violations that emanated from the policy of apartheid – namely, those that resulted in physical or mental harm or death and were incurred in the course of the political conflicts of the mandate period.[24]

The Truth and Reconciliation Commission consisted, while it was fully functional, of several organs including the Committee on Human Rights Violations, the Committee on Amnesty, and the Committee on Reparation and Rehabilitation. A brief explanation of these is necessary to take the discussion forward.

The TRC also exercised its power to establish an investigating unit, with wide-ranging powers to question under oath people who were called on to appear before it. Such witnesses were compellable and the law of perjury applied to their testimony, notwithstanding that they might incriminate themselves; such evidence, however, was inadmissible against them in criminal proceedings unless it related to a charge of perjury. Apart from the law relating to privilege, the general rules of evidence were not applicable. This is not surprising, for the whole point of the TRC is that it was not a court: the "Nuremberg option" having been rejected in the interests of reconciliation, its proceedings were not to be regarded as trials.

Arising out of investigations, notice had to be given to anyone who might have been detrimentally implicated, or who may have been a victim of a human rights violation. Such people were given an opportunity to make representations to the TRC.

[23] Asmal, *Debates of the National Assembly (Hansard)*, cols. 1381–2.
[24] Truth and Reconciliation Commission, *Report, Vol. 1*, ch. 2, para. 19.

The jurisprudence underlying the work of the committees dealing with human rights violations, amnesty, and reparations is vast. Only the sketchiest outline of their context will be offered here.

2.1. The Committee on Human Rights Violations

One of the several objectives of the TRC as a whole is to establish:

> . . . as complete a picture as possible of the causes, nature and extent of the gross violations of human rights which were committed during the period from 1 March 1960 to the cut-off date, including the antecedents, circumstances, factors and context of such violations, as well as the perspectives of the victims and the motives and perspectives of the persons responsible for the commission of the violations, by conducting investigations and holding hearings.[25]

The Committee on Human Rights Violations heard both those who wanted to appear before it, and those who were summoned by it for the purpose of its investigations.[26] In summary, its functions were derived from those of the Commission itself, which, *inter alia*, required it to conduct enquiries into the gross violations of human rights, including those which were a part of a systematic pattern of abuse: their nature, causes and extent; the identities of all persons and organisations and authorities involved; the question of whether they were deliberately planned; who was accountable for them; to gather evidence to determine who the victims were; and to facilitate and to promote amnesty for those responsible. It was required to prepare a comprehensive report of all its activities and findings.

The Committee on Human Rights Violations also had the duty of referring a matter to the Committee on Reparation and Rehabilitation if it found that a gross violation of human rights had been committed.

2.2. The Committee on Amnesty

Anyone who wished to apply for amnesty "in respect of any act, omission or offence on the grounds that it (was) an act associated with a political objective" had to apply to the Commission, and the Committee on Amnesty had to consider the application and grant or refuse it as the case may be. It had, of course,

[25] Promotion of National Unity and Reconciliation Act, 1995 (Act 34 of 1995), s. 3(1)(a). The full texts of this important document and of all others is available from the web-site of the TRC: http://www.truth.org.za.

[26] It was the exercise of the latter power which brought the TRC into conflict with ex-President P.W. Botha, who refused to appear before it; Truth and Reconciliation Commission, *Report, Vol. 5* (1998) ch. 6, paras. 10–12.

the necessary powers to call for further evidence, to conduct hearings and to deal with ancillary matters. If it felt that the act, omission or offence was one related to "a political objective committed in the course of the conflicts of the past" and that a full disclosure of all the relevant facts had been made, then it had to grant amnesty.

The Explanatory Memorandum to the Parliamentary Bill[27] set out the parameters of the granting of amnesty. It explained that:

> Amnesty may be given for acts, omissions or offences described as "acts associated with a political objective" and which is defined in the Bill. The definition also requires that such conduct must comply with the internationally accepted Norgaard principles (clause 20). Only acts associated with a political objective which were committed during the period from 1 March 1960 (the month of the Sharpeville massacre) to the last possible date specified in the interim Constitution (at present 5 December 1993) shall be considered for amnesty.

The cut-off date of 5 December was subsequently changed to a later one, following various pressures.

The "Norgaard" principles[28] are encapsulated in s. 20(3) of the TRC Act. They relate to:

> (a) The motive of the person who committed the act, omission or offence;
> (b) the context in which the act, omission or offence took place, and in particular whether the act, omission or offence was committed in the course of or as part of a political uprising, disturbance or event, or in reaction thereto;
> (c) the legal and factual nature of the act, omission or offence, including the gravity of the act, omission or offence;
> (d) the object or objective of the act, omission or offence, and in particular whether the act, omission or offence was primarily directed at a political opponent or State property or personnel or against private property or individuals;
> (e) whether the act, omission or offence was committed in the execution of an order of, or on behalf of, or with the approval of, the organisation, institution, liberation movement or body of which the person who committed the act was a member, an agent or a supporter; and
> (f) the relationship between the act, omission or offence and the political objective pursued, and in particular the directness and proximity of the relationship and the proportionality of the act, omission or offence to the objective pursued, but does not include any act, omission or offence committed by any person referred to in subsection (2) who acted-
> (i) for personal gain: Provided that an act, omission or offence by any person who acted and received money or anything of value as an informer of the State or

[27] Promotion of National Unity and Reconciliation Bill, No. 30 of 1995.

[28] Based on a specially-commissioned study by Professor C A Norgaard, independent jurist, "Advice to the United Nations Special Representative on the Entitlement of 16 Persons to Release as Political Prisoners Under para. 7 of the Namibian Settlement Proposal" (Aarhus, Denmark, Unpublished, 1989).

a former state, political organisation or liberation movement, shall not be excluded only on the grounds of that person having received money or anything of value for his or her information; or

(ii) out of personal malice, ill-will or spite, directed against the victim of the acts committed.

It is notable that the Act recognised that those who applied for amnesty – whether granted or refused – might also be victims. It accordingly provided that their cases might be referred to the Committee on Reparation and Rehabilitation.[29]

2.3. The Committee on Reparation and Rehabilitation

People who considered that they had suffered harm as a result of gross violations of human rights could apply for reparation, and if this Committee felt that the application was well-founded it was charged with the duty to "make recommendations. . . . in an endeavour to restore the human and civil dignity of such victim".[30] Parliament and the President between them have the duty of drawing up and implementing a response to the recommendations by this Committee.

In a sense, the very idea that there should be amnesties and reparations is the key to an understanding of the entire significance of the TRC. We must remember that the matters being addressed are the acts of an established state performed by a government which had lost power and had been deprived by events of any legitimacy it might ever have had. This is a remarkable and uncommon event of itself, but the distinctive feature is that the new regime had contrived to co-opt the former regime's leaders and agents into the procedure of investigating and passing judgment on that regime. More than anything else, this underlines the importance of what happened and is happening in South Africa for an understanding of the values underlying law and the rule of law.

3. THE TRC ON INTERNATIONAL LAW

An attempt will be made to draw attention to some of the themes which emerged from the TRC's proceedings and point to the paradigmatic change in the values which the South African revolution has entailed, though the material which was placed before it is overwhelming in volume and it is impossible here to do it justice. The topics on which comments are offered below were chosen simply because they seem to illustrate especially clearly some of the underlying values which the TRC and its processes embody. Part of the interest

[29] Section 22.
[30] Section 26(3).

and importance of such reflections is that they enable one to illustrate two points made frequently from the very outset of the struggle against apartheid and its repressive machinery: first, it is not possible to enforce an unjust law justly and fairly; and secondly, the laws of an unjust regime – and apartheid is only one example – and the defence of them ultimately constitute a threat to international security and peace.

Unless we address ourselves to the lessons to be learnt from South Africa's history, the collected experience of humanity will be impoverished. The TRC is concerned to give expression to one dimension of the new culture of human rights enshrined in both the interim and 1996 Constitutions, for the new South Africa was determined to start as it intended to continue. Those who led the struggle certainly seem to have sought to make it impossible to repeat the past – a point that seems to be so obvious that it will not be expanded in this essay. Applications for amnesty had[31] to be supported by the fullest disclosure of the conduct for which amnesty was sought. This means no less than that applicants had to make a complete confession to the commission of criminal offences which were often of the gravest possible nature. The Norgaard principles make it clear that no crime should be beyond consideration no matter how grave, and indeed violence of all sorts including murder was a frequent theme.

3.1. Civilian casualties and the Geneva Conventions

A strange, almost paradoxical, feature is that, after it had been elected, the party which formed the present Government of South Africa itself drew attention to incidents of its own misconduct. The ANC filed its first submission to the TRC in August 1996, and in it drew attention to the civilian casualties of the armed struggle it had led and, more to the point, also to grave acts of misconduct that had taken place in its camps. Those who had opposed the ANC throughout its life – and still do – were and are bitterly critical of the ANC's submission with regard to civilian loss of life. However, whether they like it or not, the submission engages in a sombre and extensive reflection on the history and nature of armed struggle against a regime which was brutal both in its objectives – a society founded on racism – and in the methods which it sought to implement and to defend them. In its submission, the ANC opened the subject thus:

> It was the policy of the ANC – ever since the formation of MK[32] in 1961 – to avoid unnecessary loss of life. The ANC has never permitted random attacks on civilian targets.

[31] The past tense is used as no further applications can be made. At the time of writing, over 2,000 applications for amnesty still had to be decided; of the 7,124 applications made, approximately 5,000 had been rejected and 300 granted: *Daily mail and Guardian*, 22 March 1999.

[32] uMkhonto we Sizwe ("the Spear of the Nation") – the armed wing of the ANC.

> Once MK camps were in existence, part of the training of every MK combatant was political and included an insistence that the enemy should not be defined simply in racial terms. When the ANC became a signatory to the Geneva Convention on the conduct of war in 1977 it was reported to be the first liberation movement in the world to take this step.
>
> However, the morality of the ANC, its objectives then and now, and standards it set itself dictate that we examine the conduct of struggle critically, and acknowledge where errors took place.[33]

The civilian casualties at the hands of the ANC constitute an important subject which we cannot examine in detail here. Suffice it to be said that the ANC rejected robustly any comparison between those who fell in the cross-fire at the hands of its combatants, and those who were the deliberate victims of the repressive organs of the State. The TRC, while not hesitating to express grave criticisms of the ANC and others engaged in the struggle against apartheid, acknowledged the distinction.[34]

The examination referred to was made fully in the main body of the submission. This essay is obviously not the place for an extensive review of the ANC's position as a political matter, but it is important at least to note it, and to compare it with that of the National Party because of the insight this gives of the change in fundamental values which inspires the new South Africa.

Underlying the ANC's approach is the fact that, in the armed struggle it opened against the apartheid government of South Africa, it signed the Geneva Convention on the conduct of war in 1977 – reportedly, the first liberation movement in the world to do so. In November 1980 the ANC declared its adherence to all the Protocols of 1977 to the Geneva Conventions, and the President, O R Tambo, claimed that this was done as the movement had always defined the enemy in terms of a system of domination and not of a people or a race . . . "As we have done in the past, so shall we continue, consistently and unreservedly, to support, fight for and abide by the principles of international law".[35]

Nothing could distinguish more sharply the distinction between the ANC and the apartheid government it was confronting.

After considering the basic submission by the National Party in which it made no reference to the Geneva Conventions, the TRC asked it directly[36] whether the

[33] African National Congress, *Statement to the Truth and Reconciliation Commission* (Johannesburg, African National Congress, Department of Information and Publicity, 1996), Executive Summary, para. 5, Http://www.anc.org.za.

[34] Truth and Reconciliation Commission, *Report of the Truth and Reconciliation Commission, Vol. 5* (1998), ch. 6, para. 58 ff.

[35] African National Congress, *Further Submissions and Responses by the African National Congress to Questions Raised by the Commission for Truth and Reconciliation* (Johannesburg, African National Congress, Department of Information and Publicity, 1996), para. 2.1, Http://www.anc.org.za.

[36] Truth and Reconciliation Commission, "Questions Put to the National Party", 12 December 1996, para. 4.

Government had adhered to them. In its reply – constituting the second submission it made to the TRC – the matter was not addressed at all and the conclusions in the Final Report of the TRC were almost inevitable.

For example, the TRC reviewed "Operation Reindeer" – the code-name for a massive attack by the South African Defence Force (SADF) on a camp in Angola where refugees from Namibia had gathered at an important base of the Peoples' Liberation Army of Namibia (PLAN).[37] The TRC had available the documentation and other material prepared by the SADF, including intelligence reports and operational orders.

Indeed, so important were these resources that a brief digression is appropriate. Fundamental to understanding the impact and importance of the TRC is that it was given and used successfully the authority to make available to public scrutiny vast resources which would otherwise never have been revealed. In his opening comments on the Report, Archbishop Desmond Tutu said:

> One of the unique features of the South African Commission has been its open and transparent nature. Similar commissions elsewhere in the world have met behind closed doors. Ours has operated in the full glare of publicity. This means that some of the information contained in this report is already in the public domain. Nonetheless, some significant and new insights are included in the pages that follow. . . . This material will be of great value to scholars, journalists and others researching our history for generations to come. From a research point of view, this may be the Commission's greatest legacy.[38]

The TRC had little difficulty in concluding that the SADF knew well that there would be many civilian casualties, and that these were intended:

> The fact that the operational orders for *Reindeer* included the instruction that "women and children must, where possible, not be shot" is evidence of the SADF's prior knowledge of the presence of civilians. However, this apparent intention to spare their lives was rendered meaningless by the SADF's decision to use fragmentation bombs in the initial air assault, as such weapons kill and maim indiscriminately. Their use, therefore, in the face of the knowledge of the presence of civilians, amounts to an indiscriminate and illegitimate use of force and a violation of Protocol 1 to the Geneva Conventions of 1949. The foreseeable killing of civilians at Kassinga was therefore a breach of humanitarian law.[39]

The TRC expressly made no finding about what happened to SWAPO and PLAN wounded, in view of inconsistent evidence about the matter. It drew attention to the evidence that the chief of the army, General Constand Viljoen, had been present at the raid and had ordered that no wounded were to be killed, but it also quoted contemporary reports in the South African press to a different effect: whether civilians or combatants, they were shot:

[37] This was the armed wing of the South-West African Peoples' Organisation (SWAPO).

[38] Truth and Reconciliation Commission, *Report, Vol. 1*, ch. 1, para. 3.

[39] Truth and Reconciliation Commission, *Report of the Truth and Reconciliation Commission, Vol. 2* (1998), ch. 2, para. 45.

> We were in enemy territory and had to get the hell out of there as quickly as possible. There were just too many wounded. We could have left them on the battlefield to die in pain and agony. We couldn't. I was given an AK-47 and instructed to kill those who couldn't be saved. I had to decide who was not going to live. I was the company leader, so I had to take the lead. I don't know how many people I shot that day. Some were conscious, some were not. We found this woman clutching her screaming baby. It was only when we saw the terrible wounds inflicted by an Air Force bomb. There was no hope for her. I had to shoot her. She looked at me. I can never describe what it did to me. It was too much. I later broke down.[40]

The TRC also noted evidence before it that on other occasions in the course of the war in what was then South-West Africa the SADF had shot wounded PLAN combatants.

The TRC considered Principles III, IV, and VI of the Principles of International Law Recognised in the Charter of the Nuremberg Tribunal and in the Judgment of the Tribunal 1950. Principle III provides, in brief, that it is not a defence under international law that one acted as head of state or responsible government official when committing an act which constitutes a crime under international law, and Principle IV similarly shuts out the defence of superior orders, provided a moral choice was in fact possible to the person accused.

Principle VI defines a series of crimes which the TRC clearly considered to be relevant to the issues before it:

(a) Crimes against peace:
  (i) Planning, preparation, initiation or waging of a war of aggression or a war in violation of international treaties, agreements or assurances;
  (ii) Participation in a common plan or conspiracy for the accomplishment of any of the acts mentioned under (i).

(b) War crimes:
Violations of the laws or customs of war include, but are not limited to, murder, ill-treatment or deportation to slave-labour or for any other purpose of civilian population of or in occupied territory, murder or ill-treatment of prisoners of war, of persons on the seas, killing of hostages, plunder of public or private property, wanton destruction of cities, towns, or villages, or devastation not justified by military necessity.

(c) Crimes against humanity:
Murder, extermination, enslavement, deportation and other inhuman acts done against any civilian population, or persecutions on political, racial or religious grounds, when such acts are done or such persecutions are carried on in execution of or in connexion with any crime against peace or any war crime.

No apology is given for reproducing these points in full, for it is striking how they resonate in the context of South Africa. Though they were being considered in the context of Namibia, in a sense they encapsulate the whole ethos of

[40] Truth and Reconciliation Commission, *Report, Vol.* 2, ch. 2, paras. 46, 47, quoting an interview with an anonymous soldier reported in *The Star*, 8 May 1993.

apartheid and it was inevitable that the TRC would conclude that those responsible for the atrocities described above[41] were guilty of gross human rights violations under international law. Generally, it found that the former South African Government had violated the Geneva Convention by using capital punishment against those convicted of political offences, and that it had refused to sign the 1977 addenda which extended the cover of the Conventions to captured guerrillas.

As an aside, it is interesting to note the South African status of various international instruments on human rights. The new, democratically-elected government ratified and acceded to the 1977 Protocols to the Geneva Conventions in 1995. Of a list consisting of thirty-six Conventions and Protocols, including the African Charter on Human and People's Rights, from 1922 to 1993 South Africa signed or ratified or acceded to no more than six.[42] By comparison, from 1993 to July 1998 incomplete data reveal that at least nineteen had been signed or ratified or acceded to. According to the Department of Foreign Affairs, South Africa is now a party to twenty-six human rights-related conventions and protocols.[43] The change in fundamental values seems to be patent, and the lesson clear: the commitment to a human rights culture internally leads inevitably to a respect for the standards of international law generally.

It is striking that the National Party has sought to bring itself within the new paradigms. In its own submission to the TRC, F W de Klerk was anxious to draw distinctions:

> I must also stress that a distinction should be drawn between what have become known as the "old National Party" and the "New National Party". There is a profound difference between the National Party as it is presently constituted and the party that ruled South Africa for the first decades after its election victory in 1948. The

[41] Prime Minister B J Vorster in his capacity as Head of State (Principle III); Minister of Defence P W Botha in his capacity as Political Head of the SADF; General Magnus Malan in his capacity as Chief of the SADF; Lieutenants-General Constand Viljoen and R H Rogers in their capacities as Chiefs of the Army and Air Force respectively. Constand Viljoen subsequently became a leader of the "Freedom Front" and was elected as one of its MPs to the National Assembly. It is worth noting that, despite the finding of the TRC, absolutely no inhibitions have been placed on the political life of people such as Viljoen, who is fully protected by the new Bill of Rights. Indeed, he typifies the new *status quo* in that he vigorously claims the rights enshrined in it; this factor is one of many which signals the success of the TRC and the security of the new South Africa.

[42] These included the Geneva Conventions of 1952, regulating conduct between warring parties, ratified in 1952 by the National Party Government under its then Prime Minister, J G Strijdom. At the very least this was a matter of political expediency, for the South African Air Force was at the time fighting in the Korean War under the United Nations' flag.

[43] It will be realised that when a treaty has been signed by a certain number of states (prescribed either by the treaty or by customary law), accession or ratification by a state does not require its signature. In the case of South Africa, since 1994 for ceremonial reasons a two-stage procedure has occasionally been followed even where accession would have been sufficient. A full review of South Africa's latest position on International Human Rights Instruments can be found in the *Human Rights Report*, published monthly by the Human Rights Committee (an independent NGO monitoring and reporting on human rights abuses and political violence in South Africa since 1988).

policies and philosophy of the National Party as it is today are diametrically different from those of the old party.[44]

Many South Africans reacted badly to the NP's submissions, for the claim was implicitly that the problem was not apartheid but the means used to enforce it. Moreover, the NP's evidence heard by the TRC creates a sense of unease, and the TRC's Final Report confronted it. It notes that Mr de Klerk claimed that:

> . . . things happened which were not authorised, not intended, or of which we were not aware. . . . I have never condoned gross violations of human rights . . . and reject any insinuation that it was ever the policy of my party or government.[45]

The TRC set this against the words of Eugene de Kok, the convicted Vlakplaas[46] killer, in the published confession he made:

> Yet the person who sticks most of all in my throat is former State President F W de Klerk. Not because I can prove, without a shadow of doubt, that he ordered the death of X or cross-border raid Y. Not even because of the holier than thou attitude that is discernible in the evidence he gave before the [Commission] on behalf of the National Party.
>
> It is because, in that evidence, he simply did not have the courage to declare: "yes we at the top levels condoned what was done on our behalf by the security forces. What's more, we instructed that it should be implemented. Or – if we did not actually give instructions we turned a blind eye. We didn't move heaven and earth to stop the ghastliness. Therefore let the foot soldiers be excused."

Mr de Klerk secured a court order provisionally deleting from the Report the TRC's findings against him: there is a blank space instead. What remains is a passage which bleakly notes that his appearance before the Commission was a particular disappointment to the Commission; though he had done so much to turn the tide of South African history, "his evasiveness and unwillingness candidly to acknowledge the full burden of the NP's responsibility seemed to the Commission to be a missed opportunity to take the reconciliation process forward".[47]

> Pieter-Dirk Uys, in a biting comment on the evidence to the Commission, wrote:
>
> Fifty years after the Nuremberg Trials, South Africans stand on the eve of their Truth and Reconciliation Commission. The search for the truth about the past. The demand for the guilty to step forward. To be forgiven? To be punished? A former apartheid minister takes the stand. He peers at the watching Commissioners.
>
> "Comrades," he says, his moustache twitching. "I have a clear conscience. I never used it!"[48]

[44] F W de Klerk, Leader of the National Party, "Submission to the Truth and Reconciliation Commission" (Cape Town, 1997). http://www.truth.org.za/submit/truth-np.htm.

[45] Truth and Reconciliation Commission, *Report, Vol.* 5, ch. 7, para. 18.

[46] The farm where the police established the headquarters of a death-squad.

[47] Truth and Reconciliation Commission, *Report, Vol.* 5, ch. 5, para. 6.

[48] Pieter-Dirk Uys, "The Truth, the Whole Truth and Nothing But." *Index* 25, no. 5 (September–October 1996), 46.

The hostility to what F W de Klerk wrote is not surprising. He went out of his way to put on record his "deep respect" for his predecessors who led the National Party and whom he described as "good and honourable men". He blamed the ANC for the violence of the past and claimed that it was a hindrance to, rather than the driving force of, the change to the new and democratic South Africa. The TRC had a different view; it concluded one chapter of its Final Report thus:

> To many, notably those in the leadership in the government and security forces in the 1980s, the conclusion that the State sanctioned murder may and probably will be an unpalatable assertion. It is also probably not what the Commission expected to find when it started its work two years ago. It is, however, a "truth" to which it has been drawn by the evidence.[49]

4. THE LAWYERS AND THE LEGAL SYSTEM

Lawyers should read the Final Report of the TRC with a sense of unease. Submissions from the legal profession were invited and made, oral hearings were held, and the volume of material assembled is colossal and a resource of value beyond measure for the study of the practise of law and of legal ethics. It is quite impossible to review it here comprehensively, but the findings of the TRC make for painful reading. If we are concerned about fundamental values in law we need to remind ourselves that *if the lawyers cannot be trusted, then truly we face the abyss*. The TRC drew attention to:

a) Prosecutors who knew that the police had used brutal means to extract information from suspects and then assisted such interrogators from being questioned too closely on their methods. . . .
b) Attorneys-General[50] who too easily launched prosecutions or granted "no-bail" certificates on flimsy evidence.
c) Magistrates who uncritically granted police search and seizure warrants, and who conveniently found no one responsible for injuries and deaths in detention at inquests. . . .
d) Attorneys who failed to accept an unpopular political person as a client, perhaps for fear of social ostracism or the loss of lucrative commercial clients.
e) Advocates who were willing to appear for the government in civil actions where some of the basic building blocks of apartheid, such as racial classification or influx control or Group Areas, were being attacked as the unreasonable and invalid exercise of executive discretion.
f) Law teachers who chose to concentrate on "safe" areas of the law or to teach in such a way that no critical ability was imparted to the students.

[49] Truth and Reconciliation Commission, *Report, Vol. 1*, ch. 2, para. 80.

[50] Though also responsible for prosecutions, this now-abolished position in each of the former Provinces of South Africa must not be confused in status or responsibilities with the Attorney-General in England.

g) Students who chose to be blinded by the glamour and material returns of the conventional mainstream of the profession, neglecting his or her potential role as a fighter for justice for all in South Africa.
h) In the greatest injustices of all, judges who too easily made sense of the illogical and the unjust in legislative language, and who too quickly accepted the word of the police or official witness in preference to that of the accused. . . .
i) The judiciary, which unthinkingly allowed judicial policy to be influenced by executive dictate or white male prejudice; which was intent on maintaining and protecting the *status quo*; which willingly participated in producing the highest capital punishment rate in the "Western" world by the mid-1980s and an executionrate that impacted overwhelmingly on poor black male accused. . . .
j) The organised professional bodies which were obsequious in their attitudes to government policies, hounding those of their members who chose to buck the system politically. . . .
k) The organised profession (who) took no effective initiatives to make the administration of justice more accessible to those who could not afford it, not at least until apartheid's days were numbered. Their complacency in the face of the challenges thrown up by government injustice internally, and their defensiveness in international forums when foreign lawyers' organisations dared criticise, are matters of public record.[51]

The Commission said that it believed this to have been the position during the apartheid years, and that it was acknowledged by many (in some cases, with qualifications) of those whose evidence it examined to have been the case. Shocking examples are provided. There are many matters which arise, and many of these relate to the fundamental values which must drive and inspire law and lawyers – especially in the fields of human rights. A Dutch advocate (Willem van Manen) reported to the International Commission of Jurists that no trial of a person accused of having infringed unfair "apartheid laws" could ever in itself be called fair. This was a comment made in the context of the trial of a Dutch national, Helen Pastoors, in 1986; Mr Justice Spoelstra had found her guilty of treason but not guilty of terrorism. Sentencing her to ten years' jail, he said that she was not being punished for her convictions but for the acts that arose from them.[52] The Deputy Dean of Law at the University of Cape Town, Professor Zimmerman, demurred and said that it was far too sweeping to suggest that a judiciary called to enforce "unfair" laws was incapable of conducting fair trials.[53] This brings out a fundamental tension, and the TRC has given its answer: unjust laws cannot be enforced fairly. For lawyers in South Africa, the problem was always how they should react to this tension. In what is probably the most meticulously detailed and thought-through study of judges and lawyers in South Africa, Ellman was clear: lawyers had a role to play even

[51] Truth and Reconciliation Commission, *Report of the Truth and Reconciliation Commission, Vol. 4* (1998), ch. 4, para. 34.

[52] South African Institute of Race Relations, *Race Relations Survey 1986*, Part 2 (1988), 879.

[53] South African Institute of Race Relations, *SAIRR, Survey, 1986, Part 2*, 878–83.

in the darkest years and under the worst conditions.[54] The TRC's findings are not in conflict with this; in a passionate passage which stands dramatically as a counterweight to the grim indictment of South Africa's jurists, the TRC drew attention to the few lawyers (including judges, teachers and students) who were prepared to break with the norm:

> These lawyers used every opportunity to speak out publicly and within the profession against the adoption and execution of rules of law that sanctioned arbitrary official conduct and injustice. They explored the limits of their forensic skills in defending those on trial for offences in terms of such legislation, or in arguing for the invalidity of vague or unreasonable administrative action. They worked ceaselessly to prepare the cases of those targeted by the State, often in trying conditions and for little material reward. They advised and educated those in the community most vulnerable to official excesses, such as the rural poor and workers, through advice offices and religious bodies. They challenged their students to confront the relationship between law and justice and to translate their ideals into practice. They forswore the comforts of commercial practice for the sake of the upliftment of those excluded from all forms of power. They exercised their judicial discretion in favour of justice and liberty wherever proper and possible.[55]

They had courage, strength, perseverance and clarity of purpose, ". . . and they were influential enough to be part of the reason why the ideal of a constitutional democracy as the favoured form of government for a future South Africa continued to burn brightly throughout the darkness of the apartheid era".

The South African experience must teach all lawyers, for there are no alternatives to their integrity and courage.

5. CONCLUSIONS

The wider implications of the TRC must be left to the future to be fully explored: we are still too close to these events.

However, some final observations seem to be possible. The TRC must be seen not just as a single event in history and which has now been concluded, but as the start of a process. The act of exploring those wider implications may ultimately prove to be the real inheritance of the TRC, for it is that exploration which will be as crucial as the work of the TRC itself. The TRC may have done something richer and more important for humanity than has yet been realised: perhaps even more important than Nuremberg.

It is impossible to provide an adequate review of the impact of the proceedings in this essay, and two impressions at polar extremes of experience must

[54] Stephen Ellman, *In a Time of Trouble: Law and Liberty in South Africa's State of Emergency* (New York, Oxford University Press, 1992).

[55] Truth and Reconciliation Commission, *Report, Vol.* 4, ch. 4, para. 36.

suffice. On one hand, there were times when evidence at hearings was so dramatic, tragic, and horrifying that it was reasonable that many – especially the bereaved families of victims – opposed applications for amnesty, resenting bitterly that those responsible for their anguish might not be brought to trial.

By contrast, and more needs to be said of this for the purposes of this essay, there were also moments when the conduct of those appearing before the TRC seemed to transcend the humanly possible. It is a hopeless task to find any single moment that stands out more clearly than another: they each seem to encapsulate a different aspect of the capacity of the human spirit to triumph, somehow, over the horror and evil that people are capable of committing on each other. There were acts of forgiveness and acts of regret and remorse and acts of reconciliation which brought South Africa to a stop. How those involved managed to find the strength to do what they did is a matter which must, surely, remain one of the wonderful mysteries of the human spirit. Surely too, this greatness must be given a framework and opportunity – such as the Truth and Reconciliation Commission – to become manifest if humanity can have any hope of moving forwards to a better world. Either we must accept that the evil which led to the TRC is the best that humanity can do and that it is an eternal characteristic of human history, or we can hope as individuals that humanity can evolve to something better.

The profound, moving and emotional incidents of regret and contrition and of forgiveness and pardoning were experiences of the Truth and Reconciliation Commission which demonstrate that jurisprudence has now to take into account a new vision of what is possible in relationships between people. If this essay, which claims to be about fundamental values, has any value whatever it is because it succeeds in pointing to one of the many challenges to law which the TRC has raised. Unless law is inspired by the fundamental values which drove the TRC into existence, then it betrays humanity. The greatest achievement of the TRC would be that it never again has to happen.

There are indeed fundamental values in law. In the most general terms, they are to be found where law recognises the humanity of those to whom it applies. This is something more than the recognition of human rights; it means, if the South African experience teaches anything, that individuals each have the duty to act with humanity. The matter extends beyond states and governments and political parties: it is the concern of human beings and we are our brothers' and sisters' keepers. In the new South Africa, the invocation is for the spirit of *ubuntu*[56] to prevail. The TRC drew attention to this – passionately and at length.[57]

What the TRC said about those involved in the administration of justice in South Africa must make lawyers squirm, for it is truly a shaming indictment.

[56] See n. 8 *supra*.

[57] Truth and Reconciliation Commission, *Report, Vol. 1*, ch. 5, para. 80 ff.

In the context of this essay, the fundamental values to be considered must be those which lie at the heart of what it is to be a lawyer. These are something more than the formal ethics of the practise of law, which stop short when they have defined the formal relationships – e.g. between practitioners and their clients – without helping jurists to take decisions about what they are willing to do in the first place at all.

Many anti-apartheid lawyers, during the so-called "struggle years", contributed greatly to the examination of the issues behind such problems, for they were a matter of profound and practical importance. In the past, what jurists did in South Africa frequently involved decisions of conscience: for example, should law teachers encourage students to form an opinion about the laws of apartheid – and should they express opinions themselves? Was the moral basis of laws based on racial discrimination, and the wretched, muddled rag-bag of hatred, fear, and ignorance that was used to justify it, something that one should disregard after one had taken the usual practitioner's oath to uphold the law? On elevation to the bench, how far does a judge forfeit the right to independence of opinion?

There has been much comment on the positivism which has characterised much of South African jurisprudence. In 1973, Sachs drew attention to the fact that law faculties made few attempts to introduce moral or sociological criteria into the evaluation of legal rules, and he remarked that the only substantial critique was advanced by Afrikaner jurists whose concern was to use historical and nationalist jurisprudence in an attempt to expunge English influence from the South African common law.[58] He drew attention to the inaugural lecture by John Dugard in 1971, in which Professor Dugard – an outstanding and courageous exception to the general attitude justly criticised by Sachs in law faculties – reminded his audience that it was the "servile obedience to the will of the sovereign and strict distinction between law and morals" which was exploited by Hitler and led to the debasement of the German legal system.[59] Dugard expanded on the theme in a powerful book published five years later:

> Positivism has not served South Africa well as a guide to legal thinking. It has prevented judges from fully perceiving that the judicial function is essentially an exercise in choice in the penumbral zone of legal uncertainty, and it has discouraged lawyers from playing a more active role in the protection of those principles which make up the country's legal heritage.[60]

Some of the effects were described, as the apartheid era moved towards its end, by a practitioner who wrote bitterly:

[58] Albie Sachs, *Justice in South Africa* (London, Heinemann, 1973), p. 120.

[59] John Dugard, "Justice and Civil Liberty" Inaugural lecture, *Rand Daily Mail*, 25 March 1971; quoted by Sachs, *Justice in South Africa*, p. 260.

[60] John Dugard, *Human Rights and the South African Legal Order* (Princeton, Princeton University Press, 1978), p. 397.

> If every white lawyer was required to spend one hour in the Bantu Commissioner's court every Monday, he could not fail to change his view of South African justice. Unfortunately very few would agree to represent a black in these courts especially since there is little chance of being paid. Most attorneys are far happier pretending that such courts and such proceedings do not exist.[61]

Twenty years later the TRC returned to the theme, but now there was a greater and more terrible legacy in which Sachs and Dugard and others were, sadly, the exceptions.

The legal professions did not act honourably, though there were certainly individuals who did. In its evidence to the TRC, the National Association of Democratic Lawyers (NADEL) said bluntly that "the legal system and its functionaries unquestioningly failed those whose rights were systematically violated under apartheid".[62]

Two incidents illustrate the enormous initial impact of the TRC and the changes in South Africa on legal practitioners. Even before the TRC's Report was published, the white and male-dominated Provincial Law Societies wound themselves up in March 1998 and, together with the National Association of Democratic Lawyers and the Black Lawyers' Association, founded the Law Society of South Africa (LSA). The event took place in a dramatic and moving meeting held symbolically in the old chamber of the former House of Assembly where so many of South Africa's apartheid's laws were enacted. The gathering was addressed by the Minister of Justice and a speaker on behalf of the President of the International Bar Association. The constitution of the LSA now ensures that the spirit of the new South Africa shall prevail in its affairs, and the membership of the new Council includes some of the courageous and distinguished men and women whom the TRC drew attention to. In another development, the Johannesburg Bar Council dramatically expressed its contrition that in 1964 it had moved to disbar one of South Africa's leading silks and human rights lawyers, Advocate "Bram" Fischer, in a politically-driven action. He was posthumously reinstated amid enormous acclaim.

There have been many formal changes. At the forefront is the fact that South Africa has a new Constitution with a Bill of Rights which is surely one of the most advanced in the world. The Constitution establishes equally powerful machinery to protect and to further the explicit passion for democratic and open government. There is now a Public Protector who has the power to

> investigate any conduct in state affairs, or in the public administration in any sphere of government, that is alleged or suspected to be improper or to result in any impropriety or prejudice.[63]

[61] John D Jackson, *Justice in South Africa* (London, Penguin Books, 1980), p. 22.

[62] National Association of Democratic Lawyers, *Submission by the National Association of Democratic Lawyers to the Truth and Reconciliation Commission on the Role of Lawyers and the Legal System in the Gross Human Rights Violations of Apartheid* (1998), ch. 5.

[63] Constitution of the Republic of South Africa 1966, s. 182.

There are also, *inter alia*, a Human Rights Commission, a Commission for Gender Equality, and a Commission for the Promotion and Protection of the Rights of Cultural, Religious and Linguistic Communities.[64] The Constitution prescribes that all of these, and other associated structures, are independent, subject only to the Constitution and the law, and must function without fear, favour or prejudice; and they, and their dignity and effectiveness, must be protected and furthered by all organs of the State. It is striking – and reassuring – that even the most hostile figures from the old regime invoke the new machinery readily when they feel aggrieved by the new one.

Judges are appointed by the President from a list put forward by the Judicial Service Commission. The hearings of the Judicial Commission are characterised by active public interest; in particular, would-be judges in the Constitutional Court are openly subjected to vigorous scrutiny, and are in any event appointed only if they survive both the Commission and the President's consultations which must include, *inter alia*, the leaders of the political parties in the National Assembly.[65] A great interest in judicial independence has developed rapidly; many judges from the old regime still sit, and this has led to considerable tension, vigorous criticism, and sometimes colourful public debate as South Africans come to terms with the jurisprudence of the new South Africa.

Finally, reference must be made to law teaching. This, too, has been transformed. The law schools have been caught up in the turbulent process of the reconstruction of the entire university system – indeed, of the entire education system. Students are no longer prevented from questioning the fundamental elements of their courses – often a very dangerous matter in the past, when the entire educational system was racially-divided and geared totally to apartheid's values. There is no doubt whatsoever of the great value of these challenges, though sometimes individual institutions are plunged into turmoil. The young men and women who often risked their lives in the front line during the "struggle years" and who are acutely conscious of how they were disadvantaged by the apartheid-based educational system are rightly highly sensitive to, and ruthlessly intolerant of, old values and attitudes.

The list of changes is endless. But no matter with what rhapsodies the TRC is greeted, no matter how inspiring the speeches and documents, no matter how exciting are the changes and the challenges and the hopes, South Africa today is still the child of its past. Much of the poverty, violence, corruption, division and bitter racism of the old regime are still evident: *ubuntu* is still a long way off. We need not concern ourselves with the question of whether events would have developed differently had the lawyers collectively hearkened to voices such as Dugard's and Sachs'. What matters is that lawyers should remember that past

[64] Constitution of the Republic of South Africa 1966, Chapter 9: "State Institutions Supporting Constitutional Democracy".

[65] Constitution of the Republic of South Africa 1966, s. 174.

and act accordingly, lest the country relive it. In South Africa, *ubuntu* is not a matter of choice: the new South Africa cannot survive without it, and jurists have a key part to play. They are at last actively aware of their role and concentrate deliberately on it. Truly, South African jurisprudence has become something that everyone can do.

15

The Value of Multiculturalism in Eastern Europe

ISTVAN POGANY

1. THE DEMISE OF MULTICULTURALISM IN EASTERN EUROPE

Throughout most of its history, large swathes of Eastern Europe were characterised by the wide variety of national, ethnic and religious groups who co-existed, peaceably enough, within individual villages, as well as in the towns and cities. The village of Kétegyháza, which is located in south eastern Hungary, close to the Romanian border, offers a good example of this phenomenon.[1] Even today, a majority of its 4,400 inhabitants are of Romanian "nationality", i.e. persons of Romanian national descent whose mother tongue is Romanian, although they are Hungarian citizens born in Hungary.[2] A much smaller proportion of the villagers are of German national descent, while there are also significant numbers of persons of Hungarian nationality and over three hundred Roma, or Gypsies. Most of the Roma live in the so-called "uj falu", or "new village", which is situated, quite literally, on the other side of the railway tracks that run along the northern rim of the older, larger and more prosperous part of the village.

If you spend a little time studying the war memorial in the centre of Kétegyháza, as I did on recent visits, you will discover that the cultural mix in the village was richer still before the Second World War. The war memorial records the deaths in that war, in addition to numerous Hungarian soldiers and airmen, of the "Khon family", of "Mr and Mrs Gelber", of "Mr and Mrs Freisinger" and of several other men and women with German-sounding names. These civilians, for they did not bear arms, belonged to Kétegyháza's former Jewish

[1] For details on the different national, ethnic and religious groups within the village of Kétegyháza I am grateful to its mayor, Gulyás György, whom I interviewed on a research trip to Hungary in September 1999.

[2] On the distinction between "citizenship" and "nationality", terms which are routinely treated as synonyms in the English-speaking world, but which have sharply divergent meanings in Eastern Europe and in the post-Soviet states see e.g. N Davies, *Europe a History* (Oxford, Oxford University Press, 1996), esp. at pp. 812–13.

community. They were killed during the Holocaust, the full impact of which only bore down on Hungary at a comparatively late stage of the War, after March 1944, when German forces occupied the country and a Hungarian administration was formed which energetically colluded with Hitler's murderous policies towards the Jews.[3] It was the provincial Jews of Hungary, such as those in Kétegyháza, who were the first to be rounded up and deported to the death camps in Poland. On a more random and arbitrary basis, thousands of Hungarian Roma were also killed in Hungary or despatched to concentration and extermination camps where they subsequently perished.[4] The Gypsies of Kétegyháza, as I was told by some of the older Roma in the village, escaped this fate only because of the rapid advance of the Russian troops towards the end of the War, which prevented the Hungarian *csendőrök*, or gendarmes, from rounding up the Roma in the village and sending them to the camps as they had planned. But Roma from the neighbouring village of Elek were killed by Hungarian gendarmes and tossed into a lime pit, I was informed, including a heavily pregnant woman who was casually shot by a gendarme officer.

After the War, and in accordance with the Potsdam Accords, a sizeable proportion of the *Volksdeutsche* (ethnic German) communities in the region were stripped of virtually all of their property and forcibly uprooted from the territories of Hungary, Poland and the former Czechoslovakia.[5] The legality (let alone morality) of this measure, which was supposedly "authorised" by the Allied Powers, cannot be examined here.[6] However, it is clear that hundreds of thousands of families, including women, children, the elderly, even desperately ill patients removed from hospital wards, were dumped, often after agonisingly harsh and protracted journeys, in a war-ravaged Germany which lacked the resources to provide for them.

As the village of Kétegyháza aptly illustrates, genuinely multicultural communities, small as well as large, existed in much of Eastern Europe before the impact of ideologies of racial exclusivity, in the twentieth century, resulted in drastic and irreversible demographic changes. It would be wrong, though, to present an excessively idealised picture of relations between the different ethnic

[3] For an overview by the leading authority on the subject see R Braham, "The Holocaust in Hungary: A Retrospective Analysis" in D Cesarini (ed.), *Genocide and Rescue: The Holocaust in Hungary 1944* (Oxford, Berg, 1997), ch. 2.

[4] The numbers of Hungarian Roma killed during the War remains controversial. The leading Hungarian study is: L Karsai, *A cigánykérdés Magyarországon 1919–1945* ("The Gypsy Question in Hungary 1919–1945") (Budapest, Cserépfalvi Kiadás, 1992). For an English-language analysis see D Kenrick and G Puxon, *Gypsies under the Swastika* (Hatfield, Hertfordshire, University of Herfordshire Press, 2nd ed., 1995), pp. 100–05. I examine the Roma Holocaust, Nazi attitudes towards the Roma and related issues in chapter 5 of my forthcoming book, I Pogany, *The Roma Café* (2001, forthcoming).

[5] See generally, Z Zeman, *The Making and Breaking of Communist Europe* (Oxford, Basil Blackwell, 1991), pp. 210–19.

[6] For an impassioned critique of the forcible resettlement of the *Volksdeutsche* communities of East Central Europe, see A-M de Zayas, *The German Expellees: Victims in War and Peace* (Basingstoke, Macmillan Press, 1993).

and religious communities in the era before the Second World War. Inevitably, there were a variety of resentments and tensions in such villages (as in the region as a whole) based on economic, cultural, religious or political factors. Some of these resentments are explored in the literature of the period, in works such as the sociologically informed novel, *Kiskunhalom*, by the Hungarian novelist Lajos Nagy. The book, first published in 1934, presents a blisteringly unsentimental account of the hardships and rigours of the life of landless agricultural labourers and the poorer class of peasants in Hungary's villages, in contrast to the idleness and comparative wealth of the gentry, visitors from the capital and, so the author insinuates none too subtly, certain minority groups such as Jews.[7]

In villages such as Kétegyháza, Jews were often associated with particular occupations, such as running inns, shops, mills and other fairly modest commercial ventures. Some were employed by the gentry to manage their estates while the owners enjoyed a sybaritic lifestyle in the capital or abroad; an increasing number became farmers in their own right.[8] Others, like my paternal grandfather, were schoolmasters, while many practised as pharmacists, doctors or notaries. Understandably, Jews, who were generally much better educated than the peasants, were often resented by the latter for having greater wealth and an apparently easier way of life, as well as for their heresy.

By contrast, Gypsies in village communities like Kétegyháza were frequently treated with a degree of condescension by the peasants. Some, the élite among the Roma, were professional musicians, earning a decent enough living through their work at weddings, funerals and other celebrations. Others might be employed as wooden spoon or wooden trough carvers, or as menders of copper pots. Such 'professions' would be handed down through families, who themselves belonged to distinct Roma sub-groups, or tribes, and would be learnt by the children at an early age.[9] The less fortunate among the Roma were forced to seek work on peasant smallholdings, hiring themselves out as day labourers. Some, particularly the women, would also supplement family incomes through begging, which was not perceived as in any way shameful.[10] The living conditions of the Roma were generally far worse than those of the ordinary peasants. Before the Second World War, many Roma lived in *putrik*,

[7] Lajos Nagy's *Kiskunhalom* was reisssued (in Hungarian) in 1999, in Budapest, Hungary by Osiris Kiadó, as part of its Millennium Series.

[8] For a study of one family of Jewish farmers in pre-War Hungary, see E Naves, *Journey to Vaja* (Montreal & Kingston, McGill-Queen's University Press, 1996).

[9] See generally, on the socio-economic conditions of the Roma in pre-War Eastern Europe, D M Crowe, *A History of the Gypsies of Eastern Europe and Russia* (New York, St. Martin's Griffin, 1996).

[10] A number of the older Roma women whom I interviewed in Hungary have referred to begging by their mothers and grandmothers as a supplementary source of family incomes. I was struck by the casual and unselfconscious way in which they invariably referred to this practice, as if it were the most natural of occupations. Among many Roma communities, begging clearly lacks those negative and 'shameful' connotations which it has in most *Gadzo* (i.e. non-Roma) cultures.

flimsily- constructed shacks on the edge of villages; some were reduced to living in holes dug underground.[11]

Ethnic German smallholders (*Svábok*), in villages such as Kétegyháza, were often resented by ordinary Hungarian or Romanian peasants for appearing to be arrogant and aloof while they, in turn, may well have regarded the other peasant farmers as comparatively inefficient and lazy. Romanians believed that their culture, language and Orthodox religion had not been sufficiently recognised or accommodated by the Hungarian administration, while ethnic Hungarians feared that the other nationalities would outnumber Hungarians, threatening the "historic" ascendancy of the Hungarian people in the region.[12]

Nevertheless, such resentments, while genuine, were mostly latent and contained; they did not typify daily life in villages as Kétegyháza, in the nineteenth or even in the first half of the twentieth century. In general, the ethnic or religious background of an individual was far less important than how he conducted himself – whether he was honest, hard-working and helpful to others, or whether he was self-regarding, greedy and untrustworthy. People were liked or disliked in such communities for a variety of reasons which had nothing to do with their religion, ethnicity or preferred language. Friendships and even marriages were often formed which breached these national, ethnic or religious barriers.[13]

Multiculturalism in Eastern Europe, both as a politico-philosophical value and as a practical reality, received a series of violent shocks in the first half of the twentieth century. The collapse of the Austro-Hungarian Empire at the end of the First World War and the creation of a series of "nation states" in the region were indicative of a massive underlying shift in the prevailing political ideology. Nationalism had seduced many of the peoples in the region, or at least that stratum of the various national groups which was educated and politically literate. By contrast, for the average peasant, owning a fair-sized plot of land which was sufficient to enable him to feed and clothe his family was generally more important than the political squabbles that took place in remote capital cities that he had never visited.[14] The price of grain from year to year, or whether

[11] For a visual record see e.g. P Szuhay and A Barati (eds.), *Pictures of the History of Gipsies in Hungary in the 20th Century* (Budapest, Néprajzi Múzeum, 1993).

[12] On the growing militancy of national minorities, such as the Romanians, within Hungary before the collapse of the Austro-Hungarian Empire see e.g. C A Macartney, *The Habsburg Empire 1790–1918* (London, Weidenfeld and Nicolson, 1968), pp. 721–34.

[13] In terms of inter-marriage, this was, and remains, least common between Roma and members of any of the non-Roma communities. By contrast Jews, as they became less scrupulous in their religious devotions, many abandoning Judaism altogether in favour of total assimilation, were increasingly willing and sometimes even eager to marry Gentiles, while they were also more readily accepted as marriage partners. On the assimilationist tendency among many of Hungary's secular Jews, on the eve of the First World War, see e.g. A Janos, *The Politics of Backwardness in Hungary, 1825–1945* (Princeton, New Jersey, Princeton University Press, 1982), esp. at pp. 180–1.

[14] On the distinctive psychology of peasants in Eastern Europe, and of sub-categories within the peasantry, see G Schöpflin, *Politics in Eastern Europe* (Oxford, Blackwell Publishers, 1993), pp. 25–9.

the authorities were willing to lay proper roads to his village in place of the mud-filled tracks that were impassable for several months of each year, were of more immediate concern than the abstract political arguments favoured in elegant salons.

As a political philosophy, nationalism, sometimes known as ethnic nationalism to distinguish it from its more civilised "civic" variant, is both conceptually flawed and, in practical terms, dangerous. Its intellectual shortcomings were admirably exposed by Elie Kedourie in his land-mark eponymous text:[15]

> Races, languages, religions, political traditions and loyalties are so inextricably intermixed that there can be no clear convincing reason why people who speak the same language, but whose history and circumstances otherwise widely diverge, should form one state, or why people who speak two different languages and whom circumstances have thrown together should not form one state . . . The inventors of the doctrine [nationalism] tried to prove that nations are obvious and natural divisions of the human race . . . For such a claim to be convincing, it must also be proved that similarity in one respect absolutely overrides differences in other respects.

Nevertheless, the emotional appeal of nationalism in Eastern Europe, particularly during the inter-war period, was strong. With the exception of the former Czechoslovakia, nationalist and authoritarian governments came to power in all of the countries of Eastern Europe.[16] In part, the upsurge of nationalism was due to the increasingly difficult economic conditions experienced in the region, particularly in the Great Depression. In part, it also reflected the political immaturity and volatility of the electorate in a region which had had little experience of constitutionalism, democracy, or respect for individual and minority rights.[17] Scapegoating ethnic or religious minorities as having been 'responsible' for the economic or other ills of society represented an all too easy path to electoral success for ambitious and unscrupulous politicians, or a means of deflecting attention from the lack of economic progress or genuine democratisation within societies.

In part, the rise of nationalism in Eastern Europe, together with the growing influence of theories of racial exclusivity, was fuelled by the example and influence of Nazi Germany. In economic, social and political terms, Germany had long enjoyed considerable prestige in parts of Eastern Europe, serving as a model for the generally more 'backward' countries of the region. Neo-Nazi movements, consciously modelling themselves on Germany's National Socialists, came to prominence in many states in Eastern Europe in the 1920s and 1930s, including both Hungary and Romania. Germany appeared to offer beguiling 'proof' that nineteenth century notions of economic and political liberalism, the rule of law, democracy and human rights were now obsolete

[15] E Kedourie, *Nationalism* (Oxford, Blackwell, 4th ed., 1993), p. 74.

[16] See generally, A Polonsky, *The Little Dictators* (London, Routledge & Kegan Paul, 1975).

[17] See for example, I Pogany, "A New Constitutional (Dis)Order for Eastern Europe?" in I Pogany (ed.), *Human Rights in Eastern Europe* (Aldershot, Edward Elgar, 1995), ch. 10.

concepts. Industrial efficiency, national pride and political "clout" depended on other, less humane foundations, or so Hitler's Germany had apparently shown.

The approach of war in Eastern Europe accelerated the collapse of multiculturalism. In territories occupied by, or allied to, Nazi Germany, Jews and, in a less systematic way, Gypsies, were subjected to a series of increasingly draconian restrictions. These were generally implemented and enforced by means of the 'ordinary' legal process, through the active collaboration of lawyers, whether acting as legal draftsmen, judges, prosecutors, national or local officials, or advisers. In Hungary, for example, a series of progressively more crippling anti-Jewish laws were passed by a sovereign Hungarian Parliament, beginning in 1938, which limited the participation of Jews in higher education, in the liberal professions, in the arts, media and, ultimately, in white collar sectors generally.[18] This represented a conscious attempt to proletarianise and impoverish the Jewish community, before virtually all forms of employment were denied to them. Their property, including items of personal jewellery (plain wedding rings were exempted), savings and art works (if any) were confiscated under a series of hastily issued decrees, while Jewish males were conscripted into auxiliary labour battalions attached to the Hungarian Army. These conscripts were denied the right to bear arms and were used, instead, to dig trenches, carry munitions etc. The Jewish labour auxiliaries suffered wholly disproportionate fatalities due to the lack of adequate food, clothing and other essentials supplied to them by the Hungarian military authorities, as well as because of the sadism of many of the Hungarian officers commanding them. This process culminated in the deportation, *en masse*, of Jews and, more erratically, of Roma to the death camps.[19]

After the war, *Volksdeutsche*, or ethnic German, communities in Eastern Europe were subjected to vicious reprisals by the local population, who accused them of having collaborated with the occupying German forces. This amounted to an imputation of 'collective guilt' which few individuals were able to refute, even on the grounds of age, sex or poor physical health. Tens of thousands of *Volksdeutsche*, women as well as men, were sent to the former Soviet Union as slave labourers to assist with the task of reconstruction, while the bulk of the *Volksdeutsche* communities, particularly from Poland, Hungary and the former Czechoslovakia, were forcibly "resettled" in Germany.[20]

In many ways, this period represented the nadir of multiculturalism in Eastern Europe. Only remnants of the formerly vibrant East European Jewish communities survived the Holocaust. Many of the survivors had, in any event,

[18] These are analysed in I Pogany, *Righting Wrongs in Eastern Europe* (Manchester, Manchester University Press, 1997), chs. 2, 5.

[19] For an authoritative account of the Holocaust in Hungary see R Braham, *The Politics of Genocide*, Vols. I–II (New York, Columbia University Press, 1981).

[20] For a somewhat emotive but fundamentally accurate account of the resettlement of the *Volksdeutsche* communities, see de Zayas, *supra* n.6.

opted for emigration, while those who chose to remain in (or return to) Eastern Europe, frequently lacked either the will or the resources to rebuild a Jewish cultural or religious life.[21] Anonymity, blending into the background, was often seen as a safer option, particularly as anti-Semitism rapidly regained some of its former importance in post-war Eastern Europe.[22] With the decimation of the once strong and cohesive German communities in Eastern Europe (through resettlement rather than physical annihilation), formerly heterogeneous societies had become increasingly homogeneous.

The tendency towards cultural uniformity increased significantly during the Communist era. The assertion of ethnic identities, particularly by minorities such as the Hungarians in Romania or in the former Czechoslovakia, was generally discouraged.[23] Excessive pride in one's national or ethnic heritage was viewed as politically suspect in societies which had supposedly transcended such 'bourgeois' values.

Even the Roma were denied full cultural self-expression by the Communist authorities. The new Communist administrations were frequently sympathetic to the social and economic plight of Roma communities in Eastern Europe, providing them with jobs, healthcare, education and improved housing. At the same time, Communist authorities tended to view the Roma as a social problem rather than as a distinct ethnic group with their own language, traditions and culture. Communist efforts were directed at "integrating" the Roma within the new and increasingly homogeneous socialist societies, generally in the lower echelons, where Roma proved useful as factory workers, road builders and labourers in the construction industry, often performing work which was dangerous or unhealthy.[24] Although the term was not used in public fora, this amounted to a process of *de facto* assimilation.

2. TOWARDS A NEW MULTICULTURALISM IN EASTERN EUROPE?

The collapse of communism in Eastern Europe has created the conditions, both legally and politically, in which diversity and multiculturalism can flourish once again – and to a degree never previously achieved. For an international lawyer the signs are clear, although they are frequently in the form of soft law texts rather than in instruments giving rise to immediate legal obligations for the states of the region.[25] Nevertheless, it is difficult to suppress a sense of

[21] See, generally, on Jewish life in Eastern Europe after the Second World War, B Wasserstein, *Vanishing Diaspora* (London, Penguin Books, 1997), ch. 9.

[22] P Lendvai, *Anti-Semitism Without Jews* (New York, Doubleday, 1971).

[23] See generally, G Schöpflin, "National Minorities in Eastern Europe" in G Schöpflin (ed.), *The Soviet Union and Eastern Europe* (London, Muller, Blond & White, 1986), pp. 303–12.

[24] See, generally, on Communist policies towards the Roma, A Fraser, *The Gypsies* (Oxford, Blackwell, 2nd ed., 1995), esp. at pp. 274–82. See, also, Crowe, *supra* n.9.

[25] In international law, a distinction is often made between "hard law" texts, such as binding treaties and norms of customary international law, and "soft law" instruments. The former are a

excitement, even now, in reading declarations such as the Charter of Paris for a New Europe,[26] in which a new constitutional framework for an undivided Europe was sketched out. The Charter, which was adopted in November 1990 by the thirty-four heads of state or government of the states then participating in the Conference on Security and Co-operation in Europe (now the *Organisation* for Security and Co-operation in Europe (OSCE))[27] sets out a number of key principles which can be seen as laying the foundations of a new pan-European constitutional settlement.[28] A number of these principles are of particular importance, in my view, for establishing the conditions necessary for genuine multiculturalism in Eastern Europe. These are (a) the recognition of minority rights and (b) recognition of the value of cultural diversity.

The potential importance of these principles, in expressing a renewed commitment to multiculturalism in Eastern Europe, is difficult to overstate. Eastern Europe has experienced successive historical phases in which multiculturalism was under attack. During the first half of this century, the assault was essentially fuelled by right wing ideologies which viewed the ascendancy of particular nations within individual states as of overriding philosophical and political importance. It was an ideology which resulted in genocidal campaigns against Jews and Roma, in the indiscriminate killing of Slavs in the Eastern territories occupied by German forces in the Second World War and, finally, in the mass expulsion of *Volksdeutsche* communities from Eastern Europe in the immediate aftermath of the War. The chauvinism of the right was then followed by almost half a century of leftist repression, which inhibited the expression of cultural identity and aimed at the creation of largely undifferentiated societies of quiescent workers. This Orwellian vision was never fully realised and, in Eastern Europe at least, resulted in far fewer deaths than the policies unleashed by Hitler and his allies.[29] Nevertheless, the denial of individual and group rights under communism was real and omnipresent.

source of immediate legal obligation; the latter are, at best, aspirational statements which are potentially normative and which may influence the future conduct of states and other international actors. However, the distinction between hard and soft law norms is rarely absolute. When it was adopted by the UN General Assembly, the Universal Declaration of Human Rights was viewed as merely aspirational, a provisional catalogue of rights pending the adoption of a binding multilateral treaty. Now, substantial portions of the Universal Declaration are accepted as declaratory of customary international law. See generally, M Shaw, *International Law* (Cambridge, Cambridge University Press, 4th ed., 1997), pp. 206–08; H Hillgenberg, "A Fresh Look at Soft Law" 10 *European Journal of International Law* 499.

[26] For the text of the Charter see e.g. 30 *International Legal Materials* 193.

[27] On the protection of minorities under the auspices of the Organisation for Security and Co-operation in Europe see e.g. M Estébanez, "Minority Protection and the Organisation for Security and Co-operation in Europe" in P Cumper and S Wheatley (eds.), *Minority Rights in the "New" Europe* (The Hague, Kluwer Law International, 1999), pp. 31–52.

[28] In fact, the Charter deals with a number of extra-constitutional issues as well, such as economic liberty, security and environmental matters.

[29] Of course, within the former Soviet Union, as within China, the millions killed by the Communist authorities in purges, state-induced famines etc. exceeded the numbers killed by the Nazis and their allies.

2.1. The recognition of minority rights

The Charter of Paris declares boldly that "Europe is liberating itself from the legacy of the past" and sets out a number of key principles which should form the basis of the new political and constitutional order. These include human rights, democracy and the rule of law, principles which are construed, in the Charter, as entailing a commitment to minority rights:

> We affirm that the ethnic, cultural, linguistic and religious identity of national minorities will be protected and that persons belonging to national minorities have the right freely to express, preserve and develop that identity without any discrimination and in full equality before the law.

In a later section of the Paris Charter, on the human dimension mechanism of the OSCE, the participating states affirm their determination "to foster the rich contribution of national minorities to the life of our societies" and undertake:

> . . . further to improve their situation. We reaffirm our deep conviction that friendly relations among our peoples, as well as peace, justice, stability and democracy, require that the ethnic, cultural, linguistic and religious identity of national minorities be protected and conditions for the promotion of that identity be created. We declare that questions related to national minorities can only be satisfactorily resolved in a democratic political framework. We further acknowledge that the rights of persons belonging to national minorities must be fully respected as part of universal human rights.

The Charter of Paris' ringing endorsement of minority rights, and of multiculturalism, represents a conscious departure from the view, so influential at the conclusion of the Second World War, that minority rights are undesirable and possibly even dangerous. There is no reference in the UN Charter, for example, to the rights of national or ethnic minorities.[30] The drafters of the Charter deliberately omitted such principles, preferring instead to emphasise individual rights and the nebulous and politically-charged collective right of self-determination. There was a feeling, in some quarters, that notions of minority rights had been discredited by Hitler's exploitation of the alleged abuse of *Volksdeutsche* minorities in Eastern Europe as a pretext for German military aggression.

Despite its enthusiastic affirmation in the Charter of Paris and in other texts, the recognition and protection of minority rights remains a politically-charged issue, particularly in a number of post-Communist states which have a legacy of minorities problems. In Romania, accommodation of the aspirations of the

[30] See generally, P Thornberry, *International Law and the Rights of Minorities* (Oxford, Oxford University Press, 1992), ch. 11.

sizeable Hungarian minority, the largest national minority in Europe, has been a source of intermittent tension. Even in Western Europe there remain pockets of resistance to the notion of minority rights, and hence to genuine multiculturalism. France has steadfastly declined to sign, let alone ratify, the Framework Convention for the Protection of National Minorities. This important regional treaty, which was drafted under the auspices of the Council of Europe and entered into force in February 1998, will be examined below.[31] France's refusal to become a party to the Treaty is based on the idiosyncratic view that there are *no* national or ethnic minorities on her territory. As a French social scientist, Lamia Missaoui, has despairingly commented, "[d]ans une nation constitutionnellement intégrative, la vocation de l'étranger de l'intérieur est de devenir citoyen".[32]

Nevertheless, the Charter of Paris has served as a catalyst in the growing recognition and protection of minority rights in Europe. Within the OSCE, particular mention should be made of the Human Dimension Mechanism and the work of the OSCE High Commissioner for National Minorities.[33] Parallel with these developments, which operate primarily at the political and diplomatic levels, the Council of Europe has been active in securing agreement on new legal standards with regard to the recognition and protection of minority rights. The European Convention on Human Rights and Fundamental Freedoms, in keeping with the general climate of opinion at the time when it was drafted, does not contain a minority rights clause. Minorities are only referred to expressly in Article 14, which is the non-discrimination clause.[34] Nevertheless, in recent years two multilateral treaties concerned with minority rights have been drafted under the auspices of the Council of Europe. One of these, the Framework Convention for the Protection of National Minorities, referred to above, entered into force in February 1998. At the time of writing, there are twenty-eight parties to the Framework Convention.[35] In addition, there is the European Charter for Regional or Minority Languages, which was adopted by the Committee of Ministers of the Council of Europe in June 1992 and entered into force on 1 March 1998. There are currently eight parties to the Charter.[36] Finally, reference should be made to the growing number of bilateral treaties,

[31] For the text see e.g. Framework Convention for the Protection of National Minorities and Explanatory Report, Council of Europe Doc. H (95) 10.

[32] L Missaoui, "Construction d'une catégorie sociale: 'L'étranger de l'intérieur' ", 13 *Revue Européenne de Migrations Internationales* 247.

[33] See generally, on the protection of national and ethnic minorities under the auspices of the OSCE, Estébanez, *supra* n.27.

[34] See generally, G Gilbert, "Minority Rights Under the Council of Europe" in Cumper and Wheatley, *supra* n.27, 53, at 54.

[35] For details see the Council of Europe Website at http://www.dhdirhr.coe.fr

[36] For the text of the European Charter for Regional or Minority Languages and for details concerning those states which have ratified the instrument see the Council of Europe Website, *supra* n.35.

many of which have been concluded by post-Communist states, which are concerned wholly or partially with minority rights.[37]

A detailed analysis of some or all of these treaties would be beyond the scope of the present chapter. However, a word of caution may be in order. Potentially, at least, the most important of these treaties is the Framework Convention for the Protection of National Minorities as it seeks to lay down general norms regarding the recognition and protection of minority rights throughout Europe, while providing mechanisms of monitoring if not actual enforcement. Beleaguered minorities may have hoped for an instrument that is the equal of the European Convention on Human Rights and Fundamental Freedoms. The reality, however, has been rather different. As Geoff Gilbert has trenchantly (but by no means unfairly) observed, in writing of the Framework Convention, "[t]he combination of weak obligations and weak monitoring render the Framework Convention, as it stands, almost worthless as a means of guaranteeing minority rights within the Council of Europe".[38]

Nevertheless, the proliferation of instruments concerned with minority rights, since the adoption of the Charter of Paris, is indicative of an enhanced and consolidating recognition of the legitimate interest of minorities in seeking to preserve their identities. Whatever the limitations of certain treaties, such as the Framework Convention, it is difficult to envisage that this process will be arrested or put into reverse.

2.2. Recognition of the value of cultural diversity

The Paris Charter is important in viewing national, ethnic and other minorities not only as the bearers of various rights but as representing, in their *differentness*, a contribution to the overall cultural, social and even economic wealth of a society.[39] Rather than constituting a potential threat minorities are, on this view, an asset. This conviction is clear from the phrase in the Charter in which the participating states affirm their commitment to fostering "the rich contribution of national minorities to the life of our societies". Similar sentiments are expressed, *inter alia*, in the preamble to the Council of Europe's Framework Convention for the Protection of National Minorities, which refers to "cultural diversity" as "a source and a factor, not of division, but of enrichment for each society".[40] Mention should also be made of Recommendation

[37] I have examined some of these treaties in I Pogany, "Bilateralism versus Regionalism in the Resolution of Minorities Problems in Central and Eastern Europe and in the Post-Soviet States" in Cumper and Wheatley, *supra* n.27, 105.

[38] Gilbert, *supra* n.34, 53, at 63.

[39] On the frequently overlooked economic contribution made by many minority communities see e.g. T Sowell, *Migrations and Cultures* (New York, Basic Books, 1996).

[40] For the text of the Convention see *supra* n.31.

1203 (1993) on Gypsies in Europe, which was adopted by the Parliamentary Assembly of the Council of Europe on 2 February 1993.[41] This states, in operative paragraph 1, that "Europe harbours many different cultures, all of them, including the many minority cultures, enriching and contributing to the cultural diversity of Europe". Operative paragraph 3 of the Recommendation notes that, as a "non-territorial minority, Gypsies greatly contribute to the cultural diversity of Europe . . . be it by languages and music or by their trades and crafts".

This is, in my view, the essence of multiculturalism. The mere existence of different national, ethnic or religious groups within a country is evidence of *pluralism* but not necessarily of *multiculturalism*. In some pluralist societies the various national or ethnic communities can lead rigidly separate lives, with scant opportunities for social or cultural exchanges, for engaging with or comprehending the *other*. In such circumstances, individual communities may fulfil particular economic functions within the society as a whole, but inter-communal relations will be based largely or predominantly on economic considerations. This was, in essence, the situation in South Africa under apartheid, where most relations between the various ethnic groups, outside those permitted and carefully regulated in the economic sphere, were legally proscribed.

Multiculturalism implies engagement with the *other*; the embracing of difference whether out of intellectual curiosity, aesthetic preference or human empathy. In many West European and North American societies, multiculturalism is becoming at least imperfectly realised and is evident in the growing taste for different musical idioms, foods, fashions, and even religious experiences. We are becoming genuinely multicultural societies in which it is increasingly common for individuals born into Anglican or Roman Catholic families to opt for Buddhism or for some other "alien" faith in adult life (or simply for no faith at all). Rates of inter-marriage, between members of different religious or ethnic groups, are rising, while in the realm of culture and the arts the taste for multiculturalism has become the norm. It is now very much the exception in much of Western Europe and North America for persons to choose a musical instrument, a dance form or a type of music to play or listen to simply because they happen to belong to the cultural or national group identified with that particular art form. Only where certain cultures are in danger of disappearing altogether, or where parents may be first or second generation immigrants, would such a culturally-determined decision be at all likely. I happen to like jazz and the blues more than any other form of musical expression. Given the choice, I would rather listen to Billie Holiday than Maria Callas. These tastes have nothing to do with my national or ethnic heritage, or even with my educational background.

[41] For the text see e.g. *Activities of the Council of Europe concerning Roma/Gypsies and Travellers* (Strasbourg, Council of Europe, 1998), 43.

But much of Eastern Europe remains obdurately different. In Eastern Europe the collapse of communism has not resulted, as yet, in an enthusiastic upsurge of multiculturalism. The protracted denial of national self-expression, combined with economic uncertainties and an often debased political culture, have led to a recrudescence of virulent ethnic nationalism in some countries in the region. In the former Yugoslavia, the rapid growth of ethnic nationalism resulted in massive loss of life, above all in Bosnia,[42] in widespread resort to ethnic cleansing and in the creation of states, such as Croatia and Serbia (not to mention Republika Serbska or, in the future, perhaps an independent Kosovo) with a very imperfect understanding of the culture of individual and minority rights, let alone of multiculturalism.[43]

However, these nationalist tendencies should not be over-stated. Poland, the Czech Republic, Hungary, Slovenia and, perhaps, Slovakia, have established genuine democracies in which national, ethnic and religious minorities are legally protected, at least formally.[44] A great deal of effort, time and money has been expended to this end, and there are many individual lawyers, writers, scholars, politicians and civil servants in these countries who are fervently committed to the ideals of liberalism and perhaps even multiculturalism.

But at the level of civil society there is far less evidence of a genuine shift towards, or even appetite for, multiculturalism. Engagement with the *other*, particularly if that *other* is a Rom, is much less apparent in even supposedly liberal societies such as the Czech Republic or Hungary.[45] Roma NGOs and human rights organisations such as Amnesty International, the European Roma Rights Center and Human Rights Watch believe that hostility towards the substantial Roma minorities in certain post-Communist societies has sharply increased in recent years. At the same time, evidence is overwhelming that the socio-economic position of the Roma in these countries has deteriorated drastically in the transition to capitalism. As the OSCE's much respected High Commissioner for National Minorities, Max van der Stoel stated, in a Report on the Roma (Gypsies) in the CSCE Region, "Roma have been particularly vulnerable to the impoverishing effects of economic transformation and cuts in govern-

[42] See generally, N Malcolm, *Bosnia, a Short History* (London, Papermac, 1996), esp. chs. 15–16, and Epilogue.

[43] Criticism of Croatia may no longer justified in view of the defeat of the intensely nationalistic ruling party in recent general elections. Similarly, the removal of slobodan Milosevic, following Presidential elections in the former Yugoslavia, gives cause for hope.

[44] See generally, the essays in Pogany, *supra* n 17. See, also, I Pogany, "International Human Rights Standards and the New Constitutions: Minority Rights in Central and Eastern Europe" in R Müllerson, M Fitzmaurice, M Andenas (eds.), *Constitutional Reform and International Law in Central and Eastern Europe* (The Hague, Kluwer Law International, 1998), ch. 10.

[45] On the grossly unsatisfactory and arguably racist educational policies for the Roma minority in the Czech Republic see: *A Special Remedy: Roma and Schools for the Mentally Handicapped in the Czech Republic* (European Roma Rights Center, Country Reports Series, No. 8, June 1999).

ment-sponsored social services and support".[46] At the same time, the High Commissioner noted:[47]

> the recent context of collective "scapegoating" of Roma for societal ills through anti-Roma discrimination and the persistent practice of "popular justice" by skinheads, by organised vigilantes, and in some cases, even by members of government security forces.

3. CONCLUSIONS

At the level of political rhetoric, the value of multiculturalism is now firmly recognised as one of the key principles that should guide policy making in Europe. If the principle has not yet acquired the status of an unequivocal norm of international law, it may be used as an aid to the interpretation of treaties and custom. Recognition of the value of cultural difference in, *inter alia*, the Charter of Paris and in the Preamble to the Framework Convention for the Protection of National Minorities, would allow judicial and other bodies to invoke the principle when interpreting treaties and other instruments concerned with minority rights. However, there is no guarantee that they will choose to do so. In *Buckley* v. *United Kingdom*, the European Court of Human Rights showed little inclination to accommodate the cultural requirements, or differentness, of Europe's Roma.[48] The Court chose, instead, to grant the United Kingdom a wide margin of appreciation with respect to its planning laws, even though these prevented a Roma woman from living in caravans with her young children on land which she owned. Her only realistic alternatives were to move to a designated site for Gypsies in the area, where there had been several reported cases of vandalism and violence, or to abandon a traditional Roma lifestyle and take up permanent residence with her family in a house or flat. Applying political ideals concerning the value of multiculturalism in specific judicial decisions, or in concrete political or administrative policies, is likely to prove a long, painful and uncertain process.

I returned to the village of Kétegyháza, in Hungary, in December 1999. One of the Roma families I visited complained that a Christmas party had been held some days previously for the children of the village but that the Roma had been excluded. Several Roma children had turned up, but they had been turned away with the excuse that it was a private function. The Roma parents were visibly upset, but resigned. "What's the point in complaining or in making a fuss?" one of the fathers said to me. "It won't change anything".

[46] *Roma (Gypsies) in the CSCE Region* (Report of the High Commissioner on National Minorities, September 1993), 7.

[47] *Ibid.*, at 8. See, now, Report on the situation of Roma and Sinti in the OSCE Area (OSCE High Commissioner on Nation & Minorities, March 2000).

[48] For an analysis of the *Buckley Case* see e.g. I Pogany, "Accommodating an Emergent National Identity: The Roma of Central and Eastern Europe" 6 *International Journal of Minority and Group Rights* 149, at 163–4.

16

"Culture" as a Fundamental Value of the German Constitution? The Kulturstaat Debate in German Constitutional Law

CAROLA THIELECKE

1. INTRODUCTION

Four main principles, expressly mentioned by the *Grundgesetz*, the German fundamental law, underlie the constitutional framework of the Federal Republic of Germany: according to these fundamental principles Germany is a *Rechtsstaat*, i.e. a state governed according to the rule of law, a *Sozialstaat*, which roughly translates as welfare state, a *Bundesstaat*, i.e. a federal state, as well as a democracy.

There is, however, a school of lawyers who maintain that, although not stated expressly in the constitution, there is a fifth fundamental principle on which the *Grundgesetz* is built: the principle of the *Kulturstaat*, a state committed to culture. This concept is elusive and no consensus has been reached as to its exact content or application. What exactly does *Kultur* mean? Where exactly in the Grundgesetz is the *Kulturstaat* laid down? Should the legal doctrines developed to describe the effect of the other fundamental principles be applied to the *Kulturstaat* principle, too?

1.1. Functions of the fundamental principles

The fundamental principles which are expressly mentioned have primarily what is called an objective function. This means that they bind first and foremost the legislator, the executive and the courts who are obliged to act in such a way that the fundamental principles are given maximum effect. They are therefore a blueprint for the State, they set out the ground rules and values of society and act as guidelines for legislation. Most importantly, they demand positive action from the state rather than simply prohibiting interference, as is the case with many classic civil rights.[1]

The *Bundesverfassungsgericht* (Federal Constitutional Court) has taken the fundamental principles a step further and endowed them with a subjective function by making them a possible basis for an individual's constitutional complaint. Whenever a rule of law limits the actions of an individual, he or she may lodge a constitutional complaint under article 2 I GG, the general right to liberty. If the law is found to conflict with the constitution, which includes the fundamental principles, it may be declared void and the limitation on the individual will be removed.[2]

1.2. Application to the *Kulturstaat*

Applying these doctrines to the *Kulturstaat* would have far-reaching consequences. As far as the objective function goes, the state could be obliged to work towards giving the principle maximum effect, that is not only to refrain from obstructing cultural activities, but also to take an active part in fostering them. There has indeed for a long time been a broad consensus to the effect that the furtherance and support of culture and the arts is a duty of the state and private patronage is still a relatively minor source of income for the sector in Germany. This stands in contrast with the situation in Britain, where private patronage has always been of immense importance while the State has become involved on a far smaller scale.[3] Applying the objective function would therefore seem to present no great difficulties at first sight. But if the *Kulturstaat* was accepted as a fully-blown fundamental principle, the pressure on the State to become active and drastically increase spending in this field would surely mount.

To acknowledge a subjective side to the *Kulturstaat* would have even more radical consequences. Individuals would have the right to litigate against legislation if they felt it inhibited their cultural activities; every new piece of legislation would have to stand up to the test of compatibility with the *Kulturstaat* principle. The scope of the *Bundesverfassungsgericht*'s jurisdiction would be further expanded and a whole new aspect would be added to the considerations of the legislator.

The aim of this essay is to chart the discussion which has evolved around the theme of *Kulturstaat* in Germany and to explore whether the *Kulturstaat* really is a fundamental principle of equal standing with the other principles set out above. I will not attempt to answer the question of whether in principle the state should get involved in supporting culture and the arts. Much has been written

[1] K Stern, *Staatsrecht der Bundesrepublik Deutschland*, vol III/1 (München, Beck Verlag, 1988), p. 558.

[2] Entscheidungen des Bundesverfassungsgerichts (BverfGE) vol 6, 36 at 41.

[3] M Nissel, "Financing the Arts in Great Britain" in J Myerscough (ed.), *Funding the Arts in Europe* (Studies in European Poltics 8, London, 1984).

on this issue by those engaged in the field of cultural studies[4] and political theory and to try and resolve it in the limited space available here would be unrealistic.

2. A BRIEF HISTORY OF THE CONCEPT OF *KULTURSTAAT*

2.1. The beginnings of the *Kulturstaat* idea

The history of the term *Kulturstaat* mirrors a growing awareness that cultural affairs affect society as a whole and that their administration (and funding) should therefore be a matter of public policy rather than the prerogative of certain privileged individuals or institutions. From the end of the Middle Ages up until the early nineteenth century, education was mainly the domain of the Church and all forms of patronage for culture and the arts very much a private matter for the absolutistic monarch to pursue or neglect at his whim[5]. The State, on the other hand, was considered an instrument for the preservation of public order only, a system that became famous under the name of *Polizeistaat*.[6]

The term *Kulturstaat* was first used nearly two hundred years ago by the philosopher Johann Gottlieb Fichte[7] and was snapped up by the school of German Idealism, philosophers such as Hegel, Wilhelm von Humboldt and others endowing it with a meaning that remained influential well into the second half of the twentieth century.[8] Around the theme of *Kulturstaat* they evolved a model state, in which individuals are "citizens", taking an active role in public life, rather than "subjects" to be ruled over.[9] One of the central elements of this idea-list *Kulturstaat* was education, which prepares the individual for his role as a citizen,[10] since education in the idealist sense encompasses

[4] In an Anglo-American context, any mention of the word "culture" instantly conjures up associations with "cultural studies", but so far the *Kulturstaat* debate has not been influenced deeply by this movement. Peter Häberle, in his writing on the *Kulturstaat* (*cf.* below at 4.1.1.), has made valiant efforts to make use of the insights into cultural phenomena gained by sociologists and anthropologists, however, as we shall see later, no real involvement has ensued. Similarly, Häberle is the only writer to engage at all with the work on culture and its protection in the international law field, a fact which serves to emphasise how centred on Germany and German debates the public law of the Federal Republic of Germany has remained.

[5] Or indeed at *her* whim, as for instance in the case of Anna Amalia of Sachsen-Weimar-Eisenach, the patroness of Johann Wolfgang von Goethe.

[6] H Mitteis/ H Lieberich, *Deutsche Rechtsgeschichte* (München, Beck Verlag, 1992), p. 311.

[7] J G Fichte, "Die Staatslehre" in: J G Fichte, *Sämmtliche Werke* (*Berlin Verlag* v. *Veit & Comp* 1845).

[8] M-E Geis, "Ergänzung des Grundgesetzes um eine 'Kulturklausel'" [1992] *Zeitschrift für Gesetzgebung* 7, 38 at 41.

[9] Hegel himself rarely used the word culture, but his term "Sittlichkeit", i.e. ethical living, corresponds with Fichte's "Cultur". In his view, the State, which to him is the expression of objective rationality , was the perfect embodiment of "Sittlichkeit", and as such had existed in its own right, independent of the individuals living in it. cf. G W F Hegel, *Grundlinien der Philosophie des Rechts*, §257.

[10] GWF Hegel, *idem*, §239.

not only the passing on of factual knowledge but the formation of the personalities of the young in accordance with the ethical ideas of German Idealism.[11]

Wilhelm v Humboldt, who, apart from being a philosopher, was also a leading politician of his age, put into practice elements of his *Kulturstaat*, reforming the Prussian system of education and introducing the three tier system of education in force in Germany to the present day.

2.2. Collecting ideological baggage

During the nineteenth century the word *Kulturstaat* gained a nationalist connotation. Because Germany at this point was divided into a multitude of principalities, the common cultural values and heritage and the language seemed to be the one thing all Germans shared, forming a *Kulturnation*, a cultural nation, rather than one defined by citizenship of a common state. This situation was resolved with the foundation of the *Kaiserreich*, which finally emerged in 1871, and considered itself, therefore, both a nation state and a *Kulturstaat*.[12]

In 1919, Weimar, undoubtedly one of the cultural capitals of Germany, was selected as the seat of the constitutional convention for the first German republic. This was intended as a symbol of the aspirations of the re-born state and the term *Kulturstaat* was used as a buzzword to denote a modern, enlightened approach to government, contrasting it with the authoritarian state embodied by the *Kaiserreich*.[13] In 1922, Heinrich von Treitschke writes of the Weimar Republic:

> In short, we may call our state a *Kulturstaat* and expect of it a positive input into the spiritual and economic life of its people.[14]

Accordingly, article 142 s.2 of the Weimar Constitution not only placed the arts and science under the protection of the State, but also assigned to it the task of actively supporting and nurturing them. The *Kulturstaat* seemed to have gained a firm place in constitutional theory.

Sadly, as with so many other German legal concepts and institutions, the *Kulturstaat* was hijacked by the jurists of the Third Reich. By giving *Kultur* the meaning of "Aryan culture", with all its connotations, the term was abused to justify the complete subjection of cultural life in Germany to National Socialist aims and ideas.[15] At the end of the Second World War the concept of the *Kulturstaat* had to be completely reconsidered.

[11] Mitteis/Lieberich n.6, 454.

[12] Mitteis/Lieberich n.6, 454.

[13] E R Huber, *Zur Problematik des Kulturstaats* (Tübingen, Mohr Verlag, 1958), p. 4. M-E Geis, *Kulturstaat und kulturelle Freiheit* (Baden-Baden, Nomos, 1990) p. 30; *cf.* E Kästner, *Fabian* (dtv 1999), p. 5.

14 H v Treitschke, *Vorlesungen zur Politik* vol 1 (Berlin 1922), 81 (This and all further translations from the German are the author's).

[15] E-M Geis, "Kulturklausel" n.8, 40.

2.3. The *Kulturstaat* in post-War German law

In 1946, Bavaria was the first federal state to include in its constitution the assertion that it is a "*Rechts-, Kultur- und Sozialstaat*".[16] The Federal Assembly, drafting the *Grundgesetz* in 1949, did not follow suit. The legal debate, however, did not end here. The *Bundesverfassungsgericht* fanned the flames of the discussion by referring to the Federal Republic as a *Kulturstaat* in a number of *obiter dicta*, unfortunately without ever explaining on which legal basis it did so.[17] In 1981 a federal commission on constitutional reform recommended that the following phrase be inserted into article 20 of the *Grundgesetz*:

> It [the Federal Republic] protects and fosters culture and the natural prerequisites for human life.[18]

The contentious term *Kulturstaat* was not used. However, it did find its way into a piece of federal legislation in 1990: article 35 s. 1 of the Unification Treaty, which will be discussed in more detail later, refers to it. Nevertheless, unlike the preservation of the environment, which is now guaranteed by article 20a GG, the *Kulturstaat* was never incorporated into the Constitution.

3. LEGAL TEXTS DEALING WITH CULTURE AND THE *KULTURSTAAT*

How then, considering this state of affairs, do the advocates of the *Kulturstaat* principle arrive at the conclusion that it has equal standing with the other fundamental principles? The argument is based on the legislative technique used in the *Grundgesetz*. For example, the *Rechtsstaat*[19] is mentioned in passing in article 28 s.1, but there is widespread agreement among legal scholars that it is also implied in other norms,[20] which do not name it, that indeed it is formed by this composite body of norms.[21]

A number of norms within the *Grundgesetz* bear a relation to cultural affairs, and to the advocates of the *Kulturstaat* these embody the "cultural

[16] Several other states have followed suit with the new Federal Free State of Saxony being one of the most recent additions. *cf.* B Wiegand, "Die neuen Bundesländer als Kulturstaaten" [1995] *Landes und Kommunalverwaltung*, 55.

[17] BVerfGE, vol 35, 79 at 114, vol 36, 321 at 331, vol 81, 108 at 116.

[18] Bundesministerium d. Inneren (ed.), *Staatszielbestimmungen, Gesetzgebungsaufträge: Bericht der Sachverständigenkommission* (Bonn, 1983), p. 128.

[19] This describes a system of government committed to implementing state decisions on the basis of norms enacted in accordance with the Constitution with the aim of preserving freedom and justice. *Cf.* F E Schnapp in: I v Münch/ P Kunig, *Grundgesetzkommentar* (München, C H Beck, Verlag 1992), margin no. 21.

[20] For example, Article 20 s.3, in which the legislative, executive and judicial powers are declared to be subject to the rule of law or the rights to due process laid down in articles 103 and 104.

[21] Article 20 s.3 is in fact seen as the main sedes materiae of the Rechtsstaat principle, although it does not expressly say so.

constitution", i.e. form the *Kulturstaat* principle. Since the *Rechtsstaat* is also distributed over several norms, it is then argued that the *Kulturstaat* is equally important, the sole difference being that the word *Kulturstaat* is at no point used.[22]

I will, therefore, first of all survey the norms which are said to constitute the principle and examine whether they demand positive action in cultural matters of the State, or whether they require mere non-intervention.

It needs to be pointed out at this juncture that the meaning of the word *Kultur* is not completely identical to the English word "culture". Whereas in every-day English, meanings range from something similar to civilisation or way of life, to contexts with an elitist connotation, i.e. artistic life,[23] the every-day German term *Kultur* tends to be used more in the elitist sense and as complementing the term *Zivilisation*, but this does not seem to hold true when the word is used by lawyers.[24] I will therefore also attempt to pin-point which types of cultural activity are alluded to by the *Grundgesetz*.

3.1. Direct references to culture in the *Grundgesetz*

3.1.1. Fundamental rights concerning culture

The first and perhaps most obvious example of a norm expressing the constitution's commitment to cultural affairs is article 5 s.3, which contains both the freedom of the arts and what has become known as the "fundamental rights of Higher Education". This article is often portrayed as being the constitutional *sedes materiae* for the principle of *Kulturstaat*.[25] The wording of the provision is very brief stating merely that: "The arts and science, research and [academic] teaching are free".

This has generally been construed by both scholars and the *Bundesverfassungsgericht* in a very wide manner. Art is defined as an expression of the artist's personality and experience, which is open to ongoing interpretation.[26] All aspects of the production of such forms of expression are held to be protected, from preparatory actions to the public showing of the work.[27] Similarly, the freedom of science and research is seen to protect scholarly work at all stages

[22] P Häberle, "Vom Kulturstaat zum Kulturverfassungsrecht" in P Häberle, *Kulturstaatlichkeit und Kulturverfassungsrecht* (Darmstadt, Wissenschaftliche Buchgesellschaft, 1982), p. 5. W Maihofer, "Kulturelle Aufgaben des modernen Staates" in Benda/Maihofer/Vogel (eds.), *Handbuch des Verfassungsrechts* (Berlin, Walter de Gruyter, 1994), p. 1204.

[23] A good overview of the various meanings of "culture" in common English is given by T S Eliot, *Notes towards the Definition of Culture* (London, Faber, 1962), pp. 22–3.

[24] G Marshall, *Concise Oxford Dictionary of Sociology* (Oxford, 1994), p. 105.

[25] U Steiner, "Kulturauftrag im staatlichen Gemeinwesen" [1984] *Verhandlungen des Vereins der Deutschen Staatsrechtslehrer* vol 42, 15.

[26] BVerfGE vol 67, 213 at 228.

[27] BVerfGE vol 30, 173 at 191, BVerfGE vol 77, 240 at 251.

of progress and every member of the academic community may invoke it. Academic freedom is also held to guarantee the right of universities to self government and freedom from state intervention.[28]

Article 7 grants protection to certain aspects of education, more specifically religious education in state schools (article 7 ss.2,3) and the freedom to found private schools (article 7, ss.4,5).

The activities protected by these fundamental rights are all cultural in an elitist sense, i.e. intellectual or artistic, although the interpretation of "art" in article 5 s.3 GG is, admittedly, very broad, taking in many levels of expertise. These fundamental rights create a sphere in which the arts, academia and education can develop and unfold free from state interference. But they do no more than that, providing no blanket protection to all forms of culture used in the sense of "way of life".[29] They also imply no duty of the state to take positive action.[30]

Finally, it needs to be pointed out that the right to freedom of expression as guaranteed by article 5, s.1 GG does not come into this discussion for a technical reason: in German constitutional law it is only possible to take recourse to a fundamental right, if there is no more specialised right covering the area concerned. As artistic and academic freedom, as guaranteed by article 5, s.3 GG are both specialised aspects of the freedom of expression, they override the broader freedom guaranteed by article 5, s.1 GG.[31]

3.1.2. Article 29 section 1 GG

There is one provision that actually uses the word culture, article 29 s.1 GG. Here, rules are laid down for the restructuring of the territory of the Federal Republic of Germany. Although article 79 s.3 of the *Grundgesetz* renders the complete abolition of the federal state system unconstitutional, it is possible to make changes to the actual boundaries of the existing federal states. In such a case, article 29 s.1 GG demands that cultural factors be taken into account. Here "culture" is used in the sense of "way of life". However, this is again a provision which requires no active input into cultural life from the State, in that it requires only that the State draw new borders according to existing cultural watersheds. It is also, obviously, very limited in its application.

3.1.3. Competence for legislation in matters cultural

A further part of the *Grundgesetz* which can furnish evidence of the *Kulturstaat* are the rules on legislative competence set out by articles 70 to 78. These distribute the areas of legislation between the federation and the individual federal

[28] BVerfGE vol 35, 79 at 112, 113.
[29] U Steiner, Kulturauftrag n.25 *supra*, 14.
[30] BVerfGE vol 31, 229 at 238, BverfGE vol 35, 79 at 114, 116.
[31] BVerfGE vol 75, 377.

states. In doing so, the *Grundgesetz* expressly attributes certain legislative competences to the federation, implicitly leaving the others to the federal states (article 70 s.1GG).

Thus, the federal parliament is competent to pass copyright and publishing laws, undoubtedly a matter of vital importance if the arts are to prosper in a community. Article 75 GG contains provisions for legislation in two further areas of interest: the universities (within the limits set by article 5 III GG) and the prevention of unlimited export of cultural artefacts. These norms again concern activities and artefacts which are cultural in the elitist sense. Whether they necessitate positive action on the part of the state does not become fully clear.

3.2. Interpretation of "culturally neutral" norms

At this point, express reference to anything that might be described as belonging to the field of culture ends. However, many broadly formulated norms have been interpreted to include action in the field of culture in their scope.

3.2.1. Norms on legislative competence

This is true for several of the articles on legislative competence. Article 73 for instance accords the federation the competence to legislate in matters of foreign policy. This has generally been taken to include foreign policy on cultural affairs, such as cultural exchanges, institutes etc. Similarly, article 74 GG empowers the federation to make laws concerning the economy. This is held to include the law of state aid, and the statute providing state aid to the German film industry, undoubtedly a "cultural industry", was passed on its basis.[32] Through the statute law passed using these norms the State is actively aiding cultural production, though not on the basis of the actual wording of the *Grundgesetz*, but on the basis of interpretation. The *Künstlersozialversicherungsgesetz* (Law on Social Security for Artists) also exemplifies this: it was passed on the basis of article 74 No. 12 GG, which grants the federation the right to legislate on social security. Though the effect is direct support for those culturally active, the legal basis again is "culturally neutral".

3.2.2. The responsibility of local government in the area of cultural affairs

A huge contribution to the German State's involvement in cultural affairs is made through local government bodies, funding municipal theatres, art gal-

[32] U Steiner, "Kulturpflege" in Isensee/Kirchhof (eds.), *Handbuch des Staatsrechts* vol 3 (Heidelberg, Müller Verlag, 1988), p. 1249. W Maihofer, "Kulturelle Aufgaben" n.22 *supra*, 1228.

leries, museum and arts initiatives.[33] The 1980s saw a spate of legal publications on the mandate given to local government by the *Grundgesetz* in cultural affairs.[34] So one might expect to find a reference to culture and its advancement in the constitutional rules on local government. But again, there is no outright reference. The reason for this is the so-called *Allzuständigkeit* (universal competence), laid down in article 28 of the *Grundgesetz*, making subsidiarity a key principle of German administation: whereas in England, the scope of action of local government is defined by the doctrine of *ultra vires*,[35] the exact opposite is true in Germany, with local governments having the right to decide "all matters of local community life", with the exception of those conferred on other bodies by statute.[36] This makes it unnecessary for the *Grundgesetz*, or in fact any other piece of legislation, to enumerate those affairs which fall into the ambit of self government. Ascertaining these is left to *interpretation*. So once again, although there is widespread agreement that action on matters of local cultural life, and this includes the passing of bye-laws and the provision of funding, are not only the right but also the duty of German local governments,[37] the *Grundgesetz* does not contain any hard evidence.

3.2.3. Legislation by the Federal States

Like local government, the *Länder* (federal states) have made a major input into the cultural sector. In fact, cultural policy has traditionally become regarded as a *Land* affair to a degree that has given rise to the term "*Kulturhoheit der Länder*" (cultural sovereignty/authority of the *Länder*). Many federal states have legislated substantially on cultural affairs. In Baden-Württemberg, for example, article 10 s.2 of the Local Government Act gives local governments the responsibility of catering for "the cultural welfare of inhabitants".[38] In doing so, the federal states consider that they are fulfilling the responsibility given to them by the *Grundgesetz*. But again the legislative technique of the constitution prevents us from gleaning any evidence: as pointed out above, the *Grundge-*

[33] P Ditges, *Kommunale Kulturarbeit* (Stuttgart, Boorberg, 1985), p. 13.

[34] For example, P Häberle, *Kulturpolitik in der Stadt – ein Verfassungsauftrag* (Heidelberg, Decker&Müller, Verlag 1979); F Hufen, *Kulturauftrag als Selbstverwaltungsgarantie* [1983] NVwZ, 516.

[35] J Sharland, *Local Government Law* (London Blackstone 1997), p. 70.

[36] W Löwer in I v.Münch/ P Kunig (eds.), *Grundgesetzkommentar* (München, C.H.Beck, 1995), article 28.

[37] W Maihofer, "Kulturelle Aufgaben" n.22 *supra*, 1234; U Steiner, "Kulturpflege" n.31 *supra*, 1252.

[38] One reason for this is that in acting in the field of culture, many states are actually fulfilling the demands of their state constitutions. Article 140 of the Bavarian Constitution for example requires local governments to support science and the arts and article 34 of the Saarland Constitution states that " cultural activities shall enjoy the support of the state". It must be stressed, however, that these state constitutions are on a distinct level from the *Grundgesetz*, and that the Federal Republic may include "*Kulturstaaten*" in the ranks of its federal states does not make the entire entity a "*Kulturstaat*".

setz only lays down the federal competencies, while the remaining fields of action are left to the federal states. This void is *interpreted* to include cultural affairs.

3.3. Decisions of the *Bundesverfassungsgericht*

So far, consequently, there is little evidence of the *Kulturstaat* in the actual text of the *Grundgesetz*. Where the state has become actively involved in cultural affairs, this has most often been based not on what the constitution actually says, but on how its *silences are interpreted*. As a consequence of this very insecure legal basis for a verdict on the standing of the *Kulturstaat* principle, great significance has been accorded to the rulings of that supreme interpretative authority, the *Bundesverfassungsgericht*. These relevant rulings consist, in the main, of the three cases quoted above, in which the word *Kulturstaat* was actually used.[39] All three were decisions dealing with article 5 s.3 GG, in two cases concerning the freedom of the arts and one the freedom of science. In all cases the allusion was made as an *obiter dictum*. The wording is also very similar (in two cases identical) and states that "a state, which considers itself to be a *Kulturstaat* – in the sense of a fundamental constitutional principle – has the duty to protect and foster free academic and artistic life".[40] This phrasing seems to indicate that the *Bundesverfassungsgericht* does consider the *Kulturstaat* to be on an equal level with the other fundamental principles, but some scholars believe that the court intended this observation to be limited to the context of article 5 s.3 GG.[41] The *Bundesverfassungsgericht* has however also made other statements that imply that it believes in a commitment to cultural matters based on the *Grundgesetz*. In one of its early decisions, for instance, it points out that " the modern state considers it its duty to foster the cultural development of the community".[42] On the whole, therefore, the jurisprudence of the *Bundesverfassungsgericht* does seem to point in the direction of *Kulturstaat* as a fundamental principle, even if the endorsement is somewhat lukewarm.

3.4. Article 35 Unification Treaty

The apparently most direct statement in favour of the *Kulturstaat*, finally, comes from the Unification Treaty. This Treaty, drawn up in 1990 to facilitate the legal integration necessary for the reunification of the Federal Republic of Germany

[39] BVerfGE 35, 79 at 114, BVerfGE 36, 321 at 331, BVerfGE 81, 108 at 116.
[40] BVerfGE 81, 108 at 116.
[41] U Steiner, "Kulturpflege" n.31 *supra*, 1238.
[42] BVerfGE 10, 20 at 36.

and the German Democratic Republic, is, strictly speaking, not federal legislation but an international treaty. The law it contains is, however, directly applied in Germany.[43] Article 35 s.1, 3 of the Treaty states that:

> The position and the respect accorded to a unified Germany by the world depend not only on its political power and economic output but also on its importance as a *Kulturstaat*.

While this statement appears at first as the long-awaited endorsement of the *Kulturstaat* by the legislator, it is more baffling when examined closely: the other items in the list, political power and economic output, are merely descriptive terms and not constitutional principles. It can only be deduced, therefore, that in this context *Kulturstaat* is also used in a descriptive manner, rather than referring to an existing constitutional principle.

4. THE MEANING OF *KULTUR* AND *KULTURSTAAT*

Looking back to the section above, the survey of constitutional rules on the *Kulturstaat* yielded very little concrete evidence of the principle in the text of the *Grundgesetz*, indeed it seemed to be the product of a certain interpretation of the *Grundgesetz*. Where cultural activities featured in the text of the Constitution they were usually artistic or intellectual and the state was rarely required to take an active role. However, on the basis of the interpretation, a very positive proactive role was assumed by the state players and, due to the structure of the *Grundgesetz*, such an interpretation seems legitimate.

What then, according to the modern advocates of the *Kulturstaat* does the term mean, what is required of a state to make it a *Kulturstaat*?

4.1. The meaning of Kultur in the modern German legal discussion

The first problem encountered in discussing the concept of *Kulturstaat* is the difficulty in defining the word *Kultur*. In attempting to find a legal definition,[44] German legal scholars have drawn on writings from a wide range of disciplines. The resulting definitions fall, broadly speaking, into two categories. These correspond with the extreme meanings of the common English word culture, as mentioned above, i.e. roughly define "*Kultur*/culture" as either civilisation ("universalist definitions") or a concept related to manners and the arts ("elitist definitions").

[43] K Bülow in Benda/Maihofer/Vogel no.22, 1467.
[44] T Oppermann, *Kulturverwaltungsrecht* (Tübingen Mohr Verlag 1979), p. 9.

4.1.1. *The "universalist" definition of culture*

The universalist side has been taken by a number of German legal scholars, striving to escape from what is perceived as a bourgeois concept of culture and working towards an "open" definition, more suited to the pluralist values of the modern state.[45] Peter Häberle, for example, remarks that "culture" is often equated with the arts-oriented pastimes of the middle classes, especially when practised by masters of these activities.[46] On the other hand he emphasises the need for a definition, criticising those who leave this decision to the State.[47] He therefore draws up a number of criteria which define, to him, "culture". In doing this, he refers to the sociological and anthropological schools, especially the American cultural theorists, although he does concede that not all the elements that they associate with culture can be easily transferred to a legal usage.[48]

The sociological tradition he draws from begins with the classical definition in the sociological field drawn up by E B Tylor in 1871, who stated that culture is "the complex whole, which includes knowledge, belief, art, morals, law, custom and any other capabilities and habits, acquired by man as a member of society".[49] Here, "culture" is equivalent with civilisation and includes all forms of specifically human behaviour. This definition has become the foundation for those used in modern sociology and anthropology. Consequently, culture is seen as "all that in human society which is socially, rather than biologically transmitted",[50] "the total, socially acquired lifestyle of a group of people",[51] "a term of virtually limitless application which [. . .] refers to everything that is produced by human beings as distinct from all that is part of nature".[52] In 1958 the leading scholars in the field, A L Kroeber and Talcott Parsons, summarised the previous definitions and, in a joint publication, described culture as "transmitted and created content of values, ideas and other symbolic-meaningful systems as factors in the shaping of human behaviour and the artifacts produced by behaviour".[53]

Kultur, then, to Häberle, is first of all characterised by handing down past achievements, by tradition, what Tyler calls socially acquired lifestyle. Secondly, culture involves developing these achievements further, that is to say, there must

[45] P Häberle, "Kulturstaat" n.22 *supra*, 31.
[46] P Häberle, *ibid.*
[47] P Häberle, *ibid.*
[48] P Häberle, *ibid.*
[49] E B Tylor, "Die Kulturwissenschaft" in R König/ASchmalfuss (eds.), *Kulturanthropologie* (Düsseldorf, 1972), p. 51.
[50] G Marshall, in *Concise Oxford Dictionary of Sociology* (Oxford, 1994) p. 104.
[51] M Harris, *Cultural Anthropology* (New York, Harper Collins, 1995).
[52] M Payne in M Payne (ed.), *Dictionary of Cultural and Critical Theory* (London, Blackwells, 1996).
[53] A L Kroeber, T Parsons, "The Concepts of Culture and Social System" in [1958] *American-Sociological Review* 583.

be innovation. Thirdly, he states, it is important to recognise that there may be more than one culture in society, there must be cultural pluralism. This third element is perhaps the most important, and he goes on to demand that culture must be open to all members of a society, and that not only the active "production" of culture must be protected, but that the "consumption" of culture must in future be viewed as an integral part of cultural life, rendering the division into an elite group of artists and a merely passive audience obsolete and bringing forth a more holistic approach to culture.[54] To ensure that all members of society have the possibility of participating in cultural life, the state must engage actively in making culture more universally accessible.[55] In this he partly emulates the anti-elitist approach of the school of cultural studies who believe that all forms of cultural products should be ranked as having equal value.[56]

Although Häberle does not really seem to come to grips with the diversity of (especially the newer) sociological research, he does pin-point several very important aspects of culture and his pluralist approach and his assertion that culture must not be the domain of a small privileged group are useful and suited to a contemporary discussion. But unfortunately his definition is too vague to distinguish between culture and non-culture. He does not seem to take in civilisation as a whole, but it is difficult to see where he actually draws the line. If however, the state is to take an active role, it is imperative to define the limits of this involvement, rather than having to deal with the entirety of human behaviour, as the Tylor tradition might indicate.

Werner Maihofer takes a very similar approach to Häberle, but the sources he quotes are mainly philosophical, with Pufendorff and Kant being central to his argument.

Samuel Pufendorff, one of the central figures of German legal philosophy of the renaissance age and co-founder of the natural-law movement, divided the world into two halves, the world of nature and the world of culture. Whereas the world of nature is governed strictly in his view by the rules of causation and instinct, so that all things are predictable, the world of culture is unpredictable, with many aspects and facets, governed by the freedom of the individual's will and his mental abilities. This multitude of ideas and approaches is the propelling force of human development, and is regulated only by our sense of what is morally good. Pufendorff recognises that liberty is a necessary prerequisite for human development.[57] Culture appears therefore as the product of liberty.[58] Kant shares this view of the relationship between culture and liberty.[59] In his

[54] P Häberle, "Kulturstaat" n. *supra* 22, 32.

[55] P Häberle, *idem*, 33.

[56] D Chaney, *The Cultural Turn* (London, Routledge, 1994), p. 20.

[57] H Welzel, *Naturrecht und materielle Gerechtigkeit* (Göttingen, Vandenhoek&Ruprecht, 1962), p. 132.

[58] H Welzel, *ibid*.

[59] I Kant, *Die drei Kritiken* (Leipzig, R. Schmidt, 1933), p. 324.

teleological view of the world, culture is, in fact, the ultimate end of nature, the state to which all development of mankind aims.[60] And again culture is seen as the entirety of learnt or acquired human behaviour, which not one generation alone, but only mankind as such is capable of attaining.[61] Kant notes that there are higher and lower forms of culture, with the mere "skills" of some human beings providing the necessary comforts on the basis of which others may work on the other, higher cultural achievements, such as science and the arts,[62] but culture as such encompasses all of these.[63]

Maihofer, like Häberle, states that tradition of achievements and innovation are both central to culture. Drawing on the theme of culture as a product of liberty, he adds, however, another element, pointing out that in culture and cultural achievements the individual is of paramount importance. Whereas in other areas of human activity one individual may easily be replaced by another, where culture is concerned, there is always an element of personal experience which renders the artefact or activity distinct and which is perceived as being of the highest importance. As an example he points out, that, though Raphael may have had many workers to help him paint his frescoes, it is the stamp of his personality on the resulting work which distinguishes it from a whitewash.[64]

Both Maihofer and Häberle, then, see "culture" as something distinct from civilisation itself, but have a very broad view of what falls into this category, a view that defies any sort of classification or evaluation according to merit. It certainly encompasses the arts, but goes further to cover education and religious matters and practically all "creative" activities.

4.1.2. The "elitist" or "narrow" definition of culture

The above "universalist" definition stands in contrast with the original meaning of the word culture. The earliest use of the word in the modern sense was made by Cicero. Originally, the Latin *cultura* expressed only the agri-*cultural* process of cultivating the soil. Cicero combined it with the word animus, to denote the cultivation of the mind or spirit. To him, "*cultura animi*" was identical with philosophy, i.e. culture was not simply civilisation, but one of civilisation's finest achievements.[65]

This "honorific" usage of the word was most common from the seventeenth to the nineteenth century.[66] Both Fichte and Hegel in their work on the *Kul-*

[60] I Kant, *ibid.*

[61] I Kant, "Idee zu einer allgemeinen Geschichte in weltbürgerlicher Absicht" in *Kants gesammelte Schriften* (Berlin, WdG, 1923), p. 19.

[62] I Kant, *Kritiken* n.59 *supra*, 325.

[63] There is one important exception however: Kant for the first time draws a dividing line between culture and religion. *Cf.* W Maihofer, "Kulturelle Aufgaben" n. *supra* 22, 1212.

[64] Maihofer, "Kulturelle Aufgaben" n.22 *supra*, 1220.

[65] M T Cicero, *Tusculan Disputations*, book II, 13.

[66] M Payne, *Cultural Theory* n.52 *supra*, 128.

turstaat use it this way. In the English-speaking world, Matthew Arnold has become the best-known advocate of this elitist approach. In his essay on "Culture and Anarchy", he defines culture as "the study of perfection",[67] the aim of which is to learn the best of what has been thought and said in the world and to make it "prevail".[68] He emphasises also that culture is a collective phenomenon. An individual alone cannot achieve perfection, the aim and end of culture, but this must always be done by the general whole of society.[69] Although this idea of culture as a social phenomenon is shared by other definitions, Arnold takes this a step further: as there is to him only the one ideal for which all must strive, he infers that culture must set limits to individual freedom, with individuals not being allowed to do as they think fit, but having to conform to the norms dictated by "perfection".[70] This last, extremely un-pluralistic attitude to culture has, I am glad to say, found no followers in the current German legal debate.

There are, however, a number of legal scholars who favour various versions of the "elitist" approach. Ernst Rudolf Huber, for example, who revived the concept of *Kulturstaat* after the end of the Second World War, considered as falling within *Kultur* only activities which do not contribute to sustaining man's physical existence, are not related to providing food, shelter etc, but "are of a lasting intellectual value, reaching beyond transitory physical existence".[71] This definition excludes from culture not only the activities of breadwinning, but all those achievements in the fields of literature, art, science, philosophy and so forth that are not of lasting intellectual value, thereby necessitating an evaluation of these activities. The issue he does not resolve is who makes these decisions, as practical experience has demonstrated often enough that recognition of the lasting value may come about only after a substantial period of time. Making selections worthy of a pluralist society is a dilemma which could prove insurmountable and renders the definition hardly applicable in a legal context.

Thomas Oppermann choses a more pragmatic approach, saying that, although there are many different usages of the word culture, the relevant content for a legal discussion is shaped by the constitutional and administrative tradition. In this context, he suggests, cultural affairs are understood to be the sphere in which the state comes into particularly close contact with intellectual life.[72] Areas of particular importance are quoted as being education, science and art, while religion falls into a different catogory.[73] This again is a definition which, though covering the core areas on which there seems to be no

[67] M Arnold, *Culture and Anarchy* (Cambridge, 1957), p. 45.

[68] M Arnold, *idem*, pp. 6, 46.

[69] M Arnold, *idem*, 48.

[70] M Arnold, *idem*, 50.

[71] E R Huber: "Kulturverfassung, Kulturkrise, Kulturkonflikt" in *Bewahrung und Wandlung* (Berlin, Duncker&Humblot, 1975), p. 344.

[72] T Oppermann, *Kulturverwaltungsrecht* n.44 *supra*, 8.

[73] T Oppermann, *idem*, 9.

dispute, is not very helpful in discerning the margins of culture and again raises the question of merit. The uncontroversial core of education, science and art is also emphasised by Udo Steiner, who, obviously despairing of finding an exact definition, lists all the different areas of law which to him are part of the field of culture, e.g. the arts, both amateur and professional, museums and archives, the protection of heritage, and a number of others. He summarises these as being related to intellectual or creative human activities.[74] He instantly concedes, however, that all definitions are so vague that they are hardly usable for legal puposes.[75]

4.1.3. Conclusions

This survey of the prevalent opinions on the meaning of *Kultur* leaves us with a core area, consisting of the arts, science and education, which undisputedly falls under *Kultur*, and a fringe area that is largely undefined. In the case of the universalist definition, it is very extensive, encompassing a wide range of human activities, so much so, that if applied legally as the basis for constitutional protection it might render other constitutional guarantees obsolete. In the case of the narrow interpretation, on the other hand, there is only a fairly small fringe area, but the contents is dependent on some form of assessment of the activities involved. This lack of clarity makes the definitions at best legally unpracticable, in the worst case renders them meaningless. While the core area tallies with the, somewhat scant, textual analysis produced by the survey of the Constitution, the broader, universalist definition seems to tie in better with the general legislative spirit of the *Grundgesetz*, which lays great emphasis on the personal development of the individual (guaranteed in article 2 s.1 GG) and equality of individuals (guaranteed by, among others, article 3 GG).

4.2. *Kulturstaat*

It is not only the term *Kultur* that lacks definition, the term *Kulturstaat* is also unclear. There are many different views as to what characteristics a state must have to merit the title *Kulturstaat* and a variety of positions on whether the Federal Republic of Germany is a *Kulturstaat*.

The paper which reintroduced the notion to German constitutional law in 1956, E R Huber's "Problematik des *Kulturstaats*"[76] deals with nothing but the question: what is a *Kulturstaat*? It is a beautifully argued piece, heavily influenced in content by Hegel's concept of the state and in style by his dialectic method,[77] and takes the reader through five progressive stages on the way to

[74] U Steiner, "Kulturauftrag" n.25 *supra*, 9.
[75] U Steiner, *idem*, 10.
[76] E R Huber, *Problematik*, n.13 *supra*.
[77] M-E Geis, *Kulturstaat* n.13 *supra*, 48.

Huber's ideal *Kulturstaat*. He begins by describing a state which has imposed on itself complete cultural neutrality, saying that this might be a *Kulturstaat* in that it does not hinder cultural development.[78] The second step towards perfection is a state which aims to "serve" culture, which protects and aids cultural development and ensures that the achievements of culture are handed on to younger generations.[79] But this is not enough for Huber, his next step forward is to demand that the state must take a hand in the cultural process itself and must involve itself in shaping what culture is.[80] From here it is not far to the next stage which brings about a reversal of roles, with culture becoming the dominant factor and shaping the appearance of the state.[81] At the pinnacle of this development stands the ultimate *Kulturstaat*, in which both elements merge, the state being an expression of culture and vice versa.[82] The construction, however, has major drawbacks. For one thing Huber did not actually define what *Kultur* meant, the definition quoted above being supplied in one of his later works. He also gave no indication at which of these stages he believed the (then young) Federal Republic had arrived. This limited any practical application of his ideas, and the piece has since been heavily criticised,[83] but it did trigger a lively discussion of the topic and has become something of a classic.

Of the modern scholars, R Scholz is the most forthright advocate of the *Kulturstaat*. He believes that it is part of German constitutional law, and a fully fledged fundamental principle to boot.[84] In fact his writing on the topic sounds so positive, one might be led to believe that this is the reigning opinion among German lawyers. He bases his proposition mainly on article 5 s.3 of the *Grundgesetz*, and says that the State is required not only to be culturally neutral and tolerant, giving all forms of culture equal status (although it may make a decision as to what is not *Kultur*), but also must be proactive in nurturing cultural activities. However, according to Scholz, individuals cannot make demands for state aid purely on the basis of the principle, but this does not exclude the possibility of litigation via article 2 s.I GG.[85]

Maihofer also asserts that the Federal Republic is a *Kulturstaat*, although he does point out that this view is not shared by the majority of legal scholars. He sets out, at great length, his vision of the modern, democratic and liberal *Kulturstaat*, based on his "open" definition of *Kultur*. This is a state which is "supportive" ("*solidarisch*") of all aspects of culture, at all levels from the amateur to the professional. It not only helps preserve past achievements, but

[78] E R Huber, *Problematik* n.13 *supra*, 8.
[79] E R Huber, *idem*, 11.
[80] E R Huber, *idem*, 13.
[81] E R Huber, *idem*, 21.
[82] E R Huber, *idem*, 26.
[83] M-E Geis, "Kulturstaat", n.13 *supra*, 47.
[84] R Scholz in Maunz-Dürig-Herzog, *Grundgesetz*, Vol I, Art.5 III No.8 (Munich, C.H. Beck, 1996).
[85] R Scholz, *ibid*.

also aids innovation, even where it is not economically viable according to the rules of our economic order.[86]

Häberle, on the other hand, is a little less emphatic about the *Kulturstaat*: he sees the principle as being in the process of formation, more a thing of the future than a present day institution. He claims, however, that the outlines of a "*Kulturstaat*" principle are already emerging, made visible by the jurisdiction of the *Bundesverfassungsgericht* and the great number of norms dealing with cultural matters at constitutional and subconstitutional level. These confer on both the Federation and the federal states a large scope of competencies in the cultural sector, as well as providing the individual with protection against state interference and a right to demand positive action from the State.[87] Other scholars are even more reticent about using the term *Kulturstaat*. In some cases it is used simply to describe a certain field of state activity, without elevating it to a constitutional principle, or deducing any further rights or duties from it.[88] Finally, there are those who are altogether opposed to applying the term *Kulturstaat* to the framework of the *Grundgesetz*, either because they believe that there is a good reason for the silence of the German constitution on this topic, i.e. that absolute cultural neutrality was intended and an involvement of the State in cultural matters must be prevented,[89] or else because they fear that the very material and pragmatic guarantees given by the various culture-related norms will be weakend by making these part of a larger but elusive fundamental principle.[90]

4.3. Consequences of applying these theories in practice

As mentioned above a *Kulturstaat* along universalist lines seems in some ways more suited to the *Grundgesetz*. However, the *Grundgesetz* is so open on the question that the elitist approach does not really conflict with the constitution, either. One aspect that has been little explored in the discussion so far is which effect the various theories might have if put into practice.

First, rights derived from the *Kulturstaat* would of course clash with other constitutional rights. Resolving these clashes would necessitate careful balancing actions. To take an example, the youth spraying graffiti paintings onto the wall of a privately owned house is combining traditional and acquired techniques with innovation and a "personal input", is, according to Maihofer's theory, engaged in a cultural activity. The potential for conflict with the owner's property rights under article 14 is obvious. The more inclusive a definition of culture becomes and the more activities are protected under it, the more poten-

[86] W Maihofer, "Kulturelle Aufgaben", n.22 *supra*, 1215.
[87] P Häberle, "Kulturstaat", n.22 *supra*, 25.
[88] U Scheuner, "Die Bundesrepublik als Kulturstaat" [1977/1978] *Bitburger Gespräche* 113.
[89] A Hamann/ H Lenz, *Kommentar zum Grundgesetz* (Neuwied, Luchterhand, 1970), p. 338.
[90] Steiner, "Kulturauftrag", n.25 *supra*, 12.

tial for conflict arises. Here a slightly narrower understanding would prevent much controversy.

If *Kulturstaat* means more than non-intervention and a commitment to state funding is assumed, this raises further problems. The *Bundesverfassungsgericht* has placed the *Sozialstaat* under the proviso of feasibility: the State need only give support within its financial means, but equality of distribution must be guaranteed.[91] A similar condition would surely have to be attached to the *Kulturstaat*. But if *Kultur* was understood very broadly and therefore a great number of individuals could claim some support, this would mean the actual amount received by each could become so minimal as to have no real effect. A more elitist approach might make a pooling of resources and an allotment of greater sums to individual activities or projects possible and so might lead more effectively to an advancement of culture.[92]

Then, however, one is faced with the task of selection and would have to decide on the relative merits of various activities. Under a pluralist constitution like the *Grundgesetz* with its very strong emphasis on equality, this might become an insurmountable dilemma. Both approaches consequently have grave drawbacks where practicability is concerned.

5. CONCLUSION

All in all, considering the considerable contributions made to cultural life by German government and its agencies and the body of legal writing on the topic, there can be no doubt that a commitment to culture and its advancement is a fundamental value of German public law and public policy. In fact, if one uses the word *Kulturstaat* purely descriptively, one might well class the Federal Republic as a *Kulturstaat*.

But the constitutional standing of the *Kulturstaat* is more problematic. Whereas the other fundamental principles are based on the wording of the *Grundgesetz*, the commitment to culture is based merely on its interpretation, and whereas the other fundamental principles are fully practised constitutional law, grave doubts must remain as to how the *Kulturstaat* can be put into practice. Any attempt to accord the principle equal constitutional status alongside the *Rechtsstaat*, the *Sozialstaat*, the *Bundesstaat* and democracy seems, consequently, far removed from constitutional reality.

[91] BVerfGE vol 33, 303 at 333.

[92] Oppermann has pointed out that in terms of cultural (artistic, intellectual) advancement, democracy may actually not be the most propitious system, and that the very focused attention given to the monarch's favourites in absolutistic monarchies may have been a far more efficient way of kick-starting cultural development. T Oppermann, *Kulturverwaltungsrecht*, n.43 *supra*, 16.

Part 4

Fundamental Values in Private Law

17

Professional Negligence: Free Riders and Others

ANDREW TETTENBORN

Surveyors from Lloyd's arrange to inspect a boat. They know it is for sale, and that in the nature of things the buyer is very likely to see their report. They pronounce the boat sound and fit for its class, having failed to look at it properly. Their report is indeed passed to the would-be buyer, who reads it, purchases the vessel and finds himself burdened with a rust-bucket. The classification society, even if negligent, are not liable to him.[1] Nor are they bound to pay up if a vessel they have foolishly pronounced serviceable then proceeds to sink with someone else's cargo on board: and this remains true even if they knew about the cargo, and indeed inspected the vessel partly with a view to seeing whether it could be safely allowed back into cargo service.[2] Again, accountants are engaged by a company to audit its affairs. They miss signs of a massive hole in the balance-sheet which ought to ring alarm bells in any properly-run practice, and give the operation a clean bill of health. A predator reads their conclusions, likes what he sees and takes over the concern. He then finds he has bought a pup. Even if the auditors knew a take-over might be in the offing and were clearly culpable, the predator cannot look to them for reparation.[3] (It may possibly be different, however, if the accountants had actual knowledge of both his existence and identity).[4]

Meanwhile, valuers acting for prospective financiers inspect a house which is to be bought on a mortgage. They overlook the fact that it is abominably built and apt to fall down at any moment. Satisfied, the financiers accommodate the buyer, who as a result is saddled with an expensive and unsaleable wreck. This buyer, unlike the previous ones, is lucky. He can send the valuers the bill for his

[1] *The Morning Watch* [1990] 1 Lloyds Rep 547.
[2] *Marc Rich & Co AG* v. *Bishop Rock Marine Ltd* [1996] AC 211.
[3] *Caparo plc* v. *Dickman & Ors* [1990] 2 AC 605.
[4] Cf. *Galoo* v. *Bright Grahame Murray* [1995] 1 All ER 16.

loss[5] (though, curiously, he cannot sue the builder or the architect who actually created the defect the valuer failed to spot).[6]

While all this is going on, a Lloyd's name appoints an underwriting agent, who in turn appoints a sub-agent to underwrite risks on his behalf. The sub-agent negligently exposes the name to the claims of the victims of disasters both numerous and prodigious, and the name is mulcted of many millions. The sub-agent may have had neither a contract with the name nor a claim against him for fees: nevertheless the House of Lords has said that he must make good the losses the name has suffered in the vain hope of lucre.[7]

When it comes to deciding who owes a duty of care to whom, and in respect of what, there is no doubt that actions for professional negligence raise the most awkward and intractable problems. Decisions are reconcilable one with another only on the basis of the most tortuous distinctions; and reasons, for or against liability, held good in one context are ignored elsewhere.[8] Indeed, in this area of law the hapless adviser might forgivably think it was a matter of pure chance whether or not a given proceeding is struck out as disclosing no cause of action. The object of this essay is to try to make a little more sense of the whole subject, by looking at some of the more notorious decisions from a different angle. I would like to suggest that the real justification for a great deal of professional negligence "duty of care law" – at least *sub rosa* – is a relatively simple idea: namely, that in law as elsewhere, there is no such thing as a free lunch. What causes a great many negligence plaintiffs to fall at the first fence – "no duty" – is that they are trying to use the legal process to gain a benefit at someone else's expense without paying for it, and without the consent of the person providing it.

This is a large claim. Before dealing with it in detail, we need to take a number of steps back. We start with three propositions, whose significance will appear in due course.

1. NEGLIGENCE AND GUARANTEES

My first assertion is simple. All negligence law (meaning by negligence law any rule whose effect is to make someone liable for fault, whether we classify it as tort, breach of contract, or for that matter under some more fancy rubric such as breach of trust or fiduciary duty) is really about *guarantees*. We are talking about guarantees of a very particular sort, of course (to be precise, about guar-

[5] *Smith* v. *Eric S Bush* [1990] 1 AC 831, upholding the earlier *Yianni* v. *Edwin Evans* [1982] QB 438.

[6] So held in *Dept of the Environment* v. *Thos Bates* [1991] 1 AC 499.

[7] *Henderson* v. *Merrett Syndicates Ltd* [1995] 2 AC 145.

[8] "The outcome of three decades of litigation has been a complex, uncertain and anomalous pattern of decision". – Stapleton (1991) 107 LQR 249, 258.

antees that something will be done competently, or that identifiable persons will exhibit a given level of competence or care in doing it): but about guarantees nevertheless.

Now, this proposition is deliberately combative. To a lawyer it is also counter-intuitive, since it contradicts the idea that negligence law is prescriptive, something we are subject to willy-nilly, whereas guarantees are consensual: they are spawned by contract or possibly trust, and not imposed on us by the State. But a moment's thought will show that classifying negligence liability as a kind of guarantee is not quite so outlandish as it seems. Suppose we say that A is owed a duty of care in tort by B (any duty of care will do, but take the simple case where A is crossing the road in front of B's car). To all intents and purposes, this is equivalent to saying that A has the benefit of a guarantee, or assurance, or obligation, on B's part – it matters not what we call it – allowing A to call for compensation from B in the case of default by B or others more or less connected with him. B's duty could be re-christened a "due-care guarantee" without anything other than a slight oddness of language. The thing itself would remain identical. Save that the defendant is different, the position is precisely the same as it would have been if A had insured against loss due to B's negligence.[9]

This is not to deny that the ambit of "due-care guarantees" will vary enormously. So will the events giving rise to them. Some are just there. Reinforcing the commonplace view that duties in tort are imposed by law, they take effect whether the parties like it or not and – on occasion – despite the fact that the burdened party has neither agreed to, or even done, anything whatever. At this extreme comes the city council's duty to provide safe and pedestrian-friendly pavements.[10] This depends on neither an undertaking nor even a voluntary act on the authority's part: it is a claim anyone can invoke, irrespective of the circumstances, simply because he is a pedestrian. Other due-care guarantees, by contrast, come right at the other end of the spectrum. They exist because, and only because, the potential defendant has agreed to provide them: they arise by consensus, not imposition. Take the case of the sub-contractor on a big building project who writes a "duty of care letter" to a future purchaser of the structure he is helping to erect. The rights the buyer gets are those appearing in the contractor's agreement, no more, no less (it being clear he is otherwise owed none in tort).[11] They are circumscribed entirely by the terms of the letter and the willingness of the contractor to give them.

And, of course, between these poles we find the common congeries of miscellaneous contractual, tortious and other duties, more or less consensual in origin as the case may be. But the point remains: whatever the differences

[9] Compare Atiyah, *The Damages Lottery*, p. 133 ("The third party insurance system forces [people] (in effect) to buy and to pay for this additional life insurance element".).

[10] Imposed by statute: now the Highways Act 1980, s.79.

[11] *Dept of the Environment* v. *Thos Bates* [1991] 1 AC 499.

between them, as regards the potential claimant they are all equivalent simply to guarantees of one sort or another. Save for the fact that the defendant is different, they might just as well be contained in an insurance policy against shoddy work. True it is that we tend to reserve the use of words such as "guarantee" and "assurance" to promise-based liabilities: but at bottom this is just a matter of long-standing usage. The effect as regards the beneficiary is the same even in straightforward tortious duties such as that of the highway authority. The claimant is treated as though he had the benefit of a guarantee, or assurance, or call it what you will.

2. TWO KINDS OF RIGHT

In the nature of civil obligations, legal entitlements (or rights) split pretty neatly into two camps. There are those you get automatically; and over and above these, there are extra rights which do not come as of course but which you can take steps to acquire if you want. For want of anything better I shall christen them "basic" and "supplemental" rights.

Basic rights come, as it were, as standard issue. Your right not to be murdered, brutalised, burgled, or defamed is not something you have to buy, or bargain for. It comes to you, *gratis*, for no better reason than that you are part of the community, and to that extent gives you a free legal lunch. (It might be more accurate to say that this is a lunch you are not billed for directly, since you almost certainly pay for it indirectly, through tax, etc. But that is another story we need not enter into here).

But basic rights are only part of the story. Contrast other kinds of right – to take two random examples, the right to be paid for work done, or to be compensated (other than by the burglar) for the goods that disappeared when your house is ransacked. As anyone who is unemployed or uninsured will tell you, these are claims you get only if you bought or bargained for them: only, that is, if someone – employer, insurance company or someone else – chose to sell them to you (or possibly to give them to you: this is an important point in the law of negligence, as appears below). That is a fact of political and social life. Beyond your basic entitlement, rights are commodities which may on principle be granted or withheld at will: if you want more you will have to persuade someone to provide you with them. Of course what counts as a basic right will vary between societies and legal systems, and at times may be highly controversial.[12] But the soundness of the distinction itself cannot be in serious doubt.

[12] Thus the right to expect manufactured items to be safe was once regarded as clearly supplemental. That was the point of *Winterbottom* v. *Wright* (1842) 10 M & W 109, which said, perfectly intelligibly, that if you had not bought this right as a matter of contract, you did not have it. It took *Donoghue* v. *Stevenson* [1932] AC 562 to shift it into the category of basic rights available to you in any case whether or not you had taken steps to acquire it. An interesting contemporary example of a similar argument concerns the Osman family's claim to sue the police for damages

Claims in negligence are of course a species of legal right; and a moment's thought shows that they work identically. Some are basic, included in your "citizen's package deal": for instance, your right to sue the man who carelessly knocked you down in the street, or the incompetent assembler of the lorry which demolished your house when the brakes failed. But it is often forgotten that this is only a part of the story. Suppose you buy a car which immediately fails to start, leaves you in the lurch, and costs you money as a result. Imagine in addition that this is due to inexpert manufacture, or to bad servicing by a garage employed by a previous owner. If you sue the manufacturer you will fail, in the absence of some explicit guarantee enforceable by you.[13] As for the garage, you may have a claim, but only in very limited circumstances. The mere fact that you were damnified and that it was the garage's fault will not do. You will have to show something indicating that the garage gave you that right, or should be treated as having done: for example, that you yourself commissioned and paid for the service and hence bought a no-negligence guarantee as part of it; or – conceivably – that although you did not pay for it, the person who carried it out said you could rely on his having done a proper job and he was prepared to accept liability if he hadn't.

It will, of course, be apparent that this suggested line separating basic and supplemental rights is not entirely novel. The distinction has something in common with the tort-contract divide: contract rights, after all, are generally consensual, while imposed duties are nearly always tortious. Apart from that, it also has affinities with the well-attested difference between physical and economic loss. Nor is the reason difficult to see: basic rights are appropriate where there is a social imperative to compensate, and this imperative is generally much stronger in the case of physical lesion than merely monetary loss.[14] Nevertheless, the quadration is inexact. Tort liability may be dependent on an acceptance of liability, or something similar (as in *Hedley Byrne*).[15] Indeed, one of the odder consequences of the doctrines of consideration and privity in contract is that if a professional wants to guarantee the quality of his work to someone who has not paid him, the only possible liability is tortious. And even some cases of physical damage are clearly classifiable under the head of supplemental liability: see the cases of the cargo owner who loses his cargo owing to a classification society failure.[16] or the house which falls down owing to poor design.[17]

when they failed to thwart a lunatic who later shot their son. In *Osman* v. *Ferguson* [1993] 4 All ER 344 the Court of Appeal denied the claim. By contrast, the European Court of Human Rights thought that the possibility of bringing such a claim was so important that its lack amounted to an infringement of human rights (see *Osman* v. *UK* [1999] 1 FLR 193 (Application No. 00023452/94)).

[13] That is the essential point of *Simaan General Contracting Co* v. *Pilkington Glass Ltd (No. 2)* [1988] QB 758. And compare *Hamble Fisheries* v. *Gardner* [1999] 2 Lloyd's Rep. 1.

[14] Compare *Marc Rich* v. *Bishop Rock* [1994] 1 WLR. 1071, 1077 (Savile LJ).

[15] *Hedley Byrne* v. *Heller & Partners* [1964] AC 465.

[16] *Marc Rich* v. *Bishop Rock* [1996] 1 AC 211.

[17] *Dept of the Environment* v. *Thos Bates* [1991] 1 AC 499.

3. TWO DUTIES OF CARE

My third proposition derives from the previous two. Because basic and supplemental rights are radically different, they engender (or should engender) two different approaches to the duty of care question. In other words, in deciding whether a given plaintiff is owed a duty of care, the criterion to be applied must vary, and vary radically, according to whether we are talking about basic or supplemental claims. To suggest that our tort books can continue to have one chapter headed "duty of care in negligence", or that there is one single test (be it proximity, policy, good sense, or for that matter anything else) which is capable of covering all cases (or even all cases of negligence causing economic loss) is both deceptive and counterproductive.

This will discompose tort lawyers. Apart from discussing physical and economic loss and the possible differences between them, they have been brought up to discuss the duty of care as a unified problem.[18] But the underlying reasoning is compelling. "Basic negligence" vindicates important rights, rights we all have as a matter of course. If so, it follows that in delineating the duty of care, the only real issue is one of finding the proper limits to be applied to our conception of social responsibility. Of course the way we do this, and how far we are prepared to curtail financial responsibility for practical or other reasons, will be different in different contexts. One has only to look at the principles and assumptions that have grown up to deal with particular problems, such as the presumptive needs for protection against physical lesion (*Donoghue*[19] to *Dorset Yacht*)[20] and for an efficient channelling of claims for damage to chattels (see cases such as *The Aliakmon*[21] and *The Mineral Transporter*);[22] the practical desirability of reining in claims for psychic injury (*McLoughlin* v. *O'Brien*);[23] the non-liability for disruption to utilities (*Spartan Steel*);[24] and the idea that good administration by public bodies may not be best furthered by mulcting the taxpayer in damages (see *Osman*[25] and similar cases). But for all the nuances and sub-distinctions that these cases draw, the circle they are trying to square remains essentially the same: the limitation for practical reasons of our *prima facie* entitlement to keep person and property intact.

Supplemental negligence, by contrast, is different. Return to the mechanic whose negligence leaves my car immobile, or the manufacturer who negligently

[18] For example, the current (17th) edition of *Clerk & Lindsell* devotes fourteen pages to "Duty of Care: The General Criteria", before heading the last paragraph "Universal Application of the Criteria". (See §§ 7-05–7-17). A similar attitude permeates Lord Steyn's judgment in *Marc Rich* v. *Bishop Rock* [1996] 1 AC 211; and see too *Mulcahy* v. *Min of Defence* [1996] 2 All ER 758, 771 (Neill LJ).

[19] [1932] AC 465.

[20] [1970] AC 1004.

[21] [1986] AC 785.

[22] [1986] AC 1.

[23] [1983] 1 AC 410.

[24] [1973] 1 QB 27.

[25] [1993] 4 All ER 344.

leaves out a component of my television set so that it does not work (or even quietly burns out) when I switch it on. True, his liability is limited: but the reason is nothing to do with social responsibility, or the limitations to be placed on it.[26] It makes no sense to say I am entitled, even presumptively, to a working television, or to a guarantee that care will be taken to make a car work, so that social morality demands that I should have a *prima facie* claim against you if you culpably deprive me of it. On the contrary: this is the sort of assurance that by its nature ought to be available only by way of some voluntary transaction. Hence, if I want to claim it, I will have to show that I obtained it from the mechanic or manufacturer – by purchase, or by gift, or possibly by some other conduct of his that led me to believe I was getting some legally enforceable right. In more traditional negligence terms, this means I ought to succeed only if I contracted with the mechanic, or received some express or implied assurance from him (call this an "undertaking of responsibility" if you like, on which more below), or can show something similar which takes the case out of the ordinary run of negligence actions and creates a "special relationship" between us.

4. SUPPLEMENTARY RIGHTS AND PROFESSIONAL NEGLIGENCE

So far we have not mentioned professional negligence *eo nomine*. But the alert reader will have no difficulty in seeing where the discussion is leading. Put simply, professional negligence claims – whether brought in contract or in tort – have one common characteristic. They overwhelmingly vindicate supplemental, not basic, rights. There may be a few exceptions (medical negligence is a possible candidate, at least in a society that believes every citizen has a right not only to therapy but to free therapy guaranteed by the taxpayer). But as a rule there is no such thing as a general right to high-quality service, even if there is one to (say) safe driving.

This argument is not as outrageous or outlandish as it looks. It actually mirrors the point made in section 3 above in connection with sale of goods: that is, that there is no universal right to quality merchandise. If you want a legally-enforceable assurance that something you own has been soundly and properly made, so that you can rely on it not to let you down, you have to take steps to obtain it. That is, indeed, pretty uncontroversial now. But logically, exactly the same reasoning must apply to services, where the duty to supply goods of satisfactory quality is paralleled by the duty to supply careful and competent service.[27] There can be no sensible reason to distinguish between my right to a high-quality house survey and my right to a super Saab. If in the latter case I

[26] *Pace* Hepple at [1997] CLP 69, who regards professional standards as fundamentally a matter of social morality.

[27] A point well made by Whittaker: see (1996) 16 OJLS 191, 205–6.

must bargain with someone – seller or otherwise – for quality assurance, so too with the former. The mere fact that I stand to lose if services are bungled or not properly rendered is not – or at least ought not to be – enough. It must be necessary for me to go further, and show something in the nature of a contract, or at least a serious undertaking, in my favour.

The same point can be reinforced in another way. Professionals invariably practise in a market: they use it to sell (good) service. This is one of the things that marks them off from the ordinary run of wrongdoer. You cannot, save in some mythical Chicago research institute, set up a market for the purveying of decent driving or considerate crane-operation to those prepared to pay for them.[28] But sale by its nature implies specificity. The ability to sell something to X must carry with it the possibility of selling it to X *and nobody else*, or it means nothing at all. If Y, who has not bought the service, is nevertheless enabled to sue the person providing it on the basis that it was badly rendered, the whole idea of purchase is set at nought. You do not pay for something if you can get it for nothing. Yet this is the necessary effect of liability based on foreseeability, whatever its guise. Allowing someone to whom a professional service was not rendered to complain that it was negligently rendered *ipso facto* creates a class of "free riders" and gives them, gratis, what others have been prepared to pay for.

5. DUTY OF CARE: SOME EXISTING ARGUMENTS

All this no doubt explains why such an astonishing number of duty of care issues have arisen in professional negligence cases. Judges and lawyers alike have tried long and hard to make sense of the mystery ingredient known as "proximity" which must be added to foreseeability in order to decide whether someone claiming against a lawyer, accountant or other professional comes within the class of those owed a duty. What the analysis above tells us is not so much that this way of looking at things is alarmingly unspecific (although it is): but, more importantly, that it asks the wrong questions. The rest of the law of tort may depend on ideas of social responsibility and the reasonable contemplation of the defendant. But if services fail to come up to the standard expected, the natural starting-point for enquiry is not "Who was foreseeably likely to be affected?" It is "Who were those services provided or guaranteed to?"

[28] There is a related, if slightly more esoteric, point here. Financial and legal advice, house surveys and the like are not only a saleable commodity, but a commodity of a specialised kind, in that their value consists in large measure precisely in the provider's subjoined undertaking to show due diligence. To buy a car is to buy a thing, with a guarantee thrown in as it were as a sideline. To buy professional advice, by contrast, is to some extent to purchase an abstraction. The guarantee itself forms a large part of what the customer is paying for.

If the scheme suggested above is accepted, a good many ideas put forward in professional negligence jurisprudence become much more comprehensible.

First, oddly enough, we find that the word "proximity" begins to make sense in something like its natural meaning of a close and intimate connection. Elsewhere in the law of negligence, it has largely been reduced to a clumsy shorthand expression referring to other, more or less imponderable, reasons for accepting or denying a duty of care.[29] In the professional negligence context, by contrast, to say "no proximity – no duty" is to make the perfectly reasonable point that professionals do not normally evince an intent to benefit persons not pretty closely connected with them – at least in the sense of giving such people a right to claim if something goes wrong. A solicitor works for his client: *prima facie*, at least, he does not work for anyone else, however much that person may stand to lose in the event of his failing to provide a proper service.[30] Of course, professionals can show a different intention if they want to: there is nothing to stop them stating that remoter parties should feel free to rely on the quality of their services and claim against them in the event of dissatisfaction. Nevertheless, the presumption must be that they do not.

Secondly, the bugbear of open-ended liability to an uncomfortably wide class, cemented unhealthily fast in legal minds by a too-quotable epigram from a 1930s New York judge,[31] comes neatly into context. In non-professional cases, it is difficult to avoid concluding that this currently operates as a rough-and-ready limitation device, akin to remoteness of damage. In the electricity cut-off cases, to take the best-known example, potential plaintiffs suffering loss are deprived of a claim not because of any particular undeservingness on their part, but simply because liability must stop somewhere.[32] With professional negligence, by contrast, the idea falls much more naturally into place. Absent specific agreement to the contrary, it is inherently implausible that a person rendering professional services intends to guarantee their proper execution to a large number of claimants solely on the basis of their foreseeability as victims. Professionals simply do not work that way.

Thirdly, a similar tidying-up process can be applied to the vexed issue of "assumption of responsibility". In general negligence cases, this concept has

[29] *Caparo* v. *Dickman* [1990] 2 AC 605, 618 (Lord Bridge); 633 (Lord Oliver).

[30] See below, and cases such as *Hemmens* v. *Wilson Browne* [1993] 4 All ER 826 (solicitor advising X how to make an enforceable promise to Y owes no duty to Y when, owing to his negligence in drawing up the documentation, the promise turns out to be unenforceable by Y).

[31] *I.e.*, Cardozo J's reference to liability "in an indeterminate amount for an indeterminate time to an indeterminate class": *Ultramares Corp* v. *Touche* 255 N.Y. 170, 179; 174 N.E. 441, 450 (1931). It is referred to by Lord Bridge in *Caparo* v. *Dickman* [1990] 2 AC 605, 621 and in other cases too numerous to mention. Professor Stapleton has quite rightly cautioned against over-use of this argument as a substitute for serious thought: see (1991) 107 LQR 249, 254.

[32] *Spartan Steel* v. *Martin & Co (Contractors) Ltd* [1973] QB 27, 37 (Lord Denning MR). Similar reasoning, though sometimes with different results, appears in cases such as *Caltex Oil* v. *The Willemstad* (1976) 136 CLR 529 and *Canadian National Rly Co* v. *Norsk Pacific SS Co* (1992) 91 DLR (4th) 289.

been correctly criticised as meaning very little: indeed, at times it sounds frankly bizarre.[33] A statement that there was, or was not, an assumption of responsibility in a given case is about as informative as a determination that there is "proximity" between the parties.[34] On the other hand, no such difficulty arises if one accepts the idea that professional liability should depend on some manifested intent on the defendant's part to provide reassurance or protection to this particular plaintiff. Indeed, an intent of this sort is precisely the idea lying behind an "assumption of responsibility". It is a way of saying that, even though X may not have provided services under a contract with Y, he nevertheless provided them for the benefit of Y and in so doing vouched for their quality.

6. PROFESSIONAL LIABILITY: CONCRETE APPLICATIONS

The time has now come to apply theory to practice. I am not contending, of course, that the ideas just outlined explain all the authorities on duty of care, or even all the cases dealing with that subject in the context of professional negligence. That would be inconceivable. Rather, what I would like to suggest is that it helps to explain and simplify at least a number of the authorities that at present are puzzling or awkward, and that it provides a better guide than we now have to how the point should be approached in future. For reasons of space, I will concentrate on three classes of professionals: accountants, solicitors and valuers.

Take first accountants. We have known for thirty years and more that there is no doctrinal objection to making an accountant liable in tort for professional negligence to a foreseeable victim other than his direct client.[35] Nevertheless, in 1980 *Caparo plc* v. *Dickman*[36] made it clear that this liability was to be treated with care. It holds in effect that, if you hazard your money by buying into a company on the basis of its auditor's report, this is *prima facie* something you do at your own risk. Hence a predator failed to recover against auditors when all it could prove was that it had foreseeably relied on an ailing company's negligently-audited accounts in deciding to take it over. What matters, of course, is the emphasis in *Caparo* that foreseeability, even high foreseeability,

[33] For example, in *White* v. *Jones* we find Lord Nolan discussing, apparently with a straight face, whether drivers assume a responsibility to other road users like pedestrians. See [1995] 2 AC 207, 294.

[34] "I do not think that voluntary assumption of responsibility is a helpful or realistic test. . . . The phrase . . . can only have any real meaning if it is understood as referring the circumstances in which the law will deem the maker of the statement to have assumed responsibility. . . ." – Lord Griffiths *in Smith* v. *Eric S Bush* [1990] 1 AC 831, 862, quoted by Lord Roskill in *Caparo* ([1990] 2 AC 605, 628). See generally Barker (1993) 109 *LQR* 461, 462 ff, making much the same point.

[35] See *Hedley Byrne & Co Ltd* v. *Heller & Partners Ltd* [1964] AC 465, overruling the contrary decision in *Candler* v. *Crane Christmas* [1951] 2 QB 164. And see too *JEB Fasteners Ltd* v. *Marks Bloom* [1981] 3 All ER 289, [1983] 1 All ER 583.

[36] [1990] 2 AC 605.

was not enough to engender liability. Caparo's action in buying Fidelity was, after all, neither surprising or unusual: the accountants had known perfectly well that a takeover was on the cards, and indeed that Caparo was a front runner in the line of potential predators. Since that case, non-clients asserting tortious duties against accountants or auditors have faced an uphill task. True, some have succeeded, at least to the extent of avoiding a strike-out. But, in order to recover, they have all had to show some kind of more direct relationship: some "proximity", "assumption of responsibility", or what you will.[37]

Why, then, deny liability? The reason given was that there was no "proximity" between the parties; that there was a danger of open-ended or indeterminate liability;[38] and lastly, the legal and commercial context showed no intent by the auditors concerned to comfort future investors.[39]

It is submitted that this is a classic case of a right result reached for a wrong reason. As the House of Lords itself recognised, the ideas of proximity and assumption of responsibility which they chose to invoke operated more as verbal formulae than anything else.[40] Nor can the idea of indeterminate liability bear much weight. It could have been easily sidestepped by confining liability to a limited class (i.e. existing shareholders) – a solution which, indeed, the Court of Appeal had been happy to adopt.[41] And in any case the converse assumption lying behind it – that if liability had not been unmanageable that would have militated, at least *prima facie*, in favour of making the defendants pay – is itself tendentious. It is by no means clear, even given an ideal world and an impeccably circumscribed class of potential plaintiffs, that outsiders damnified by an accountant's negligence ought to be able to pass their losses on to him.

Nor can much more comfort be drawn from arguments based on the purpose of making the accounts available. If this refers to the purposes of the statute requiring proper company accounts, this latter gives no reliable indication of whether, and if so to whom, delinquent auditors should be liable.[42] If it means the purpose of the auditors in supplying them, this is equally problematical. Assuming this means purpose objectively determined,[43] in practice we are talking about "purpose" inferred from the foreseeable, or perhaps the very foreseeable use of the accounts by the plaintiff. But this in turn brings foreseeability in by the back door when it has just been ejected at the front.

[37] See for example, *JEB Fasteners Ltd* v. *Marks Bloom* [1981] 3 All ER 289, [1983] 1 All ER 583 and *Galoo* v. *Bright Grahame Murray* [1995] 1 All ER 16, dealt with below.

[38] For example, Lord Bridge (at [1990] 2 AC 607, 621).

[39] Lord Bridge, *ibid.* at pp. 622, 625; Lord Roskill at p. 629, Lord Oliver at pp. 631, 653; Lord Jauncey at p. 661.

[40] See Lord Roskill at p. 628; Lord Oliver at p. 639.

[41] See [1989] QB 653.

[42] And besides, given that the action is for negligence at common law and not breach of statutory duty, statutory meaning is of limited relevance anyway: see *X* v. *Bedfordshire CC* [1995] 2 AC 633, 731 ff.

[43] A mere subjective intention not to be liable clearly cannot exonerate anyone.

Much of the difficulty disappears, however, if one asks the slightly different question: "Who were the accountants in *Caparo* working for, and to whom can they be taken to have guaranteed their work?" Put the issue in those terms, and there can only be one sensible answer: it must have been Fidelity, the target company. It was that company which paid them, and to whom the accountants reported. It could not be Caparo: Caparo might have potentially stood to benefit from the auditors' services, but that was something different.[44] Seeing the matter from the other side and bringing it closer to the general argument advanced above, the real objection to Caparo's claim was that it was trying to use the auditors as free investment advisers: to take advantage of a guarantee of good service which it had not paid for and which had clearly not been intended to enure to its benefit. Put it shortly, Caparo were in the same position as the borrower of a BMW who misses a meeting because it breaks down and then seeks to sue the person who sold it to the owner. And they deserved as little sympathy.

Not only does this give an eminently plausible reason why investors and others in a similar position[45] cannot generally sue negligent accountants, it also goes some way towards explaining those cases where the plaintiff has succeeded.

One such class involves investors who can show that, although the accountants or auditors were employed and paid by the company whose finances they investigated, there were in addition negotiations or contacts with themselves directly. The early decision in *Candler* v. *Crane Christmas*[46] exemplifies this type of situation. A Cornish tin-miner needed extra capital. He not only commissioned accountants to prepare the necessary statements, but (significantly) told them to advertise in the financial press for likely investors, and deal with any takers. Candler took the bait, put £2,000 into the business and lost it. His complaint that he had been misled by the accounts failed in the Court of Appeal, but (it is now accepted) ought to have succeeded.[47] And this is hardly surprising. Although Denning LJ's dissent bases recovery on foreseeability, which is untenable since *Caparo*, a much more plausible point is that the accountants were working for, in the sense of providing their services directly to, Candler: he, after all, negotiated directly with them, and it was to him that they showed the accounts.[48] And a similar analysis goes, at least arguably, for a later series

[44] There is yet another way of putting it: the accountants may have intended to benefit Caparo, but clearly evinced no intention to create legal relations with it or to give it any enforceable rights. If England had abolished privity of contract, Caparo would indubitably have been incidental beneficiaries under their contract with Fidelity, not third parties intended to obtain a right to sue pursuant to it. Compare Lord Mustill, dissenting, in *White* v. *Jones* [1995] 2 AC 206, 290: undertaking responsibility means agreeing to accept it, not setting about a task which may give rise to a loss.

[45] Such as those who do not buy into the company but simply advance credit to it (see *Al Saudi Banque* v. *Clarke Pixley* [1989] 2 All ER 361). There is by parity of reasoning no reason why they should be allowed to use the auditors as a free credit reference agency.

[46] [1951] 2 KB 164.

[47] *Hedley Byrne* v. *Heller* [1964] AC 465; *Caparo* v. *Dickman* [1990] 2 AC 605.

[48] A point made in connection with *Candler* by Lord Jauncey in *Smith* v. *Eric S Bush*: see [1990] 1 AC 831, 870.

of takeover cases where the accounts have been sent directly to the would-be predator and the accountants have been involved, to a greater or lesser extent, in subsequent discussions. Examples include *JEB* v. *Marks Bloom*,[49] and the later decision *in Galoo* v. *Bright Grahame Murray*.[50] In such a situation the accountant is rightly held liable, at least presumptively. Of course even here he may do something to negative liability (for example, he may explicitly state that he cannot vouch for the information he is providing):[51] but that does not alter the general proposition.

Secondly, there are those cases where although an accountant is paid by the organisation whose records he audits, he is really acting entirely – or almost entirely – in someone else's interest. Take, for example, the Privy Council's decision in *Deloitte Haskins & Sells* v. *National Mutual Life*.[52] The auditors to a licensed New Zealand deposit-taker allegedly failed to spot financial weaknesses while doing the statutory audit which that institution was required by law to have conducted for its depositors' information. Despite a superficial similarity to *Caparo*, in that these depositors too had hazarded their money on a speculation in reliance on a statutory auditors' report, it is difficult to fault the Privy Council's view that they were at least potentially owed a duty of care.[53] Given that the accountants' services were provided at all, they were explicable only on the basis that the defendants had provided them for the plaintiffs' behoof, and there was nothing peculiar in regarding the plaintiffs as the beneficiaries of a guarantee of good service.

Thirdly, the connection between the claimant and the person paying the accountant may be so close that the former can plausibly be regarded as standing in the latter's shoes. A couple of recent cases illustrate the idea nicely. In *BCCI* v. *Price Waterhouse (No 2)*[54] the auditors to a subsidiary company in the ill-fated BCCI group had allegedly failed to spot alarming irregularities in its accounts which might have indicated something seriously amiss in the group as a whole. They were sued by the holding company, which argued that had the problem been nipped in the bud its own losses attributable to the group collapse would have been much less. The Court of Appeal declined to strike out, despite the accountants' plea (which was admittedly quite true) that they had been employed by the subsidiary and not the holding company. In general, indeed, such a plea will succeed.[55] The reason why it failed here was that unlike

[49] [1983] 1 All ER 289. The action failed on causation grounds, but a duty of care was held to have existed.

[50] [1995] 1 All ER 16. A company was to be sold for a multiple of its earnings as declared by its auditors: the auditors prepared the accounts and provided them directly to the buyers. The Court of Appeal had little difficulty in allowing the action to proceed.

[51] As happened in *Peach Publishing* v. *Slater* [1998] PNLR 364.

[52] [1993] AC 774.

[53] Or rather, would have but for the terms of a (New Zealand) protective statute.

[54] [1998] PNLR 564.

[55] See *Prudential Assurance Co* v. *Newman Industries* [1982] Ch 204, 222; *Barings plc* v. *Coopers & Lybrand (A Firm)* [1997] PNLR 179, 186.

the run-of-the-mill conglomerate, BCCI had been run and robbed entirely as one unit, and audited on a largely similar basis. Hence (using the argument above) it was not implausible to regard the auditors as having provided their services to the members of the group as a whole. A similar case except that it involved advice rather than auditing, is *Coulthard* v. *Neville Russell*.[56] A company's accountants advised on a financing deal which in fact involved the making of illegal loans to the directors. The scheme fell apart, the company collapsed and in the resulting fall-out its directors found themselves disqualified. The Court of Appeal refused to strike out their claims against the accountants for negligence. The ostensible reason was that the law on accountants' liability was so much in flux that no-one had any clear idea what it was, and hence a strike-out would be wrong. This was on any account a pretty desperate argument; on the other hand, the result is eminently defensible. It is hardly implausible that where accountants advise a smallish private company entirely controlled by its shareholders and directors, they should be regarded as working for the latter as well as the former: if so, then the result reached by the Court of Appeal seems eminently sensible.

So much for the accountants It is true that they are the category of professional which fits most neatly into the scheme mooted in this chapter. There is, however, a simple reason for this. The issues affecting whether accountants ought to be liable for providing bad advice or service are, on the whole, straightforwardly commercial. With other professions there are distractions. Solicitors owe duties to the court or society as a whole,[57] and this may cause them to face liabilities to unconnected third parties even where strictly commercial reasoning might indicate otherwise. Similarly with surveyors. Notably, for example, consumer protection issues have at times come to the fore, such as the perceived desirability of giving middle-class homeowners protection against substandard housing (witness *Smith* v. *Eric S Bush*,[58] discussed below). Nevertheless, subject to that caveat, it is perfectly possible to find equally instructive examples from other professions.

Take, first, solicitors. Laying aside *White* v. *Jones*,[59] admittedly problematical, it is not difficult to find results bearing out the thesis advanced here. Solicitors, for example, do not generally owe duties to their opponents in contentious business.[60] Where, exceptionally, they have been held to do so it has been on the basis of their duty to the court, rather than any failure to provide proper service to an individual: see, for example, the statutory "wasted costs" jurisdiction,[61]

[56] [1998] PNLR 267.

[57] Most graphically illustrated by the wasted costs jurisdiction under s.51 of the Supreme Court Act 1981.

[58] [1990] 1 AC 831.

[59] [1995] 2 AC 207.

[60] *Business Computers International* v. *Registrar of Companies* [1988] Ch 229; *cf. NZ Social Credit League* v. *O'Brien* [1984] 1 NZLR 84; *Connolly-Martin* v. *Davis* [1999] PNLR 826 (a barrister's case, but similar principles apply).

[61] Supreme Court Act 1981, s.51. Jackson & Powell, *Professional Negligence*, 4th ed., §§ 4–102 ff.

and at common law the cases where they have been held liable for negligently allowing undertakings given to the court to be set at nought.[62] Nor, as a rule, are they under any duty *vis-à-vis* third parties whose interests are incidentally affected by the way they serve their clients.[63] A solicitor advising his client how to make an enforceable promise of a gift owes no duty to the donee if he so bungles it that the promise is unenforceable by him.[64] Again, where a solicitor helps a client dispose of property forgetting that it has already been willed to a legatee, that is (as one might expect) simply the legatee's bad luck.[65] True, in these cases the ostensible reason for denying a duty of care in such cases was lack of proximity:[66] but a far simpler point is that the solicitor had in no sense been working for, or giving any assurance to, the claimant. My solicitor works for me: he is not employed to keep a watching brief on behalf of the objects of my largesse. By contrast, cases where third parties have succeeded have tended to be where there is, or appears to be, some direct contact between the two. This no doubt explains why a solicitor instructed to act for husband and wife owes a duty to the latter to make sure that her instructions are actually genuine;[67] and why it now seems not unlikely that solicitors answering enquiries before contract owe a duty to the purchaser who relies on them.[68]

White v. *Jones*[69] is admittedly awkward. It obliges solicitors who fail to do a proper will-drawing job for a client to compensate the would-be legatees; and it does this even though the latter have neither employed them nor paid them anything, in all likelihood have had no previous contacts or dealings with them, and for good measure are claiming in respect of legacies to which they had no vested right anyway as against the testator. To say that in such a case the solicitors are working for the legatees or should be regarded as having given them some kind of guarantee of proper service is far-fetched.

On the other hand, there is one very significant point about *White* v. *Jones*: the majority who decided it realised that the case was highly peculiar and

[62] Notably *Al-Kandari* v. *J.R. Brown* [1988] QB 665 (solicitor holding passport as stakeholder negligently releases it to client who uses it to abduct child). And see too *Welsh* v. *Chief Constable of Merseyside* [1995] 1 All ER 833 (as explained in *Elguzouli-Daf* v. *Comm'r of Police* [1995] QB 335, 348 ff).

[63] ". . . the general rule today is that, subject to his duties to the court and the professional duties imposed on his profession, a solicitor when acting for his client owes no duty to third parties." (Lord Goff in *White* v. *Jones* [1995] 2 AC 207, 259).

[64] *Hemmens* v. *Wilson Browne* [1993] 4 All ER 826. See too *Cancer Research Campaign* v. *Ernest Brown* [1998] PNLR 592.

[65] *Clark* v. *Bruce Lance & Co* [1988] 1 All ER 364.

[66] See *Clark* at [1988] 1 All ER 364, 369; *Hemmens* at [1993] 4 All ER 826, 837.

[67] *Penn* v. *Bristol & West BS*, *The Times*, 2 May 1995. Strictly speaking, of course, this involved a solicitor who had pointedly *not* been instructed by the plaintiff. However, it hardly lay in his mouth to say this when he himself had proceeded all along on the basis that he had been.

[68] *Contra*, admittedly, *Gran Gelato Ltd* v. *Richcliff (Group) Ltd* [1992] Ch 560. But this decision has since met telling scepticism in England (*First National Commercial Bank* v. *Loxleys* [1997] PNLR 211) and downright rejection in the Irish Supreme Court (see *Doran* v. *Delaney* [1998] 2 ILRM 1), and is now of doubtful authority.

[69] [1995] 2 AC 207.

demanded a special solution. They also accepted that their decision was difficult to justify on the basis of the previous authority. They concurred in the result only because of their intuition (an intuition that some might regard as specious)[70] that the solicitors had been negligent and ought not to be allowed to escape scot free.[71] Moreover, it is also worth noting that the decision remains in fairly narrow compass. It does not apply, for example, where donors' solicitors have bungled arrangements for *inter vivos* gifts.[72] Ostensibly this is because a live donor, unlike a dead one, can put things right if and when he finds out what has happened.[73] But since on the facts this is hardly ever on the cards (otherwise, indeed, the matter would never have come to litigation) a far more convincing explanation is a feeling that the plaintiff simply does not deserve any intervention on his behalf; and in the absence of any compelling reason to make an exception the loss should be allowed to lie where it falls.

The third topic, the question of surveyors' liability to third parties, has arisen less often. As with solicitors and *White* v. *Jones*,[74] there is one difficult decision, *Smith* v. *Eric S. Bush*,[75] where, it will be remembered, surveyors appraising a house on behalf of prospective mortgagees were held liable to the purchasers when they failed to notice serious defects, even though the purchasers had not employed them and indeed their terms of engagement had made it clear that their duty was limited to the lenders. On the other hand, it is difficult to deny that consumer protection issues loomed large there[76] (and, furthermore, it must be remembered that a great deal of the argument was about the application of the Unfair Contract Terms Act 1977, which is of limited relevance here). Elsewhere, by contrast, it is suggested that the above suggestion holds good: surveyors are not generally held liable to those who did not in fact employ them. Thus, those valuing commercial property for mortgagees owe no duty to other participants in the same loan,[77] or to assignees buying out the lender's rights.[78] A surveyor employed by the lessor to make sure the terms of a building lease are complied with cannot be made liable to a mortgagee who foreseeably relies

[70] And one which has, incidentally, been ignored with equanimity elsewhere. Exactly the same point – that the incompetent should not be allowed to escape scot-free – applies to the accountants' cases such as *Caparo* v. *Dickman*: yet it hardly seems to have worried their Lordships.

[71] See [1995] 2 AC 207, 259, 268 (Lord Goff), 275–6 (Lord Browne-Wilkinson).

[72] *Hemmens* v. *Wilson Browne* [1993] 4 All ER 826, referred to above: *cf. White* v. *Jones* [1995] 2 AC 207, 256 (Lord Goff) ("... a solicitor advising a client about a proposed dealing with his property in his lifetime owes no duty of care to a prospective beneficiary ...").

[73] See *Hemmens* v. *Wilson Browne* [1993] 4 All ER 826, 838.

[74] [1995] 2 AC 207.

[75] [1990] 1 AC 831. *Yianni* v. *Edwin Evans* [1982] QB 438 is to similar effect: but as Smith was effectively an appeal against the correctness of that case it need not be dealt with separately.

[76] "Consumers who have need of manufactured articles and services are not in a position to bargain" – Lord Templeman at [1990] 1 AC 831, 846–7. See too p. 865, where Lord Griffiths regarded the fact that the house was a modest one as important to the existence of a duty of care as against the purchaser.

[77] *Omega Trust* v. *Wright, Son & Pepper* [1997] PNLR 424.

[78] *Barex Brokers* v. *Morris* [1999] PNLR 344.

on his advice;[79] and those surveying property for defects on behalf of the owner owe no duty to a purchaser, even though it might be foreseeable that any report might be shown to him.[80]

The exceptions are equally explicable. Most of them involve situations broadly analogous to those where accountants have faced liability to non-clients. Thus, surveyors paid by mortgagors but reporting direct to lenders have long been held to owe the latter a duty.[81] Again, there are situations where the person engaging the services of the surveyor is so closely connected with the eventual plaintiff that it would be unrealistic not to regard the surveyor as having worked for the latter. Thus, where an owner of property who wants to borrow money against it engages a surveyor and makes it clear to him that his report is as much for the benefit of the lender as himself, the surveyor will readily be held to owe a duty to the lender.[82]

7. CONCLUSIONS

This essay has only scratched the surface of what I see as a vital division of function within the law of negligence. On one side there is tortious negligence as protection against outside interference with one's vital social interests – life, limb, property (sometimes) and money (very occasionally).[83] On the other we see – or should see – negligence being used as a form of extra-contractual quality assurance: a guarantee, more or less freely given, that a given service is of satisfactory quality and may be relied on with the prospect of legal redress if it fails to come up to scratch. The difficulty with treatments of the duty of care hitherto, both academic and decisional, has been precisely that they have failed to draw this distinction properly. It has simply assumed that a single essay on the duty of care can cover everything under some such rubric as "liability for pure economic loss". It can't: and if this essay has managed to demonstrate this and set lawyers thinking on the right lines it will not have been entirely in vain.

[79] *Le Lievre* v. *Gould* [1893] 1 QB 491 (accepted as correct in *Hedley Byrne* v. *Heller* [1964] AC 465, despite over-wide dicta re impossibility of liability in tort for negligent misrepresentation).

[80] *Machin* v. *Adams* (1997) 84 Build. LR 79 (the survey there was done by an architect, but the principle must be the same). The marine survey case of *The Morning Watch* [1990] 1 Lloyds Rep 547, referred to at the beginning of this chapter, is to the same effect (however foreseeable it may be that a classification survey may be relied on by a potential purchaser, the latter cannot sue).

[81] See *Cann* v. *Wilson* (1888) 39 Ch.D 39 (valuation): *Western Trust* v. *Strutt & Parker* [1999] PNLR 154.

[82] See *Singer & Friedlander* v. *John D. Wood* (1977) 243 EG 212 (admitted); *Corisand Investments* v. *Druce & Co* (1978) 248 EG 315.

[83] *Ministry of Housing* v. *Sharp* [1970] 2 QB 223.

18

Fairness in Tax Law

ROBERT MITCHELL

1. FAIRNESS AS A VALUE

> *"Fair . . . Of conduct, actions, arguments, methods: . . . equitable, legitimate . . ."*[1]

This essay explores the resonance of a word – "fair" – in the context of the United Kingdom tax system. Few dispute that the tax system should be as fair as possible.[2] At the same time, many recognise a tension between that objective and others, including most topically those of simplicity, comprehensibility and certainty. Indeed, that very tension may be found within the concept of fairness itself whose many meanings[3] include not only equal treatment (more properly, perhaps, appropriate recognition of similarities and differences) and clarity,[4] but also a sense of imprecision or approximation.[5]

Two major aspects of fairness must be left for debate by others. First, there is what might be called the "substantive fairness" of the particular tax burdens borne by different taxpayers. While lawyers cannot ignore this type of fairness, politicians and economists probably have more to say about it. Secondly, there is "administrative fairness", covering procedures for assessment, investigation and appeal. This is very much lawyers' (and accountants') territory and debate

[1] *Oxford English Dictionary*, 2nd ed., (Oxford, Clarendon Press, 1989) ("OED"), definition 10 a.

[2] The theme of fairness in taxation was taken up by the Chancellor of the Exchequer in presenting his March 1999 budget as one for "enterprise and fairness"; very little content was given to the term "fairness" however, and cynics may see it as implying nothing more than minimal constraints on the workings of the free market. The Finance Bill debates were notable for acrimonious allegations as to the misleading nature of some of the budget announcements: this was not a "budget for fairness" in the sense that citizens (or Members of Parliament) could easily see "what was going on", as to which see section 3 below.

[3] The OED definition of fair runs to some seven closely typed columns.

[4] *Cf.* Lord Oliver, "Judicial Approaches to Revenue Law" in Gammie (ed.), *Striking the Balance* (London, The Institute for Fiscal Studies, 1996), p. 174: "Elementary fairness dictates that if rules are to be imposed in an area in which there is no universal moral imperative to aid understanding, they shall be clear and unequivocal . . ."

[5] A similar contradiction between precision and approximation may be inherent in the terms "reasonable" and "equitable".

about the fairness of Inland Revenue procedures is highly topical; however, space does not permit consideration of those debates here.

Instead, this essay looks at the tax system as a set of rules for the determination of tax liabilities. The multifarious meanings of "fairness" in this context are explored in connection with various current developments, and an argument is developed in favour not only of recognising but also of analysing and understanding the inevitability of an appropriate degree of imprecision at various points within the machinery of taxation. Finally, a view is reached as to whether it is helpful to regard fairness as a "fundamental value" in the context of tax law.

2. IS TAX LAW SPECIAL? – WORDS AND NUMBERS

> *"Fair . . . Unquestionable, absolute, complete, thorough . . . 'A fair nark' or, more emphatically, 'a fair cow' is anything inexpressibly tedious or baffling".*[6]

The professional press is full of complaints about particular instances of "unfairness" in tax legislation and in the conduct of the Revenue authorities. On the other hand, it is often said that there is little room for any concept of fairness, equity or morality elsewhere in the tax system particularly with regard to the interpretation of tax legislation and the conduct expected of taxpayers.[7] Such attitudes may be due to a number of factors, none of which is unique to tax law but which collectively have a special impact on the way tax law, as a system of rules, works.

Of those factors, four are worth mentioning at the outset. First, there is the near universal dislike of paying taxes. Taxation is regarded by many as being at best an evil necessity, and very few would see it as part of a citizen's duty to go any further than bare compliance with legal obligations.[8] Partly this is due to the politics of individualism which sees state activity as something to be restricted rather than willingly supported. But even among those who accept the need for state funding, taxation may be objectionable because the process of tax collection is experienced as an intrusion. Interestingly, the most vociferous opposition to the introduction of income tax two hundred years ago was

[6] OED, definition 11 c.

[7] For classic quotations, see *Ayrshire Pullman Motor Services* v. *IRC* [1929] 14 TC 754 at p. 763: "No man in this country is under the smallest obligation, moral or other, so to arrange his legal relations to his business or to his property as to enable the Inland Revenue to put the largest possible shovel into his stores". (Lord Clyde); and *Ensign Tankers (Leasing) Ltd* v. *Stokes* [1992] 1 AC 655 at p. 668B: "There is no morality in a tax and no illegality or immorality in a tax avoidance scheme". (Lord Templeman).

[8] *Cf.* the suggestion of Neville Chamberlain in 1932 (cited by Roger White, "The Practitioner's Perspective" in Gammie (ed.), *Striking the Balance* (London, The Institute for Fiscal Studies, 1996), at p. 59) that it was the duty of the taxpayer to pay his tax and to pay it as early as he can: quaint to the point of laughability now, but apparently not so at the time.

grounded (ostensibly, at least) not so much in reluctance to pay as in the perceived invasion of privacy. Such opposition was responsible for some of the archaic features which persist in the present system, including the schedular basis of income tax. Concerns about privacy are replaced today, perhaps, by the sheer burden of compliance, exacerbated for many by the system of self-assessment for income tax introduced in 1996.[9]

A second feature of tax law is its arbitrariness and changeability. To a greater or lesser extent, tax law necessarily makes distinctions (e.g. between income and capital) which are neither physically nor morally obvious.[10] Tax law may thus be seen by many as lacking not only moral legitimacy but also internal moral coherence. No wonder, therefore, that there seem to be no "fundamental principles" of tax law to aid interpretation or ensure continuity.[11]

A third special feature of tax law is that its principal function is not to guide behaviour but to arrive at a precise monetary conclusion in every case. It is true that a function of taxation in some cases may be to influence behaviour (for instance, by encouraging investment or discouraging smoking).[12] But the logical focus of a tax charging rule, and the outcome which, as an algorithm, it is designed to produce, is not the underlying behaviour but the ascertainment and payment of an amount of tax. It is also true that many other legal rules could be regarded as producing precise monetary outcomes in the sense that the rules, if litigated to final judgment, will result in an order for the payment of a precise amount of money (debt, damages or fine). However, it would obviously be a distortion to regard the production of such orders as the main purpose or logical focus of the rules.

For present purposes, the process of translating "real life" into a precise monetary conclusion may be divided into three broad stages – those of classification, valuation and computation. These categories are not philosophically absolute or comprehensive, nor will they necessarily be applied consecutively or distinctly in any particular case.[13]

[9] *Cf.* Atkinson in *The Guardian*, 6 April 1999: "[T]he biggest complaint from business and tax professionals is not how much tax has to be paid – the tax burden in the UK is lower than in the rest of the EU – but the complexity of the system . . . In a self-assessment era, [Richard Mannion, vice-president of the Chartered Institute of Taxation] said, it was becoming increasingly difficult for taxpayers to work out their bills accurately. 'The system is unfair to the point of dishonesty', he said. 'Nobody can be expected to get their tax return 100 per cent right and if you get it wrong it's either negligence or fraud. If the Inland Revenue get it wrong, it's human error' ".

[10] This point is entertainingly developed by Prebble, "Why Is Tax Law Incomprehensible?" [1994] *British Tax Review* 380.

[11] On the lack of "fundamental principles", see the discussion in *Taxation*, 18/25 December 1997, pp. 313–15; on changeability of tax law, see, e.g., Oerton, "Is Tax Law Tolerable?" (1990) 134 *Sol. Jo*. 178.

[12] For difficulties associated with such projects, see Ogus, "Nudging and Rectifying: the Use of Fiscal Instruments for Regulatory Purposes" (1999) 19 *Legal Studies* 245.

[13] This analysis of the application of rules may be said to overlook other important stages, including perhaps proof of the underlying facts and establishment of what the rule to be applied *is* (as distinct from what it *means*). These stages do not, however, raise particular problems for tax law.

"Classification" may be regarded as the process of determining that a situation has arisen to which a particular operation should be applied – e.g. that a transaction is such that tax of a certain kind should be charged. This is a linguistic exercise requiring the interpretation both of facts and of the wording of the relevant rule. Because of the fluid and fractal nature of words, the process will always involve a degree of discretion. Two problems in tax law are, first, the lack of moral principle to guide the exercise of such discretion, as noted above, and, second, the insistence that such discretion should be exercised only by Parliament, i.e. at the rule-writing stage of the process and not at the application stage. These difficulties are explored further below.

"Valuation" is the process by which a monetary value is attributed to facts which have been classified as relevant. Although the principles of valuation may be highly contentious, the fact that the process involves a degree of negotiation and estimation is not controversial. It is noteworthy that uncertainty and approximation are accepted here while, in tax law, being regarded as highly unacceptable at the classification stage. Perhaps this is because the necessary discretion can often be guided by the same principles as apply in non-tax contexts.

"Computation" is the process of carrying out the operation required by the rule. The need for finely differentiated monetary outcomes means that the operation required by the rule is often both linguistically and numerically complex. Furthermore, the nature of tax law is such that resolution of those complexities cannot be delegated to non-lawyer experts at the valuation stage as it might be in other areas of law. This, then, is a fourth special feature of tax law, namely that some facility with numbers is required to make sense of many of the rules. For this reason, tax law is both unattractive and incompletely comprehensible to most lawyers (and politicians).

3. LAW AND POLITICS

"Fair . . . Of external manifestations, words, promises: Attractive or pleasing at the first sight or hearing; specious, plausible, flattering".[14]

The design of a tax system is subject to political and economic considerations which are beyond the specialist remit of a lawyer. In particular, arguments about fairness play a large part in any debate about how the burden of tax should be distributed. Such arguments about "substantive fairness" are not examined in detail here except insofar as most people would accept that, to be "fair", a tax system must have some sensitivity to the citizen's ability to pay.[15] At its

[14] OED, definition 5 a.

[15] For fuller discussion of the fairness of tax burdens, see James and Nobes, *The Economics of Taxation*, (Harlow, England, Financial Times, Prentice Hall, 2000), ch. 5 and materials there cited.

minimum, this requires that a citizen should not be required to pay so much tax that he has insufficient left to live on. Some method, more or less refined, of measuring ability to pay is therefore needed.

However, the measurement of ability to pay will inevitably be complex and contentious, and is likely to complicate the tax system by introducing a need for various reliefs whose conceptual structure will not necessarily fit neatly with the basic structure of the tax. One response to the ensuing complexity is to suggest that reliefs be replaced by some kind of direct subsidy (perhaps in the form of a means tested benefit). There are various reasons, however, why this is unlikely to be satisfactory. Leaving aside issues of efficiency, there is an argument of principle which objects to the differential treatment of what are perceived as "tax" rules as compared with "welfare" rules.[16] If, to be fair, tax needs to be sensitive to ability to pay, then that sensitivity needs to be embedded in the structure of the tax and not hived off in a separate system to which different canons of construction may apply.

Whether or not the foregoing argument is accepted as philosophically sound, it may well be true as political fact that a tax will not be *perceived* to be fair unless it can be seen that the particular tax itself acknowledges ability to pay to at least a minimum extent.[17] The distinction between "actual" fairness and perceived fairness is important. Whatever debate there may be as to how actual fairness should be measured, the politically important fact is how a tax is popularly perceived. Popular perception is likely to be based on crude outlines fed to the public by politicians via spin doctors and headline writers. Consequently, there is huge emphasis on those aspects of a tax which are easy to see, such as the basic rate of income tax whose rising or falling may bear little direct relation to the overall burden of tax. Complicated tax rates at least have the merit that the public are not misled into thinking they understand them.

At a political level, fairness may thus be seen to comprise two limbs. The first concerns substantive fairness. The second requires that the tax system be sufficiently transparent for citizens to judge, at least in broad outline, how far their own conception of substantive fairness is satisfied.[18] Political fairness in this second sense might be advanced in a number of ways. There are issues here about education and journalism, and more generally about whom we should trust to interpret government policy for us. There is a role for ground-rules as to how the overall tax burden, for example, should be measured so that proper comparisons can be made between one period and another. Simplification of tax policy would also help. As to the latter, however, it should be noted not only

[16] For wide-ranging discussion of differential responses to tax law and welfare law, see Cook, *Rich Law, Poor Law* (Milton Keynes, Open University Press, 1989). There are, indeed, strong arguments in favour of further amalgamation, not separation, of the tax and benefits systems.

[17] Or, more precisely, the tax can be expected to be perceived as unfair if it seems clear that it does not so reflect ability to pay. The experience of the community charge, introduced in 1990 and abandoned after great popular protest in 1993, perhaps illustrates this.

[18] See generally Tiley, "Away from a Virtuous Tax System?" (1998) *British Tax Review* 317.

that substantive fairness is likely to work against simplification, but also that the simplification which might help citizens to assess substantive fairness – to see, generally, "what is going on" – is not necessarily the same as that which might facilitate the computation of their own tax liabilities.

4. ELEGANCE AND SIMPLICITY

> *"Fair . . . Beautiful to the eye; of pleasing form or appearance; good-looking . . . Of language, diction: Elegant . . . Of a line, curve, or surface: free from roughness or irregularities; smooth, even".*[19]

Few would place great importance on making a system of rules "elegant", or "beautiful to the eye", as an end in itself. More might be persuaded, however, that rules are better to the extent that it is easier for the eye to find its way around them (in various metaphorical senses). A distinction must be drawn between simplicity and comprehensibility. While the distinction is not philosophically absolute, simplicity may be taken to refer to system design while comprehensibility refers to the manner in which the system's rules are expressed.[20] For present purposes, "simpler" will be taken to mean less complicated, capable of expression in fewer rules, or in rules with fewer exceptions. A simpler system will be better to the extent (if any) that its increased simplicity makes it easier to use – that is, easier to understand, easier to apply, easier to change.

Why is tax law so complicated? Three complicating factors have already been noted: the confusion of legislative objectives, the demands of substantive fairness and the difficulty of translating "real life" into numbers. In addition, the demand for precision requires more and more exceptions to basic rules to be made in order to acknowledge significant differences of circumstance and to avoid abuse of the grey area on the fringes of words. Unless the demand for precision can be acceptably moderated, this will always remain a complicating factor for tax law.

The factors mentioned in the previous paragraph might perhaps be regarded as impinging at the "classification" stage of the process. A different type of complication arises at the "computation" stage as a result of the need for mathematical processes to be expressed in terms which are comprehensible to, or at least usable by, non-mathematicians.[21]

A major cause of complication at this stage is the desire to impose progressive rates of taxation whereby the rate of tax varies in some relation to the

[19] OED, definitions 1, 4, and 8 e.

[20] As to the latter, see section 5 below.

[21] Including legislators, tax officials, tax professionals and taxpayers (not to mention judges).

amount on which tax is being charged. The complication is compounded when the "amount on which tax is being charged" is itself composed of a number of elements (e.g. earned income and investment income) with different rates applicable to each element. Traditionally, progressive rates of tax have been imposed in steps, or "bands", which enables the rate of tax chargeable on any given taxable amount to be fairly easily visualised and computed. However, such banding necessitates rather clumsy procedures when it comes to operations such as "grossing up" (whereby one works backwards from a given net amount to calculate the gross sum which, after deduction of tax at the prescribed rate, would leave the net amount). This problem is perhaps most graphically illustrated by the lengthy rate tables and grossing tables published in connection with pre-1988 rates of inheritance tax and capital transfer tax,[22] and the tortuous drafting of Inheritance Tax Act 1984, s 38.[23]

It would not require advanced mathematics to express a smoothly progressive rate of tax in a single mathematical formula occupying the equivalent of two or three lines of text.[24] Such formulae avoid the inconsistencies and ambiguities to which verbally dictated procedures are prone; they can easily be manipulated (without the need for express statutory direction) to deal with grossing up and related matters; and they can very easily be amended to change the rate of tax in various ways.

Why, then, are such formulae not more commonly used? One reason may be historical, in that when electronic calculators were less readily available than they are now, all but the crudest formulae would have required tiresomely lengthy sums to be done. While that reason may no longer be valid, a second reason has as much force as ever, namely most people's inability to deal with algebra, either in terms of applying it or of being able to see "what is going on". What is simple to the mathematician is the very opposite to everyone else.

5. COMPREHENSIBILITY

"Fair . . . Open to view, plainly to be seen, clear, distinct".[25]

The Tax Law Rewrite project was launched in 1996 with a view to rewriting "most of the UK's primary direct tax legislation in order to make it clearer and

[22] See for example, Greenfield and Barton, *Dymond's Capital Taxes* (London, Sweet & Maxwell, 1999), Vol. 3, Part 8.

[23] Which prescribes at length a rough and ready iterative method for solving some of the problems which banded rates cause: see Mitchell, "The Avoidance of Algebra: Why *Re Benham* Is Wrong" (1995) *British Tax Review* 602.

[24] Banded rates can also be expressed in mathematical formulae, thus achieving brevity but probably without the other benefits of genuine simplification. *Cf.* Casen and Steiner, "Mathematical Functions and Legal Drafting" (1986) 102 *Law Quarterly Review* 585.

[25] OED, definition 17.

easier to use. The main aim of the project is not to simplify the current tax system, but to restructure and rewrite the existing legislation without changing its general effect".[26] Much has been written about the feasibility of the project.[27] The most pertinent issue here concerns its motivation: to whom is tax law to be made more comprehensible and why?

It seems highly likely that the Government's motive for tax simplification was connected with the move towards self assessment.[28] If the object of the latter was to transfer the burden of computing individual tax liabilities from government agencies onto taxpayers and their advisers, then it no doubt followed that tax law should be made (or made to appear) more accessible to such people. The prime motivation for tax simplification thus seems to be to make the rules easier for tax professionals to use, and perhaps even for taxpayers themselves to apply.

What is really going on? An interesting way of viewing the matter is to suggest that, in the period before self-assessment, tax legislation was in fact addressed primarily to tax officials who had the responsibility and the privilege of interpreting it, the role of tax professionals being to keep watch on official interpretations and transmit them to taxpayers. By contrast, we might now begin to understand the legislation as being addressed to taxpayers in theory, but to tax advisers in fact, with the tax agencies now having more of the supervisory role.

Such analysis is highly theoretical, but it does draw attention to some important questions about the purpose of tax simplification. It also casts light on another issue, namely the role of information technology. In the not too distant future, it is likely that the whole of the "computation" stage will be hidden behind a user-friendly screen. For the purpose of calculating actual or hypothetical tax liabilities, it will not be necessary for anyone to understand the computation process at all; taxpayers and their advisers will simply need to put the right numbers in the right boxes: a computer will do the rest. A comprehensive system of this kind would require a huge number of boxes, and that in itself would prevent the system being user-friendly unless the boxes were organised

[26] See www.inlandrevenue.gov.uk/rewrite.

[27] See in particular, Jones, "Tax Law: Rules or Principles" (1996) *British Tax Review* 580; James and Wallschutzky, "Tax Law Improvement in Australia and the UK: the Need for a Strategy for Simplification" (1997) 18 *Fiscal Studies* 445; and Williams, "Solving Problems with Words" (1998) *British Tax Review* 14. The article by Jones is relevant to several of the issues discussed in this paper. However, it is submitted that he overemphasises the courts as the primary audience for tax legislation. His suggestion that Value Added Tax illustrates the possibilities for "general principles drafting" is interesting, but it should be noted (a) that VAT is, by comparison with income tax and capital gains tax, a fairly simple tax (at the systemic level, anyway, even if it gives rise to some fine and, to the layman, extraordinary distinctions at the classification stage) and (b) that the general principle of economic neutrality which is said to inform the interpretation of VAT legislation is possibly undesirable in other contexts, and may be found to delegate undue authority to economists!

[28] For a general discussion of the implications of self-assessment, see James and Nobes, *The Economics of Taxation* (Harlow, England, Financial Times, Prentice Hall, 2000), pp. 199–203.

in a highly sophisticated hierarchy. As with the computation process itself, it would not be necessary for users to have the slightest understanding of the hierarchy in order to use the system. Thus the "computation" stage and large parts of the "classification" stage would be hidden from view, and the system's user-friendliness would depend on that very hiddenness.[29]

Who should be in charge of any such system? In one scenario, the Government continues to legislate in the traditional manner, with tax agencies and tax professionals designing their own, possibly competing, systems to calculate liabilities efficiently. An intermediate position might have the tax agencies becoming responsible for the production of a publicly available system, leaving it to professionals and commentators to judge whether the system properly implements the legislation. At the extreme, the Government legislates directly for the system, so that debate about the effect of the system becomes the responsibility of Parliament itself.

It is not suggested that this kind of comprehensive computerisation is an imminent prospect. However, two things do seem clear. First, the Tax Law Rewrite project risks being wasted effort unless it takes proper account of the implications of computerisation. Second, computerisation, if only by way of analogy, shows how, far from being synonymous, user-friendliness and openness may in fact be contradictory objectives: the constitutional and practical implications of this need close attention.

6. FAIR PLAY AND FAIR GAME – STATUTORY CONSTRUCTION AND ANTI-AVOIDANCE

"Fair . . . Equitable; not taking undue advantage; disposed to concede every reasonable claim . . . Of objects: That may be legitimately aimed at; often in fair game".[30]

"Fair play: upright conduct in a game".[31]

Another recent Government project has been the attempt to develop a statutory "general anti-avoidance rule". The main object of such a rule seems to be to give legislative legitimacy to the courts' jurisdiction to impose tax according to the "real" effect of a transaction rather than its avoidance-led form.[32] The

[29] No doubt many aspects of the "valuation" stage could be similarly computerised, although the need for a bank of comparable values raises additional issues.

[30] OED, definition 10 a.

[31] OED, "fair" definition 10 c.

[32] See for example, Lord Oliver, "Judicial Approaches to Revenue Law" in Gammie (ed.), *Striking the Balance* (London, The Institute for Fiscal Studies, 1996), p. 173; Arnold, "Responses to Tax Avoidance", *ibid*, 201; and Appleton, "The Interaction between Paragraph 13 and *McGuckian*: A Descent into the Maelström" (1999) *British Tax Review* 86.

project has, however, been adjourned generally, largely because of the prohibitive cost to the Government of providing for pre-transaction rulings which would have been a necessary (if not sufficient) step towards securing acceptance of the rule.[33]

The mischief at which such a rule would be directed is obvious but difficult to define. At its heart, it seems, is the unfair gamesmanship of those whose dealings are within the spirit of a tax charge but who are able to structure the dealing so as to fall outside the letter of the law. This may be objectionable on grounds of morals, economics or disincentive effect on other taxpayers.

Closely connected with the mischief of tax avoidance is the more general problem of the courts' traditionally strict approach to the construction of tax legislation, resulting in what has been called "tax rule madness".[34] This syndrome is exacerbated by technological developments. As computerisation engulfs more and more of life, we may become more and more inclined to expect that life is naturally divided into the neat boxes which computers require, and thus to demand that laws should have similarly neat and incontestable boundaries. We then find that the proliferation of laws to which this gives rise does not in fact reduce the scope for dispute and uncertainty, but merely the level of detail at which they arise.

Two main arguments are made against relaxation of the strict construction of tax statutes. One is based on a demand for certainty: the fiscal consequences of a transaction should be determinable in advance and not subject to retrospective discretion by whomever exercised. The other is that, regardless of timing, no person other than Parliament should have any discretion as to the extent of tax liabilities.

The argument on the basis of certainty is undermined by other sources of inevitable uncertainty. As noted above, the valuation process must often involve an element of estimation which precludes pre-transaction certainty. Furthermore, following Finance Act 1998, s. 42, taxable trading profits are now to be

[33] Adjournment of the project was announced in an Inland Revenue / Customs and Excise Press Release, CW3, of 9.3.99. See Bartlett, "The Duty to Pay Taxes" in Lasok et al (ed.), *Fundamental Duties* (Oxford, Pergamon Press, 1980) for general discussion; his recommendations are, in essence, to reduce the incentive for avoidance by reducing marginal rates, to simplify where possible, and to change the "rules about the construction of tax statutes so that substance should take precedence over form in dealing with facts". More recently, see Masters, "Is There a Need for General Anti-Avoidance Legislation in the UK?" (1994) *British Tax Review* 647; Goldberg, "Between the Taxpayer and the Executive: Law's Inadequacy; Democracy's Failure?" (1996) *British Tax Review* 9; and Troup, "The consultative document on a general anti-avoidance rule for the United Kingdom – a view from a practising lawyer" (1999) *British Tax Review* 5. It is submitted that Goldberg in particular makes too much of the issue of parliamentary sovereignty.

[34] Vann, "Improving Tax Law Improvement: an International Perspective" (1995) *Australian Tax Forum* 193, 222, cited in Jones, "Tax Law: Rules or Principles" (1996) *British Tax Review* 580. See further Ghosh, "The Construction of Fiscal Legislation" (1994) *British Tax Review* 126; Ward, "A Comparative Study of the Interpretation of Tax Statute in the UK and the Republic of Ireland" (1994) *British Tax Review* 42 and 160.

computed on "an accounting basis which gives a true and fair view . . .". This process, which was already the statutory basis for the preparation of the accounts required by company law,[35] involves more estimation and discretion than an outsider might assume.[36] And in any event, the nature of language is such that it can never perfectly map reality: there will always be gaps and fuzzy edges.

It is that aspect of language which also undermines the appeal to parliamentary sovereignty. Indeed, Parliament's intention is more likely to be frustrated than fulfilled by denying any elasticity in the interpretation of its words. The difficulties are enormous. On the one hand, sovereignty is diminished, if Parliament is denied the ability to speak in natural, non-rigid language. On the other, the absence of easily discernible general principles in tax law may make it hard to know how any flexibility of construction should be exercised.

Three things, perhaps, are needed. The first is a general recognition that words are not necessarily rigid. The second is an acceptance that different degrees of flexibility may be appropriate at different stages of the tax process.[37] And finally, an understanding, or morality, is needed as to how the elasticity of words is to be managed. Such morality has to be a sort of meta-language which cannot be legislated for in the language to which it is to apply, any more than the rules of cricket can define what is "not cricket". Whether today's problems can be mitigated by means of a statutory anti-avoidance rule, by simplification of tax policy or by a move towards general principles drafting is a matter for technical debate. Little progress will be made, however, unless it is realised that the system cannot be wholly mechanical, and therefore some degree of trust has to be placed in, and appropriately exercised by, those tax officials, tax professionals, judges and taxpayers who together have to make the system work.[38]

[35] Companies Act 1985, s. 226(2).

[36] See Macdonald, "Substance, Form and Equity in Taxation and Accounting" (1991) 54 *Modern Law Review* 830; British Tax Review Special Issue, "Accounting Standards and Taxable Profits" (1995) *British Tax Review* 433–98; most recently, see Chandler and Edgley, "Certainly reasonable or reasonable certainty" (1999) *British Tax Review* 309, commenting on *Herbert Smith* v. *Honour* [1999] STC 173.

[37] The classification / valuation / computation analysis may not be the best approach, but it does highlight the point that some matters can be left more open-ended than others. The *Benham* debate, mentioned above, illustrates this well: what should have been approached as a technical, systemic, computation issue was thoroughly confused by appeals to tax policy and testator's intention.

[38] See White, "The Practitioner's Perspective " in Gammie (ed.), *Striking the Balance* (London, The Institute for Fiscal Studies, 1996) for exploration of the analogy between the tax process and the game of cricket, and for acknowledgement of the continuing importance of appropriately gentlemanly conduct. On the latter point, see more recently Sabine, "The Need for Co-operation" *Taxation* 29 January 1998, p. 421.

7. CONCLUSION – CAN TAX LAW BE "FAIR"?

"Fair . . . Expressing moderate commendation: Free from grave objection; of tolerable though not excellent quality . . ."[39]

A tax system needs to be fair in a number of different senses:

- it needs to distribute the burden of taxation in an acceptable manner; the parameters of acceptability are wide, but the system is unlikely to be adequately acceptable if it fails to respond at least minimally to ability to pay, or if it imposes punitive rates of tax on any group of taxpayers;
- it needs to be sufficiently simple in design that the electorate can see broadly "what is going on"; this may be a largely unattainable ideal, but it is a consideration which should inform tax policy; it is quite distinct from user-friendliness;
- the system needs to be sufficiently certain and precise that taxpayers can plan their affairs and settle their liabilities without excessive expense or dispute; however, the demand for absolute certainty is foolish and illegitimate;
- there needs to be sufficient flexibility to prevent abuse; for this purpose, some degree of controlled discretion has to be delegated to tax officials and judges;
- the system as a whole needs to be user-friendly; this requires attention not only to the text of tax legislation but also to administrative processes and relationships between all involved.

All these ideals are important, but none is capable of complete attainment without prejudice to others. Excessive emphasis on one only of these ideals will result in yet another way to fail to make law.[40]

Is it, then, helpful to regard "fairness" as a "fundamental value" in the context of tax law, or at all? It is hoped that appreciation of the many, sometimes contradictory, meanings of fairness might induce appropriate caution in the use of such concepts in debate. (A similar point could be made about many of the other concepts which might be proposed as "fundamental values"). More positively, it is suggested that "fairness" is a useful heading for various considerations which should inform the writing of rules,[41] helping as it does to bring out the elusive nature of language and of the morality which governs its use. Finally, the concept of fairness offers an interesting perspective on a system such as the tax system within which, as a result above all of computerisation, the roles of text – the raw tax legislation in particular – and players are changing fundamentally.

[39] OED, definition 11 a.

[40] *Cf.* Fuller, *The Morality of Law* (New Haven and London, Yale University Press, 1964), p. 33ff.

[41] Parallel points could be made about other uses of legal language, such as advocacy.

19

Fundamental Values in Employment

VIVIEN SHRUBSALL

1. PROPERTY IN EMPLOYMENT

If one reduced the employment contract to the minimum of obligation on either side, one would identify an obligation to work on the part of the employee and an obligation to pay on the part of the employer. That positive mutuality of performance is the essence of the employment agree-ment; when all that which is peripheral is stripped away from the employment agreement and relationship, that minimum mutual performance remains.[1] The employer has work to be performed, the employee is selling his labour. But, traditionally, there has been a negative mutuality as well: the employee's access to work endures only so long as the employer wishes to make work available; it does not translate to any enforceable "property" in the job or right to work.[2] The employment relationship is regarded as being founded on personal service and mutual trust and confidence and neither side can compel specific performance by the other. The purpose of this essay is to consider the extent to which modern law has altered that traditional view so as to recognise any sense of property right in employment.

[1] Without that irreducible minimum of obligation, there is no contract of employment. See Stephenson LJ in *Nethermere (St Neots) Ltd* v. *Gardiner* [1984] IRLR 240; Sir Christopher Slade in *Clark* v. *Oxfordshire Health Authority* [1998] IRLR 125 and Lord Irvine in *Carmichael* v. *National Power plc* [2000] IRLR 43.

[2] While the contract continues and in the absence of any express agreement, the employer is not under any duty to provide work so long as he continues to pay wages or salary. See Lord Asquith in *Collier* v. *Sunday Referee Publishing Co Ltd* [1940] 2 KB 647, "Provided I pay my cook her wages regularly she cannot complain if I choose to take all my meals out". But where work and wages go together so that unavailability of work means forfeiture of wages, or where the opportunity to perform is regarded as part of the remuneration for the contract, the obligation to provide work remains. See *Devonald* v. *Rosser* [1906] KB 728, *Bauman* v. *Hulton Press Ltd* [1952] 2 All ER 1121, *Clayton* v. *Oliver* [1930] AC 209.

2. WRONGFUL DISMISSAL

At common law, there is nothing to stop an employer from terminating a contract of employment for an indefinite term provided reasonable notice is given.[3] If an employer terminates without reasonable or due contract notice, in the absence of repudiatory breach of contract by the employee, the employee has an action for breach of contract for wrongful dismissal but, normally, an award of damages is regarded as the appropriate remedy. The damages due are usually limited to the wages or salary which would have been earned if the employee had been allowed to work out the notice to which he was entitled.[4] Traditionally, subject only to due contract notice or damages for loss of wages in that notice period,[5] an employer can terminate the employment relationship at will and cannot be compelled to continue to employ a particular worker or workers. Similarly, the employee cannot be compelled to work for a particular employer against his wishes. Contracts of employment are not specifically enforceable.[6] The justification from the employee's side is a repugnance of bonding the servant to a particular master,[7] and from the employer's side the principle endorses the personal trust and confidence which is reposed in the employee.

Modern departures from the principle that contracts of employment are not specifically enforceable have occurred but they have been limited to enforcement of contractual disciplinary procedures. Where the employer has terminated improperly by ignoring, short-cutting or otherwise failing to comply with the contractual procedure, courts have been willing to grant injunctions to stop unlawful termination and/or declarations that the employment continues.[8] Such a remedy is usually only available where damages would not be an adequate

[3] Statutory minimum periods of notice were introduced in 1963 and are now contained in the Employment Rights Act 1996, s. 86.

[4] See *Addis* v. *Gramophone Co Ltd* [1909] AC 488, House of Lords, reconsidered and endorsed by the Court of Appeal as recently as December 1998 in *Johnson* v. *Unisys Ltd* [1999] IRLR 90. But if failure to give due notice or failure to follow the contract procedure for termination means that service is foreshortened and the employee loses the appropriate service to qualify for unfair dismissal protection, damages in wrongful dismissal will reflect that loss. For a recent illustration see *Raspin* v. *United News Shops Ltd* [1999] IRLR 9.

[5] But where the employment is very specialised and the employee's unique skills require frequent exercise, the employer may be required to provide work during the notice period. See *William Hill Organisation Ltd* v. *Tucker* [1998] IRLR 313. (In the absence of an express "garden leave" clause, a senior dealer in the specialised business of spread betting was entitled to be provided with work during the notice period and could not be sent home on full pay).

[6] See *Lumley* v. *Wagner* (1852) 1 De GM&G 604; *Whitwood Chemical Co* v. *Hardman* [1891] 2 Ch 416, *Warner Bros Pictures Inc* v. *Nelson* [1937] 1 KB 209. The common law position is reflected in s. 236 Trade Union & Labour Relations (Consolidation) Act 1992.

[7] See the famous dictum of Fry J in *De Francesco* v. *Barnum* (1890) 45 Ch D 430 at p. 438, "The courts are bound to be jealous lest they turn contracts of service into contracts of slavery".

[8] See *Gunton* v. *Richmond on Thames Borough Council* [1980] ICR 755; *Irani* v. *Southampton & South West Hampshire AHA* {1985} IRLR 590; *Wadcock* v. *London Borough of Brent* [1990] IRLR 223.

remedy and the evidence shows that mutual trust and confidence has not broken down, so that a workable relationship still subsists between the parties.[9] The effect is that the employment continues for so long as it takes the employer to go through the contractual procedure for proper termination. This limited development in specific performance of employment has not been without its critics[10] but it has become established in modern employment law.[11] Though it remains true that no court will force parties to a contract of employment to continue on a permanent basis in a practical working relationship against the will of one of them, this approach recognises that modern employment contracts may include a range of provisions which may be specifically enforced during the subsistence of the contract. A distinction can be made between enforcing the employment relationship, which the law will not allow, and enforcing a supplementary term of the contract while the employment subsists. Enforcement need not be limited to disciplinary provisions but could extend to other contract terms. For example, in 1999 the High Court accepted that an employee has a free-standing contractual right under the Working Time Regulations and can bring a claim for a declaration of rights and an injunction prohibiting the employer from requiring work in excess of the limits imposed by the Regulations.[12] The scope of enforcement orders is limited,[13] but even as far as it goes at present, this is a significant development in the recognition of "property in employment" since there is a real possibility in cases of procedurally defective dismissals that the employer might be unable to satisfy the contractual disciplinary procedure when required to do so, with the result that the employment might continue long-term. There is a difference in having a complaint against an employee on the one hand and, on the other, proving to an independent and objective panel or forum that the complaint is not only made out but that termination of employment is the appropriate reaction. And if enforcement injunctions are available to ensure the employer's compliance with

[9] But see *Robb* v. *London Borough of Hammersmith and Fulham* [1991] IRLR 514 for an example of an injunction being awarded to restrain implementation of a procedurally defective dismissal even where the employers *had* lost trust and confidence in the employee.

[10] See judgments in the Court of Appeal in *Boyo* v. *London Borough of Lambeth* [1995] IRLR 50, particularly that of Staunton LJ at p. 59 where he stated his view plainly that neither an employee nor an employer should be compelled to treat a contract of employment as still in existence against his will and that he would have departed from the *Gunton* development if he could.

[11] See *Peace* v. *City of Edinburgh Council* [1999] IRLR 417 for recent endorsement from the Scottish Court of Session. A teacher was held entitled to an interdict restraining the employer from using a disciplinary procedure different from that contained in the contract of employment. The contractual procedure provided for all stages to be heard before elected members of the relevant authority; the employer purported to put the initial stage before a senior officer.

[12] See *Barber* v. *RJB Mining (UK) Ltd* [1999] IRLR 308. In the case, the application for a declaration of rights was granted but the injunction was denied on the grounds that its effect would be disproportionate to the benefit to the plaintiffs. The Court accepted that an injunction could be awarded in such a case.

[13] Note that s. 205 Employment Rights Act 1999 expressly restricts an employee's remedy for infringement of most of the statutory rights under that Act to proceedings in the employment tribunals and "not otherwise".

other agreed contract terms, even though that availability is limited by mutual willingness to continue with the employment relationship itself, the employee's protection is strengthened considerably.

3. UNFAIR DISMISSAL

The creation of the right not to be unfairly dismissed appeared to be a major step towards recognising that the worker acquired some right other than that merely to be paid for work done and as a major limitation on the employer's right to terminate the employment contract. Statute[14] recognised the worker's right not to lose his job, with or without notice, save for provable fault, incapability or incompetence on his own part or objective commercial reasons justifying redundancy or re-organisation and dismissal. And even where one of the acceptable reasons for dismissal is established by the employer, the structure of the right not to be unfairly dismissed still requires that the tribunal has to be satisfied that dismissal was reasonable, in accordance with equity and the substantial merits of the case. Add to those provisions the principle that the primary remedy for successful claims of unfair dismissal is an order for re-instatement or re-engagement and, almost thirty years on from the introduction of the right not to be unfairly dismissed, we should have a substantial body of case law and practice endorsing the sense of property in the job. It has not turned out quite like that.

Although the employer has the burden of proving the reason for dismissal, the unqualified heads of capability, qualifications or conduct are so wide that an employer has no difficulty in practice in bringing his defence within one of them and, in their application of the additional "some other substantial reason" defence, tribunals have emphasised managerial discretion in reorganisation cases and upheld frequently the employer's right to manage,[15] so limiting the employee's likely success in insisting on observance of the contract on the agreed terms. If the employee resigns and claims constructive dismissal, or if he is dismissed for declining to accept any substantial change in terms, subject to

[14] Unfair dismissal protection was first enacted in The Industrial Relations Act 1971. Current consolidated provisions are in Part X Employment Rights Act 1996. In claims of unfair dismissal the employee has the burden of proving dismissal (which includes expiry and non-renewal of fixed term contract and constructive dismissal), the employer has the burden of showing that the reason for dismissal falls within one of the specified categories (conduct or capability, competence, redundancy, contravention of an enactment or some other substantial reason) and the tribunal determines fairness or otherwise against what is claimed to be a neutral burden of proof.

[15] See *Hollister* v. *National Farmers Union* [1979] IRLR 238 and *Evans* v. *Elemeta Holdings Ltd* [1982] ICR 323 where the Appeal Tribunal upheld the finding that it was not unfair to dismiss for "some other substantial reason" where the employee refused to accept a standard form of contract which included a new term for limited, compulsory overtime working. The tribunal recognised a "commercial need of discernible advantage" to standardise employment contracts for "harmony of relationships in the workforce".

fair procedure and consultation, the dismissal is likely to be held not unfair.

Since the reasons are so wide, any real employment protection afforded by the right not to be unfairly dismissed turns on the interpretation and application of the provisions governing the third stage of the claim, the determination of fairness. The approach to that crucial issue has been similarly in favour of the employer. That is partly because of the wording of the statutory provision itself[16] but mostly because, for much of the period during which tribunals and higher courts have been adjudicating on unfair dismissal claims, they have adopted and applied a band of reasonable responses test.[17] This translates to findings that dismissals are not unfair if, though the tribunal members themselves might well not have dismissed, the employer was not outside the range of reasonable responses in dismissing for the reason shown. Under the band of reasonable responses test a dismissal is not unfair unless it is extreme, i.e. sufficiently unreasonable as to be outside the outer limit of the range of reasonable responses. Under this test, tribunals are exhorted not to substitute their managerial view for that of the employer by judging fairness in terms of whether they would have dismissed in the same circumstances. The correct question is whether the employer's action in dismissing is inside, albeit just inside, the range of reasonable responses. In practice, this amounts to a perversity test of the fairness of dismissal, with the inevitable result that cases have less chance of success.[18] If the employment tribunal judges by reference to extremes, rather than by measuring reasonableness of dismissal against what they would have done in the same circumstances, the intended function of the tribunal as an industrial jury is lost and the scope for objective checks on improper employment termination is reduced.

In September 1999, towards the end of his tenure as President of the Employment Appeal Tribunal, Morison J highlighted those results of the band of reasonable responses test and declared it unhelpful and erroneous.[19] In his opinion, the issue of fairness is a pure question of fact for the tribunal. Because the tribunal are applying an objective test, that is, a test of reasonableness, it is not sufficient for them simply to say that they would, or would not, have done the same in the same circumstances. They must go further and take account of their knowledge and experience of employment practice generally in adjudicating on the reasonableness of dismissal. Morison J says that the mantra that "the

[16] Fairness of dismissal is judged by reference to the reasonableness of the employer's action in dismissing, not by reference to the reasonableness to the employee in having been dismissed; s. 98 (4) Employment Rights Act 1996. For illustrations of the distinction see *Monie* v. *Coral Racing Ltd* [1980] IRLR 464 and *Parr* v. *Whitbread plc* [1990] IRLR 39.

[17] This test of whether the dismissal is fair or unfair was first established by the Court of Appeal in *British Leyland* v. *Swift* [1981] IRLR 91 and the classic formulation of it is in the judgment of Browne-Wilkinson P in *Iceland Frozen Foods Ltd* v. *Jones* [1982] IRLR 439.

[18] Less than 10 per cent of claims of unfair dismissal registered with tribunals in 1997–8 and 1998–9 were upheld. See Labour Market Trends, Department of Trade & Industry September 1999.

[19] *Haddon* v. *Van Den Bergh Foods Ltd* [1999] IRLR 672.

tribunal must not substitute their own decision for that of the employer" amounts to no more than that but it is exactly the function of the tribunal members to substitute their judgment for that of the employer. The tribunal is composed of people chosen because of their experience and expertise in employment and industrial relations. It is right that they should determine the objective question of reasonableness by reference to what they would have done in those circumstances because it is likely that what the tribunal themselves would have done will often coincide with their judgment as to what a reasonable employer would have done. Whenever a complaint of unfair dismissal is upheld, the tribunal are in effect substituting their own judgment for that of the employer. Provided that they apply the test of reasonableness, it is their duty to determine their own judgment and to substitute it where appropriate.

If it were to be followed, this new approach would have a marked effect on the determination of reasonableness of dismissal and protection of property in employment. The case could become a landmark decision in changing the trend of unfair dismissal claims. However, there are strong, established authorities approving and applying the band of reasonable responses test[20] and the justification in this judgment for sweeping them away is rather thin. It amounts to little more than a reliance on *obiter dicta* of the Court of Appeal[21] and an assertion that the tribunal's application of the test depends on their interpretation of the facts. It could be argued that the force of Mr Justice Morison's judgment is weakened further by his statement that the reference to equity in s. 98 (4) of the Employment Rights Act 1996 requires a consideration of the case from the employee's perspective. The House of Lords directly addressed this point in *Polkey*[22] and concluded that injustice to the dismissed employee was irrelevant to the fairness or otherwise of dismissal, though it is important in relation to the compensatory award. It would be premature to assume on the basis of Morison's judgment, however brave, that tribunals will no longer apply the range of reasonable responses test to the question of fairness of dismissal.[23]

Even where an application for unfair dismissal is upheld, it is unusual for the employee to be put back into the employment from which he was dismissed. Although the primary remedy for unfair dismissal is an order for reinstatement or re-engagement, in practice such orders are made in a very small proportion of successful cases. Reinstatement or re-engagement was awarded in only

[20] For Court of Appeal or Court of Session cases see *Hereford & Worcester CC* v. *Neale* [1986] IRLR 168; *Conlin* v. *United Distillers* [1994] IRLR 169; *British Gas* v. *McCarrick* [1991] IRLR 305; *Gair* v. *Bevan Harris Ltd* [1983] IRLR 368.

[21] Morison J relied heavily on *obiter dicta* of the Court of Appeal in *Gilham* v. *Kent CC* [1985] IRLR 18 which stressed the factual nature of the tribunal's determination of fairness and stated that the band of reasonable responses test is not helpful.

[22] *Polkey* v. *AE Dayton Services* [1987] IRLR 503 . See also n. 6 *supra*.

[23] Indeed, Mr Justice Lindsay, the new President of the EAT, declared in *Midland Bank* v. *Madden* [2000] IRLR 288 that it is not open to any court short of the Court of Appeal to deny reference to the band of reasonable responses, not only as a guide but as a determinative test.

twenty-six of the 35,183 unfair dismissal claims registered in 1997–8 and in twenty-eight of 32,632 claims in 1998–9. Deducting claims conciliated by ACAS and claims withdrawn, reinstatement or re-engagement was awarded in less than 0.1 per cent of cases heard by tribunals, and in less than 0.9 per cent of claims upheld by tribunals.[24] It is that final statistic which is remarkable, giving the lie to any assertion that re-employment is a real remedy in an unfair dismissal claim. Several commentators have drawn attention to the missed opportunity to deliver re-employment[25] as the appropriate remedy, citing as reasons the tribunals' perpetuation of historical antipathy towards specific performance of employment contracts and the inquisitorial nature of tribunal proceedings which entrenches hostility between the parties and discourages renewal of the employment relationship. The very wording of the source statutory provision militates against re-employment, requiring the tribunal, when exercising its discretion on the appropriate remedy, to consider whether it is practicable for the employer to comply with a re-employment order That leads to heavy reliance on the employer's evidence and assessment of practicability from a managerial perspective. It is true that the statutory provision has the appearance of even-handedness since it takes account of the employee's wish for re-employment but, given the substantive finding that dismissal is unfair, re-employment might be seen as the presumptive remedy, unless the employee has caused or contributed to the dismissal. There is a strong case for a provision which assumes re-employment of an unfairly dismissed employee and puts the employer to the proof of impracticability.

Under present provisions, even in the few cases in which tribunals do make orders for re-employment, the Employment Appeal Tribunal shows a readiness to overturn them.[26] One can easily see the practical difficulties in the way of re-engagement of the employee: the fact that there has been a dispute at all damages the mutual trust and confidence that is regarded as the foundation of the employment relationship; there is an inevitable time delay between severance of the relationship and any tribunal hearing with the result that the employer will have had to make alternative arrangements to cover business needs and the employee will have sought, and may have secured, new employment; there is the perception that management loses face and authority if obliged to take back a dismissed worker; the worker himself commonly will be

[24] Statistics from Labour Market Trends, Department of Trade and Industry, September 1999.

[25] See Dickens et al, *Re-employment of unfairly dismissed workers: the lost remedy* (1981) 10 ILJ 160; Williams and Lewis *The aftermath of tribunal reinstatement and re-engagement* DE Research Paper No 23 (1981).

[26] See for example, *Wood Group Heavy Industrial Turbines Ltd* v. *Crossnan* [1998] IRLR 680 where, though the tribunal which had had the benefit of seeing and hearing the parties at the hearing made an order for re-engagement, the EAT upset it on appeal on the grounds that the employers genuinely, though erroneously, believed in the allegations against the employee and the breakdown of the employers trust and confidence in the employee made re-engagement "not practical".

reluctant to return to employment where he has been treated so badly. The problem is recognised[27] by central government and the attempt at solution is the promotion of a new voluntary arbitration scheme under the auspices of ACAS[28] which the Government "hopes will create a change of culture so that individuals who have been dismissed unfairly are more likely to get their jobs back". The scheme envisages the making of "re-employment orders" in arbitrations conducted in accordance with the scheme which would be enforceable by employment tribunals. It remains to be seen whether such "orders" will be truly mandatory but a non-adversarial arbitration forum has some chance of addressing the difficulties noted above.

The level of damages commonly awarded in unfair dismissal claims also has relevance to the frequency and effectiveness of orders for re-employment. If an employer is likely to have to pay a substantial sum by way of alternative remedy, compliance with a re-employment order might seem rather more practicable than it does if the award is likely to be modest. Most of the apparent difficulties of compliance have a price perspective. Much publicity has been given to the increase in the maximum limit to the compensatory element of unfair dismissal damages.[29] However, every year's statistics show the median award of unfair dismissal damages falling far short of the current statutory maximum.[30] Tribunal attitudes to the computation of damages must change, particularly in respect of the award for lost continuity (frequently only about £200) and the award for future loss (where the forward period is commonly only three or six months). Unless this change occurs, the increase in the statutory maximum will provide little incentive to employers to consider re-employment more readily. The prospect of practical recognition of property in employment recedes accordingly.

4. EMPLOYMENT PROTECTION ON BUSINESS TRANSFERS

It can be argued that European law has promoted a property in employment effectively, at least in the context of business transfers. European Directive 77/187[31] safeguards the rights of workers whenever a business undertaking is transferred by ensuring entitlement to continue working for the transferee

[27] See paragraphs 3.4 and 3.5 of the *Fairness at Work White Paper*, Cm 3968, May 1998.

[28] The Employment Rights (Dispute Resolution) Act 1998 inserted provision in the Trade Union and Labour Relations (Consolidation) Act 1992 for the creation of an arbitration scheme as an alternative to tribunal proceedings.

[29] Section 34 Employment Relations Act 1999 substituted £50,000 for the previous figure of £12,000 in respect of dismissals on or after 25 October 1999.

[30] The median award in 1998–9 was £2,388.

[31] Council Directive of February 1977 on the approximation of the laws of the Member States relating to the safeguarding of employees' rights in the event of transfers of undertakings, businesses or parts of undertakings or businesses, usually referred to in the UK as the Acquired Rights Directive. The Directive was amended in July 1998 by Council Directive 98/50.

employer on the same terms and conditions as those agreed with the transferor employer. Whenever a transfer is within the Directive, contracts of employment run with the undertaking. The purchaser cannot take the business without the employees and must take those employees on existing employment terms. Further, a transfer cannot constitute grounds for dismissal, whether carried out by the transferor or the transferee, unless there is an economic, technical or organisational reason entailing changes in the workforce. The provisions of the European Directive were carried into national law by the 1981 TUPE Regulations.[32] Those national regulations have to be interpreted purposively to comply with the Directive[33] and, where the regulations are inadequate to carry into effect the protection intended by the Directive, they can be challenged by the Commission[34] or relied on directly by individuals in accordance with emerging constitutional principles on the superiority of European law.

We have now almost twenty years experience of the TUPE Regulations and that period has seen a cyclical attitude to their interpretation and application and a significant impact on preservation of employment. In the early years, there was reluctance to accept the width of circumstances which could be a transfer within the scope of the Directive, and therefore within the TUPE Regulations. However, decisions of the European Court of Justice established that a transfer did not have to be direct, that it could involve an ancillary or peripheral service and need not be the main, or even a main, business activity. ECJ rulings established that the undertaking did not have to have a profit-making objective, that the criteria for determining whether a transfer has taken place are wide and no one of them is conclusive, and there can be a relevant transfer between competitors for a commercial contract with the result that the transferee is obliged to take on the workforce assigned by the transferor to the performance of that contract.[35] These principles were applied in national courts and tribunals so that by the late 1990s there was almost a presumption that TUPE applied whenever part of an undertaking was sold or otherwise assigned and where services were contracted-out and even where a contract for the provision of services was withdrawn from one contractor and awarded to another.[36] The result was that workers engaged in those undertakings enjoyed job protection; they

[32] Transfer of Undertakings (Protection of Employment) Regulations SI 1981/1794, amended by SI 1995/2587 and SI 1999/1925.

[33] See *Litster* v. *Forth Dry Dock & Engineering Co Ltd* [1989] IRLR 161, House of Lords.

[34] See *Commission of the European Communities* v. *UK* [1994] IRLR 392. The challenge led to amendment of the regulations so that the exclusion of non-commercial ventures was withdrawn, obligations to consult with employee representatives were strengthened and sanctions for breach of consultation obligations were extended.

[35] *Foreningen of Arbejdsledere i Danmark* v. *Daddy's Dance Hall A/S* [1988] IRLR 315; *Rask* v. *ISS Kantineservice A/S* [1993] IRLR 133; *Dr Sophie Redmond Stichting* v. *Bartol* [1992] IRLR 366; *Spijkers* v. *Gebroeders Benedik Abattoir CV* [1986] IRLR 1119; *Schmidt* v. *Spar-und-Leihkasse* [1994] IRLR 302.

[36] See for example, *Dines* v. *Initial Health Care Services Ltd & Pall Mall Services Group Ltd* [1993] IRLR 521.

had a right to transfer to the incoming proprietor on the same terms and conditions of service as previously enjoyed.[37] The effect on the public sector of the UK workforce was especially significant because of the wide-scale implementation of compulsory competitive tendering required by the Local Government Act 1988.

This widening of employment protection appeared to be checked by the *Suzen*[38] decision in 1997, so far as service contacts are concerned. That case established that where the business does not involve any significant tangible or intangible assets, an organised grouping of workers performing a labour-intensive service can be identified as an "economic entity" capable of transfer under the Directive, but that there is no transfer in such a case, and so no obligation to take on employees on the same terms and conditions of employment, unless the new contractor takes over not only the activity but also a major part of the workforce in terms of their numbers and skills. There has to be a transfer of the economic entity; a transfer of the activity only is not sufficient to trigger the Directive.[39] The *Suzen* principle does not affect the usual type of business transfer so that employment rights will transfer in such a case whenever, by balancing the resources deployed in the economic unit, the national court or tribunal concludes that sufficient of those resources have moved across for a transfer to be found. But where the economic entity is composed merely of an organised grouping of workers performing services, the effect of the *Suzen* decision is that there is no transfer unless the transferee takes sufficient of the workforce, as well as the right to perform the activity, so show that the "entity" has moved across. If he does take "a major part of the workforce", he cannot decline to take all of them on the same terms and conditions because now the Directive applies and he may not pick and choose. But if he takes none of them, there is no transfer and the Directive does not apply.[40] In other words, after the *Suzen* decision, the applicability of the Directive to labour-intensive service contracts involving nothing, or nothing significant, in the way of supporting assets is voluntary!

[37] There is an exception in respect of pension' rights under occupational pension schemes; see TUPE Regulation 7, permitted by Article 3 of the Acquired Rights Directive. The 1998 amendments (Council Directive 98/50) permit Member States to provide for the internal compulsory transfer of pension benefits and the UK is expected to adopt a scheme for their transfer when the new version of the TUPE Regulations is published during the year 2000.

[38] *Suzen* v. *Zeknacker Gebaudereinigung GmbH Krankenhausservice* [1997] IRLR 255, ECJ. See Shrubsall, ACompetitive Tendering, Out-sourcing and the Acquired Rights Directive (1998) 61 *Modern Law Review* 85 for comment.

[39] Subsequent references confirmed that the same approach should be adopted to original contracting-out arrangements and to the taking back of previously contracted-out services. See *Francisco Hernandez Vidal SA* v. *Gomez Perez* [1999] IRLR 132; *Sanchez Hidalgo* v. *Association De Servicios Aser* [1999] IRLR 136.

[40] Council Directive 77/187 was amended by Directive 98/50 so as to provide that "there is a transfer within the Directive where there is a transfer of an economic entity which retains its identity, meaning an organised grouping of resources which has the objective of pursuing an economic activity" i.e. a *transfer* of the entity has to take place; there is no automatic transfer for labour-intensive service contracts.

The national Employment Appeal Tribunal and Court of Appeal have not arrived at the same conclusion. In *ECM (Vehicle Delivery Service)* v. *Cox*[41] the EAT held that the TUPE Regulations could not be avoided by the transferee's refusal to take on the workforce on a change of a service contract. Morison J said that a purposive approach should be adopted to the Regulations because it would not be "proper" for a transferee to be able to control the extent of his obligations under the regulations by refusing to comply with them in the first place. The Court of Appeal dismissed the appeal, but on the basis that the Employment Tribunal had considered the appropriate factors[42] and had concluded that there was a transfer. There was no endorsement of Morison's J's anti-avoidance approach. But the decision is unsatisfactory in its acceptance of the Employment Tribunal's finding of a transfer. The Tribunal made its determination before the decision in *Suzen* was promulgated and it is hard to reconcile the Tribunal's finding with it. If the economic entity was a combination of organisational methods, assets (i.e. the car transporters) and the drivers and yardmen, it is difficult to see how there could be a finding that a transfer had taken place given that the new contractor changed the organisational methods, did not take any of the assets and did not take any of the workers.[43] And if the economic entity was merely the organised grouping of workers performing the service, that is exactly the situation to which the *Suzen* principle applies so that there can be no transfer unless both elements of the entity move across. Findings that the work is the same and the customer is the same will not do. It remains to be seen whether the national reluctance to accept the *Suzen* restriction on the width of application of the Directive will be permitted long term.

Assuming that there is a transfer, employment protection is afforded by statutory novation of the employees contracts. The transferee is substituted for the transferor in respect of all contracts of employment existing at the time of the transfer[44] and must honour all terms and conditions of employment, save for occupational pension terms. Employees cannot agree to waive their rights to transfer on the existing terms[45] and they are protected against dismissal because

[41] [1998] IRLR 416, EAT; [1999] IRLR 559, Court of Appeal. The case involved the loss of a delivery contract with *VAG Ltd* under which Audi and VW cars imported through Grimsby docks were driven onwards to delivery centres and dealers in different parts of England. The issue was whether twenty-four car transporter drivers and yardmen employed by the outgoing contractor were entitled to transfer on the same employment terms to the new contractor.

[42] Set out in *Spijkers*. See n. 35 *supra*.

[43] It looks now very like *Betts* v. *Brintel Helicopters Ltd* [1997] IRLR 361 where the Court of Appeal held that since no assets, infrastructure or staff were taken on by the new contractor who took over a contract to supply transport services to oil rigs, there was no transfer.

[44] *Litster* v. *Forth Dry Dock & Engineering Co Ltd* [1989] IRLR 161, House of Lords, establishes that employees who are dismissed immediately before the transfer but because of the transfer are still within the protection of the regulations.

[45] See *Wilson* v. *St Helens Borough Council* [1998] IRLR 707. Even if the changed terms are better for the employee overall, the employee can renege on an agreement to accept any inferior term; see *Credit Suisse First Boston (Europe) Ltd* v. *Padiachy* [1998] IRLR 504. The employee can

of the transfer, whether that dismissal is effected by the transferor or transferee employer. There is a qualification to this protection where there is an economic, technical or organisational (ETO) reason entailing changes to the workforce but that defence, so far, has been applied somewhat restrictively. It has been given the same meaning as that given to redundancy under normal employment law. The employer will have an ETO defence only where his technical, organisational or economic changes result in changes of demand on the workforce in terms of structure, numbers or skills. For example, if the transferee employer introduces new technology or automates some part of the production process with the result that he needs fewer workers to do the work available, the ETO defence will apply. It might also apply where the transferee is merging the workforce of the undertaking taken over with his existing workforce. Economies of scale might easily result in a need for a reduced workforce, although in that case the pool of selection for dismissal has to be the merged workforce, not just the workers transferred. But if he has the same amount of work to do, though at lower rates of pay, perhaps because the market permits the engagement of cheaper workers, that is an "economic" reason but not an economic reason "entailing changes in the workforce" and the ETO defence does not apply.

Even where there is an ETO defence for dismissal, s. 98(4) of the Employment Rights Act 1996 still applies so that the employer has to consider redeployment and must satisfy the usual consultation procedures.

Where the transfer, and not an ETO , is the reason for the dismissal, or where an ETO dismissal does not satisfy s. 98(4), the employee is improperly dismissed. However, it is now established that such dismissals are effective, even though unlawful.[46] The dismissals are not nullities and those dismissed cannot compel the transferee to employ them on their old employment terms. They have a remedy against the transferee but that remedy is in unfair dismissal[47] and, as we have already seen, that remedy translates in practice to a compensation award rather than to re-employment. Effective employment protection breaks down here in the same way as it does under the normal law of unfair dismissal.

compromise his claim under the TUPE Regulations, but it has to be a genuine compromise agreement meeting the requirements of the Employment Rights Act 1996 s. 203 (f) and the employee must have taken independent advice.

[46] *British Fuels Ltd* v. *Baxendale & Meade* (joined in the House of Lords with *Wilson* v. *St Helens Borough Council*) [1998] IRLR 706.

[47] The employee has a right to object to transferring as part of the business, see Reg 5 (4A). Where he does object, the transfer operates as an automatic termination of his contract but not as a dismissal, see Reg 5 (4B), so the employee has no entitlement to unfair dismissal nor redundancy compensation. However, Reg 5 (5) preserves the employee's common law right to terminate if a substantial change is made in his working conditions to his detriment. The Court of Appeal held in *Humphreys* v. *Oxford University*, *Times Law Report*, 18 January 2000, that if the transfer would result in detrimental changes, the employee can object to the transfer and bring a wrongful dismissal claim against the transferor.

5. CONCLUSION

While the last three decades have seen considerable growth in rules, practices and policies which establish minimum standards of employment protection, there is still little recognition of an employee's "property" in the job. Even where the employee can show that his dismissal is outside the range of reasonable responses to the complaint against him, he cannot insist on re-employment in an action for unfair dismissal. The process of enforcement militates against a willing resumption of the employment relationship, and the concept that employment is based on personal service and mutual trust and confidence militates against a forced resumption. Though the business transfer regulations have provided real protection for workers caught up in acquisitions, mergers and competitive tendering exercises, in the face of a recalcitrant employer that protection too is reduced to entitlement to compensation payment. A more robust attitude needs to be taken by tribunals towards the computation of loss so that the risk of heavy damages acts as a real incentive to employers to accept the unfairly dismissed employee back into employment. In modern employment law the brightest hope of a realistic remedy for improper termination of employment is a limited, yet definite, development in the remedies available in the traditional wrongful dismissal action.

20

Fundamental Values in Company Law?

ROBERT DRURY

1. INTRODUCTION

The area chosen for investigation in this essay is that of company law. If the work of Otto von Gierke in the last century had achieved universal recognition there would be little doubt that every system of company law would have to adhere to certain fundamental values. He argued that certain groups and associations, including companies, had a personality that was just as real as that of a human individual and should be recognised by the law as such. He saw the corporation as a manifestation of the collective will of its members, and it was this distinctive element that gave rise to its separate legal personality. If a corporation could claim legal personality "as of right" then there would have to be something inherent in the nature of the corporation which related to the fundamental values adopted by the society of which it formed a part. One would then be able to investigate precisely what it was in the essential nature of the corporation that merited this treatment, and it could be hoped that certain values would emerge that were not only fundamental, but also common to all systems of company law. However, this is not the case, and different systems of company law have adopted very different perspectives on this issue. While it is true to say that Gierke's emphasis on the real nature of a company has struck a chord with some systems, in others it has struck a very discordant note indeed.

Gierke's theories are not the only ones in the field, and many others, including the Concession Theory which takes the line that corporations only obtain legal personality when the State decides to give it to them, have enjoyed considerable popularity. It is the Fiction Theory above all that stands in sharpest contrast to the Realist theories. This has been expressed in the following way:

> Whatever may be the nature of corporations, foundations and so on, all that interests us is that they are endowed by law with legal capacity as if they were human

> beings. . . . The value of the fiction formula is that it starts from a natural, extra judicial conception of personality, as founded in ethics and religion and then adds that certain groups and institutions determined by law, though lacking in supreme, that is human dignity, are nevertheless treated by law as if they were human persons.[1]

While this has links with fundamental values, it almost expressly denies them to corporations because they are only included by way of some sort of analogy to human beings, and not because of anything inherent in their nature. The logical consequence of this is that "It is for each legal system to decide whether it is advisable to endow certain bodies not human beings with personality or not. The decisions differ in the various legal systems".[2] Because these decisions have differed in various jurisdictions with some, for example, extending corporate personality to partnerships and others not, a search for fundamental values can best be carried out in relation to individual jurisdictions rather than by finding some universal factors common to the corporate form.

It may therefore be useful to examine several systems of company law to see if they do espouse any values inherent in the system that can be described as fundamental. If we, like charity, begin at home, we find some difficulties in discovering any values at all, still less any fundamental ones. Other systems thus need to be selected for comparison. If one considers their influence on other systems of company law, then those of France and Germany can be considered as paradigm systems. The French has, for example, had a profound influence on those of Belgium, Spain, Luxembourg, Italy, and through them on other systems in the developing world, especially South America and some parts of the Far East. German company law has influenced systems in Austria, The Netherlands, Portugal, Greece (where some French influence is also apparent), Switzerland and Japan. For these reasons our search will concentrate on what appears to be fundamental in those two systems

2. A BARE ENGLISH CUPBOARD

If we begin the search for fundamental values in our own backyard, as it were, we find that unlike many civil law jurisdictions English company law does not really place much, if any, emphasis on the role of sweeping theories or concepts that might help to elucidate the fundamental values of the subject. This is a difficult assertion to justify without writing a thesis on the whole area. One could cite the words of Martin Wolff when, in a company law context, he stated, "It has very often been said that English law has never taken dogmatic theories of any kind much to heart and does not adopt any speculative opinion".[3] An

[1] Martin Wolff, *On the Nature of Legal Persons* (1938) 54 *LQR* 494, 506–7.
[2] *Ibid.*
[3] Wolff, *op.cit.* at 521.

example of this can be found in the work of H L A Hart in this area. He would prefer to "put aside the question 'What is a corporation?' and ask instead 'Under what types of conditions does the law ascribe liabilities to corporations?' This is likely to clarify the actual working of a legal system and bring out the precise issues at stake when judges, who are supposed not to legislate, make some new extension to corporate bodies of rules worked out for individuals".[4] English law tends to take a pragmatic approach to these issues which inclines towards the Fiction Theory if anything, but really has little time for such theories. Another way of supporting the assertion might be to look at textbooks on company law and to investigate their structure. A brief survey of the layout of some of the leading student textbooks on English Company Law[5] indicates that they had an average of 7.2 per cent devoted to matters other than an exposition of the details of specific and technical company law. If we compare this with a similar selection of French student textbooks we see that they take an average of 21.4 per cent of the work to deal with the general principles before moving on to consider the detailed specific law on different types of companies.[6] In Germany the position is similar with a leading work there devoting 34 per cent to such general principles and concepts.[7]

If no real assistance in our search for fundamental values is to be gained from the way in which the system of company law is presented and taught, then perhaps those values will emerge from a study of the detailed provisions of that law. While it is possible to discern parts of this company law which embrace values such as equality of treatment and fairness, in the final analysis these do not pervade the whole system in a fundamental way and do not constitute what

[4] H L A Hart, *Definition and Theory in Jurisprudence* (1954) 70 LQR 37, 56.

[5] Half of the leading student textbooks on English company law begin with an outline of the typology of companies and sometimes other business forms, before moving on to their characteristics and history, sometimes dallying with the European dimension, but very soon getting on with the real business of the detail of the formation and running of companies. The other half just start with formation and have no more general aspect at all. There is no real theoretical introduction to the fundamental aspects of a company, and this lack of interest in the subject is typical of the system as a whole. Out of the five books surveyed only two had anything of any substance in the area of theory, and much of that was devoted to the history of the legislation.

The books included in this survey were:

Gower's Principles of Modern Company Law 6th ed., Paul L Davies, London, 1997;
Farrar's Company Law. 4th ed., J H Farrar, B Hannigan, London, 1998;
Pennington's Company Law, 7th ed., R R Pennington, London, 1995;
Company Law, S Mayson, D French and C Ryan, 11th ed., London 1994;
Principles of Company Law, S Goulding, London, 1996.

[6] These works were:

Droit des Affairs, Y Guyon, 9th ed., Paris, 1996 with 23 per cent;
Droit des Sociétés, M Cozian & A Viandier, 7th ed., Paris 1994, with 35 per cent;
Traité de Droit Commercial, G Ripert par R Roblot, 13th ed., Paris 1989, with 9.3 per cent plus further theoretical sections under the separate headings of specific types of company;
Droit Commercial: Sociétés Commerciales, P Merle, 4th ed., Paris 1994, with 21.4 per cent.

[7] *Gesellschaftsrecht*, K Schmidt, Köln, 1986.

one could describe as fundamental values. Just to take one example, one can find in the textbooks references to "the presumption of equality between shareholders" which looks like some sort of fundamental principle to the effect that "all shares confer the same rights and impose the same liabilities".[8] However, all that this so-called principle now involves[9] is the idea that if some shares are to have priority over others this must be stated in the terms of issue. Otherwise they will be presumed to rank equally with existing ones. As these rights are many and varied and can be created and subsequently altered with comparative ease during the life of the company, we cannot grace this minimal presumption with the label of a principle, still less a fundamental value. It would be where a system of company law makes it an absolute rule that the shareholders must at all times be treated equally, where there can only be one class of shares, where every share must have a vote and where each share can only have one vote, that we would begin to have elements of fundamental values of equality within that system. Such rules have existed in other jurisdictions and some still do.[10] This is not so in England. It is difficult to prove a negative, but it appears at first sight that the English cupboard is rather bare of fundamental values. We therefore need to look elsewhere.

3. FUNDAMENTAL VALUES IN FRENCH COMPANY LAW

In order to further our search for fundamental values in French company law it is necessary to begin by explaining the structure of that law. In France we have as the basic building block the concept of the *société*. This is provided by the Code Civil and is the root structure for all forms of business organisation. It should be distinguished from the *association*, which is not required to have a profit making or economic purpose and must have some object other than the distribution of profits among its members.[11] The common core concept of the *société* is used for organisations which have an economic objective or *but lucratif* and which can be either commercial or non-commercial (i.e. civil) according to

[8] *Gower's Principles of Modern Company Law*, 6th ed., Paul L Davies, London 1997, at p. 303.

[9] After the case of *Andrews* v. *Gas Meter Co.* [1897] 1 Ch 361, C.A. which permitted a subsequent alteration of the constitution to authorise an issue of shares carrying rights preferential to those initially created, in contrast to the earlier rule which did not.

[10] See for example, article 58 of the French law of 24 July 1966 which specifies that each member has a vote equal to the number of shares (*parts*) that they hold.

[11] These can be formed by a simple declaration and a deposit of their constitution with the local prefecture, or formed with legal personality as Registered Associations under the law of 1 July 1901. They can be used for social and domestic purposes, and are, for example used by professional football clubs, which do have a business dimension, as well as small shooting or fishing clubs, which do not. They are also used in the area of political, religious, artistic and charitable activities. The fundamental characteristic of all of them is that they must not have as an objective the distribution of their profits to their members, although they can allow their members to share in certain economic advantages flowing from their membership of the association.

the definitions laid down by French law. Certain *sociétés* are commercial because of the legal form that they have adopted. Thus the law of 24 July 1966, the major piece of company legislation, states in its first article that the following are commercial by reason of their form whatever object they have: *sociétés en nom collectif* (general partnerships), *sociétés en commandite simple* (limited partnerships), *sociétés á responsabilité limitée* (private companies) and *sociétés par actions* (other companies with a share capital – public companies especially). If one of these forms is not adopted then much will depend upon the objects for which the *société* is established. There is the important form of the *société civile* that is used by businesses whose activities fall outside the definition of *actes de commerce* in the Code de Commerce. These are extensively used for purposes of agricultural, forestry, building construction and exploitation and the so-called liberal professions (lawyers, doctors, dentists, accountants etc.). There are other types where their civil or commercial status is dependent upon their objects alone – e.g. *sociétés en participation* (silent partnerships), *sociétés créées de fait* (*de facto* or unregistered companies) and *groupments d'intérêt économique* (economic interest groupings). There are also many specialised types of *société*[12] as well as specialised sub-types of several of these forms, especially the *sociétés civiles*[13] and the diverse forms of the *sociétés cooperatives*.[14]

Given this structure, it can readily be perceived that any values in the system which are to be considered truly fundamental will be found in this basic concept of the *société*. This area is described in many French texts as the law common to all *sociétés*, and to this we must turn in our search for fundamental values. The definition set out initially in the Civil Code was "A partnership (*société*) is a contract by which two or more persons agree to place in common some assets or their skill, for the purpose of dividing the profits or benefiting from the economy that may result therefrom. The partners commit themselves to make contributions in the event of losses".[15] From this definition we can see that the concept of the *société* embraces several distinct ideas which are crucial to its existence. There must be two people involved who pool part of their assets by way of a contractual agreement in a common venture, which has a profit making or at least an economic function. Several aspects of this are worth pursuing in our search for fundamentals.

[12] Among these can be found the many *sociétés á capital variable, sociétés agricoles, sociétés d'assurance mutuelle, sociétés mutuelle d'assurance*, as well as the *sociétés anonyme á participation ouvrière, sociétés anonyme d'expertise comptable, sociétés de gèométres experts, sociétés de presse, sociétés de contrepartie* and the *sociétés anonymes d'habitation á loyer modérée*.

[13] These include the *sociétés civiles professionelles* and the *sociétés civiles immobilieres* both of which have many sub-types, and the *sociétés civiles de placement immobilier autorisées á faire publiquement appel á l'epargne*.

[14] There are separate regimes for *coopératives agricoles, coopératives de commercants détaillants, coopératives de banque, coopératives ouvriéres de production* and *coopératives artisanales*.

[15] This translation is from *French Business Enterprises*, by John H Crabb (Colorado 1979). The definition was later amended in 1985 to make provision for the creation of a one-person *société* something which gave strict theorists many conceptual problems.

The bonding force of a contract means that all *sociétés* should involve a bilateral agreement between parties of full legal capacity, whose legal consent to the transaction is not vitiated in any way. They must agree to share both the profits and the losses arising from their economic activities. Clauses which relieve one party from losses while arrogating to them the major or lion's share of the profits (called leonine clauses) are not acceptable and void (deemed not written) and may in some forms of *société* be a ground for causing the nullity of the *société* itself. From this we can see that some notions of equality begin to emerge, in the sense that all parties must have a financial involvement in the enterprise, although this need not be of the same amount. This contribution or *apport* must be a real one, in the sense that if it is not a valid contribution the very existence of the *société* is challenged and it could be declared a nullity. As Guyon says "*La mise en commun des apports est une condition indispensable á la constitution d'une* société. *En effet, faute de moyens, les associés ne pourraient pas agir en commun. Donc, s'il n'y a pas d'apport, il ne peut pas y avoir de* société".[16] Contributions can be in cash, in kind and, in some types of *société*, in labour. Examples of defective contributions include cases where the asset does not exist,[17] has already been sold,[18] or is already subject to an encumbrance for more than its value.[19] If a person does not make a valid contribution, or even if their contribution is merely nominal then their commitment to the *société* is regarded as being in grave doubt.

The necessity for every party to make a real contribution is linked to two other concepts that are also fundamental to the idea of the *société*. The first is that the contribution of assets from each member generates a pool of property that belongs to the *société*, and this is known as its *patrimoine*. As Ripert par Roblot precisely states "*Ce sont les apports qui constituent le patrimoine initial de la* société. *Toute* société *doit avoir un patrimoine puisqu'elle est une personne morale. Ces deux notions sont généralement liées dans le droit français*".[20] Thus certain assets are separated from the individual *patrimoine* of each of the members and set aside as belonging to the enterprise itself. As the genus "*société*" embraces partnerships with unlimited liability one cannot link the concept of patrimony to the idea of a fund from which the interests of creditors must be met. Instead, one can suggest that it is a fundamental feature of

[16] *Droit des Affairs*, Y Guyon (9th ed. Paris, 1996) at p. 94. "The bringing together of contributions is an indispensable condition for the formation of a *société*. As a matter of fact, without resources the members are not able to act in common. Consequently, if there is no contribution there cannot be a *société*". [Author's translation]

[17] Amiens, 30 avril 1975, *Journ. Agréés*, 1978, 310; note Sortais. Honfleur company, 20 novembre 1970. J.C.P., 1971.2.16628.

[18] Lyon, 3 fèvrier 1949, *J. Société.*, 1949, 277.

[19] Com. 18 juin 1974: *Rev. Trim. Dr. Com.*, 1975, 525, note Houin.

[20] *Traité de Droit Commercial*, G Ripert par R Roblot, 13th ed., Paris 1989, at p. 577. "It is the contributions that constitute the initial patrimony of a *société*. Every *société* must have a patrimony since it is a legal person. These two ideas are generally linked in French law". [Author's translation]

legal personality.[21] However, not all *sociétés* are endowed with legal personality, although those that lack it – *sociétés en participation* (silent partnerships) and *sociétés de fait* (*de facto* or unregistered companies) – are somewhat exceptional for various reasons. The patrimony in such cases cannot belong to the *société* itself and is held either by one member or by all the members as *la propriété indivise* – tenants in common. For this reason, while the existence of a patrimony is fundamental, we cannot say that it is only a fundamental characteristic of legal persons. It may well be that ownership of a patrimony is a fundamental attribute of a *société*, and that one can see in the fact of this essential requirement a link to the need for a real existence for the *société* as a whole. Certainly the absence of a patrimony may lead to a *société* being condemned as *fictive* and being made liable to annulment. The necessity for a real or substantive existence for the *société* could be a truly fundamental value. As will be seen later, it is a value that is arguably shared by the *gesellschaft* in Germany.

The second concept, which derives in many ways from the requirement of a real and substantive contribution from every member of a *société*, is the crucial factor of *affectio societatis*. This in essence is the will to act together with others, on an equal footing i.e. without subordination,[22] towards the success of the common enterprise undertaken. Its origins certainly lie in Roman law where it was used to distinguish mere common ownership of assets from a *societas* in which the members must have *affectio societatis*.[23] The concept as used in French law describes an essential quality of the relationship between the participants in the enterprise. For one author the participants in the *contrat de société* or company contract must act not as adversaries discussing their interests, but as collaborators animated by a spirit of fraternity.[24] For another they must march side by side rather than engaging in hand-to-hand combat.[25] In one way this concept relates to the quality of the free consent that every member of the *société* must give to the *contrat de société*. They must wish truly to work together for their common objective. This too has overtones of equality in the sense that one person is not permitted to take for themselves all of the profits generated by the enterprise, nor to absolve themselves from any contribution to the losses sustained nor, on the other hand, to be regarded totally in a subordinate role without the right to participate in some way in the conduct of the

[21] "*Un groupement est doté de la personnalité morale lorsqu'il possède un patrimoine; les deux notions de personnalité et de patrimoine sont traditionellement liées dans la conception juridique française*". *Ibid.* at p. 523. "A grouping is endowed with legal personality when it possesses a patrimony; the two ideas of personality and patrimony are traditionally linked in French legal thinking". [Author's translation]

[22] See the decision reported at Paris, 4e ch. 22 May 1976, inedit: Juris-Data, n.250.

[23] Dig., 17, 2, fr. 32.

[24] G Ripert par R Roblot, *op.cit.* at p. 568.

[25] Put much more elegantly in the original French as "*c'est le 'coude à coude' – sinon le corps à corps – entre associés, qui finissent parfois dos à dos.*" *Droit des Sociétés*, M Cozian and A Viandier, 7th ed., Paris 1994 at p. 70.

enterprise. The concept of *affectio societatis* reinforces the need for a substantive reality about every *société* in another way. It is necessary that two or more persons make a genuine commitment, backed up as we have seen with a financial stake, to participate in the business of the *société*. If such a commitment is absent we find that the *société* will be condemned as fictive and be subject to annulment. As one author has put it "A *société fictive* (and one can speak also of a *société de façade* or a *société ecran*) has only the appearance of a *société*, manipulated by a single person who is the controlling proprietor of the business; whose associates are only nominees (men of straw)". [Present author's translation].[26] Such a company is a nullity.[27] Another use for the concept occurs if there is an onset of great animosity between the members of a *société*, and this can be a ground for its dissolution. One can say though that the force of *affectio societatis* is greater in some types of *société* than in others. It is obviously at its strongest in partnerships and family companies and at its weakest in large public companies where the concept of individual shareholders participating in the running of the enterprise is a little far fetched. However, the concept could help to explain the reluctance of French law for a long time to accept the idea of the non-voting share, which might effectively deny the right to participate in any sort of controlling role, merely retaining the right to participate in profits.

All of these factors point towards the need for the real existence of a collaborative entity with some substance as a fundamental value of French company law. There are several other factors supporting this contention. The *société* must be a potentially durable liaison and not merely a temporary one. French law requires the constitution of a company to state its duration,[28] but this must not exceed ninety-nine years.[29] The body of funds represented by the *patrimoine* of a *société* must be dedicated towards a lawful objective. The value placed upon the existence of a real and substantial corporate entity links in well with the *Realitätstheorie* espoused by German law to which we will now turn.

4. FUNDAMENTAL VALUES IN GERMAN COMPANY LAW

When we begin to consider whether there are any fundamental values evident in German company law we cannot take the same approach as in France. This is because the German system does not use the idea of *gesellschaft*[30] in the same unified way as the French use the concept of the *société*. There is a greater

[26] *Ibid.* at p. 73.
[27] Cass. Civ. 3e, 22 June 1976: D. 1977, 619, note P Dienier.
[28] Code Civil Article 1835.
[29] Code Civil Article 1838.
[30] Essentially this is the association of persons by contract to realise a common purpose, and is a very wide concept because it is not necessarily a "business" association.

distinction in Germany between partnerships and companies than is immediately apparent in France. Almost all partnerships in France have corporate personality, but none do in Germany, and therefore use of a unified concept is not possible. In fact in Germany there are two models or building blocks used in the field of commercial associations. There is the Civil Code partnership or *BGB* (*Bürgerliches Gesetzbuch*)-*Gesellschaft* which is the model also for other partnership forms including the *Offene Handelsgesellschaft* (OHG – partnership under the Commercial Code), the *Kommandit Gesellschaft* (KG – Limited Partnership), and the *stille Gesellschaft* (silent partnership). Hence the rules on the *BGB-Gesellschaft*[31] apply to the OHG, the KG and the *stille Gesellschaft* where the Commercial Code provides no specific rules. The model for associations with corporate personality is the *rechtsfähige Verein* (association with legal capacity) which is regulated under the law of persons in articles 21–79 of the BGB. This group includes the *Aktien Gesellschaft* (AG) and the *Gesellschaft mit beschränkter Haftung* (GmbH) which are classified as capital companies (*Kapitalgesellschaften*) as well as the *eingetragener Verein* (registered association under the Civil Code). We therefore cannot derive any common features for the *Gesellschaft* which are universally applicable to the whole range of business associations.

There are other approaches that may prove more useful in trying to elucidate the fundamental values of the German system. One approach might be a philosophical one looking at some of the ideas that might have informed the German system and seeing how, if at all, they are represented in the law of today. The other approach could loosely be described as an historical one that looks at the development of the system and tries to assess the values that have been influential in that development. If we try to perceive what the legislators and judges have tried to achieve or protect we can better estimate whether these are fundamental values or merely transient concerns.

If we start with the philosophical approach we must come back to the important work of Otto von Gierke.[32] He, more than anyone, has been responsible for the development of the group personality theory. He has suggested that the emergent personality of certain groups in society must be recognised by the law as a real entity, which is just as real as the personality of a human individual. While he applied this idea to various groups such as a church, an educational or charitable foundation and a professional association, it is particularly relevant for us that he especially applied it to a company. He took the line that once such a group had organised itself in such a way as to manifest its separate identity as an institution distinct from its members, it became entitled, as of right,

[31] Articles 705 *et seq*. of the BGB.

[32] In English the work has been extensively dealt with in Maitland, *Introduction to Gierke's Political Theories of the Middle Ages*, 1900; and in his *Collected Papers*, 1911, III, pp. 304. *et seq*. In German see Otto von Gierke, *Das deutsche Gennoschenschaftrexhts*, 4 vols 1868–1913; *Die Genossenschaftstheorie und die deutsche Rechtsprechung*, 1887; *Privatrecht*, I, pp. 456–660 esp. p. 466 *et seq*. (1895); *Das Wesen der menschlichen Verbände* (Berlin 1902).

to legal recognition of its personality without the need for any official, or State, grant of legal personality. When applied to companies, this view was sharply opposed to the prevailing views in Germany at the end of the century, which in many ways adopted the State concession theory of corporate personality, claiming that it could only come into existence when granted by the State itself. It is also in direct conflict with the Fiction Theory, which found many adherents in this country, and which would claim that a group such as a company had no real existence worth talking about, and which would hold that a company was to be regarded as a legal person purely by way of a legal fiction to make the concept workable in society. Gierke wrote about the real existence of the *Gemeinwille* or collective will of the corporation becoming the manifestation of its separate identity. I would argue that there are several ways today in which emphasis is placed on the reality of the organisation in German company law and in particular on the real existence of the group at a time when the State has not intervened to confer legal personality upon a company.

German courts have recognised the real existence of a group of individuals who are actively engaged in the task of forming a company. The legislative position is simply stated in Article 11 (1) of the *GmbH-Gesetz* as "[B]efore registration in the commercial register of the domicile of the company the company with limited liability does not as such exist".[33] Those acting in the name of the company before this registration are personally liable.[34] However, in practice, many weeks or even months can elapse between the time of taking the initial steps on the road to the formation of the company, such as the notarised signing of the statutes, and the completion of this registration process. It may well be an economic necessity for the founder of the company to take some business actions during that time. Hence, "the courts have decided to yield to the needs of economic reality and to protect creditors' interests by developing an intricate case law system of liability governing the period before the GmbH is entered in the commercial register".[35] There are two stages of liability in the formation process. The first stage arises where the founders of the company agree to co-operate to form the company with a view to achieving specific objectives. At this stage the so-called pre-formation company is regarded as a civil law partnership (*BGB-Gesellschaft*) governed by the Civil Code. While the reality of the situation is recognised in a way not normally contemplated by English law there is in principle only the reality of the contractual agreement in place. When the next stage is reached, and the founders have actually signed the provisional articles of association in notarised form, the courts recognise that something has come into existence that is not merely a contract to form a company. The would-be shareholders are at this stage obliged to pay into an

[33] Translation from Peltzer, Brooks, Hopcroft, *German Law Pertaining to Companies with Limited Liability GmbH-Gesetz* (3rd ed. 1996) at p. 74.

[34] GmbH-G § 11(2).

[35] Daniela Weber-Rey and Thomas Krecek, *Liability during the Process of Formation of a German Limited Liability Company ("Pre-GmbH")* [1997] 3 *ICCLR* 95 at p. 95.

account in the name of the future GmbH the contributions due on the shares that they have agreed to take. A body of assets arises which is intended to be regulated by the *GmbH-Gesetz*. To take account of the difficulties that would be presented if one was to describe this entity as a civil code partnership, "the Federal Supreme Court (*Bundesgerichtshof* – 'BGH') avoided all these problems by simply declaring that the pre-GmbH constituted an entity 'of its own kind' (*sui generis*)".[36] The Court gave the entity a hybrid status applying to it the provisions of the *GmbH-Gesetz* which do not assume or require the existence of corporate personality. "Due to its status as an entity *sui generis* the pre-GmbH is preliminarily granted capacity to hold rights and incur obligations".[37] We thus find that this right and duty bearing entity has come into existence endowed with the ability to appoint managers and through them to enter into contracts, before official registration in the commercial register and before the formal attribution of corporate personality. If we view this through the concepts of Otto von Gierke, surely we can say that this entity is created out of the reality of the *Gemeinwille* of its participants and that it has already achieved some semblance of a separate entity without the participation of the State. What this seeks to establish is that there is an emphasis on the reality of the corporate situation in Germany that is far removed from the Fiction Theory and the emphasis on form and artificiality found in English cases such as *Salomon* v. *Salomon & Co Ltd*.[38] Such an emphasis on reality could be one of the fundamental values adopted by German company law.

There are several other distinctive features of German company law that could be pointers in the direction of what this system regards as its fundamental values. In order to elucidate them it is necessary to adopt an historical perspective because, for various reasons, they are not all totally apparent in the current legislation. The sorts of things in question here include the adoption of the two tier system of management, the separation of the system of representation of the company from the system of management, the absence of any *ultra vires* doctrine and the emphasis placed both on the position of workers within the company's structure and on the capitalisation of the company. The kingdoms and principalities that were later to be united into the German State began to make legislative responses to the industrial revolution in the middle and latter half of the nineteenth century. There was a move to enable the creation of corporations by way of compliance with the requirements of a general statute rather than only by way of creation by and under the supervision of the State. By 1870 the provisions relating to corporations in the general Commercial Code ("*Handelsgesetzbuch*" or "HGB") had been amended to remove the state concession approach to incorporation, and to permit the creation of companies if they complied with certain objective standards. Ercklentz remarks:

[36] *Ibid.* at p. 96 citing the decision BGH NJW 1956, 1435.

[37] *Ibid.* at p. 97, citing, *inter alia*, T Raiser, *Recht der Kapitalgesellschaften* 2nd ed., 1992.

[38] [1897] AC 22.

> This change marked the shift from incorporation as a matter of state discretion to incorporation as a matter of right upon the satisfaction of defined legal standards. However, since these first standards were rather loose, many abuses soon became evident. . . . In response to these abuses, more stringent incorporation requirements were imposed in 1884 and it thereafter became more difficult to form an AG.[39]

This was to have profound consequences because "the more control that was introduced, the less flexible this type of corporation became"[40] and pressure arose for the creation of a simpler form. In 1892 the statute for a limited liability company – *Gesellschaft mit beschränkter Haftung* (GmbH) Gesetz was passed, and became a model for the private company in a great many other jurisdictions. In the 1920s shareholders in the AG or public company became increasingly excluded from effective participation in management by serious abuses in the area of corporate management and control.[41] During the economic depression of the 1930s pressure built for a reform of corporation law which resulted in the stock corporation law of 1 October 1937 as a statute separate from the Commercial Code. Bearing in mind the period in which this law was debated and passed, it could not, according to Ercklentz, "entirely escape the impact of the then prevailing political philosophy",[42] although much of what it did was a response to earlier pressures arising before the National Socialist era. This act imposed a high minimum capital of RM 500,000, increased the reporting requirements, strengthened the position of management and placed a greater emphasis on the interests of the community and of the State.[43] After the development of laws relating to the inclusion of workers in the decision-making processes of companies – the "co-determination laws" – the Act was reformed in 1965. "It might be stated, therefore, that the impetus for the 1965 law was the desire to promote as extensive as possible an ownership interest on the part of the general public in the larger enterprises in Germany and to protect the investment of this broader group accordingly".[44]

What emerges from this historical review is that Germany has frequently forged its own response to the problems that it encountered, and not borrowed solutions from other jurisdictions. These solutions, many quite original, were no doubt influenced by the prevailing political ideas of the day and hence reflect what are the fundamental values of the system. It is therefore very instructive to look at how the 1937 Stock Corporation Law dealt with the issue of the obligations imposed on the management of an AG. This Act required management to be conducted in a manner "consistent with the welfare of the enterprise and its employees and consistent with the common interest of the people and the

[39] E Ercklentz, *Modern German Corporation Law*, 1979, New York, Vol. I, at p. 4.

[40] B Rüster, *Business Transactions in Germany*, New York, looseleaf – updated to 1999, Vol. II § 24.01.

[41] Ercklentz, *op.cit.* at p. 4.

[42] *Ibid.* at p. 6.

[43] *Ibid.*

[44] *Ibid.* at p. 10.

state".[45] This was not repeated in the 1965 revision of the *Aktiengesetz* partly because of the feeling that "an enumeration of principles to govern the management of the AG is superfluous on the ground that such principles should be self-evident and thus require no specific articulation".[46] The 1937 law was said at the time to be the transfer of the "*Führer* principle" to corporate law because it so strengthened the dominant position of the board.[47] There lingers the suspicion that the reference to the common interest and the State might have been omitted in part also because of the opprobrium attached to that era of German history. However, it is still true today that the obligations imposed upon the management board of an AG include the duty to take into account the interests of the company and its shareholders as well as the interests of its employees and the community in which the company operates, the latter being understood to refer to the State and its citizens. Ercklentz comments that "the foregoing concepts may be said to derive from the same philosophical base as does the comprehensive social legislation existing in the Federal Republic of Germany and its commitment to a 'social' market economy and state".[48]

If we take the interests of the State to include the interests of the citizens of the State who deal with companies a clearer picture begins to emerge, and it is possible to suggest that there is a threefold concern at the heart of German company law. Like all systems of company law, the German structure attempts "to reconcile the differing interests of the shareholders, the creditors, and possibly the employees and the public".[49] It is the comparative weighting given to these interests that is particularly interesting in the German system. Those managing the company have a threefold obligation to take into account the interests of the company including its shareholders, those of the employees and those of the community at large. It "appears to be the accepted view that these three interests are of equal weight, with the consequence that none is to be granted priority over any other".[50] The overall priority given to the interests of the shareholders, which has characterised the development of the system of company law in England and many other jurisdictions, is notably absent in Germany. This emphasis on the interests of the employees and the community, placing them alongside those of the shareholders, is not something that only arises in relation to the duties of the management. It can be suggested that such a threefold emphasis can also be said to apply to the values espoused by the company legislation at large.

[45] *Ibid.* at p. 196, citing s. 70(1), *Aktiengesetz* vom 30, January 1937.

[46] *Ibid.* at p. 197, citing *Aktiengesetz*, ed. Dr Bruno Kropff, *Verlagsbuchhandlung des Instituts der Wirtschaftspruefer GmbH*, (Düsseldorf 1965), pp. 96–8.

[47] F Klausing, *Aktiengesetz* 20–37 (Berlin 1937), cited in R Buxbaum and K Hopt *Legal Harmonization and the Business Enterprise* (1988 Berlin, New York), p. 183.

[48] Ercklentz, *op.cit.* at p. 198.

[49] R Buxbaum and K Hopt, *op.cit.* at p. 174.

[50] Ercklentz, *op.cit.* at p. 197.

Examples can be given of how these ideas have been reflected in practice. We can rather take it for granted that German company law looks after the interests of the shareholders because all systems of company law do this. It is when we look particularly at those areas where German law is distinctive – where it departs from the broad European paradigmatic norm – that we get some insight into those values that can be described as fundamental. In doing this we must take into account the fact that in many ways German law has led the field in terms of finding solutions to corporate law problems. It has greatly influenced other systems[51] and hence it has played a very influential part in determining the shape of that European norm. Indeed we can perceive that solutions applied in German law have found their way into other countries and also into the company law harmonisation Directives of the European Community and thence had an application across the whole Community. What began as something distinctively German has now become in several instances, distinctively European.

Perhaps the first distinctive element can be sought in the supervisory board (*Aufsichtsrat*) that is found in the legislation governing both the AG and the GmbH. For what reason did German law adopt this concept? If we take the foundation concept from the 1937 Stock Corporation Law that the company exists for three purposes – to benefit the shareholders, to benefit the workers and to benefit the community and the State – we can see that the role of the State is an important but generalised one in this context. It was to reflect the role of the State that the supervisory board (*Aufsichtsrat*) was created in 1861 in the German Commercial Code (*Allgemeines Deutsches Handelsgesetzbuch*) and "was made compulsory in 1870 as a substitute for the state assent until then required for the creation of corporations and for a government representative on the board of directors. The underlying idea was that the function of controlling management – formerly exercised by the state – should be taken over by the shareholders".[52] As far as one can ascertain, this was the first time that the idea of the supervisory board had been applied to a company.[53] Although such a board perhaps appears today as a device for protecting the interests of shareholders, it was in fact, in its original conception, regarded as a means of safeguarding the interests of the community at large because it was substituted for the requirement of having an appointee of the State sitting on the board of every AG.

It can also be suggested that it is a feature of German company law that particular attention is paid to the need to protect third parties dealing with the

[51] For example, the limited liability company was introduced in Germany by a separate statute in 1893 as the GmbH. Similar entities have subsequently been introduced in a separate statute in France (SARL), Belgium (Sprl), Italy, Luxembourg, the Netherlands (BV), Spain, Portugal etc.

[52] *International Encyclopaedia of Comparative Law*, Vol. XIII ch. 4, Management and Control of Marketable Share Companies, Bernhard Grossfeld, pp. 6–7, Tübingen 1971.

[53] Although according to A Viandier, *La société en commandite entre son passé et son avenir* Paris, 1983, at pp. 50 *et seq*., cited in R Buxbaum and K Hopt, *op.cit.* at p. 178, it was originally introduced for the share partnership in France in 1856.

company, and that this reflects certain values in its general commercial law promoting the security of commercial transactions. Such third parties are citizens of the State and members of the community at large and hence thus within these threefold interests mentioned above. Horn, Kötz and Leser[54] states "Ever since 1884 company law has imposed strict rules on public limited companies so as to protect creditors and investors against fraudulent and incompetent promoters and directors, and to make them suitable investments for the public". We can thus perceive that protection of the public through certain mechanisms is a central part of German company law philosophy. It has been distinctive in several areas including the following:

(i) German law provides very carefully, and at times almost obsessively, for the capitalisation of companies. Hence we see rules requiring a minimum capital for both the AG and the GmbH forms, insisting that the contributions to capital are paid in before the formation of the company, insisting that the initial capital is totally available to the directors of the new company, providing that a failure to state the capital in the foundation documents shall be one of the only two grounds for the nullity of the company and so on. Other systems have some of these rules, but German law in having them all does place a particular emphasis on this factor when other systems may well regard it as being an ineffective mechanism for achieving the objective of protecting third parties.

(ii) There is a complete absence of any rule specifying that transactions beyond the objects of the company are *ultra vires* and hence beyond the capacity of the company. Such a rule was used in England to protect shareholders, where their company's directors had gone beyond the objects that the shareholders stated in the corporate constitution that they wanted to pursue. The transaction was held to be void, and this was therefore at the expense of third parties dealing with the company on whom the risk of not investigating the company's objects clause was thrown. Germany placed the emphasis on the protection of third parties, and on the security of transactions.

(iii) The separation of the systems of management and representation is also distinctive of the German approach which focuses on boards of directors as organs of the company rather than treating them just as agents. German agency law "generally makes a clear distinction between the external relationship, that is, the power of the agent to represent the principal, and the internal relationship. . . . It is the same with *Organe*".[55] Directors and managers of companies are given extensive powers to run those companies by the company legislation itself. The power to represent the company in dealings with third parties is

[54] N Horn, H Kötz and H Leser, *German Private and Commercial Law*, Oxford, 1982, p. 240.
[55] *Ibid*. at p. 242.

> dealt with separately by the legislation. Certain limitations may be placed on the authority of those authorised to represent the company by the company's constitution and they will be liable to the members of the company if they exceed any such limitations. However, it is an important feature of German company law that such limitations are not effective against third parties. This absence of an externally enforceable limitation on the powers of the organs of the company (which would act against the interests of third parties) has played a fundamental part in the development of German company law.

The preoccupation with the rights and position of the workers in the company is another feature of German company law. Although the actuality of consultation of the employees, particularly through works councils, has a long history in Germany the "legal requirement that employees should be represented on the supervisory board was the result of post-war Anglo-American policy regarding the re-building of German industry".[56] In a series of laws dealing with co-determination (*Mitbestimmung*) spanning the years 1951–76 German law introduced the rules which require the mandatory participation of the employees on the supervisory boards of companies which fall within certain parameters. The legislation is well documented and requires no additional comment here. It covers what could be regarded as labour law in other jurisdictions, but, because of this threefold purpose of German company law, it is strongly held to be a part of the company law system. This then is the third leg of our tripod, and completes the range of measures that between them protect the company and its shareholders, the employees and the community at large, especially those dealing with the company.

On the basis of the foregoing argument it can be suggested that we can identify two areas of fundamental values in German company law. The first would be an appreciation of the reality of the company and a concern for substantive compliance with the rules governing companies. This can be contrasted with a concern only for the formal nature of the entity and for compliance with the form rather than the substance of these rules which can be found in other systems, particularly in that of England. The second area would be that of the threefold beneficiaries of the rules of German company law and the distinctive way in which values are placed on the interests of each of these three groups.

5. THE BENFITS OF FUNDAMENTAL VALUES

One could ask the question "How have those jurisdictions which have these fundamental values benefited from them?" Do they purvey any significant advantages to the system that embraces them? Looking first of all at the French

[56] M C Oliver *The Private Company in Germany* (2nd ed., Antwerp, 1986), p. 11.

system, we do find that it has reacted to social and economic changes rather more by way of creating new forms of *société*, as was mentioned earlier, than by adapting the law, especially the principles governing the traditional forms of SA and SARL. When pressure began to build for the creation of a French corporate form which could be adopted by an individual entrepreneur there were enormous problems caused, for the most part, by the rigidity of the concept of the *société*.[57] A *société* is defined in terms of the existence of a contract between at least two persons. How could this basic legal vehicle be utilised for a one-person entity that needed to have a legal personality? The legal personality was needed in practice to separate the *patrimoine* of the company from that of the entrepreneur as a private individual. The difficulty of separating the two bodies of assets proved a considerable theoretical problem that needed to be overcome if the goal of the creation of a one-member company was to be realised. Another, and very major problem, was the fact that you cannot have a contract with only one party, and such a contract lies at the very heart of the concept of the *société*. Also if there is only one party there are significant problems with discovering the existence of *affectio societatis* in this singular context. All of these theoretical problems and the academic fervour that they generated took many years to resolve, and were only overcome by the somewhat artificial device of calling the new company an "*entreprise*" rather than a *société*. Hence the *Entreprise unipersonnelle à responsabilité limitée* (EURL) came on the scene.[58] The fundamental values inherent in the French system militated against an easy response to social and economic change. One could contrast the way in which English law dealt with the emergence of the one-person company. The decision in *Salomon* v. *Salomon & Co Ltd*[59] was not only the foundation case for establishing the separate corporate personality of the company, it was also the case in which the one-person company obtained the highest judicial recognition. The court found that there was no need for other members of the company to have a separate and independent mind and will, the legitimacy of the use of nominee shareholders was accepted, and it was only necessary to see their names written on the relevant documents. The emphasis here, as in many other areas of English company law, has been on form not substance. The reality of the existence of a separate entity was not regarded as a necessary element in this case, and this has set the scene for the subsequent development of the law. Until recently the one-person company was in practice formed by merely putting the name of the entrepreneur's domestic partner, or that of an obliging solicitor or accountant on the documents. No real contribution in cash, time or labour was required. Such flexibility in the law rendered the introduction of the

[57] See for example, Yves Guyon, *Droit des affaires* (9th ed., Paris 1996), Vol. I, pp. 136–8.

[58] Created or permitted by the law of 11 July 1985. There was a similar response in the field of agricultural activity for which another special form had to be created because such an enterprise falls under the civil rather than the commercial code. The result was the *Exploitation Agricole à Responsabilité Limitée* (EARL) which is a *société civile*.

[59] [1897] AC 22.

single member company almost completely unnecessary in practice, and were it not for the need to comply with a European Community Directive such an alteration in the law would not have seen the light of day.[60]

We see in the situation that led to the introduction of another French company form – the *Société par actions simplifiée* (SAS)[61] another example of the way in which adherence to fundamental values or principles has created a rigidity which restricts the ability of the French system to react to economic and social changes. This came about as a private initiative emanating from large French companies. It was sponsored by the CNPF[62] and piloted through by M Bernard Field, the chairman of its legal committee and the director of legal affairs of the huge Saint Gobain Industries group. It was because of the rigidity and formalism of French company law that many French companies looked abroad, particularly to The Netherlands and its private company (BV), for a vehicle to use for their joint ventures with each other and with foreign partners.[63] A vehicle offering sufficient flexibility and contractual freedom was thought to be necessary to persuade such companies that they did not need to look abroad for a suitable instrument for their co-operation. French companies could not make use of the *Société Anonyme* "*qui laisse trop peu de place á la liberté statutaire*"[64] or other forms and so a completely new one was created. In England company legislation freely permits the restrictions on transfer of shares and other features, which were so sought after in the French initiative, without the need to create any special forms. As one author has said on the topic of lack of flexibility in French company law – "*Cette rigidité des mécha-nismes sociétaires se justifie par la nécessité de protéger tant les associés minoritaires que les tiers qui contractent avec la société. Mais elle va parfois au-delá du nécessitaire, en imposant des contraintes artificielles*".[65] In 1996 the Marini Report on The Modernising of Company Law (July 13 1996) called for the introduction of greater flexibility into French company law to promote its relative competitiveness in the international business community. The conclusion of the Marini Report was that French company law was too rigid and gave too high a priority to the protection of the public interest and too little weight

[60] Implemented by Companies (Single Member Private Limited Companies) Regulations 1992 (SI 1992/1699).

[61] This was introduced by law No. 94-1 of 3 January 1994.

[62] Confederation National du Patronat Français, which plays a role similar in many respects to that of the Confederation of British Industry.

[63] BRDA No. 1 of 15 January 1994 at p. 17.

[64] M Germaine, *La société par actions simplifiée*, La Semaine Juridique [JCP], Ed. G. No. 12 at p. 3749. "which leaves too little room for contractual freedom in the corporate constitution". [Author's translation]

[65] Yves Guyon, *op.cit.* Vol. I, p. 92. "This rigidity in corporate mechanisms justifies itself by the necessity to protect minority shareholders as much as third parties who contract with the company. But it sometimes goes further than necessary in imposing these artificial constraints". [Author's translation]

to the need for entrepreneurs to be given an opportunity to design business structures best suited to their needs.[66] One might also point to the increasing demand from French and other European businesses for the formation of an English company through which to pursue their affairs.[67] This is not exactly a thumping endorsement of the merit of the fundamental values inherent in the French system of company law.

When we turn to Germany, something of a similar picture emerges. It is not quite so severe because the GmbH is itself a reasonably flexible vehicle. According to practitioners Wittuhn and Stucken "The main advantage of the GmbH is the low degree of regulation. The articles of incorporation or by-laws of a GmbH can be structured very freely according to the needs of the specific business and the shareholders".[68] The same though cannot be said for the AG, where the freedom to modify its structure is pretty severely restricted by the legislation. To put the matter in a simplistic, but not inaccurate way, it could be said that the basic attitude adopted by the *AktienGesetz* of 1965 is that founders and shareholders can only modify the structure of the company's constitution to the extent permitted by the legislation.[69] In stark contrast the English position might be stated in terms that the founders and shareholders can do anything that they want with their company's constitution except to the extent that this conflicts with the mandatory provisions of the Companies Acts. The rigidity of the rules regulating the AG has discouraged many businesses from using it, and most have opted for the GmbH as an alternative. This form though does not have access to the stock market and could thus be deprived of access to

[66] *Company Law In Europe: Recent Developments: A survey of recent developments in core principles of companies regulation in selected national systems.* Produced for the Department of Trade and Industry by the Centre for Law and Business, Faculty of Law, University of Manchester, February 1999.

[67] *The Times*, 16 April 1998. This article followed up on a previous headline in *The Times* two days earlier which proclaimed "*Boulangerie* and *coiffeuse* find fortune in Britain". The headline was over an article which described how some fifty local firms in the south-east of France, including a hairdressing salon in Valence and a nearby bakery, had registered British companies to run their businesses in the optimistic hope of reducing overheads, especially social security contributions. According to the French newspaper *Libération "Le dumping fiscal is in fashion"*. German companies too have been taking the same line and indulging in what is there called "social dumping". There are also some six thousand Dutch companies which have incorporated in England to avoid the unwelcome restrictions which they find in their "home" country. Witness also the scenario which led to the celebrated *Centros* decision of the ECJ (Case C-212/97 9/3/1999). This was the creation in England of a company which immediately, and without trading in the UK, set up a branch office in Denmark through which to carry out the entire operation of the business. Again the impetus was to avoid Danish company law restrictions.

[68] G Wittuhn and R Stucken, *Deregulation of German Company Law: the Small Stock Company*, 17 *The Comparative Law Yearbook of International Business* (1995), 39.

[69] Wittuhn and Stucken *op.cit.* at p. 40 state "The AG is heavily regulated, and the articles of incorporation may not deviate from these regulations in most cases. . . . With regard to the high degree of regulation and the ensuing clumsiness of the AG, most corporations use the form of the GmbH. Even large enterprises have avoided the AG and have preferred the GmbH. Foreign investors especially tend to opt for the GmbH unless forced by other statutes to choose the AG".

equity capital in this way. The German response has been the introduction of a statute on 2 August 1994 that is referred to as the *kliene Aktiengesellschaft* statute. This statute does not create a new form, but deregulates several important aspects of the old AG law and introduces certain advantages for AGs that are not listed on a stock exchange.[70] It could be suggested that this lack of f lexibility is rooted in the care that the German system takes over the protection of third parties dealing with such a company, and the protection of those who invest in it.

The third element in the German pantheon of protection is that of the employees. The importance of the co-determination legislation requiring employee representatives on the supervisory boards of medium to large companies cannot be overstated. It was the need to ensure that German workers were not deprived of this protection that led the German Government to insist that any European Community proposal that could allow this to happen should be resolutely opposed. Hence, German insistence on employee representation provisions in the Fifth company law harmonisation Directive on the structure of public companies in the Community, has led to the non-acceptance of that Directive by many other Member States. The fear that German companies might merge with a foreign company in a manner that ended up with the resultant enterprise being subject to a foreign law which did not have such employee protection provisions may well explain German insistence that the draft Tenth Directive on cross-border mergers contained provisions to prevent this from happening. Unfortunately the other Member States could not accept such proposals and the idea still languishes well short of completion. The long-term proposal for a European company law has for many years foundered on the German insistence that it contained employee protection provisions equivalent to those in Germany. If it did not, the worry was that German companies might use this device to avoid the employee protection provisions of German law. A similar concern might explain some German opposition that has been expressed to the proposal for a Fourteenth Directive on the transfer of a company's head office. This too could be a device whereby the position of German employees could be worsened if a German company moved its head office, but not its operative workforce, to a country that did not have mandatory co-determination and other provisions. These positions and the strength of feeling that lies behind them are perfectly understandable in the context that employee protection is one of the fundamental values adopted by German company law. Such a fundamental value though has had a very deleterious effect on the success of the European Community's company law harmonisation programme.

In the light of all this we might be justified in thinking that the unprincipled, flexible, maid-of-all-work that is the English company may not be so short of

[70] Also of relevance is a further complementary statute, the *Zweites Finanzmarktförderungsgesetz*, BGBl. I § 1749 *et.seq.* of 26 July 1994 which amends and further deregulates the AG, and introduces insider-dealing rules.

disadvantages. Indeed it could even be suggested that there is one fundamental value espoused by English company law, and that this value is flexibility. It is not so grand or ethical as many of the others that we have discussed, but it is nevertheless a value that has repeatedly proved its worth in the English context, and one that is now being adopted by other more principled systems.